The Elements of Moral Philosophy

SEVENTH EDITION

JAMES RACHELS

Editions 5–7 by

STUART RACHELS

The McGraw-Hill Companies

Connect
Learn
Succeed™

THE ELEMENTS OF MORAL PHILOSOPHY, SEVENTH EDITION

Published by McGraw-Hill, a business unit of The McGraw-Hill Companies, Inc., 1221 Avenue of the Americas, New York, NY 10020. Copyright © 2012 by The McGraw-Hill Companies, Inc. All rights reserved. Previous editions © 2010, 2007, and 2003. Printed in the United States of America. No part of this publication may be reproduced or distributed in any form or by any means, or stored in a database or retrieval system, without the prior written consent of The McGraw-Hill Companies, Inc., including, but not limited to, in any network or other electronic storage or transmission, or broadcast for distance learning.

Some ancillaries, including electronic and print components, may not be available to customers outside the United States.

This book is printed on acid-free paper.

2 3 4 5 6 7 8 9 0 DOC/DOC 1 0 9 8 7 6 5 4 3 2

ISBN 978-0-07-803824-2
MHID 0-07-803824-3

Vice President & Editor-in-Chief: *Michael Ryan*
Vice President & Director of Specialized Publishing: *Janice M. Roerig-Blong*
Sponsoring Editor: *Jessica Cannavo*
Marketing Coordinator: *Angela R. FitzPatrick*
Project Manager: *Jolynn Kilburg*
Design Coordinator: *Margarite Reynolds*
Buyer: *Louis Swaim*
Media Project Manager: *Sridevi Palani*
Compositor: *Laserwords Private Limited*
Typeface: *11/12 New Baskerville*
Printer: *R. R. Donnelley*

Cover painting: Aleksandr Rodchenko. (Russian, 1891–1956). Non-Objective Painting no. 80 (Black on Black). 1918. Oil on canvas, 32 1/4 × 31 1/4" (81.9 × 79.4 cm). Gift of the artist, through Jay Leyda. The Museum of Modern Art, New York. Digital Image © 2006 The Museum of Modern Art/Licensed by Scala/Art Resource, NY. © Alexander Rodchenko/RAO, Moscow/VAGA, New York

All credits appearing on page or at the end of the book are considered to be an extension of the copyright page.

Library of Congress Cataloging-in-Publication Data

Rachels, Stuart, 1969–
    The elements of moral philosophy/James Rachels.—7th ed. by Stuart Rachels.
        p. cm.
    Includes bibliographical references and index.
    ISBN 978-0-07-803824-2 (alk. paper)
        1. Ethics—Textbooks. I. Rachels, James, 1941–2003. Elements of moral philosophy. II. Title.
    BJ1012.R29 2013
    170—dc23   2011042104

www.mhhe.com

A*bout the Authors*

JAMES RACHELS (1941–2003) wrote *The End of Life: Euthanasia and Morality* (1986), *Created from Animals: The Moral Implications of Darwinism* (1990), *Can Ethics Provide Answers? And Other Essays in Moral Philosophy* (1997), *Problems from Philosophy* (first edition, 2005), and *The Legacy of Socrates: Essays in Moral Philosophy* (2007). His website is www.jamesrachels.org.

STUART RACHELS is Associate Professor of Philosophy at the University of Alabama. He has revised several of James Rachels' books, including *Problems from Philosophy* (third edition, 2012) and *The Right Thing to Do* (sixth edition, 2012), which is the companion anthology to this book. Stuart won the United States Chess Championship in 1989, at the age of 20, and today he is a Bronze Life Master at bridge. His website is www.jamesrachels. org/stuart.

Contents

Preface

Socrates, one of the first and best moral philosophers, said that morality is about "no small matter, but how we ought to live." This book is an introduction to moral philosophy, conceived in that broad sense.

In writing this book, I have been guided by the following thought: Suppose that someone has never studied ethics but wants to do so now. What are the first things he or she should learn? This book is my answer to that question. I do not try to cover every topic in the field, nor is my coverage of any particular topic complete. Instead, I try to discuss the ideas that a newcomer should encounter first.

The chapters have been written so that they may be read independently of one another—they are, in effect, separate essays. Thus someone who is interested in Ethical Egoism could go straight to Chapter 5 and find a self-contained introduction to that theory. When read in order, however, the chapters tell a more or less continuous story. The first presents a "minimum conception" of what morality is; the middle chapters cover the most important ethical theories; and the last chapter presents my own view of what a satisfactory moral theory would be like.

The point of this book is not to provide a neat, unified account of "the truth" about ethics. That would be a poor way to introduce the subject. Philosophy is not like physics. In physics, there is a large body of established truth that beginners must patiently master. (Physics teachers rarely invite their students to make up their own minds about the laws of thermodynamics.) There are, of course, unresolved controversies in physics, but these take place against a background of broad agreement. In philosophy, by contrast, everything is controversial—or almost everything. Some of the fundamental issues are still up for grabs. A good introduction will not try to hide that somewhat embarrassing fact.

You will find, then, a survey of contending ideas, theories, and arguments. I find some of these proposals more appealing than others, and a philosopher who made different assessments would no doubt write a different book. Thus, my own views inevitably color the presentation. But I try to present the contending ideas fairly, and when I pass judgment on an argument, I do my best to explain why. Philosophy, like morality itself, is first and last an exercise in reason; we should embrace the ideas that are best supported by the arguments. If this book is successful, then the reader can begin to assess where the weight of reason rests.

A bout the Seventh Edition

The seventh edition includes no major changes, but many parts of the book have been improved.

- In Chapter 1, "What Is Morality?" I added detail to the claim that our concept of death has changed over the last 50 years (section 1.2).
- In Chapter 2, "The Challenge of Cultural Relativism," I expanded the discussion of monogamy (section 2.9).
- In Chapter 3, "Subjectivism in Ethics," I replaced the Jerry Falwell quote with a Michele Bachmann quote (section 3.1); I corrected some terminology about beliefs and attitudes stemming from Charles L. Stevenson's work (section 3.4); and I expanded our discussion of homosexuality (section 3.7).
- In Chapter 4, "Does Morality Depend on Religion?" I corrected our account of the history of Catholic thought on abortion. In previous editions, we erroneously said that the alleged spotting of "homunculi" under primitive microscopes had a profound effect on the Church's position.
- In Chapter 5, "Ethical Egoism," the Principle of Equal Treatment has been reformulated to say: "We should treat people in the same way unless there is a good reason not to."
- Chapter 6 is now called "The Social Contract Theory" (rather than "The Idea of a Social Contract").
- In Chapter 8, "The Debate over Utilitarianism," I reformulated the account of Classical Utilitarianism that opens the chapter. The new account explains what "equal consideration" is. Also, I now mention the charge that Utilitarianism would support "the tyranny of the majority" in its trampling of individual rights (section 8.3). Finally, the first defense of Utilitarianism has

been renamed "Contesting the Consequences" (from "Denying That the Consequences Would Be Good") (section 8.5).

- At the end of Chapter 10, "Kant and Respect for Persons," I now explain why the debate between retributivists and utilitarians may hinge on the debate over free will.
- Chapter 12 is now called "Virtue Ethics" (rather than "The Ethics of Virtue"). I rewrote the subsection on honesty (section 12.2).

Other changes are too small to mention.

For their help, I thank Keith Augustine, Thomas Avery, Luke Barber, Matthew Brophy, Michael Huemer, Kaave Lajevardi, Sean McAleer, Cayce Moore, Filimon Peonidis, Howard Pospesel, Brian Schimpf, Stephen J. Sullivan, Steve Sverdlik, and McGraw-Hill's outstanding anonymous reviewers. My biggest debts are to my research assistant, Daniel Hollingshead; to my wife, Professor Heather Elliott; and to my mother, Carol Rachels, whose advice again proved enormously helpful.

We all miss James Rachels, who was the sole author of this book in its first four editions. To learn more about him, visit www.jamesrachels.org.

Tell me your thoughts about the book: srachels@bama.ua.edu.

—Stuart Rachels

CHAPTER 1

What Is Morality?

We are discussing no small matter, but how we ought to live.
SOCRATES, IN PLATO'S *REPUBLIC* (ca. 390 B.C.)

1.1. The Problem of Definition

Moral philosophy is the study of what morality is and what it requires of us. As Socrates said, it's about "how we ought to live"—and why. It would be helpful if we could begin with a simple, uncontroversial definition of what morality is, but that turns out to be impossible. There are many rival theories, each expounding a different conception of what it means to live morally, and any definition that goes beyond Socrates's simple formulation is bound to offend at least one of them.

This should make us cautious, but it need not paralyze us. In this chapter, I will describe the "minimum conception" of morality. As the name suggests, the minimum conception is a core that every moral theory should accept, at least as a starting point. First, however, we will examine some moral controversies having to do with handicapped children. Our discussion will bring out the features of the minimum conception.

1.2. First Example: Baby Theresa

Theresa Ann Campo Pearson, an infant known to the public as "Baby Theresa," was born in Florida in 1992. Baby Theresa had anencephaly, one of the worst genetic disorders. Anencephalic infants are sometimes referred to as "babies without brains," but that is not quite accurate. Important parts of the brain—the cerebrum and cerebellum—are missing, as is the top of the skull. The brain stem, however, is still there, and so the baby can still breathe and possess a heartbeat. In the United States,

1

most cases of anencephaly are detected during pregnancy, and the fetuses are usually aborted. Of those not aborted, half are stillborn. About 350 are born alive each year, and they usually die within days.

Baby Theresa's story is remarkable only because her parents made an unusual request. Knowing that their baby would die soon and could never be conscious, Theresa's parents volunteered her organs for immediate transplant. They thought her kidneys, liver, heart, lungs, and eyes should go to other children who could benefit from them. Her physicians agreed. Thousands of infants need transplants each year, and there are never enough organs available. But Theresa's organs were not taken, because Florida law forbids the removal of organs until the donor is dead. By the time Baby Theresa died, nine days later, it was too late—her organs had deteriorated too much to be harvested and transplanted.

Baby Theresa's case was widely debated. Should she have been killed so that her organs could have been used to save other children? A number of professional "ethicists"—people employed by universities, hospitals, and law schools, who get paid to think about such things—were asked by the press to comment. Most of them disagreed with the parents and physicians. Instead, they appealed to time-honored philosophical principles to oppose taking the organs. "It just seems too horrifying to use people as means to other people's ends," said one such expert. Another explained: "It's unethical to kill person A to save person B." And a third added: "What the parents are really asking for is, Kill this dying baby so that its organs may be used for someone else. Well, that's really a horrendous proposition."

Is it horrendous? Opinions were divided. These ethicists thought so, while the parents and doctors did not. But we are interested in more than what people happen to think. We want to know what's true. Were the parents right or wrong to volunteer their baby's organs for transplant? To answer this question, we have to ask what reasons, or arguments, can be given on each side. What can be said to justify the parents' request or to justify opposing their request?

The Benefits Argument. The parents believed that Theresa's organs were doing her no good, because she was not conscious and would die soon anyway. The other children, however, could benefit from them. Thus, the parents seem to have reasoned: *If we can benefit someone without harming anyone else, we ought to do so. Transplanting the organs would benefit the other children without harming Baby Theresa. Therefore, we ought to transplant the organs.*

Is this correct? Not every argument is sound. In addition to knowing what arguments can be given for a view, we also want to know whether those arguments are any good. Generally speaking, an argument is sound if its assumptions are true and the conclusion follows logically from them. In this case, we might wonder about the assertion that Theresa wouldn't be harmed. After all, she would die, and isn't being alive better than being dead? But on reflection, it seems clear that, in these tragic circumstances, the parents were right. Being alive is a benefit only if it enables you to carry on activities and have thoughts, feelings, and relations with other people—in other words, if it enables you to *have a life.* Without such things, biological existence has no value. Therefore, even though Theresa might remain alive for a few more days, it would do her no good.

The Benefits Argument, therefore, provides a powerful reason for transplanting the organs. What arguments exist on the other side?

The Argument That We Should Not Use People as Means. The ethicists who opposed the transplants offered two arguments. The first was based on the idea that *it is wrong to use people as means to other people's ends.* Taking Theresa's organs would be using her to benefit the other children; therefore, it should not be done.

Is this argument sound? The idea that we should not "use" people is obviously appealing, but this is a vague notion that needs to be clarified. What exactly does it mean? "Using people" typically involves violating their *autonomy*—their ability to decide for themselves how to live their own lives, according to their own desires and values. A person's autonomy may be violated through manipulation, trickery, or deceit. For example, I may pretend to be your friend, when I am only interested in going out with your sister; or I may lie to you so you'll give me money; or I may try to convince you that you will enjoy going to the movies, when I only want you to give me a ride. In each case, I am manipulating you in order to get something for myself. Autonomy is also violated when people are forced to do things against their will. This explains why "using people" is wrong; it is wrong because it thwarts people's autonomy.

Taking Baby Theresa's organs, however, could not thwart her autonomy, because she has no autonomy—she cannot make decisions, she has no desires, and she cannot value anything. Would taking her organs be "using her" in any other morally significant sense? We would, of course, be using her organs for someone else's benefit. But we do that every time we perform a transplant. We would also be using her organs without her permission. Would that make it wrong? If we were using them *against* her wishes, then that would be a reason for objecting—it would violate her autonomy. But Baby Theresa has no wishes.

When people are unable to make decisions for themselves, and others must do it for them, there are two reasonable guidelines that might be adopted. First, we might ask, *What would be in their own best interests?* If we apply this standard to Baby Theresa, there would be no objection to taking her organs, for, as we have already noted, her interests will not be affected. She is not conscious, and she will die soon no matter what.

The second guideline appeals to the person's own preferences: We might ask, *If she could tell us what she wants, what would she say?* This sort of thought is useful when we are dealing with people who have preferences (or once had them) but cannot express them—for example, a comatose patient who signed a living will before slipping into the coma. But, sadly, Baby Theresa has no preferences about anything, nor has she ever had any. So we can get no guidance from her, even in our imaginations. The upshot is that we are left to do what we think is best.

The Argument from the Wrongness of Killing. The ethicists also appealed to the principle that *it is wrong to kill one person to save another*. Taking Theresa's organs would be killing her to save others, they said; so, taking the organs would be wrong.

Is this argument sound? The prohibition against killing is certainly among the most important moral rules. Nevertheless, few people believe it is *always* wrong to kill—most people think there are exceptions, such as killing in self-defense. The question, then, is whether taking Baby Theresa's organs should be regarded as an exception to the rule. There are many reasons to think so: Baby Theresa is not conscious; she will never have a life; she is going to die soon; and taking her organs would help the other babies. Anyone who accepts this will regard the argument as flawed. Usually, it is wrong to kill one person to save another, but not always.

There is another possibility. Perhaps we should regard Baby Theresa as already dead. If this sounds crazy, bear in mind that our conception of death has changed over the years. In 1967, the South African doctor Christiaan Barnard performed the first heart transplant in human beings. This was an exciting development; heart transplants could potentially save many lives. It was not clear, however, whether any lives could be saved in the United States. Back then, American law understood death as occurring when the heart stops beating. But once a heart stops beating, it quickly degrades and becomes unsuitable for transplant. Thus, under American law, it was not clear whether any hearts could be legally harvested for transplant. So, American law changed. We now understand death as occurring, not when the heart stops beating, but when the brain stops functioning: "brain death" is our new end-of-life standard. This solved the problem about transplants, because a brain-dead patient can still have a healthy heart, suitable for transplant.

Anencephalics do not meet the technical requirements for brain death as it is currently defined; but perhaps the definition should be revised to include them. After all, they lack any hope for conscious life, because they have no cerebrum or cerebellum. If the definition of brain death were reformulated to include anencephalics, we would become accustomed to the idea that these unfortunate infants are born dead, and so taking their organs would not involve killing them. The Argument from the Wrongness of Killing would then be moot.

On the whole, then, the arguments in favor of transplanting Baby Theresa's organs seem stronger than the arguments against it.

1.3. Second Example: Jodie and Mary

In August 2000, a young woman from Gozo, an island south of Italy, discovered that she was carrying conjoined twins. Knowing that the health-care facilities on Gozo were inadequate to deal with such a birth, she and her husband went to St. Mary's

Hospital in Manchester, England. The infants, known as Mary and Jodie, were joined at the lower abdomen. Their spines were fused, and they had one heart and one pair of lungs between them. Jodie, the stronger one, was providing blood for her sister.

No one knows how many sets of conjoined twins are born each year, but the number has been estimated at 200. Most die shortly after birth, but some do well. They grow to adulthood and marry and have children themselves. But the outlook for Mary and Jodie was grim. The doctors said that without intervention the girls would die within six months. The only hope was an operation to separate them. This would save Jodie, but Mary would die immediately.

The parents, who were devout Catholics, refused permission for the operation on the grounds that it would hasten Mary's death. "We believe that nature should take its course," they said. "If it's God's will that both our children should not survive, then so be it." The hospital, hoping to save Jodie, petitioned the courts for permission to perform the operation anyway. The courts agreed, and the operation was performed. As expected, Jodie lived and Mary died.

In thinking about this case, we should distinguish the question of *who should make the decision* from the question of *what the decision should be.* You might think, for example, that the decision should be left to the parents, and so the courts should not have intruded. But there remains the separate question of what would be the wisest choice for the parents (or anyone else) to make. We will focus on that question: Would it be right or wrong to separate the twins?

The Argument That We Should Save as Many as We Can. The rationale for separating the twins is that we have a choice between saving one infant or letting both die. Isn't it plainly better to save one? This argument is so appealing that many people will conclude, without further thought, that the twins should be separated. At the height of the controversy, the *Ladies' Home Journal* commissioned a poll to discover what Americans thought. The poll showed that 78% approved of the operation. People were obviously persuaded by the idea that we should save as many as we can. Jodie and Mary's parents, however, believed that there is an even stronger argument on the other side.

The Argument from the Sanctity of Human Life. The parents loved both of their children, and they thought it would be wrong to kill one of them even to save the other. Of course, they were not alone in thinking this. The idea that all human life is precious, regardless of age, race, social class, or handicap, is at the core of the Western moral tradition. It is especially emphasized in religious writings. In traditional ethics, the prohibition against killing innocent humans is absolute. It does not matter if the killing would serve a good purpose; it simply cannot be done. Mary is an innocent human being, and so she may not be killed.

Is this argument sound? The judges who heard the case did not think so, for a surprising reason. They denied that the operation would kill Mary. Lord Justice Robert Walker said that the operation would merely separate Mary from her sister and then "she would die, not because she was intentionally killed, but because her own body cannot sustain her life." In other words, the operation wouldn't kill her; her body's weakness would. And so, the morality of killing is irrelevant.

The Lord Justice, however, has missed the point. It doesn't matter whether we say that Mary's death is caused by the operation or by her body's own weakness. Either way, she will be dead, and we will knowingly have hastened her death. *That's* the idea behind the traditional prohibition against killing the innocent.

There is, however, a more natural objection to the Argument from the Sanctity of Life. Perhaps it is *not* always wrong to kill innocent human beings. For example, such killings may be right when three conditions are met: (a) the innocent human has no future because she is going to die soon no matter what; (b) the innocent human has no wish to go on living, perhaps because she has no wishes at all; and (c) this killing will save others, who can go on to lead full lives. In these rare circumstances, the killing of the innocent might be justified.

1.4. Third Example: Tracy Latimer

Tracy Latimer, a 12-year-old victim of cerebral palsy, was killed by her father in 1993. Tracy lived with her family on a prairie farm in Saskatchewan, Canada. One Sunday morning while his wife and other children were at church, Robert Latimer put Tracy in the cab of his pickup truck and piped in exhaust fumes until she died. At the time of her death, Tracy weighed less than 40 pounds, and she was described as "functioning at the mental level of a three-month-old baby." Mrs. Latimer said that she was relieved to find Tracy dead when she arrived home and added that she "didn't have the courage" to do it herself.

Robert Latimer was tried for murder, but the judge and jury did not want to treat him harshly. The jury found him guilty of only second-degree murder and recommended that the judge ignore the mandatory 10-year sentence. The judge agreed and sentenced him to one year in prison, followed by a year of confinement to his farm. But the Supreme Court of Canada stepped in and ruled that the mandatory sentence must be imposed. Robert Latimer entered prison in 2001 and was paroled in 2008.

Legal questions aside, did Mr. Latimer do anything wrong? This case involves many of the issues that we saw in the other cases. One argument against Mr. Latimer is that Tracy's life was morally precious, and so he had no right to kill her. In his defense, it may be said that Tracy's condition was so catastrophic that she had no prospects of a "life" in any but a biological sense. Her existence had been reduced to pointless suffering, and so killing her was an act of mercy. Considering those arguments, it appears that Robert Latimer acted defensibly. There were, however, other points made by his critics.

The Argument from the Wrongness of Discriminating against the Handicapped. When Robert Latimer was given a lenient sentence by the trial court, many handicapped people felt insulted. The president of the Saskatoon Voice of People with Disabilities, who has multiple sclerosis, said: "Nobody has the right to decide my life is worth less than yours. That's the bottom line." Tracy was killed because she was handicapped, he said, and that is unconscionable. Handicapped people should be given the same respect and the same rights as everyone else.

What are we to make of this? Discrimination is always a serious matter, because it involves treating some people worse than others, for no good reason. Suppose, for example, that a blind person is refused a job simply because the employer doesn't like the idea of hiring someone who can't see. This is no better than refusing to hire someone because she is Hispanic or Jewish or female. Why is this person being treated differently? Is she less able to do the job? Is she less intelligent or less industrious? Does she deserve the job less? Is she less able to benefit from employment? If there is no good reason to exclude her, then it is arbitrary to do so.

Should we think of the death of Tracy Latimer as a case of discrimination against the handicapped? Robert Latimer argued that Tracy's cerebral palsy was not the issue: "People are saying this is a handicap issue, but they're wrong. This is a torture issue. It was about mutilation and torture for Tracy." Just before her death, Tracy had undergone major surgery on her back, hips, and legs, and more surgery was planned. "With the combination of a feeding tube, rods in her back, the leg cut and flopping around and bedsores," said her father, "how can people say she was a happy little girl?" At the trial, three of Tracy's physicians testified about the difficulty of controlling her pain. Thus, Mr. Latimer denied that Tracy was killed because of her disability; she was killed because she was suffering, and because there was no hope for her.

The Slippery Slope Argument. When the Canadian Supreme Court upheld Robert Latimer's sentence, the director of the Canadian Association of Independent Living Centres said that she was "pleasantly surprised." "It would have really been the slippery slope, and opening the doors to other people to decide who should live and who should die," she said.

Other disability advocates echoed this idea. We may feel sympathy for Robert Latimer, it was said; we may even think that Tracy Latimer is better off dead. However, it is dangerous to think like this. If we accept any sort of mercy killing, we will slide down a "slippery slope," and at the bottom of the slope, all life will be held cheap. Where will we draw the line? If Tracy's life is not worth protecting, what about the lives of other disabled people? What about the elderly, the infirm, and other "useless" members of society? In this context, Hitler's program of "racial purification" is often mentioned, implying that we will end up like the Nazis if we take the first step.

Similar "slippery slope arguments" have been used on other issues. Abortion, in vitro fertilization (IVF), and human cloning have all been opposed because of what they might lead to. Sometimes, in hindsight, it is evident that the worries were unfounded. This has happened with IVF, a technique for creating embryos in the lab. When Louise Brown, the first "test tube baby," was born in 1978, there were dire predictions about what might be in store for her and for society as a whole. But none of those predictions came true, and IVF has become routine. Since Louise Brown's birth, over 100,000 American couples have used IVF to have children.

Without the benefit of hindsight, however, slippery slope arguments are hard to assess. As the old saying has it, "It's tough to make predictions, especially about the future." Reasonable people may disagree about what would happen if mercy killing were allowed in cases like Tracy Latimer's. Those inclined to defend Mr. Latimer may find the dire predictions unrealistic, while those who want to condemn him may insist that the predictions are sensible. This kind of disagreement can be hard to resolve.

It is worth noting, however, that slippery slope arguments are easy to abuse. If you are opposed to something but have no good arguments against it, you can always make up a prediction about what it might lead to; and no matter how implausible your prediction is, no one can prove you wrong. That is why such arguments should be approached with caution.

1.5. Reason and Impartiality

What can we learn from all this about the nature of morality? As a start, we may note two main points: first, moral judgments must be backed by good reasons; and second, morality requires the impartial consideration of each individual's interests.

Moral Reasoning. The cases of Baby Theresa, Jodie and Mary, and Tracy Latimer are liable to arouse strong feelings. Such feelings are often a sign of moral seriousness and may be admired. But they can also get in the way of discovering the truth: When we feel strongly about an issue, it is tempting to assume that we just *know* what the truth is, without even having to consider arguments on the other side. Unfortunately, however, we cannot rely on our feelings, no matter how powerful they may be. Our feelings may be irrational; they may be nothing but the products of prejudice, selfishness, or cultural conditioning. At one time, for example, people's feelings told them that members of other races were inferior and that slavery was God's plan.

Moreover, people's feelings can be very different. In the case of Tracy Latimer, some people feel strongly that her father deserved a long prison term, while others feel equally strongly that he should never have been prosecuted. But both of these feelings cannot be correct.

Thus, if we want to discover the truth, we must let our feelings be guided as much as possible by reason. This is the essence of morality. The morally right thing to do is always the thing best supported by the arguments.

This is not a narrow point about a small range of moral views; it is a general requirement of logic that must be accepted by everyone, regardless of their position on any particular issue. The fundamental point may be stated simply. Suppose someone says that you ought to do such-and-such. You may legitimately ask why you should do it, and if no good reason can be given, you may reject the advice as arbitrary or unfounded.

In this way, moral judgments are different from expressions of personal taste. If someone says, "I like coffee," she does not need to have a reason—she is merely stating a fact about her preferences, and nothing more. There is no such thing as "rationally defending" one's like or dislike of coffee. So long as she is accurately reporting her taste, what she says must be true. On the other hand, if someone says that something is morally wrong, he does need reasons, and if his reasons are legitimate, then other people must acknowledge their force. By the same logic, if he has no good reason for what he says, then he is simply making noise, and we may ignore him.

Of course, not every reason that may be advanced is a good reason. There are bad arguments as well as good ones, and much of the skill of moral thinking consists in discerning the difference. But how do we tell the difference? How do we go about assessing arguments? The examples we have considered point to some answers.

The first thing is to get one's facts straight. Often this is not as easy as it sounds. Sometimes key facts are unknown. Other times, matters are so complex that even the experts disagree. Yet another problem is human prejudice. Often we *want* to believe something because it supports our preconceptions. Those who disapprove of Robert Latimer's action, for example, will want to believe the dire predictions of the Slippery Slope Argument; those who approve of his actions will want to reject them. It is easy to think of other examples: People who do not want to give to charity often say that charities are inefficient and corrupt, even when they have no good evidence for this; and people who dislike homosexuals may say that gay men are all pedophiles, even though very few are. But the facts exist independently of our wishes, and responsible moral thinking begins when we try to see things as they are.

Next, we can bring moral principles into play. In our three examples, a number of principles were involved: that we should not "use" people; that we should not kill one person to save another; that we should do what will benefit the people affected by our actions; that every life is sacred; and that it is wrong to discriminate against the handicapped. Most moral arguments consist of principles being applied to particular cases, and so we must ask whether the principles are justified and whether they are being applied correctly.

It would be nice if there were a simple recipe for constructing good arguments and avoiding bad ones. Unfortunately, there is not. Arguments can go wrong in many ways, and we must always be alert to the possibility of new complications and new kinds of error. But that is not surprising. The rote application of routine methods is never a satisfactory substitute for critical thinking, in any area. Morality is no exception.

The Requirement of Impartiality. Almost every important moral theory includes the idea of impartiality. This is the idea that each individual's interests are equally important; no one should get special treatment. At the same time, impartiality requires that we not treat the members of particular *groups* as inferior, and thus it condemns forms of discrimination like sexism and racism.

Impartiality is closely connected with the idea that moral judgments must be backed by good reasons. Consider the racist who thinks that white people deserve all the good jobs. He would like all the doctors, lawyers, business executives, and so on, to be white. Now we can ask for reasons; we can ask why this is thought to be right. Is there something about white people that makes them better fitted for the highest-paying and most prestigious positions? Are they inherently brighter or more industrious? Do they care more about themselves and their families? Would they benefit more from such employment? In each case, the answer is no; and if there is no good reason for treating people differently, then discrimination is unacceptably arbitrary.

The requirement of impartiality, then, is at bottom nothing more than a rule against treating people arbitrarily. It forbids treating one person worse than another when there is no good reason to do so. But if this explains what is wrong with racism, it also explains why, in some cases, it is *not* racist to treat people differently. Suppose a movie director were making a film about Fred Shuttlesworth (1922–2011), the heroic African-American civil rights leader. This director would have a good reason not to cast Christian Bale in the starring role. Such "discrimination" would not be arbitrary or objectionable.

1.6. The Minimum Conception of Morality

We may now state the minimum conception: Morality is, at the very least, the effort to guide one's conduct by reason—that is, to do what there are the best reasons for doing—while giving equal weight to the interests of each individual affected by one's decision.

This gives us a picture of what it means to be a conscientious moral agent. The conscientious moral agent is someone who is concerned impartially with the interests of everyone affected by what he or she does; who carefully sifts facts and examines their implications; who accepts principles of conduct only after scrutinizing them to make sure they are justified; who is willing to "listen to reason" even when it means revising prior convictions; and who, finally, is willing to act on the results of this deliberation.

As one might expect, not every ethical theory accepts this "minimum." This picture of the moral agent has been disputed in various ways. However, theories that reject the minimum conception encounter serious difficulties. Most philosophers realize this, and so most theories of morality incorporate the minimum conception, in one form or another.

CHAPTER 2

*T*he Challenge of Cultural Relativism

Morality differs in every society, and is a convenient term for socially approved habits.

RUTH BENEDICT, *PATTERNS OF CULTURE* (1934)

2.1. Different Cultures Have Different Moral Codes

Darius, a king of ancient Persia, was intrigued by the variety of cultures he met in his travels. He had found, for example, that the Callatians, who lived in India, ate the bodies of their dead fathers. The Greeks, of course, did not do that—the Greeks practiced cremation and regarded the funeral pyre as the natural and fitting way to dispose of the dead. Darius thought that a sophisticated outlook should appreciate the differences between cultures. One day, to teach this lesson, he summoned some Greeks who happened to be at his court and asked what it would take for them to eat the bodies of their dead fathers. They were shocked, as Darius knew they would be, and replied that no amount of money could persuade them to do such a thing. Then Darius called in some Callatians and, while the Greeks listened, asked them what it would take for them to burn their dead fathers' bodies. The Callatians were horrified and told Darius not to speak of such things.

This story, recounted by Herodotus in his *History*, illustrates a recurring theme in the literature of social science: Different cultures have different moral codes. What is thought right within one group may horrify the members of another group, and vice versa. Should we eat the bodies of the dead

14

or burn them? If you were a Greek, one answer would seem obviously correct; but if you were a Callatian, the other answer would seem equally certain.

There are many examples of this. Consider the Eskimos of the early and mid-20th century. The Eskimos are the native people of Alaska, northern Canada, Greenland, and northeastern Siberia, in Asiatic Russia. Today, none of these groups call themselves "Eskimos," but the term has historically referred to that scattered Arctic population. Prior to the 20th century, the outside world knew little about them. Then explorers began to bring back strange tales.

The Eskimos lived in small settlements, separated by great distances, and their customs turned out to be very different from ours. The men often had more than one wife, and they would share their wives with guests, lending them out for the night as a sign of hospitality. Moreover, within a community, a dominant male might demand—and get—regular sexual access to other men's wives. The women, however, were free to break these arrangements simply by leaving their husbands and taking up with new partners—free, that is, so long as their former husbands chose not to make too much trouble. All in all, the Eskimo custom of marriage was a volatile practice that bore little resemblance to our custom.

But it was not only their marriages and sexual practices that were different. The Eskimos also seemed to care less about human life. Infanticide, for example, was common. Knud Rasmussen, an early explorer, reported meeting one woman who had borne 20 children but had killed 10 of them at birth. Female babies, he found, were especially likely to be killed, and this was permitted at the parents' discretion, with no social stigma attached. Moreover, when elderly family members became too feeble, they were left out in the snow to die. In Eskimo society, there seemed to be remarkably little respect for life.

Most of us would find these Eskimo customs completely unacceptable. Our own way of living seems so natural and right to us that we can hardly conceive of people who live so differently. When we hear of such people, we might want to say that they're "backward" or "primitive." But to anthropologists, the Eskimos did not seem unusual. Since the time of Herodotus, enlightened observers have known that conceptions of right and wrong differ from culture to culture. If we assume that our ethical ideas will be shared by all cultures, we are merely being naïve.

2.2. Cultural Relativism

To many people, this observation—"Different cultures have different moral codes"—seems like the key to understanding morality. There are no universal moral truths, they say; the customs of different societies are all that exist. To call a custom "correct" or "incorrect" would imply that we can judge that custom by some independent standard of right and wrong. But no such standard exists; every standard is culture-bound. The sociologist William Graham Sumner (1840–1910) put it like this:

> The "right" way is the way which the ancestors used and which has been handed down. . . . The notion of right is in the folkways. It is not outside of them, of independent origin, and brought to test them. In the folkways, whatever is, is right. This is because they are traditional, and therefore contain in themselves the authority of the ancestral ghosts. When we come to the folkways we are at the end of our analysis.

This line of thought, more than any other, has persuaded people to be skeptical about ethics. Cultural Relativism says, in effect, that there is no such thing as universal truth in ethics; there are only the various cultural codes, and nothing more. Cultural Relativism challenges our belief in the objectivity and universality of moral truth.

The following claims have all been made by cultural relativists:

1. Different societies have different moral codes.
2. The moral code of a society determines what is right within that society; that is, if the moral code of a society says that a certain action is right, then that action *is* right, at least within that society.
3. There is no objective standard that can be used to judge one society's code as better than another's. There are no moral truths that hold for all people at all times.
4. The moral code of our own society has no special status; it is but one among many.
5. It is arrogant for us to judge other cultures. We should always be tolerant of them.

These five propositions may seem to go together, but they are *independent* of one another, meaning that some of them may be true even while others are false. Indeed, two of the propositions appear to be inconsistent with each other. The second says that right and wrong are determined by the norms of a society; the fifth says that one should always be tolerant of other cultures. But what if the norms of one's society favor intolerance? For example, when the Nazi army invaded Poland on September 1, 1939, thus beginning World War II, this was an intolerant action of the first order. But what if it conformed to Nazi ideals? A cultural relativist, it seems, cannot criticize the Nazis for being intolerant, if all they're doing is following their own moral code.

Given that cultural relativists take pride in their tolerance, it would be ironic if their theory actually supported the intolerance of warlike societies. However, their theory need not do that. Properly understood, Cultural Relativism holds that the norms of a culture reign supreme *within the bounds of the culture itself.* Thus, once the German soldiers entered Poland, they became bound by the norms of Polish society—norms that obviously excluded the mass slaughter of innocent Poles. "When in Rome," the old saying goes, "do as the Romans do." Cultural relativists agree.

2.3. The Cultural Differences Argument

Cultural Relativists often employ a certain *form of argument.* They begin with facts about cultures and end up drawing a conclusion about morality. Thus, they invite us to accept this reasoning:

(1) The Greeks believed it was wrong to eat the dead, whereas the Callatians believed it was right to eat the dead.

(2) Therefore, eating the dead is neither objectively right nor objectively wrong. It is merely a matter of opinion, which varies from culture to culture.

Or:

(1) The Eskimos saw nothing wrong with infanticide, whereas Americans believe infanticide is immoral.

(2) Therefore, infanticide is neither objectively right nor objectively wrong. It is merely a matter of opinion, which varies from culture to culture.

Clearly, these arguments are variations of one fundamental idea. They are both examples of a more general argument, which says:

(1) Different cultures have different moral codes.

(2) Therefore, there is no objective truth in morality. Right and wrong are only matters of opinion, and opinions vary from culture to culture.

We may call this the Cultural Differences Argument. To many people, it is persuasive. But is it a good argument—is it *sound?*

It is not. For an argument to be sound, its premises must all be true, and the conclusion must follow logically from them. Here, the problem is that the conclusion does not *follow from* the premise—that is, even if the premise is true, the conclusion might still be false. The premise concerns what people *believe—* in some societies, people believe one thing; in other societies, people believe something else. The conclusion, however, concerns what *really is the case.* This sort of conclusion does not follow logically from that sort of premise. In philosophical terminology, this means that the argument is *invalid.*

Consider again the example of the Greeks and Callatians. The Greeks believed it was wrong to eat the dead; the Callatians believed it was right. Does it follow, *from the mere fact that they disagreed,* that there is no objective truth in the matter? No, it does not follow; it could be that the practice was objectively right (or wrong) and that one of them was simply mistaken.

To make the point clearer, consider a different matter. In some societies, people believe the earth is flat. In other societies, such as our own, people believe that the earth is a sphere. Does it follow, from the mere fact that people disagree, that there is no "objective truth" in geography? Of course not; we would never draw such a conclusion, because we realize that the members of some societies might simply be wrong. There is no reason to think that if the world is round, everyone must know it. Similarly, there is no reason to think that if there is moral truth, everyone must know it. The Cultural Differences Argument tries to derive a substantive conclusion about a subject from the mere fact that people disagree. But this is impossible.

This point should not be misunderstood. We are not saying that the conclusion of the argument is false; for all we have said, Cultural Relativism could still be true. The point is that the conclusion does not follow from the premise. This means that the Cultural Differences Argument is invalid. Thus, the argument fails.

2.4. What Follows from Cultural Relativism

Even if the Cultural Differences Argument is unsound, Cultural Relativism might still be true. What would follow if it were true?

In the passage quoted earlier, William Graham Sumner states the essence of Cultural Relativism. He says that the only measure of right and wrong is the standards of one's society: "The notion of right is in the folkways. It is not outside of them, of independent origin, and brought to test them. In the folkways, whatever is, is right." Suppose we took this seriously. What would be some of the consequences?

1. *We could no longer say that the customs of other societies are morally inferior to our own.* This, of course, is one of the main points stressed by Cultural Relativism. We should never condemn a society merely because it is "different." This attitude seems enlightened, so long as we concentrate on examples like the funerary practices of the Greeks and Callatians.

However, we would also be barred from criticizing other, less benign practices. For example, the Chinese government has a long history of repressing political dissent within its own borders. At any given time, thousands of political prisoners in China are doing hard labor, and in the Tiananmen Square episode of 1989, Chinese troops slaughtered hundreds, if not thousands, of peaceful protesters. Cultural Relativism would preclude us from saying that the Chinese government's policies of oppression are wrong. We could not even say that a society that respects free speech is *better* than Chinese society, for that would also imply a universal standard of comparison. The failure to condemn *these* practices does not seem enlightened; on the contrary, political oppression seems wrong wherever it occurs. Nevertheless, if we accept Cultural Relativism, we have to regard such practices as immune from criticism.

2. *We could no longer criticize the code of our own society.* Cultural Relativism suggests a simple test for determining what is right and what is wrong: All we need to do is ask whether the action is in line with the code of the society in question. Suppose a resident of India wonders whether her country's caste system—a system of rigid social hierarchy—is morally correct. All she has to do is ask whether this system conforms to her society's moral code. If it does, there is nothing to worry about, at least from a moral point of view.

This implication of Cultural Relativism is disturbing because few of us think that our society's code is perfect—we can think of ways in which it might be improved. Moreover, we can think of ways in which we might learn from other cultures. Yet Cultural Relativism stops us from criticizing our own society's code, and it bars us from seeing ways in which other cultures might be better. After all, if right and wrong are relative to culture, this must be true for our own culture, just as it is for all other cultures.

3. *The idea of moral progress is called into doubt.* We think that at least some social changes are for the better. Throughout most of Western history, the place of women in society was narrowly defined. Women could not own property; they could not vote or hold political office; and they were under the almost absolute control of their husbands or fathers. Recently, much of this has changed, and most people think of it as progress.

But if Cultural Relativism is correct, can we legitimately view this as progress? Progress means replacing the old ways with new and improved ways. But by what standard do we judge the new ways as better? If the old ways conformed to the standards of *their* time, then Cultural Relativism would not judge them by *our* standards. Sexist 19th-century society was a different society from the one we now inhabit. To say that we have made progress implies that present-day society is better—just the sort of transcultural judgment that Cultural Relativism forbids.

Our ideas about social *reform* will also have to be reconsidered. Reformers such as Martin Luther King Jr. have sought to change their societies for the better. But according to Cultural Relativism, there is only one way to improve a society: to make it better match its own ideals. After all, the society's ideals are the standard by which reform is assessed. No one, however, may challenge the ideals themselves, for they are by definition correct. According to Cultural Relativism, then, the idea of social reform makes sense only in this limited way.

These three consequences of Cultural Relativism have led many people to reject it. Slavery, we want to say, is wrong wherever it occurs, and one's own society can make fundamental moral progress. Because Cultural Relativism implies that these judgments make no sense, it cannot be right.

2.5. Why There Is Less Disagreement Than It Seems

Cultural Relativism starts by observing that cultures differ dramatically in their views of right and wrong. But how much do they really differ? It is true that there are differences, but it is easy to exaggerate them. Often, what seemed at first to be a big difference turns out to be no difference at all.

Consider a culture in which people believe it is wrong to eat cows. This may even be a poor culture, in which there is not enough food; still, the cows are not to be touched. Such a society would appear to have values very different from our own. But does it? We have not yet asked *why* these people won't eat cows. Suppose they believe that after death the souls of humans inhabit the bodies of animals, especially cows, so that a cow may be someone's grandmother. Shall we say that their values differ from ours? No; the difference lies elsewhere. The difference is in our belief systems, not in our value systems. We agree that we shouldn't eat Grandma; we disagree about whether the cow could be Grandma.

The point is that many factors work together to produce the customs of a society. Not only are the society's values important, but so are its religious beliefs, its factual beliefs, and its physical environment. Thus, we cannot conclude that two societies differ in value just because they differ in custom. After all, customs may vary for a number of different reasons. Thus, there may be less moral disagreement than there appears to be.

Consider again the Eskimos, who killed perfectly healthy infants, especially girls. We do not approve of such things; in our society, a parent who kills a baby will be locked up. Thus, there appears to be a great difference in the values of our two cultures. But suppose we ask why the Eskimos did this. The explanation is not that they lacked respect for human life or did not love their children. An Eskimo family would always protect its babies if conditions permitted. But the Eskimos lived in a harsh environment, where food was scarce. To quote an old Eskimo saying: "Life is hard, and the margin of safety small." A family may want to nourish its babies but be unable to do so.

As in many traditional societies, Eskimo mothers would nurse their infants over a much longer period than mothers in our culture—for four years, and perhaps even longer. So, even in the best of times, one mother could sustain very few children. Moreover, the Eskimos were nomadic; unable to farm in the harsh northern climate, they had to keep moving to find food. Infants had to be carried, and a mother could carry only one baby in her parka as she traveled and went about her outdoor work. Finally, the Eskimos lacked birth control, so unwanted pregnancies were common.

Infant girls were more readily killed for two reasons. First, in Eskimo society, the males were the primary food providers—they were the hunters—and food was scarce. Males were thus more valuable to the community. Second, the hunters suffered a high casualty rate, so the men who died prematurely far outnumbered the women who died young. If male and female infants had survived in equal numbers, then the female adult population would have greatly outnumbered the male adult population. Examining the available statistics, one writer concluded that "were it not for female infanticide . . . there would be approximately one-and-a-half times as many females in the average Eskimo local group as there are food-producing males."

Thus, Eskimo infanticide was not due to a fundamental disregard for children. Instead, it arose from the recognition that drastic measures were needed to ensure the group's survival. Even then, however, killing the baby would not be the first option considered. Adoption was common; childless couples were especially happy to take a fertile couple's "surplus." Killing was the last resort. I emphasize this in order to show that the raw data of anthropology can be misleading; it can make the differences in values between cultures seem greater than they are. The Eskimos' values were not all that different from our own. It is only that life forced choices upon them that we do not have to make.

2.6. Some Values Are Shared by All Cultures

It should not surprise us that the Eskimos were protective of their children. How could they not be? Babies are helpless and cannot survive without extensive care. If a group did not protect its young, the young would not survive, and the older members of the group would not be replaced. Eventually the group would die out. This means that any culture that continues to exist must care for its young. Neglected infants must be the exception, not the rule.

Similar reasoning shows that other values must be more or less universal across human societies. Imagine what it would be like for a society to place no value on truth telling. When one person spoke to another, there would be no presumption that she was telling the truth, for she could just as easily be lying. Within that society, there would be no reason to pay attention to what anyone says. If I want to know what time it is, why should I bother asking anyone, if lying is commonplace? Communication would be extremely difficult, if not impossible, in such a society. And because societies cannot exist without communication among their members, society would become impossible. It follows that every society must value truthfulness. There may, of course, be situations in which lying is thought to be okay, but the society will still value honesty in most situations.

Consider another example. Could a society exist in which there was no prohibition against murder? What would this be like? Suppose people were free to kill one another at will, and no one disapproved. In such a "society," no one could feel safe. Everyone would have to be constantly on guard, and everyone would try to avoid other people—those potential murderers—as much as possible. This would result in individuals trying to become self-sufficient. Society on any large scale would thus collapse. Of course, people might band together in smaller groups where they could feel safe. But notice what this means: They would be forming smaller societies that did acknowledge a rule against murder. The prohibition against murder, then, is a necessary feature of society.

There is a general point here, namely, that *there are some moral rules that all societies must embrace, because those rules are necessary for society to exist.* The rules against lying and murder are two examples. And, in fact, we do find these rules in force in all cultures. Cultures may differ in what they regard as legitimate exceptions to the rules, but this disagreement exists against a broad background of agreement. Therefore, we shouldn't over-estimate the extent to which cultures differ. Not every moral rule can vary from society to society.

2.7. Judging a Cultural Practice to Be Undesirable

In 1996, a 17-year-old named Fauziya Kassindja arrived at Newark International Airport in New Jersey and asked for asylum. She had fled her native country of Togo, in West Africa, to escape what people there call "excision." Excision is a permanently disfiguring procedure. It is sometimes called "female circumcision," but it bears little resemblance to male circumcision. In the Western media, it is often referred to as "female genital mutilation."

According to the World Health Organization, excision is practiced in 28 African nations, and about 135 million females have been painfully excised. Sometimes, excision is part of an elaborate tribal ritual performed in small villages, and girls look forward to it as their entry into the adult world. Other times, the practice is carried out in cities on young women who desperately resist.

Fauziya Kassindja was the youngest of five daughters. Her father, who owned a successful trucking business, was opposed to excision, and he was able to defy the tradition because of his wealth. Thus, his first four daughters were married with-out being mutilated. But when Fauziya was 16, he suddenly died. Fauziya then came under the authority of her aunt, who arranged a marriage for her and prepared to have her excised. Fauziya was terrified, and her mother and oldest sister helped her escape.

In America, Fauziya was imprisoned for nearly 18 months while the authorities decided what to do with her. During this time, she was subjected to humiliating strip searches, denied medical treatment for her asthma, and generally treated like a criminal. Finally, she was granted asylum, but not before her case aroused a great controversy. The controversy was not about her treatment in America, but about how we should regard the customs of other cultures. A series of articles in *The New York*

Times encouraged the idea that excision is barbaric and should be condemned. Other observers were reluctant to be so judgmental. Live and let live, they said; after all, our culture probably seems just as strange to outsiders.

Suppose we say that excision is wrong. Are we merely imposing the standards of our own culture? If Cultural Relativism is correct, that is all we can do, for there is no culture-independent moral standard to appeal to. But is that true?

Is There a Culture-Independent Standard of Right and Wrong?

Excision is bad in many ways. It is painful and results in the permanent loss of sexual pleasure. Its short-term effects can include hemorrhage, tetanus, and septicemia. Sometimes it causes death. Its long-term effects can include chronic infection, scars that hinder walking, and continuing pain.

Why, then, has it become a widespread social practice? It is not easy to say. The practice has no obvious social benefits. Unlike Eskimo infanticide, it is not necessary for group survival. Nor is it a matter of religion. Excision is practiced by groups from various religions, including Islam and Christianity.

Nevertheless, a number of arguments are made in its defense. Women who are incapable of sexual pleasure are less likely to be promiscuous; thus, there will be fewer unwanted pregnancies in unmarried women. Moreover, wives for whom sex is only a duty are less likely to cheat on their husbands; and because they are not thinking about sex, they will be more attentive to the needs of their husbands and children. Husbands, for their part, are said to enjoy sex more with wives who have been excised. Unexcised women, the men feel, are unclean and immature.

It would be easy, and perhaps a bit arrogant, to ridicule these arguments. But notice an important feature of them: They try to justify excision by showing that excision is beneficial— men, women, and their families are said to be better off when women are excised. Thus, we might approach the issue by asking whether excision, on the whole, is helpful or harmful.

This points to a standard that might reasonably be used in thinking about any social practice: *Does the practice promote or hinder the welfare of the people affected by it?* But this looks like the sort of independent moral standard that Cultural Relativism forbids. It is a single standard that may be brought to bear in judging the practices of any culture, at any time, including our own. Of course, people will not usually see this principle as being "brought in from the outside" to judge them, because all cultures value human happiness.

Why, Despite All This, Thoughtful People May Be Reluctant to Criticize Other Cultures. Many people who are horrified by excision are nevertheless reluctant to condemn it, for three reasons. First, there is an understandable nervousness about interfering in the social customs of other peoples. Europeans and their descendants in America have a shameful history of destroying native cultures in the name of Christianity and enlightenment. Because of this, some people refuse to criticize other cultures, especially cultures that resemble those that were wronged in the past. There is a difference, however, between (a) judging a cultural practice to be deficient and (b) thinking that we should announce that fact, apply diplomatic pressure, and send in the troops. The first is just a matter of trying to see the world clearly, from a moral point of view. The second is something else entirely. Sometimes it may be right to "do something about it," but often it will not be.

Second, people may feel, rightly enough, that we should be tolerant of other cultures. Tolerance is, no doubt, a virtue—a tolerant person can live in peace with those who see things differently. But nothing about tolerance requires us to say that all beliefs, all religions, and all social practices are equally admirable. On the contrary, if we did not think that some things were better than others, then there would be nothing for us to tolerate.

Finally, people may be reluctant to judge because they do not want to express contempt for the society being criticized. But again, this is misguided: To condemn a particular practice is not to say that the culture on the whole is contemptible. After all, the culture could still have many admirable features. Indeed, we should expect this to be true of most human societies—they are mixtures of good and bad practices. Excision happens to be one of the bad ones.

2.8. Back to the Five Claims

Let us now return to the five tenets of Cultural Relativism that were listed earlier. How have they fared in our discussion?

1. Different societies have different moral codes.

This is certainly true, although there are some values that all cultures share, such as the value of truth telling, the importance of caring for the young, and the prohibition against murder. Also, when customs differ, the underlying reason will often have more to do with the factual beliefs of the cultures than with their values.

2. The moral code of a society determines what is right within that society; that is, if the moral code of a society says that a certain action is right, then that action *is* right, at least within that society.

Here we must bear in mind the difference between what a society *believes* about morals and what is *really true*. The moral code of a society is closely tied to what people in that society believe to be right. However, that code, and those people, can be in error. Earlier, we considered the example of excision—a barbaric practice endorsed by many societies. Consider three more examples, all of which involve the mistreatment of women:

- In 2002, an unwed mother in Nigeria was sentenced to be stoned to death for having had sex out of wedlock. It is unclear whether Nigerian values, on the whole, approved of this verdict, given that it was later overturned by a higher court. However, it was overturned partly to appease the international community. When the Nigerians themselves heard the verdict being read out in the courtroom, the crowd shouted out their approval.
- In 2005, a woman from Australia was convicted of trying to smuggle nine pounds of marijuana into Indonesia. For that crime, she was sentenced to 20 years in prison—an excessive punishment. Under Indonesian law, she might even have received a death sentence.
- In 2007, a woman was gang-raped in Saudi Arabia. When she complained to the police, the police discovered in the course of their investigation that she had recently been alone with a man she was not related to. For that crime, she was sentenced to 90 lashes. When she appealed her conviction, this angered the judges, and they increased

her sentence to 200 lashes plus a six-month prison term. Eventually, the Saudi king pardoned her, although he said he supported the sentence she had received.

Cultural Relativism holds, in effect, that societies are morally infallible—in other words, that the morals of a culture can never be wrong. But when we see that societies can and do endorse grave injustices, we see that societies, like their members, can be in need of moral improvement.

3. There is no objective standard that can be used to judge one society's code as better than another's. There are no moral truths that hold for all people at all times.

It is difficult to think of ethical principles that hold for all people at all times. However, if we are to criticize the practice of slavery, or stoning, or genital mutilation, and if such practices are really and truly wrong, then we must appeal to principles that are not tethered to any particular society. Earlier I suggested one such principle: that it always matters whether a practice promotes or hinders the welfare of the people affected by it.

4. The moral code of our own society has no special status; it is but one among many.

It is true that the moral code of our society has no special status. After all, our society has no heavenly halo around its borders; our values do not have any special standing just because they happen to be ours. However, to say that the moral code of one's own society "is merely one among many" seems to imply that all codes are the same—that they are all more or less equally good. In fact, it is an open question whether a given code "is merely one among many." That code might be among the best; it might be among the worst.

5. It is arrogant for us to judge other cultures. We should always be tolerant of them.

There is much truth in this, but the point is overstated. We *are* often arrogant when we criticize other cultures, and tolerance *is* generally a good thing. However, we shouldn't tolerate everything. Human societies have done terrible things, and it is a mark of progress when we can say that those things are in the past.

2.9. What We Can Learn from Cultural Relativism

So far, in discussing Cultural Relativism, I have dwelt mostly on its shortcomings. I have said that it rests on an unsound argument, that it has implausible consequences, and that it suggests greater moral disagreement than exists. This all adds up to a rejection of the theory. Nevertheless, you may have the feeling that this is a little unfair. The theory must have something going for it—why else has it been so influential? In fact, I think there is something right about Cultural Relativism, and there are two lessons we should learn from it.

First, Cultural Relativism warns us, quite rightly, about the danger of assuming that all of our practices are based on some absolute rational standard. They are not. Some of our customs are merely conventional—merely peculiar to our society—and it is easy to lose sight of that fact. In reminding us of this, the theory does us a service.

Funerary practices are one example. The Callatians, according to Herodotus, were "men who eat their fathers"—a shocking idea, to us at least. But eating the flesh of the dead could be understood as a sign of respect. It could be seen as a symbolic act which says, "We wish this person's spirit to dwell within us." Perhaps this is how the Callatians saw it. On this way of thinking, burying the dead could be seen as an act of rejection, and burning the corpse as positively scornful. Of course, the idea of eating human flesh may repel us, but so what? Our revulsion may be only a reflection of our society. Cultural Relativism begins with the insight that many of our practices are like this—they are only cultural products. Then it goes wrong by inferring that, because some practices are like this, all of them must be.

Or consider modesty of dress. In America, a woman is not supposed to display her breasts in public. For example, during the 2004 Super Bowl halftime show, Justin Timberlake ripped off part of Janet Jackson's costume, exposing one of her breasts to the audience. CBS quickly cut to an aerial view of the stadium, but it was too late. Half a million viewers complained, and the federal government fined CBS $550,000. In some cultures, however, it is considered unremarkable for a woman to show her upper torso in public. Objectively speaking, such displays are neither right nor wrong.

Finally, consider an even more complex and controversial example: that of monogamous marriage. In our society, the ideal is to fall in love with, and to marry, one person, and then one is expected to remain faithful to that person forever. But aren't there other ways to pursue happiness? The advice columnist Dan Savage lists some possible drawbacks of monogamy: "boredom, despair, lack of variety, sexual death and being taken for granted." For such reasons, many people regard monogamy as an unrealistic goal—and as a goal whose pursuit would not make them happy.

What are the alternatives to this ideal? Some married couples reject monogamy by giving each other permission to have the occasional extramarital fling. Allowing one's spouse to have an affair is risky—the spouse might not come back—but greater openness in marriage might work better than our current system, in which many people feel sexually trapped and, on top of that, feel guilty for having such feelings. Other people deviate from monogamy more radically by practicing *polyamory*, which is having more than one long-term partner, with the consent of everyone involved. Polyamory includes group marriages such as "triads," involving three people, or "quads," involving four people. Some of these arrangements might work better than others, but this is not really a matter of morality. If a man's wife gives him permission to have an affair, then he isn't "cheating" on her—he isn't betraying her trust, because she has consented to the affair. Or, if four people want to live together and function as a single family, with love flowing from each to each, then there is nothing morally wrong with that. But most people in our society would disapprove of any deviation from the cultural ideal of monogamy.

The second lesson has to do with keeping an open mind. As we grow up, we develop strong feelings about things: We learn to see some types of behavior as acceptable, and other types as outrageous. Occasionally, we may find those feelings challenged. For example, we may have been taught that homosexuality is immoral, and we may feel uncomfortable around gay people. But then someone suggests that this may be prejudice; that there is nothing wrong with being gay; and that gay people are just people, like anyone else, who happen to be attracted to members of the same sex. Because we feel so strongly about this, we may find it hard to take this line of reasoning seriously.

Cultural Relativism provides an antidote for this kind of dogmatism. When he tells the story of the Greeks and Callatians, Herodotus adds:

> For if anyone, no matter who, were given the opportunity of choosing from amongst all the nations of the world the set of beliefs which he thought best, he would inevitably, after careful consideration of their relative merits, choose that of his own country. Everyone without exception believes his own native customs, and the religion he was brought up in, to be the best.

Realizing this can help broaden our minds. We can see that our feelings are not necessarily perceptions of the truth— they may be due to cultural conditioning and nothing more. Thus, when we hear it suggested that some element of our social code is *not* really the best, and we find ourselves resisting the suggestion, we might stop and remember this. Then we will be more open to discovering the truth, whatever it might be.

We can understand the appeal of Cultural Relativism, then, despite its shortcomings. It is an attractive theory because it is based on a genuine insight: that many of the practices and attitudes we find natural are really only cultural products. Moreover, keeping this thought in mind is important if we want to avoid arrogance and remain open to new ideas. These are important points, not to be taken lightly. But we can accept them without accepting the whole theory.

CHAPTER 3

Subjectivism in Ethics

> Take any [vicious] action. . . . Wilful murder, for instance.
> Examine it in all lights, and see if you can find that matter of fact,
> or real existence, which you call vice. . . . You can never find it,
> till you turn your reflexion into your own breast, and find a
> sentiment of [disapproval], which arises in you, toward this action.
> Here is a matter of fact; but 'tis the object of feeling, not reason.
> DAVID HUME, *A TREATISE OF HUMAN NATURE* (1740)

3.1. The Basic Idea of Ethical Subjectivism

In 2001 there was a mayoral election in New York, and when it came time for the city's Gay Pride Day parade, every single Democratic and Republican candidate showed up to march. Matt Foreman, the director of a gay rights organization, described all the candidates at the march as "good on our issues." He said, "In other parts of the country, the positions taken here would be extremely unpopular, if not deadly, at the polls." The national Republican Party apparently agrees; for decades, it has opposed the gay rights movement.

What do people around the country actually think? Since 2001, the Gallup Poll has been asking Americans whether they personally believe gay relations to be morally acceptable or morally wrong. In 2001, 53% of Americans considered gay relations to be "morally wrong," with only 40% calling them "morally acceptable." By 2011, these numbers had changed dramatically: 56% called gay relations "morally acceptable," and only 39% deemed them "morally wrong."

People on both sides have strong feelings. Michele Bachmann, a Republican congresswoman from Minnesota, once told a conservative audience, "If you're involved in the gay and lesbian lifestyle, it's bondage. It is *personal* bondage, *personal* despair, and

32

personal enslavement." Bachmann and her husband offer troubled gays a way to break free from their alleged chains: they run a "Christian Counseling Center" in Minnesota, which offers its clients "Reparative Therapy" as a "cure" for homosexuality. Ms. Bachmann is an evangelical Lutheran. The Catholic view may be more nuanced, but it agrees that gay sex is wrong. According to the *Catechism of the Catholic Church,* homosexuals "do not choose their homosexual condition" and "must be accepted with respect, compassion, and sensitivity. Every sign of unjust discrimination in their regard should be avoided." Nonetheless, "homosexual acts are intrinsically disordered" and "under no circumstances can they be approved." Therefore, if gay people want to be virtuous, then they must resist their desires.

What attitude should we take? We might say that homosexuality is immoral, or we might say that it is all right. But there is a third alternative. We might say:

> People have different opinions, but where morality is concerned, there are no "facts," and no one is "right." People just feel differently, and that's all there is to it.

This is the basic thought behind Ethical Subjectivism. Ethical Subjectivism is the idea that our moral opinions are based on our feelings and nothing more. On this view, there is no such thing as "objective" right or wrong. It is a fact that some people are homosexual and some are heterosexual; but it is not a fact that one is good and the other is bad. So, when someone such as Bachmann says that homosexuality is wrong, she is not stating a fact about homosexuality. Instead, she is merely saying something about her feelings.

Of course, Ethical Subjectivism is not merely an idea about the assessment of homosexuality. It applies to all moral matters. To take a different example, it is a fact that the Nazis exterminated millions of innocent people; but according to Ethical Subjectivism, it is not a fact that what they did was evil. When we call their actions "evil," we are only saying that we have negative feelings toward them. The same applies to any moral judgment whatever.

3.2. The Evolution of the Theory

A philosophical theory may go through several stages. At first, it is put forward in simple terms, which many people find attractive. That simple formulation, however, is examined and found to have defects. At this point, some people are so impressed with the objections that they abandon the theory. Others, however, retain confidence in the basic idea, and so they refine it. For a while, it looks like they can rescue the theory. But then further arguments cast doubt on the new version. Those new objections, like the old, cause some people to abandon the idea, while others keep the faith and propose another "improved" version. The whole process of revision and criticism then begins again.

The theory of Ethical Subjectivism has developed in just this way. It began as a simple idea—in the words of David Hume, that morality is a matter of sentiment rather than fact. But as objections were raised to the theory, and its defenders tried to answer them, the theory became more sophisticated.

3.3. The First Stage: Simple Subjectivism

The simplest version of the theory is this: When a person says that something is morally good or bad, this means that he or she approves of that thing, or disapproves of it, and nothing more. In other words:

"X is morally acceptable"
"X is right"
"X is good"
"X ought to be done"

all mean: "I (the speaker) approve of X"

And similarly:

"X is morally unacceptable"
"X is wrong"
"X is bad"
"X ought not to be done"

all mean: "I (the speaker) disapprove of X"

We may call this version of the theory Simple Subjectivism. It expresses the basic idea of Ethical Subjectivism in a plain, uncomplicated form, and many people have found it attractive. However, it is open to some serious objections.

Simple Subjectivism Cannot Account for Disagreement. Gay rights advocate Matt Foreman does not believe that homosexuality is immoral. Congresswoman Michele Bachmann, however, believes it is. So, Foreman and Bachmann appear to disagree. But consider what Simple Subjectivism implies about this situation.

According to Simple Subjectivism, when Foreman says that homosexuality is not immoral, he is merely making a statement about his attitudes—he is saying, "I, Matt Foreman, do not disapprove of homosexuality." Would Bachmann disagree with that? No, Bachmann would agree that Foreman does not disapprove of homosexuality. At the same time, when Bachmann says that homosexuality is immoral, she is only saying, "I, Michele Bachmann, disapprove of homosexuality." And how could anyone disagree with that? Thus, according to Simple Subjectivism, there is no disagreement between them; each should acknowledge the truth of what the other is saying. Surely, though, this is incorrect, because Bachmann and Foreman *do* disagree about homosexuality.

There is a kind of eternal frustration implied by Simple Subjectivism: Bachmann and Foreman are deeply opposed to one another, yet they cannot even state their positions in a way that gets at the issue. Foreman may try to deny what Bachmann says, but according to Simple Subjectivism, he succeeds only in talking about himself.

The argument may be summarized like this: When one person says, "X is morally acceptable," and someone else says, "X is morally unacceptable," they are disagreeing. However, if Simple Subjectivism were correct, there could be no disagreement. Therefore, Simple Subjectivism cannot be correct.

Simple Subjectivism Implies That We're Always Right. We are sometimes wrong in our moral evaluations. But if Simple Subjectivism were correct, this would be impossible.

Again, consider Bachmann, who said that being gay is like being enslaved. In saying this, she probably meant that homosexuals are "slaves" to their wicked desires; they are living in the bonds of sin. According to Simple Subjectivism, when Bachmann called homosexuality "enslavement," she was merely saying that she, Bachmann, disapproves of homosexuality. Of course, she might have been speaking insincerely—it is possible that she didn't really mind homosexuality but was merely playing to her conservative audience. However, if Bachmann was speaking sincerely, then what she said was true. So long as someone is honestly representing her own feelings, her moral judgments will always be correct. But this contradicts the plain fact that we sometimes make mistakes about ethics. Therefore, Simple Subjectivism cannot be correct.

These arguments, and others like them, suggest that Simple Subjectivism is a flawed theory. In the face of such arguments, some philosophers have chosen to reject the whole idea of Ethical Subjectivism. Others, however, have worked to improve the theory.

3.4. The Second Stage: Emotivism

The improved version came to be known as Emotivism. Emotivism was popular during the mid-20th century, largely due to the work of the American philosopher Charles L. Stevenson (1908–1979).

Language, Stevenson said, is used in many ways. One way is to make statements—that is, to state facts. Thus we may say:

"Gas prices are rising."

"Lance Armstrong beat cancer and then won the Tour de France bike race seven times."

"Shakespeare wrote *Hamlet.*"

In each case, we are saying something that is either true or false, and the purpose of our utterance is, typically, to convey information to the listener.

However, language is also used for other purposes. Suppose I say, "Close the door!" This utterance is neither true nor false. It is not a statement, intended to convey information; it is a command. Its purpose is to get the listener to do something.

Or consider utterances such as these, which are neither statements nor commands:

"Aaargh!"

"Way to go, Lance!"

"Damn Hamlet!"

We understand these sentences easily enough. But none of them can be true or false. (It makes no sense to say, "It is true that 'way to go, Lance'" or "It is false that 'aaargh.'") These sentences are not used to state facts or to influence behavior. Their purpose is to express the speaker's attitudes—about gas prices, about Lance Armstrong, or about Hamlet.

Now think about moral language. According to the first theory, Simple Subjectivism, moral language is about stating facts—ethical statements report the speaker's attitudes. According to Simple Subjectivism, when Bachmann says, "Homosexuality is immoral," her utterance means "I (Bachmann) disapprove of homosexuality"—a statement of fact about Bachmann's attitude.

According to Emotivism, however, moral language is not fact-stating language; it is not used to convey information or to make reports. It is used, first, as a means of influencing people's behavior. If someone says, "You shouldn't do that," he is trying to *persuade you not to do it.* Thus, his utterance is more like a command than a statement of fact; "You shouldn't do that" is like saying "Don't do that!" Also, moral language is used to express one's attitudes. Calling Lance Armstrong "a good man" is thus like saying "Way to go, Lance!" And so, when Bachmann says, "Homosexuality is immoral," emotivists interpret her utterance as equivalent to something like "Homosexuality—gross!" or "Don't be gay!"

This difference between Simple Subjectivism and Emotivism may seem trivial. But it is important. To see why, consider again the arguments against Simple Subjectivism. While those arguments were severely embarrassing to Simple Subjectivism, they are less effective against Emotivism.

1. The first argument had to do with moral disagreement. If Simple Subjectivism is correct, then when one person says, "X is morally acceptable," and someone else says, "X is morally unacceptable," they are not really disagreeing. They are, instead, talking about different things: each person is making a claim about his or her own attitude—a claim which the other person doesn't dispute. But, the argument goes, such people really do disagree. Thus, Simple Subjectivism cannot be correct.

In response, Emotivism emphasizes that disagreement comes in different forms. Compare these two kinds of disagreement:

- I believe that Lee Harvey Oswald acted alone in the assassination of President John F. Kennedy, and you believe there was a conspiracy. This is a disagreement about the facts—I believe something to be true which you believe to be false.

- I am rooting for the Atlanta Braves to win, and you want them to lose. Our beliefs are not in conflict, but our desires are—I want something to happen which you want not to happen.

In the first case, we believe different things, both of which cannot be true. Stevenson calls this *disagreement in belief.* In the second case, we want different outcomes, both of which cannot occur. Stevenson calls this *disagreement in attitude.* As Stevenson observes, we may disagree in attitude even if we don't disagree in belief. For example, you and I may have all the same beliefs regarding the Atlanta Braves baseball team: we both believe that the Braves' players are overpaid; we both believe that I am rooting for the Braves just because I am from the South; and we both believe that Atlanta is not a great baseball town. Yet despite all this common ground—despite our agreement *in belief*—we may still differ *in attitude*: I may still want the Braves to win, and you may still want them to lose.

According to Stevenson, moral disagreement is disagreement in attitude only. Matt Foreman's attitudes about homosexuality are very different from Michele Bachmann's, even if Foreman and Bachmann agree about all the facts. For Emotivism, then, moral conflict is real. By contrast, Simple Subjectivism interprets moral disagreement as disagreement in *belief*—moral judgments express beliefs about the speaker's attitudes—so, when people disagree, they must disagree about what attitudes the speaker has. However, this gets things wrong. Foreman and Bachmann do disagree about homosexuality, but they do not disagree about what their own attitudes are.

   2. The second argument was that if Simple Subjectivism is correct, then we are always right in our moral judgments. But, of course, we are not always right. Therefore, Simple Subjectivism cannot be correct.

This argument is effective only because Simple Subjectivism interprets moral judgments as statements that can be true or false. "Always right" means that one's judgments are always true; and Simple Subjectivism assigns moral judgments a meaning that *will* always be true, so long as the speaker is sincere. That is why, on that theory, people turn out to be right all the time. Emotivism, on the other hand, does not interpret moral judgments as statements that are true or false. Because commands and expressions of attitude cannot be true or false, people cannot "be right" with respect to them, much less "be right all the time."

Emotivism, then, also avoids this objection to Simple Subjectivism. However, it is susceptible to a related complaint. Although we're not always right in our evaluations, we're right some of the time. Sometimes our moral judgments are true and sometimes they are false. Emotivists, however, cannot say this, because they deny that moral discourse is about stating facts.

Consider this example. On January 26, 2004, an 8-year-old girl named Katie Shelton was walking down a street in Seymour, Indiana. Suddenly she was confronted by two rottweilers, each weighing over 80 pounds. The dogs knocked Katie down and bit her repeatedly. The little girl's life, however, was saved by the heroic actions of 14-year-old Mark Friedrich, who lived nearby. When Mark saw what was going on, he rushed out of his family's house with two sticks and attacked the dogs. Predictably, Mark got bitten, but he was able to keep the dogs off Katie until a police officer arrived with a gun. Both children recovered from their wounds (the dogs were not so lucky).

Now suppose that, upon hearing this story, someone said that Mark Friedrich acted badly: "If he was a good kid, he would have minded his own business and stayed in his house." As long as this strange person was speaking sincerely, the Simple Subjectivist would have to say that his moral judgment was *true*. The emotivist's position is different, but like the Simple Subjectivist, she is barred from saying that this person's judgment is false. She must say that he is merely expressing his feelings.

Although Emotivism is an improvement on Simple Subjectivism, both theories imply that our moral judgments are, in a sense, beyond reproach. For Simple Subjectivism, our judgments cannot be criticized because they will always be true. For Emotivism, our moral judgments cannot be criticized because they are not judgments at all; they are mere expressions of attitude, which cannot be false. That is one problem for Emotivism. Another problem is that Emotivism cannot explain the role reason plays in ethics.

3.5. The Role of Reason in Ethics

If someone says, "I like peaches," she does not need to have a reason; she may be making a statement about her personal taste and nothing more. But moral judgments are different. If someone tells you that a particular act would be wrong, you may ask why, and if there is no satisfactory answer, then you may reject that advice as unfounded. A moral judgment—or for that matter, any kind of value judgment—must be supported by good reasons. Any adequate theory of ethics should be able to explain how reasons can support moral judgments.

What do emotivists say about reasons? Remember that for the emotivist, moral judgments have two functions: to express one's attitudes, and to try to influence other people's attitudes and conduct. Can the expressive function of moral language find a place for reasons? Insofar as moral judgments are mere expressions of attitude, they are like personal preferences. When I say, "Letting people be free is morally better than enslaving them," the emotivist hears this as similar to "Peaches are better than apples." The emotivist can recognize some differences between those two utterances. However, they are basically alike. Reason can play no important role here.

Thus, emotivists have usually looked to the command function of moral language to find a role for reasons. Suppose I had said to you in 2008, "You shouldn't vote for Barack Obama." If this utterance is like a command—if it is like saying, "Don't vote for Obama"—then what role can reasons play in such a judgment? If I am trying to influence your conduct, then perhaps the emotivist should say that a reason is any consideration that will influence your conduct. But consider what this means. Suppose I know that you are prejudiced against Muslims. And I say, "Obama, you know, is a Muslim." That does the trick; you now decide not to vote for Obama. For the emotivist, the claim that Obama is a Muslim would be, given the right audience, a moral reason not to vote for him. In fact, Stevenson takes exactly this view. In his classic work *Ethics and Language* (1944), he says, "*Any* statement about *any* matter of fact which *any* speaker considers likely to alter attitudes may be adduced as a reason for or against an ethical judgment."

Obviously, something has gone wrong. Not just any claim can count as reason in support of just any judgment. For one thing, it must be relevant to the judgment, and psychological influence does not always bring relevance with it. Being Muslim is irrelevant to one's ability to be a good president, regardless of the psychological connections in anyone's mind. Also, to be a legitimate reason, a claim must be true, and yet false claims can be persuasive. President Obama is not in fact a Muslim. There are two lessons to be learned from this. The small lesson is that a particular moral theory, Emotivism, is flawed, which casts doubt on the whole idea of Ethical Subjectivism. The larger lesson has to do with the importance of reason in ethics.

Hume said that if we examine wicked actions—"wilful murder, for instance"—we will find no "matter of fact" corresponding to the wickedness. The universe, apart from our attitudes, contains no such facts. What can we conclude from this? Admittedly, value is not a tangible thing like a planet or a spoon. But this does not mean that ethics has no objective basis. A fundamental mistake, which many people fall into, is to assume just two possibilities:

1. There are moral facts, in the same way that there are planets and spoons.
2. Our values are nothing more than the expression of our subjective feelings.

This is a mistake because it overlooks a third possibility. People have not only feelings but reason, and that makes a big difference. It may be that

3. Moral truths are truths of reason; that is, a moral judgment is true if it is backed by better reasons than the alternatives.

On this view, moral truths are objective in the sense that they are true independently of what we might want or think. We cannot make something good or bad just by wishing it so, because our will cannot determine what the reasons are. And this also explains our fallibility: We can be wrong about what is good or bad because we can be wrong about what reason recommends. Reason says what it says, regardless of our opinions or desires.

3.6. Are There Proofs in Ethics?

If Ethical Subjectivism is not true, why are so many people attracted to it? One reason is that science provides our paradigm of objectivity, and when we compare ethics to science, ethics seems lacking. For example, there are proofs in science, but there are no proofs in ethics. We can prove that the earth is round, that dinosaurs lived before humans, and that there is no largest prime number. But we can't prove that abortion is acceptable or unacceptable.

The general idea that moral judgments can't be proved sounds appealing. Anyone who has ever argued about something like abortion knows how frustrating it can be to try to "prove" one's opinion. However, if we inspect this idea more closely, it turns out to be flawed.

Suppose we consider something much simpler than abortion. A student says that a test was unfair. This is clearly a moral judgment—fairness is a basic moral value. Can this judgment be proved? The student might point out that the test covered a lot of material that was trivial while ignoring material the teacher had stressed as important. The test also included questions that were not covered in either the readings or the class discussions. Moreover, the test was so long that nobody could finish it in the time allowed.

Suppose all this is true. And further suppose that the teacher, when asked to explain, can offer no defense. In fact, the teacher, who is rather inexperienced, seems confused about the whole thing. Now, hasn't the student proved that the test was unfair? What more in the way of proof could we want? It is easy to think of other examples that make the same point:

- *Jones is a bad man:* Jones is a habitual liar; he toys with people; he cheats at cards; he once killed someone in a dispute over 27 cents; and so on.
- *Dr. Smith is irresponsible:* He bases his diagnoses on superficial considerations; he refuses to listen to other doctors' advice; he drinks beer before performing delicate surgery; and so on.
- *A certain used-car dealer is unethical:* She conceals defects in her cars; she tries to pressure people into paying too much; she runs misleading ads on the Web; and so on.

The process of giving reasons might even be taken one step further. If we criticize Jones for being a habitual liar, we can go on to explain why lying is bad. Lying is bad, first, because it harms people. If I give you false information, and you rely on it, things may go wrong for you in all sorts of ways. Second, lying is bad because it is a violation of trust. Trusting another person means leaving oneself vulnerable and unprotected. When I trust you, I simply believe what you say, without taking precautions; and when you lie, you take advantage of my trust. And finally, the rule requiring truthfulness is necessary for society to exist—if we could not assume that other people would speak truthfully, communication would be impossible, and if communication were impossible, society would fall apart.

So we can support our judgments with good reasons, and we can explain why those reasons matter. If we can do all this, and, for an encore, show that no comparable case can be made on the other side, what more in the way of "proof" could anyone want? In the face of all this, it is absurd to say that ethical judgments are nothing but "opinions."

Nevertheless, the impression that moral judgments are "unprovable" is remarkably persistent. Why do people believe this? Three points might be raised.

First, when proof is demanded, people often want scientific proof. They want something like experimental verification, and because ethical judgments cannot be experimentally tested, they say there is no proof. But in ethics, rational thinking consists in giving reasons, analyzing arguments, setting out and justifying principles, and so on. The fact that ethical reasoning differs from scientific reasoning does not make it deficient.

Second, when we think about proving our ethical opinions, we tend to think of the most difficult issues. The question of abortion, for example, is enormously complicated. If we consider only issues like abortion, it is easy to believe that "proof" in ethics is impossible. But the same could be said of the sciences. There are complicated matters that physicists cannot agree on; and if we focused entirely on them, we might conclude that there are no proofs in physics. But, of course, there are many simpler issues on which all physicists agree. Similarly, in ethics, there are many simple issues about which all reasonable people agree.

Finally, it is easy to run together two matters that are really very different:

1. Proving an opinion to be correct
2. Persuading someone to accept your proof

When your argument fails to persuade your audience, it is tempting to think, "Well, that argument didn't work." But the argument might have failed merely because your audience was stubborn, or biased, or not really listening. As a proof, your argument might have been perfect.

3.7. The Question of Homosexuality

Let's return to the dispute about homosexuality. If we consider the relevant reasons, what do we find? The most pertinent fact is that gays are pursuing the only kind of life that can make them happy. Sex, after all, is a particularly strong urge, and few people can be happy without satisfying their sexual needs. But we should not focus solely on sex. Homosexuality is not merely about who you have sex with; it's about who you fall in love with. Gay people fall in love in the same way that straight people do. And, like straights, gays often want to be with, live with, and build a life with, the person they love. To say that homosexuals shouldn't act on their desires is thus to condemn them to frustrating lives. It should be added that gay people cannot avoid the frustration by choosing to become straight. Both homosexuals and heterosexuals discover who they are, once they reach a certain age; nobody decides which sex to be attracted to.

Why do people oppose gay rights? Some people think that homosexuals pose a danger to others. Often the charge, whether stated or not, is that gay men are likely to be child molesters. There have, for example, been several campaigns in America to get gay public schoolteachers fired, and the fear of pedophilia has always loomed large in these discussions. Congresswoman Bachmann exploited this fear when she said of gay marriage, "This is a very serious matter, because it is our children who are the prize for this community—[the gay community] are specifically targeting our children." Such a fear, however, has never had any basis in fact. It is a mere stereotype, like the idea that blacks are lazy or that Muslims are terrorists. There is no difference between gays and heterosexuals in their moral characters or in their contributions to society.

The most common objection to homosexuality may be that it is "unnatural." What should we make of this? To assess the argument, we need to know what "unnatural" means. There seem to be three possibilities.

First, "unnatural" might be taken as a statistical notion. In this sense, a human quality is unnatural if most people don't have it. Being gay would be unnatural in this sense, but so would being left-handed, being tall, and even being immensely nice. Clearly, this is no reason to criticize homosexuality. Rare qualities are often good.

Second, the meaning of "unnatural" might be connected with the idea of a thing's *purpose*. The parts of our bodies seem to serve particular purposes. The purpose of the eyes is to see, and the purpose of the heart is to pump blood. Similarly, the purpose of our genitals is to procreate: Sex is for making babies. It may be argued, then, that gay sex is unnatural because it is sexual activity that is divorced from its natural purpose.

This seems to express what many people have in mind when they object to homosexuality as unnatural. However, if gay sex were condemned for this reason, then a number of other, widely accepted practices would also have to be condemned: masturbation, oral sex, sex using condoms, and even sex by women during pregnancy or after menopause. These practices would be just as "unnatural" (and, presumably, just as bad) as gay sex. But there is no reason to accept these conclusions, because this whole line of reasoning is faulty. It rests on the assumption that *it is wrong to use parts of one's body for anything other than their natural purposes.* Why should we accept that assumption? The "purpose" of the eyes is to see; is it therefore wrong to use one's eyes for flirting or for giving a signal? The "purpose" of the fingers may be to grasp and poke; is it therefore wrong to snap one's fingers to get someone's attention? The idea that things should be used only in "natural" ways cannot be maintained, and so this version of the argument fails.

Third, because the word *unnatural* has a sinister sound, it might be understood simply as a term of evaluation. Perhaps it means something like "contrary to what a person ought to be." But if that is what "unnatural" means, then to say that homosexuality is wrong because it is unnatural would be vacuous. It would be like saying that homosexuality is wrong because it is wrong. That sort of empty remark provides no reason for condemning anything.

The idea that homosexuality is unnatural, and so it must be immoral, seems right to many people. Nevertheless, it is an unsound argument. It fails on every interpretation.

But what about the claim, often made, that homosexuality is "contrary to family values"? James Dobson, founder of the conservative Christian group, Focus on the Family, told his followers: "For more than 40 years, the homosexual activist movement has sought to implement a master plan that has had as its centerpiece the utter destruction of the family." But how, exactly, are homosexuals trying to destroy the family? Gay activists are actually trying to *expand* the family. They do not wish to take any rights away from heterosexual couples. Instead, they want to make it easier for gays to form families— they support same-sex marriage, domestic partner benefits, the right of gay couples to adopt children, and so on. Gays find it ironic that supporters of "the family" want to prevent them from having families.

Perhaps all this talk of "family values" really amounts to saying, "Let's make sure we don't have families *like that.*" But if so, then the question arises: What is wrong with a family in which the children are raised by two mothers, or two fathers? Common sense suggests that two parents are better than one: raising a child is a huge task, and two people can perform big tasks more easily than one. But even if the *number* of parents in a household matters, it is not clear why their gender should. The largest study of gay families is the U.S. National Longitudinal Lesbian Family Study, which has followed a group of gay mothers since the 1980s. Their data suggest that the teenage children of lesbians actually do *better* than teenagers from traditional homes. Sometimes the children of gay parents are made fun of at school, and this is difficult for them. But, in general, these children have fewer behavioral problems, and they do better both socially and academically than their peers. There is no good reason to be against gay families.

Meanwhile, homosexuals in America continue to be disadvantaged. Sometimes the disadvantage is a matter of law. Legally, heterosexuals can tie the knot in any state, but gay marriage exists in only a half-dozen states. Moreover, the federal government does not recognize gay marriage as legitimate, and so it provides marital benefits to heterosexual couples only. There are hundreds of such benefits, including the social security benefits that a spouse may receive after the other spouse's death. Finally, in Florida and Arkansas, gay people cannot legally adopt children, although, of course, heterosexuals can. The law in America certainly discriminates against gays. Yet, in many other places, the laws are even more extreme.

In 76 countries, gay sex is illegal. In some countries, the punishment is death.

Apart from the law, there are social drawbacks to being gay in America. It is tough to grow up in a place where four-tenths of your neighbors believe that something is wrong with you. Even worse, you find that some of your neighbors are hateful—they are repulsed by you and see you as less than human. It is especially sad when a young person who has been taught to despise homosexuality begins to realize that he or she is gay. Many gays, whether out of fear or shame, choose to live in the closet. But in the long run, it is almost impossible to hide one's sexuality from friends, family members, and co-workers. Gays in America lead stressful lives. Among American college students, gays are twice as likely to attempt suicide as their straight classmates. And *closeted* gays are *six times* more likely to try it.

One more argument must be discussed, namely, that homosexuality is condemned in the Bible. For example, Leviticus 18:22 says, "You may not lie with a man as with a woman; it is an abomination." Some commentators have said that, contrary to appearances, the Bible is really not so harsh toward homosexuality; and they explain how each relevant passage (there seem to be nine of them) should be understood. But suppose we accept that the Bible condemns homosexuality. What may we infer from this? Are we supposed to believe what the Bible says, simply because it says it?

This question will offend some people. To question the Bible, they believe, is to challenge the word of God. And this, they think, is an act of arrogance coming from creatures who should be showing gratitude to the Almighty. Questioning the Bible can also make people feel uncomfortable, because it may seem to challenge their whole way of life. However, thoughts like these cannot hold us back. Philosophy *is* about questioning whole ways of life. When the argument is given that homosexuality must be wrong because the Bible says so, this argument must be assessed on its own terms.

The problem with the argument is that, if we look at *other* things the Bible says, it does not appear to be a reliable guide to morality. Leviticus condemns homosexuality, but it also forbids eating sheep's fat (7:23), letting a woman into the church's sanctuary who has recently given birth (12:2–5), and seeing your uncle naked. The latter, like homosexuality, is deemed an abomination (18:14, 26). Even worse, Leviticus condemns to death those who curse their parents (20:9) and those who commit adultery (20:10). It says that a priest's daughter, if she "plays the whore," shall be burned alive (21:9), and it says that we may purchase slaves from nearby nations (25:44). In Exodus, it even says that it's okay to beat your slaves, so long as you don't kill them (21:20–21).

The point of all this is not to ridicule the Bible; the Bible, in fact, contains much that is true and wise. But we can conclude from examples like these that the Bible is not always right. And because it's not always right, we can't conclude that homosexuality is an abomination just because it says so in Leviticus.

At any rate, nothing can be morally right or wrong *simply* because an authority says so. If the precepts in a sacred text are not arbitrary, there must be some reason for them—we should be able to ask *why* the Bible condemns homosexuality and then to get an answer. That answer will then give the real explanation of why the thing is wrong.

But the main point of this chapter is not about homosexuality. The main point concerns the nature of moral thinking. Moral thinking and moral conduct are a matter of weighing reasons and being guided by them. But being guided by reason is very different from following one's feelings. When we have strong feelings, we may be tempted to ignore reason and go with the feelings. But in doing so, we would be opting out of moral thinking altogether. That is why, in focusing on attitudes and feelings, Ethical Subjectivism seems to be going in the wrong direction.

CHAPTER 4

Does Morality Depend on Religion?

The Good consists in always doing what God wills at any particular moment.

EMIL BRUNNER, *THE DIVINE IMPERATIVE* (1947)

I respect deities. I do not rely upon them.

MUSASHI MIYAMOTO, AT ICHIJOJI TEMPLE (ca. 1608)

4.1. The Presumed Connection between Morality and Religion

In 1995 the American Civil Liberties Union (ACLU) sued Judge Roy Moore of Gadsden, Alabama, for displaying the Ten Commandments in his courtroom. Such a display, the ACLU said, violates the separation of church and state, which is guaranteed by the U.S. Constitution. The ACLU might not have liked Moore, but Alabama voters did. In 2000, Moore successfully campaigned to become chief justice of the Alabama Supreme Court, running on a promise to "restore the moral foundation of law." Thus the "Ten Commandments judge" became the most powerful jurist in the state of Alabama.

Moore was not through making his point, however. In the wee hours of July 31, 2001, he had a granite monument to the Ten Commandments installed in the Alabama state judicial building. This monument weighed over 5,000 pounds, and anyone entering the building could not miss it. Moore was sued again, but the people were behind him: 77% of Americans thought that he should be allowed to display his monument. Yet the law did not agree. When Moore disobeyed a court order to remove the monument, the Alabama Court of the Judiciary fired him, saying that he had placed himself above the law. Moore, however, believed that he was putting *God* above the law. The United States is a religious country. Nearly 80% of Americans say they believe in God, and another 12% say they believe in a universal spirit or higher power. The main religion in America is Christianity; 41% of Americans report believing that Jesus Christ will return to earth by 2050. In America, members of the Christian clergy are often treated as moral experts: Hospitals ask them to sit on ethics committees; reporters interview them on the moral dimensions of a story; and churchgoers look to them for guidance. The clergy even help decide whether movies will be rated "G," "PG," "PG-13," "R," or "NC-17." Priests and ministers are assumed to be wise counselors who will give sound moral advice.

Why are the clergy regarded in this way? The reason is not that they have proven themselves to be better or wiser than other people—as a group, they seem to be neither better nor worse than the rest of us. There is a deeper reason why they are thought to have special moral insight. In popular thinking, morality and religion are inseparable: People commonly believe that morality can be understood only in the context of religion. Thus the clergy are assumed to be authorities on morality.

It is not hard to see why people think this. When viewed from a nonreligious perspective, the universe seems to be a cold, meaningless place, devoid of value and purpose. In his essay "A Free Man's Worship," written in 1902, Bertrand Russell expressed what he called the "scientific" view of the world:

> That Man is the product of causes which had no prevision of the end they were achieving; that his origin, his growth, his hopes and fears, his loves and his beliefs, are but the outcome of accidental collocations of atoms; that no fire, no heroism, no intensity of thought and feeling, can preserve an individual life beyond the grave; that all the labours of the ages, all the devotion, all the inspiration, all the noonday brightness of human genius, are destined to extinction in the vast death of the solar system, and that the whole temple of Man's achievement must inevitably be buried beneath the debris of a universe in ruins—all these things, if not quite beyond dispute, are yet so nearly certain that no philosophy which rejects them can hope to stand.

From a religious perspective, however, things look very different. Judaism and Christianity teach that the world was created by a loving, all-powerful God to provide a home for us. We, in turn, were created in his image, to be his children. Thus, the world is not devoid of meaning and purpose. It is, instead, the arena in which God's plans are realized. What could be more natural, then, than to think of "morality" as part of religion, while the atheist's world has no place for values?

4.2. The Divine Command Theory

Christians, Jews, and Muslims all believe that God has told us to obey certain rules of conduct. God does not force these rules on us. He created us as free agents; so, we may choose what to do. But if we live as we should, then we must follow God's laws. This idea has been expanded into a theory known as the Divine Command Theory. The basic idea is that God decides what is right and wrong. Actions that God commands are morally required; actions that God forbids are morally wrong; and all other actions are permissible or merely morally neutral.

This theory has a number of attractive features. It immediately solves the old problem of the objectivity of ethics. Ethics is not merely a matter of personal feeling or social custom. Whether something is right or wrong is perfectly objective: It is right if God commands it and wrong if God forbids it. Moreover, the Divine Command Theory explains why anyone should bother with morality. Why not forget about "ethics" and just look out for yourself? If immorality is the violation of God's commandments, there is an easy answer: On the day of final reckoning, you will be held accountable.

There are, however, serious problems with the theory. Of course, atheists would not accept it, because they do not believe that God exists. But there are difficulties even for believers. The main problem was identified by Plato, a Greek philosopher who lived 400 years before Jesus of Nazareth. Plato's books are written as conversations, or dialogues, in which Plato's teacher Socrates is always the main speaker. In one of them, the *Euthyphro*, there is a discussion of whether "right" can be defined as "what the gods command." Socrates is skeptical and asks, Is conduct right because the gods command it, or do the gods command it because it is right? This is one of the most famous questions in the history of philosophy. The British philosopher Antony Flew (1923–2010) suggests that "one good test of a person's aptitude for philosophy is to discover whether he can grasp [the] force and point" of this question.

Socrates's question is about whether God *makes* the moral truths true or whether he merely *recognizes* that they're true. There's a big difference between these options. I know that the Burj Khalifa building in the United Arab Emirates is the tallest building in the world; I recognize that fact. However, I did not make it true. Rather, it was made true by the designers and builders in the city of Dubai. Is God's relation to ethics like my relation to the Burj Khalifa building or like the relation of the builders? This question poses a dilemma, and either way out leads to trouble.

First, we might say that *right conduct is right because God commands it*. For example, according to Exodus 20:16, God commands us to be truthful. Thus, we should be truthful simply because God requires it. God's command makes truthfulness right, just as the builders of a skyscraper make the building tall. This is the Divine Command Theory. It is almost the theory of Shakespeare's character Hamlet. Hamlet said that nothing is good or bad, but thinking makes it so. According to the Divine Command Theory, nothing is good or bad, except when *God's* thinking makes it so.

This idea encounters several difficulties.

1. *This conception of morality is mysterious.* What does it mean to say that God "makes" truthfulness right? It is easy enough to understand how physical objects are made, at least in principle. We have all made something, if only a sand castle or a peanut-butter-and-jelly sandwich. But making truthfulness right is not like that; it could not be done by rearranging things in the physical environment. How, then, could it be done? No one knows.

To see the problem, consider some wretched case of child abuse. On the theory we're now considering, God could make *that* instance of child abuse right—not by turning a slap into a friendly pinch of the cheek, but *by commanding that the slap is right*. This proposal defies human understanding. How could merely saying, or commanding, that the slap is right make it right? If true, this conception of morality would be a mystery.

2. *This conception of morality makes God's commands arbitrary.* We assume that God has good reasons for what he does.

But suppose God commands truthfulness to be right. On this theory, he could have given different commands just as easily. He could have commanded us to be liars, and then lying, and not truthfulness, would be right. After all, before God issues his commands, no reasons for or against lying exist—*God is the one who creates the reasons.* And so, from a moral point of view, God's commands are arbitrary. He could command anything whatsoever. This result may seem not only unacceptable but impious from a religious point of view.

3. *This conception of morality provides the wrong reasons for moral principles.* There are many things wrong with child abuse: It is malicious; it involves the unnecessary infliction of pain; it can have unwanted long-term psychological effects; and so on. However, the theory we're now considering cannot recognize any of these reasons as important. All it cares about, in the end, is whether child abuse runs counter to God's commands.

There are two ways of confirming that something is wrong here. First, notice something the theory implies: *If God didn't exist, child abuse wouldn't be wrong.* After all, if God didn't exist, then God wouldn't be around to make child abuse wrong. However, child abuse would still be malicious, so it would still be wrong. Thus, the Divine Command Theory fails. Second, keep in mind that even a religious person might be genuinely in doubt as to what God has commanded. After all, religious texts disagree with each other, and sometimes there seem to be inconsistencies even within a single text. So, a person might be in doubt as to what God's will really is. However, a person needn't be in doubt as to whether child abuse is wrong. What God has commanded is one thing; whether hitting children is wrong is another.

There is a way to avoid these troublesome consequences. We can take the second of Socrates's options. We need not say that right conduct is right because God commands it. Instead, we may say that God commands us to do certain things *because they are right.* God, who is infinitely wise, recognizes that truthfulness is better than deceitfulness, and so he commands us to be truthful; he sees that killing is wrong, and so he commands us not to kill; and so on for the other moral rules.

If we take this option, we avoid the consequences that spoiled the first alternative. We needn't worry about how God makes it wrong to lie, because he doesn't. God's commands are not arbitrary; they are the result of his wisdom in knowing what is best. Furthermore, we are not saddled with the wrong explanations for our moral principles; rather, we are free to appeal to whatever justifications of them seem appropriate.

Unfortunately, this second option has a different drawback. In taking it, we abandon the theological conception of right and wrong. When we say that God commands us to be truthful *because* truthfulness is right, we acknowledge a standard that is independent of God's will. The rightness exists prior to God's command and is the reason for the command. Thus, if we want to know why we should be truthful, the reply "because God commands it" does not really tell us. We may still ask, "*Why* does God command it?" and the answer to *that* question will provide the ultimate reason.

Many religious people believe that they must accept a theological conception of right and wrong because it would be sacrilegious not to do so. They feel, somehow, that if they believe in God, then right and wrong must be understood in terms of God's wishes. Our arguments, however, suggest that the Divine Command Theory is not only untenable but impious. And, in fact, some of the greatest theologians have rejected the theory for just this reason. Thinkers such as Saint Thomas Aquinas connect morality with religion in a different way.

4.3. The Theory of Natural Law

In the history of Christian thought, the dominant theory of ethics is not the Divine Command Theory. That honor instead goes to the Theory of Natural Law. This theory has three main parts.

1. The Theory of Natural Law rests on a particular view of the world. On this view, the world has a rational order, with values and purposes built into its very nature. This conception derives from the Greeks, whose way of understanding the world dominated Western thinking for over 1,700 years. The Greeks believed that *everything in nature has a purpose.*

Aristotle (384–322 B.C.) built this idea into his system of thought when he said that, in order to understand anything, four questions must be asked: What is it? What is it made of? How did it come to be? And what is it for? The answers might be: This is a knife; it is made of metal; it was made by a craftsman; and it is used for cutting. Aristotle assumed that the last

question—What is it for?—could be asked of anything whatever. "Nature," he said, "belongs to the class of causes which act
for the sake of something."

Obviously, artifacts such as knives have purposes, because
craftsmen have built them with a purpose in mind. But what
about natural objects that we do not make? Aristotle believed
that they have purposes, too. One of his examples was that we
have teeth so that we can chew. Biological examples are quite
persuasive; each part of our bodies does seem, intuitively, to
have a special purpose—our eyes are for seeing, our heart is
for pumping blood, our skin is there to protect us, and so on.
But Aristotle's claim was not limited to organic beings. According to him, *everything* has a purpose. To take a different sort
of example, he thought that rain falls so that plants can grow.
He considered other alternatives, such as that the rain falls "of
necessity" and that this helps the plants only "by coincidence."
However, he rejected them.

The world, therefore, is an orderly, rational system, with
each thing having its own proper place and serving its own special purpose. There is a neat hierarchy: The rain exists for the
sake of the plants, the plants exist for the sake of the animals,
and the animals exist—of course—for the sake of people. Aristotle says: "If then we are right in believing that nature makes
nothing without some end in view, nothing to no purpose, it
must be that nature has made all things specifically for the
sake of man." This worldview is stunningly anthropocentric, or
human-centered. But Aristotle was hardly alone in having such
thoughts; almost every important thinker in our history has
advanced such a thesis. Humans are a remarkably vain species.

The Christian thinkers who came later found this worldview congenial. Only one thing was missing: God. Thus, the
Christian thinkers said that the rain falls to help the plants
because that is what God intended, and the animals are for human
use because *that is what God made them for.* Values and purposes
were thus conceived to be part of the divine plan.

2. A corollary to this way of thinking is that the "laws of
nature" describe not only how things *are* but also how things
ought to be. The world is in harmony when things serve their
natural purposes. When they do not, or cannot, things have
gone wrong. Eyes that cannot see are defective, and drought is
a natural evil; the badness of both is explained by reference to

natural law. But there are also implications for human conduct. Moral rules are now viewed as deriving from the laws of nature. Some ways of behaving are said to be "natural" while others are said to be "unnatural"; and "unnatural" acts are regarded as morally wrong.

Consider, for example, the duty of beneficence. We are morally required to care about our neighbors. Why? According to the Theory of Natural Law, beneficence is natural for us, given the kind of creatures we are. We are by nature social and need the company of other people. Someone who does not care at all for others—who really does not care, through and through—is seen as deranged. Modern psychiatry says that such people suffer from *antisocial personality disorder*, and such people are commonly called *psychopaths* or *sociopaths*. A malicious personality is defective, just as eyes are defective if they cannot see. And, it may be added, this is true because we were created by God, with a specific "human" nature, as part of his overall plan.

The endorsement of beneficence is relatively uncontroversial. Natural-law theory has also been used, however, to support more contentious moral views. Religious thinkers often condemn "deviant" sexual practices, and they usually justify this by appealing to the Theory of Natural Law. If everything has a purpose, what is the purpose of sex? The obvious answer is procreation. Sexual activity that is not connected with making babies can therefore be seen as "unnatural," and practices like masturbation and gay sex may be condemned for this reason. This view of sex dates back at least to Saint Augustine (A.D. 354–430), and it is explicit in the writings of Saint Thomas Aquinas (1225–1274). The moral theology of the Catholic Church is based on natural-law theory.

Outside the Catholic Church, the Theory of Natural Law has few advocates today. It is generally rejected for three reasons.

First, the idea that "what's natural is good" seems open to obvious counterexamples. Sometimes what's natural is bad. People naturally care much more about themselves than about strangers, but this is regrettable. Disease occurs naturally, but disease is bad. Children are naturally self-centered, but parents don't think this is a good thing.

Second, the Theory of Natural Law seems to confuse "is" and "ought." In the 18th century, David Hume pointed out that *what is the case* and *what ought to be the case* are logically different notions, and no conclusion about one follows from the other. We can say that people are naturally disposed to be beneficent, but it does not follow that they *ought* to be beneficent. Similarly, it may be true that sex produces babies, but it does not follow that sex *ought* or *ought not* to be engaged in only for that purpose. Facts are one thing; values are another.

Third, the Theory of Natural Law is now widely rejected because its view of the world conflicts with modern science. The world as described by Galileo, Newton, and Darwin has no need for "facts" about right and wrong. Their explanations of natural phenomena make no reference to values or purposes. What happens just happens, due to the laws of cause and effect. If the rain benefits the plants, this is because the plants have evolved by the laws of natural selection in a rainy climate.

Thus, modern science gives us a picture of the world as a realm of facts, where the only "natural laws" are the laws of physics, chemistry, and biology, working blindly and without purpose. Whatever values may be, they are not part of the natural order. As for the idea that "nature has made all things specifically for the sake of man," well, that is only vanity. To the extent that one accepts the worldview of modern science, one will be skeptical of the Theory of Natural Law. It is no accident that the theory was a product, not of modern thought, but of the Middle Ages.

3. The third part of the theory addresses the question of moral knowledge. How can we determine what is right and what is wrong? The Divine Command Theory says that we must consult God's commandments. The Theory of Natural Law gives a different answer. The "natural laws" that specify what we should do are laws of reason, which we are able to grasp because God has given us the power to understand them. Therefore, the Theory of Natural Law endorses the familiar idea that the right thing to do is whatever action has the best reasons backing it up. To use the traditional terminology, moral judgments are "dictates of reason." As Saint Thomas Aquinas, the greatest natural-law theorist, wrote in his masterpiece the *Summa Theologica*, "To disparage the dictate of reason is equivalent to condemning the command of God."

This means that the religious believer has no special access to moral truth. The believer and the nonbeliever are in the same position. God has given everyone the ability to listen to reason and follow its directives. In an important sense, this leaves morality independent of religion. Religious belief does not affect the calculation of what is best, and the results of moral inquiry are religiously "neutral." Even though they may disagree about religion, believers and nonbelievers inhabit the same moral universe.

4.4. Religion and Particular Moral Issues

Some religious people will find the preceding discussion unsatisfying. It will seem too abstract to have any bearing on their actual lives. For them, the connection between morality and religion is an immediate, practical matter that centers on particular moral issues. It doesn't matter whether right and wrong are understood in terms of God's will or whether moral laws are laws of nature. What matters are the moral teachings of one's religion. The Scriptures and the church leaders are regarded as authorities; if one is truly faithful, one must accept what they say. Many Christians, for example, believe that they must oppose abortion because the church condemns it and (they assume) the Scriptures do too.

Are there distinctively religious positions on major moral issues that believers must accept? The rhetoric of the pulpit suggests so. But there is good reason to think otherwise.

For one thing, it is often difficult to find specific moral guidance in the Scriptures. We face different problems than our ancestors faced 2,000 years ago; thus, the Scriptures may be silent on matters that seem pressing to us. The Bible does contain a number of general precepts—for example, to love one's neighbor and to treat others as one wishes to be treated. And those are fine principles, which have practical application in our lives. However, it is not clear what they imply about the rights of workers, or the extinction of species, or the funding of medical research, and so on.

Another problem is that the Scriptures and church tradition are often ambiguous. Authorities disagree, leaving the believer in the awkward position of having to choose which element of the tradition to accept. For instance, the New Testament condemns being rich, and there is a long tradition of self-denial and charitable giving that affirms this teaching. But there is also an obscure Old Testament figure named Jabez who asked God to "enlarge my territories" (1 Chronicles 4:10), and God did. A recent book urging Christians to adopt Jabez as their model became a best-seller.

Thus, when people say that their moral views come from their religion, they are often mistaken. What's really going on is this. They are making up their minds about the moral issues and then interpreting the Scriptures, or church tradition, in a way that supports the conclusions they've already reached. Of course, this does not happen in every case, but it seems fair to say that it happens a lot. The question of riches is one example; abortion is another.

In the debate over abortion, religious issues are never far from the discussion. Religious conservatives hold that the fetus is a person from the moment of conception, and so abortion is murder. The fetus, they believe, is not merely a *potential* person but is an *actual* person, possessing a full-fledged right to life. Liberals, of course, deny this—they say that the fetus is something less than that, at least at the beginning of the pregnancy.

The abortion debate is complex, but we are concerned only with how it relates to religion. Conservatives sometimes say that fetal life is sacred. Is that the Christian view? *Must* Christians condemn abortion? To answer those questions, one might look to the Scriptures or to church tradition.

The Scriptures. It is difficult to derive a prohibition against abortion from either the Jewish or the Christian Scriptures. Certain passages, however, are often quoted by conservatives because they seem to suggest that fetuses have full human status. One of the most frequently cited passages is from the first chapter of Jeremiah, in which Jeremiah quotes God as saying, "Before I formed you in the womb I knew you, and before you were born I consecrated you." These words are presented as though they were God's endorsement of the conservative position: it is wrong to kill the unborn because the unborn are consecrated to God.

In context, however, these words obviously mean something different. Suppose we read the whole passage in which they occur:

> Now the word of the Lord came to me, saying, "Before I formed you in the womb I knew you, and before you were born I consecrated you; I appointed you a prophet to the nations."

Then I said, "Ah, Lord God! Behold, I do not know how to speak, for I am only a youth." But the Lord said to me,
"Do not say, 'I am only a youth'; for to all to whom I send you, you shall go, and whatever I command you, you shall speak. Be not afraid of them, for I am with you to deliver you."

The sanctity of fetal life is not discussed in this passage. Instead, Jeremiah is asserting his authority as a prophet. He is saying, in effect, "God authorized me to speak for him; even though I resisted, he insisted." But Jeremiah puts the point more poetically; he says that God had intended him to be a prophet even before he was born.

This often happens when the Scriptures are cited in connection with controversial moral issues. A few words are lifted from a passage that is concerned with something else entirely, and those words are then construed in a way that supports a favored moral position. When this happens, is it accurate to say that the person is "following the moral teachings of the Bible"? Or is it more accurate to say that he has searched the Scriptures to find support for a moral view he already believes, and then has read the desired conclusion into the Scriptures? If the latter, it suggests an arrogant attitude—the attitude that God himself must share one's own moral opinions!

Other biblical passages seem to support a *liberal* view of abortion. Three times the death penalty is recommended for women who have had sex out of wedlock, even though killing the woman would also kill her fetus (Genesis 38:24; Leviticus 21:9; Deuteronomy 22:20–21). This suggests that the fetus has no right to life. Also, in Exodus 21, God tells Moses that the penalty for murder is death; however, the penalty for causing a woman to miscarry is only a fine. The Law of Israel seemed to regard the fetus as something less than a person.

Church Tradition. Today, the Catholic Church strongly opposes abortion. When the Pope visits America, where abortions are performed routinely, his main message is always: *Stop killing unborn children.* In many Protestant churches, too, abortion is routinely denounced from the pulpit. It is no surprise, then, that many people feel that they must condemn abortion "for religious reasons," regardless of how Scripture is interpreted. What lies behind the Church's current position on abortion?

To some extent, the Vatican has always opposed abortion for the same reason that it has always condemned condoms, birth control pills, and other forms of contraception: All of these activities thwart natural processes. According to natural-law theory, sex is supposed to lead to the birth of a healthy baby. Condoms and birth control pills prevent this from happening by preventing pregnancy; and abortion, whenever it occurs, puts a man-made end to the fetus's natural course of development. Thus, by the lights of traditional Catholic thinking, abortion is wrong because it disrupts natural processes. This type of argument, however, can hardly show that Christians "must" oppose abortion. The argument depends on natural-law theory, and, as we have seen, natural-law theory is based on a worldview that predates modern science. Christians today need not reject modern science—the Pope himself, for example, believes in Charles Darwin's 19th-century theory of evolution as well as the 20th-century idea that the universe began with a "Big Bang." Thus, Christians are not required to oppose abortion based on natural-law considerations.

At any rate, to say that abortion disrupts a natural process is to say nothing about the moral status of the fetus. The Pope does not merely believe that abortion is immoral, like using a condom; he believes that abortion is *murder*. How did this position become dominant within the Catholic Church? Have Church leaders always regarded the fetus as enjoying a special moral status?

For most of the Church's history—until around A.D. 1200—little of relevance is known. Back then, there were no universities, and the Church was not especially intellectual. People believed all kinds of things, for all kinds of reasons. But in the 13th century, Saint Thomas Aquinas constructed a philosophical system that became the bedrock of later Catholic thought. The key question, Aquinas believed, is whether the fetus has a soul: if it does, then abortion is murder; if it doesn't, then abortion is not murder. Does the fetus have a soul? Aquinas accepted Aristotle's idea that the soul is the "substantial form" of man. Let's not worry about exactly what that means; what's important is that human beings are supposed to acquire a "substantial form" only when their bodies take on human shape. So now the key question is: When do human beings first look human?

When a baby is born, anyone can see that it has a human shape. In Aquinas's day, however, nobody knew when fetuses begin to look human—after all, fetal development occurs in the mother's womb, out of sight. Aristotle had believed, for no good reason, that males acquire a soul 40 days after conception and females do after 90 days. Presumably, many Christians accepted his view. At any rate, for the next several centuries, it was natural for Catholics to strongly oppose abortion at any stage of pregnancy, because the fetus *might* have already acquired a human form, and so abortion *might* be murder.

Contrary to popular belief, the Catholic Church has never officially maintained that the fetus acquires a soul at the moment of conception. Around 1600, however, some theologians began to say that the soul enters the body a few days after conception, and so abortion is murder even at an early stage. This monumentally important change in Catholic thinking occurred without extended theological debate. Perhaps it seemed unimportant because the Church already opposed early-term abortions. Yet we understand little about why the Church changed its position.

Today we know a lot about fetal development. We know, through microscopes and ultrasounds, that fetuses do not look human until several weeks into the pregnancy. Thus, a follower of Aquinas should now say that fetuses do not have a soul during the first month or two of pregnancy. However, there has been no movement inside the Catholic Church to adopt that position. For reasons that remain murky, the Church adopted a conservative view of the status of the fetus in the 1600s, and it has held fast to that view ever since.

The purpose of reviewing this history is not to suggest that the contemporary church's position is wrong. For all I have said, it may be right. My point, rather, is this: every generation interprets its traditions to support its favored moral views. Abortion is but one example of this. We could also have discussed the church's shifting views on slavery, or the status of women, or capital punishment. In each case, the moral stance taken by the Church seems not to be derived from the Bible so much as imposed on it.

The arguments in this chapter point to a common conclusion: Right and wrong are not to be understood in terms of God's will; morality is a matter of reason and conscience, not religious faith; and in any case, religious considerations do not provide definitive solutions to most of the moral problems that we face. Morality and religion are, in a word, different. Of course, religious beliefs do sometimes bear on moral issues. Consider, for example, the doctrine of eternal life. If some people go to heaven when they die—so that dying is a good thing for them—then this might affect the morality of killing these people. Or suppose we believe, upon studying ancient prophecies, that the world is about to end. This might diminish our fear of climate change. The relationship between morality and religion is complicated, but it is a relationship between two different subjects.

This conclusion may strike some readers as antireligious. However, it has not been reached by questioning the validity of religion. The arguments we have considered do not assume that Christianity or any other theological system is false; they merely show that, even if such a system is true, morality remains an independent matter.

CHAPTER 5

*E*thical Egoism

The achievement of his own happiness is man's highest moral purpose.

AYN RAND, *THE VIRTUE OF SELFISHNESS* (1961)

5.1. Is There a Duty to Help the Starving?

Each year millions of people die from health problems brought on by malnutrition. Often, those who die are children. Every day, around 22,000 children under the age of 5 die, almost always from preventable causes. That comes to over 8 million deaths each year. Even if this estimate is too high, the number who die is staggering.

Poverty poses an acute problem for many of us who are not poor. We spend money on ourselves, not only on necessities but on luxuries—DVDs, jewelry, concert tickets, iPods, and so on. In America, even people with modest incomes enjoy such things. But we could forgo our luxuries and give the money for famine relief instead. The fact that we don't suggests that we regard our luxuries as more important than the lives of the starving.

Why do we let people starve when we could save them? Few of us actually believe our luxuries are that important. Most of us, if asked the question directly, would probably be a bit embarrassed, and we might say we should do more to help. One reason we don't do more is that we rarely think about the problem. Living our own comfortable lives, we are insulated from it. The starving people are dying at some distance from us; we do not see them, and we can avoid even thinking about them. When we do think of them, it is only abstractly, as statistics. Unfortunately for the hungry, statistics have little power to move us.

64

We respond differently when there is a "crisis," as when an earthquake struck Japan in 2011, killing thousands, triggering a tsunami, and causing meltdowns at several nuclear power plants. Then the crisis is big news and relief efforts are mobilized. But when the needy are scattered, the situation does not seem so pressing. The 8 million children who die every year would probably be saved if they were all gathered in, say, Chicago.

But leaving aside the question of why we behave as we do, what is our duty? What *should* we do? Common sense might tell us to balance our own interests against the interests of others. It is understandable, of course, that we look out for ourselves, and people cannot be blamed for attending to their own basic needs. But at the same time, the needs of others are important, and when we can help others—especially at little cost to ourselves—we should do so. So, if you have an extra $10, and giving it to charity would help save a child's life, then commonsense morality would say that you should do so.

This way of thinking assumes that we have duties to others simply because *they are people who could be helped or harmed by what we do.* If a certain action would benefit (or harm) other people, then that is a reason why we should (or should not) perform that action. The commonsense assumption is that other people's interests *count,* from a moral point of view.

But one person's common sense is another person's naïve platitude. Some people believe that we have no duties to others. On their view, known as Ethical Egoism, each person ought to pursue his or her own self-interest exclusively. This is the morality of selfishness. It holds that our only duty is to do what is best for ourselves. Other people matter only insofar as they can benefit us.

5.2. Psychological Egoism

Before we discuss Ethical Egoism, we should discuss a theory it is often confused with—Psychological Egoism. Ethical Egoism claims that each person *ought* to pursue his or her own self-interest exclusively. Psychological Egoism, by contrast, asserts that each person *does in fact* pursue his or her own self-interest exclusively. Thus, these theories are very different. It is one thing to say that people are self-interested and that our neighbors will not give to charity. It is quite another thing to say that people *ought* to be self-interested and that our neighbors *ought* not to give to charity. Psychological Egoism makes a claim about human nature, or about the way things are; Ethical Egoism makes a claim about morality, or about the way things should be.

Psychological Egoism is not a theory of ethics; rather, it is a theory of human psychology. But ethicists have always worried about it. If Psychological Egoism were true, then moral philosophy itself would seem pointless. After all, if people are going to behave selfishly *no matter what*, then what's the point of discussing what they "ought" to do? Whatever it is they "ought" to do, they aren't going to do it. It might be naïve of us to think that our moral theories can matter in the real world.

Is Altruism Possible? When World War II began, Raoul Wallenberg was an unknown businessman living in Sweden. Sweden was a good place to be during the war. As a neutral country, it was never bombed, blockaded, or invaded. Yet, in 1944, Wallenberg voluntarily left Sweden for Nazi-controlled Hungary. Officially, Wallenberg was going to be just another Swedish diplomat in Budapest. However, his real mission was to save lives. In Hungary, Hitler had begun implementing his "final solution to the Jewish problem": Jews were being rounded up, deported, and then murdered at Nazi killing stations. Wallenberg wanted to stop the slaughter.

Wallenberg did help to persuade the Hungarian government to halt the deportations. However, the Hungarian government was soon replaced by a Nazi puppet regime, and the mass killing resumed. Wallenberg then issued "Swedish Protective Passes" to thousands of Jews, insisting that they all had connections to Sweden and were under the protection of his government. Wallenberg helped many people hide. When they were discovered, he would stand between them and the Nazis, telling the Germans that they would have to shoot him first. Wallenberg saved thousands of human lives. At the end of the war, when chaos prevailed, he stayed behind as other diplomats fled. After the war, Wallenberg disappeared, and for a long time his fate was unknown. Now we believe that he was killed, not by the Germans, but by the Soviets, who imprisoned him after taking over Hungary.

Wallenberg's story is especially dramatic, but it is not unique. The Israeli government recognizes over 22,000 Gentiles who risked their lives trying to save Jews from being murdered in the Holocaust. The Israelis call these women and men "The Righteous among the Nations." And though few of us have saved lives, acts of altruism appear to be common. People do favors for one another. They give blood. They build homeless shelters. They volunteer in hospitals. They read to the blind. Many people give money to worthy causes. In some cases, the amount given is extraordinary. Warren Buffett, an American businessman, gave $37 billion to the Bill and Melinda Gates Foundation to promote global health and education. Zell Kravinsky, an American real estate investor, gave his entire $45-million fortune to charity. And then, for good measure, Kravinsky donated one of his kidneys to a complete stranger. Oseola McCarty, an 87-year-old African-American woman from Hattiesburg, Mississippi, gave $150,000 to endow a scholarship fund at the University of Southern Mississippi. For 75 years, she had saved up money, working as a maid. She never owned a car, and at the age of 87 she still walked over a mile to the nearest grocery store, pushing her own shopping cart.

These are remarkable deeds, but should they be taken at face value? According to Psychological Egoism, we may believe ourselves to be noble and self-sacrificing, but that is only an illusion. In reality, we care only for ourselves. Could this theory be true? Why have people believed it, in the face of so much evidence to the contrary? Two arguments are often given for Psychological Egoism.

The Argument That We Always Do What We Want to Do. "Every act you have ever performed since the day you were born was performed because you wanted something." So wrote Dale Carnegie, author of the first and best self-help book, *How to Win Friends and Influence People* (1936). Carnegie thought of desire as the key to human psychology. Thus, when we describe one person's action as altruistic and another person's action as self-interested, we may be overlooking the fact that in each case *the person is merely doing what he or she most wants to do.* For example, if Raoul Wallenberg chose to go to Hungary, then he wanted to go there more than he wanted to remain in Sweden—and why should he be praised for altruism when he was only doing what he wanted to do? His action sprang from his own desires, from his own sense of what he wanted. Thus, he was moved by his own self-interest. And because the same may be said about any alleged act of kindness, we can conclude that Psychological Egoism must be true.

This argument, however, is flawed. There are things that we do, not because we want to, but because we feel that we *ought* to. For example, I may write my grandmother a letter because I promised my mother I would, even though I don't want to do it. It is sometimes suggested that we do such things because we most want to keep our promises. But that is not true. It is simply false to say that my strongest desire is to keep my promise. What I most want is to break my promise, but I don't, as a matter of conscience. For all we know, Wallenberg was in this position: Perhaps he wanted to stay in Sweden, but he felt that he had to go to Hungary to save lives. In any case, the fact that he chose to go does not imply that he most wanted to do so.

The argument has a second flaw. Suppose we concede that we always act on our strongest desires. Even if this were so, it would not follow that Wallenberg acted out of self-interest. For if Wallenberg wanted to help others, even at great risk to himself, then that is precisely what makes his behavior contrary to Psychological Egoism. The mere fact that you act on your own desires does not mean that you are looking out for yourself; it all depends on *what* you desire. If you care only about yourself and give no thought to others, then you are acting out of self-interest; but if you want other people to be happy, and you act on that desire, then you are not. To put the point another way: In assessing whether an action is self-interested, the issue is not *whether* the action is based on a desire; the issue is *what kind of desire it is based on.* If you want to help someone else, then your motive is altruistic, not self-interested.

Therefore, this argument goes wrong in just about every way that an argument can go wrong: The premise is not true—we don't always do what we most want to do—and even if it were true, the conclusion would not follow from it.

The Argument That We Always Do What Makes Us Feel Good. The second argument for Psychological Egoism appeals to the fact that so-called altruistic actions produce a sense of self-satisfaction in the person who performs them. Acting "unselfishly" makes people feel good about themselves, and that is the real point of it.

According to a 19th-century newspaper, this argument was made by Abraham Lincoln. The Springfield, Illinois, *Monitor* reported:

> Mr. Lincoln once remarked to a fellow-passenger on an old-time mud coach that all men were prompted by self-ishness in doing good. His fellow-passenger was antagoniz-ing this position when they were passing over a corduroy bridge that spanned a slough. As they crossed this bridge they espied an old razor-backed sow on the bank making a terrible noise because her pigs had got into the slough and were in danger of drowning. As the old coach began to climb the hill, Mr. Lincoln called out, "Driver, can't you stop just a moment?" Then Mr. Lincoln jumped out, ran back, and lifted the little pigs out of the mud and water and placed them on the bank. When he returned, his companion remarked: "Now, Abe, where does selfishness come in on this little episode?" "Why, bless your soul, Ed, that was the very essence of selfishness. I should have had no peace of mind all day had I gone on and left that suffer-ing old sow worrying over those pigs. I did it to get peace of mind, don't you see?"

In this story, Honest Abe employs a time-honored tactic of Psychological Egoism: *the strategy of reinterpreting motives.* Every-one knows that people sometimes seem to act altruistically; but if we look deeper, we may find that something else is going on. And usually it is not hard to discover that the "unselfish" behavior is actually connected to some benefit for the person who does it. Thus, Lincoln talks about the peace of mind he got from rescuing the pigs.

Other examples of alleged altruism can also be reinter-preted. According to some of Raoul Wallenberg's friends, before traveling to Hungary he was depressed and unhappy that his life wasn't amounting to much. So he undertook deeds that would make him a heroic figure. His quest for a more significant life was spectacularly successful—here we are, more than 60 years after his death, talking about him. Mother Teresa, the nun who spent her life working among the poor in Calcutta, is often cited as a perfect example of altruism—but, of course, she believed that she would be handsomely rewarded in heaven. And as for Zell Kravinsky, who gave away both his for-tune and a kidney, his parents never gave him much praise, so he was always trying to do things that even they would admire. Kravinsky himself said that, as he began to give away his money, he came to think of a donation as "a treat to myself. I really thought of it as something pleasurable."

Despite all this, Lincoln's argument is badly flawed. It may be true that one of Lincoln's motives in saving the pigs was to preserve his own peace of mind. *But the fact that Lincoln had a self-interested motive doesn't mean that he didn't have benevolent motives as well.* In fact, Lincoln's desire to help the pigs might have been even greater than his desire to preserve his peace of mind. And if this isn't true in Lincoln's case, it will be true in other cases: If I see a child drowning, my desire to help that child will usually be greater than my desire to avoid a guilty conscience. Cases like these are counterexamples to Psychological Egoism.

In some instances of altruism, we may have *no* self-interested motives. For example, in 2007, a 50-year-old construction worker named Wesley Autrey was waiting for a subway train in New York City. Autrey saw a man near him collapse, his body convulsing. The man got up, only to stumble to the edge of the platform and fall onto the train tracks. At that moment, the headlights of a train appeared. "I had to make a split[-second] decision," Autrey later said. He then leapt onto the tracks and lay on top of the man, pressing him down into a space a foot deep. The train's brakes screeched, but it could not stop in time. People on the platform screamed. Five cars passed over the men, smudging Autrey's blue knit cap with grease. When onlookers realized that both men were safe, they broke out into applause. "I just saw someone who needed help," Autrey later said. He had saved the man's life, never giving a thought to his own well-being.

There is a general lesson to be learned here, having to do with the nature of desire. We want all sorts of things— money, friends, fame, a new car, and so on—and because we desire these things, we may derive satisfaction from getting them. But the object of our desire is typically *not* the feeling of satisfaction—that is not what we are after. What we want is simply the money, the friends, the fame, and the car. It is the same with helping others. Our desire to help others often comes first; the good feelings we may get are merely a by-product.

Conclusion about Psychological Egoism. If Psychological Egoism is so implausible, why have so many intelligent people been attracted to it? Some people like the theory's cynical view of human nature. Others may like its simplicity. And, indeed, it would be pleasing if a single factor could explain all human behavior. But human beings seem to be too complicated for that. Psychological Egoism is not a credible theory.

Thus, morality has nothing to fear from Psychological Egoism. Given that we *can* be moved by regard for others, it is not pointless to talk about whether we *should* help our neighbors. Moral theorizing need not be a naïve endeavor, based on an unrealistic view of human nature.

5.3. Three Arguments for Ethical Egoism

Ethical Egoism, again, is the doctrine that each person ought to pursue his or her own self-interest exclusively. This is not the commonsense idea that one should promote one's own interests *in addition to* the interests of others. Ethical Egoism is the radical idea that the principle of self-interest accounts for *all* of one's obligations.

However, Ethical Egoism does not tell you to *avoid* helping others. Sometimes your interests will coincide with the well-being of others, so by helping yourself you'll help them too. For example, if you can convince your teacher to cancel the assignment, this will benefit you *and* your classmates. Ethical Egoism does not forbid such actions; in fact, it may recommend them. The theory insists only that in such cases the benefit to others is not what makes the act right. Rather, the act is right because it is to your own advantage.

Nor does Ethical Egoism imply that in pursuing your interests, you should always do what you want to, or what offers you the most short-term pleasure. Someone may want to smoke cigarettes, or bet all his money at the racetrack, or set up a meth lab in his basement. Ethical Egoism would frown on all this, despite the short-term benefits. Ethical Egoism says that a person ought to do what really is in his or her own best interests, over the long run. It endorses selfishness, not foolishness.

Now let's discuss the three main arguments for Ethical Egoism.

The Argument That Altruism Is Self-Defeating. The first argument has several variations:

- Each of us is intimately familiar with our own individual wants and needs. Moreover, each of us is uniquely placed to pursue those wants and needs effectively. At the same time, we understand the desires and needs of other people only imperfectly, and we are not well situated to pursue them. Therefore, if we try to be "our brother's keeper," we will often bungle the job and end up doing more harm than good.
- At the same time, the policy of "looking out for others" is an offensive intrusion into other people's privacy; it is essentially a policy of minding other people's business.
- Making other people the object of one's "charity" is degrading to them; it robs them of their dignity and self-respect. The offer of charity says, in effect, that they are not competent to care for themselves; and the statement is self-fulfilling. They cease to be self-reliant and become passively dependent on others. That is why the recipients of "charity" are often resentful rather than appreciative.

In each case, the policy of "looking out for others" is said to be self-defeating. If we want to do what is best for people, we should not adopt so-called altruistic policies. On the contrary, if each person looks after his or her own interests, everyone will be better off.

It is possible to object to this argument on a number of grounds. Of course, no one favors bungling, butting in, or depriving people of their self-respect. But is that really what's going on when we feed hungry children? Is the starving child in Niger really harmed when we "intrude" into "her business" by giving her food? It hardly seems likely. Yet we can set this point aside, for this way of thinking has an even more serious defect.

The trouble is that it isn't really an argument for Ethical Egoism at all. The argument concludes that we should adopt certain policies of behavior, and on the surface, they appear to be egoistic policies. However, the *reason* we should adopt those policies is decidedly unegoistic. It is said that adopting those policies will promote the betterment of society—but according to Ethical Egoism, that is not something we should care about. Spelled out fully, the argument says:

(1) We ought to do whatever will best promote everyone's interests.

(2) The best way to promote everyone's interests is for each of us to pursue our own interests exclusively.

(3) Therefore, each of us should pursue our own interests exclusively.

If we accept this reasoning, then we are not Ethical Egoists. Even though we might behave like egoists, our ultimate principle is one of beneficence—we are trying to help everyone, and not just ourselves. Rather than being egoists, we turn out to be altruists with a peculiar view of what promotes the general welfare.

Ayn Rand's Argument. Ayn Rand (1905–1982) is not read much by philosophers. The ideas associated with her name—that capitalism is a morally superior economic system and that morality demands absolute respect for the rights of individuals—are developed more rigorously by other writers. Nevertheless, she was a charismatic figure who attracted a devoted following during her lifetime. Today, roughly 30 years after her death, the Ayn Rand industry is still going strong. Ethical Egoism is associated with her more than with any other 20th-century writer.

Ayn Rand regarded the "ethics of altruism" as a totally destructive idea, both in society as a whole and in the lives of those taken in by it. Altruism, to her way of thinking, leads to a denial of the value of the individual. It says to a person: Your life is merely something to be sacrificed. "If a man accepts the ethics of altruism," she writes, "his first concern is not how to live his life, but how to sacrifice it." Those who promote the ethics of altruism are beneath contempt—they are parasites who, rather than working to build and sustain their own lives, leech off those who do. Rand continues:

> Parasites, moochers, looters, brutes and thugs can be of no value to a human being—nor can he gain any benefit from living in a society geared to *their* needs, demands and protections, a society that treats him as a sacrificial animal and penalizes him for his virtues in order to reward *them* for their vices, which means: a society based on the ethics of altruism.

By "sacrificing one's life," Rand does not mean anything so dramatic as dying. A person's life consists, in part, of projects undertaken and goods earned and created. Thus, to demand that a person abandon his projects or give up his goods is to demand that he "sacrifice his life."

Rand also suggests that there is a metaphysical basis for Ethical Egoism. Somehow, it is the only ethic that takes seriously the *reality* of the individual person. She bemoans "the enormity of the extent to which altruism erodes men's capacity to grasp . . . the value of an individual life; it reveals a mind from which the reality of a human being has been wiped out."

What, then, of the hungry children? It might be said that Ethical Egoism itself "reveals a mind from which the reality of a human being has been wiped out," namely, the human being who is starving. But Rand quotes with approval the answer given by one of her followers: "Once, when Barbara Brandon was asked by a student: 'What will happen to the poor . . . ?' she answered: 'If *you* want to help them, you will not be stopped.'"

All these remarks are part of one continuous argument that goes something like this:

(1) Each person has only one life to live. If we value the individual, then we must agree that this life is of supreme importance. After all, it is all one has, and all one is.

(2) The ethics of altruism regards the life of the individual as something that may be sacrificed for the good of others. Therefore, the ethics of altruism does not take seriously the value of the individual.

(3) Ethical Egoism, which allows each person to view his or her own life as being of ultimate value, does take the individual seriously—it is, in fact, the only philosophy that does.

(4) Thus, Ethical Egoism is the philosophy that we ought to accept.

One problem with this argument, as you may have noticed, is that it assumes we have only two options: Either we accept the ethics of altruism, or we accept Ethical Egoism. The choice is then made to look obvious by depicting the ethics of altruism as an insane doctrine that only an idiot would accept. The ethics of altruism is said to be the view that one's own interests have *no* value and that one must be ready to sacrifice oneself *totally* whenever *anybody* asks it. If this is the alternative, then any other view, including Ethical Egoism, will look good by comparison.

But that is hardly a fair picture of the options. What we called the commonsense view stands between the two extremes. It says that one's own interests and the interests of others are *both* important, and must be balanced against each other. Sometimes, one should act in the interests of others; other times, one should take care of oneself. So, even if we should reject the extreme ethics of altruism, it does not follow that we must accept the other extreme of Ethical Egoism. There is a middle ground.

Ethical Egoism as Compatible with Commonsense Morality.
The third argument takes a different approach. Ethical Egoism is usually presented as a *revisionist* moral philosophy, that is, as a philosophy that says our commonsense moral views are mistaken. It is possible, however, to interpret Ethical Egoism as a theory that accepts commonsense morality.

This interpretation goes as follows: Ordinary morality consists in obeying certain rules. We must speak the truth, keep our promises, avoid harming others, and so on. At first glance, these duties appear to have little in common—they are just a bunch of discrete rules. Yet there may be a unity to them. Ethical Egoists would say that all these duties are ultimately derived from the one fundamental principle of self-interest.

Understood in this way, Ethical Egoism is not such a radical doctrine. It does not challenge commonsense morality; it only tries to explain and systematize it. And it does a surprisingly good job. It can provide plausible explanations of the duties mentioned above, and more:

- *The duty not to harm others:* If we do things that harm other people, other people will not mind doing things that harm us. We will be shunned and despised; others will not be our friends and will not help us out when we need it. If our offenses are serious enough, we may end up in jail. Thus, it is to our own advantage to avoid harming others.

- *The duty not to lie:* If we lie to other people, we will suffer all the ill effects of a bad reputation. People will distrust us and avoid doing business with us. People will be dishonest with us once they realize that we have been dishonest with them. Thus, it is to our own advantage to be truthful.
- *The duty to keep our promises:* It is to our own advantage to enter into mutually beneficial arrangements with other people. To benefit from those arrangements, we need to be able to rely on others to keep their word. But we can hardly expect them to do that if we do not keep our promises to them. Therefore, from the point of view of self-interest, we should keep our promises.

Pursuing this line of reasoning, Thomas Hobbes (1588–1679) suggested that the principle of Ethical Egoism leads to nothing less than the Golden Rule: We should "do unto others" because if we do, others will be more likely to "do unto us."

Does this argument succeed in establishing Ethical Egoism as a viable theory of morality? It may be the best try. However, there are two serious problems with it. First, the argument does not prove as much as it needs to. It shows only that it is *mostly* to one's advantage to tell the truth, to keep one's promises, and to avoid harming others. But a situation might arise in which you could profit from doing something horrible, like killing someone. In such a case, Ethical Egoism cannot explain why you shouldn't do the horrible thing. Thus, it looks like some of our moral obligations cannot be derived from self-interest.

Second, suppose it is true that giving money to famine relief is somehow to one's own advantage. It doesn't follow that this is the *only* reason to do so. Another reason might be *to help the starving people.* Ethical Egoism says that self-interest is the only reason to help others, but nothing in the present argument really supports that.

5.4. Three Arguments against Ethical Egoism

The Argument That Ethical Egoism Endorses Wickedness. Consider these wicked actions, taken from various newspaper stories: To make more money, a pharmacist filled prescriptions for cancer patients using watered-down drugs. A paramedic gave emergency patients injections of sterile water rather than morphine, so he could sell the morphine. Parents fed a baby acid so they could fake a lawsuit, claiming the baby's formula was tainted. A nurse raped two patients while they were unconscious. A 73-year-old man kept his daughter locked in a cellar for 24 years and fathered seven children with her, against her will. A 60-year-old man shot his letter carrier seven times because he was $90,000 in debt and thought that being in federal prison would be better than being homeless.

Suppose that someone could actually benefit by doing such things. Wouldn't Ethical Egoism have to approve of such actions? This seems like enough to discredit the doctrine. However, this objection might be unfair to Ethical Egoism, because in saying that these actions are wicked, it assumes a nonegoistic conception of wickedness. Thus, some philosophers have tried to show that there are deeper logical problems with Ethical Egoism. The following argument is typical of such proposals.

The Argument That Ethical Egoism Is Logically Inconsistent. In his book *The Moral Point of View* (1958), Kurt Baier argues that Ethical Egoism cannot be correct, on purely logical grounds. Baier thinks that the theory leads to contradictions. If this is true, then Ethical Egoism is indeed mistaken, for no theory can be true if it contradicts itself.

Suppose, Baier says, two people are running for president. Let's call them "D" and "R," to stand for "Democrat" and "Republican." Because it would be in D's interest to win, it would be in D's interest to kill R. From this it follows, on Ethical Egoism, that D ought to kill R—it is D's moral duty to do so. But it is also true that it is in R's interest to stay alive. From this it follows that R ought to stop D from killing her—that is R's duty. Now here's the problem. When R protects herself from D, her act is both wrong and not wrong—wrong because it prevents D from doing his duty, and not wrong because it is in R's best interests. But one and the same act cannot be both morally wrong and not morally wrong.

Does this argument refute Ethical Egoism? At first glance, it seems persuasive. However, it is complicated, so we need to set it out with each step individually identified. Then we will be in a better position to evaluate it. Spelled out fully, it goes like this:

(1) Suppose it is each person's duty to do what is in his own best interest.

(2) It is in D's best interest to kill R so that D will win the election.

(3) It is in R's best interest to prevent D from killing her.

(4) Therefore, D's duty is to kill R, and R's duty is to prevent D from doing it.

(5) But it is wrong to prevent someone from doing his duty.

(6) Therefore, it is wrong for R to prevent D from killing her.

(7) Therefore, it is both wrong and not wrong for R to prevent D from killing her.

(8) But no act can be wrong and not wrong; that is a contradiction.

(9) Therefore, the assumption with which we started— that it is each person's duty to do what is in his own best interest—cannot be true.

When the argument is set out in this way, we can see its hidden flaw. The logical contradiction—that it is wrong and not wrong for R to prevent D from killing her—does not follow simply from the principle of Ethical Egoism as stated in step (1). It follows from that principle *together with* the premise expressed in step (5), namely, that "it is wrong to prevent someone from doing his duty." By putting step (5) in the argument, Baier has added his own assumption.

Thus, we need not reject Ethical Egoism. Instead, we could simply reject this additional premise and thereby avoid the contradiction. That is surely what the Ethical Egoist would do, for the Ethical Egoist would never say, without qualification, that it is always wrong to prevent someone from doing his duty. He would say, instead, that whether one ought to prevent someone from doing his duty depends entirely on whether it would be to one's own advantage to do so. Regardless of whether we like this idea, it is at least what the Ethical Egoist would say. And so, this attempt to convict the egoist of self-contradiction fails.

The Argument That Ethical Egoism Is Unacceptably Arbitrary.
This argument may refute Ethical Egoism. It is at least the deepest of the arguments we'll consider, because it tries to explain *why* the interests of other people *should* matter to us. But before presenting this argument, we need to look at a general point about moral values.

There is a whole family of moral views that have this in common: They divide people into groups and say that the interests of some groups count more than the interests of other groups. Racism is the most conspicuous example. Racists divide people into groups according to race and assign greater importance to the well-being of one race than to the well-being of other races. All forms of discrimination work like this—anti-Semitism, nationalism, sexism, ageism, and so on. People in the sway of such attitudes will think, in effect, "*My* race counts for more," or "Those who believe in *my* religion count for more," or "*My* country counts for more," and so on.

Can such ideas be defended? The people who accept such views don't usually give arguments for them—racists, for example, rarely try to offer a rational justification for racism. But suppose they did. What could they say?

There is a general principle that stands in the way of any such justification. Let's call it the Principle of Equal Treatment: *We should treat people in the same way unless there is a good reason not to.* For example, suppose we're considering whether to admit two students to law school. If both students graduated from college with honors and aced the entrance exam—if both are equally qualified—then it is merely arbitrary to admit one but not the other. However, if one graduated with honors and scored well on the admissions test while the other dropped out of college and never took the test, then it is acceptable to admit the first student but not the second.

At root, the Principle of Equal Treatment is a principle that requires fairness in our dealings with others: like cases should be treated alike, and only unalike cases may be treated differently. Two points should be made about the principle. The first is that treating people in the same way does not always mean ensuring the same outcome for them. During the Vietnam War, young American men desperately wanted to avoid getting drafted into the armed services, and the government had to decide the order in which draft boards would call people up. In 1969, the first "draft lottery" was televised to a national audience. Here is how it worked: The days of the year were written on 366 slips of paper (one slip for February 29) and inserted into blue plastic capsules. Those capsules were placed in a glass jar and mixed up. Then, one by one, the capsules were drawn. The first was for September 14—young men with that birthday, age 18–26, would be drafted first. The winners of the lottery, drawn last, were born on June 8. These young men never got drafted. In college dormitories, groups of students watched the drawings live, and it was easy to tell whose birthday had just come up—whoever just groaned or swore. Obviously, the outcomes were different: In the end, some people got drafted and others didn't. However, the process was fair. By giving everyone an equal chance in the lottery, the government treated everyone in the same way.

A second point concerns the *scope* of the principle, or what situations it applies to. Suppose you're not going to use your ticket to the big game, so you give it to a friend. In doing so, you are treating your friend better than everyone else you could have given the ticket to. Does your action violate the Principle of Equal Treatment? Does it need justification? Moral philosophers disagree on this question. Some think that the principle does not apply to cases like this. The principle applies only in "moral contexts," and what you should do with your ticket is not important enough to count as a moral question. Others think that your action does require justification, and various justifications might be offered. Your action might be justified by the nature of friendship; or by the fact that it would be impossible for you to hold a lottery at the last minute for all the ticketless fans; or by the fact that you own the ticket, so you can do what you want with it. It doesn't matter, from our point of view, whether the Principle of Equal Treatment applies only in so-called "moral contexts." Suffice it to say that everyone accepts the principle, under one interpretation or another. Everyone believes in treating people similarly, unless the facts demand otherwise.

Let's now apply that principle to racism. Can a racist point to any differences between, say, white people and black people that would justify treating them differently? In the past, racists have sometimes tried to do this by portraying blacks as lazy, unintelligent, and threatening. In doing so, the racists show

that even they accept the Principle of Equal Treatment—
the point of such stereotypes is to supply the "good reasons"
needed to justify differences in treatment. If such accusations
were true, then differential treatment would be justified in
some circumstances. But, of course, they are not true; there are
no such differences between the races. Thus, racism is an arbitrary doctrine—it advocates treating people differently even
though there are no good reasons to do so.

Ethical Egoism is a moral theory of the same type. It
advocates dividing the world into two categories of people—
ourselves and everyone else—and it urges us to regard the
interests of those in the first group as more important than
the interests of those in the second group. But each of us can
ask, What is the difference between me and everyone else that
justifies placing myself in this special category? Am I more
intelligent? Are my accomplishments greater? Do I enjoy life
more? Are my needs and abilities different from the needs and
abilities of others? In short, *what makes me so special?* Failing an
answer, it turns out that Ethical Egoism is an arbitrary doctrine,
in the same way that racism is arbitrary. Both doctrines violate
the Principle of Equal Treatment.

Thus, we should care about the interests of other people
because their needs and desires are comparable to our own.
Consider, one last time, the starving children we could feed
by giving up some of our luxuries. Why should we care about
them? We care about ourselves, of course—if we were starving,
we would do almost anything to get food. But what is the difference between us and them? Does hunger affect them any less?
Are they less deserving than we are? If we can find no relevant
difference between us and them, then we must admit that, if our
needs should be met, then so should theirs. This realization—
that we are on a par with one another—is the deepest reason
why our morality must recognize the needs of others. And that
is why, ultimately, Ethical Egoism fails as a moral theory.

CHAPTER 6

The Social Contract Theory

Wherever law ends, tyranny begins . . .
JOHN LOCKE, *THE SECOND TREATISE OF GOVERNMENT* (1690)

6.1. Hobbes's Argument

Suppose we take away all the traditional props for morality. Assume, first, that there is no God to issue commands and reward virtue. Next, suppose that there are no "natural purposes"—objects in nature have no inherent functions or intended uses. Finally, assume that human beings are naturally selfish. Where, then, could morality come from? If we cannot appeal to God, natural purpose, or altruism, is there anything left to base morality on?

Thomas Hobbes, the leading British philosopher of the 17th century, tried to show that morality does not depend on any of those things. Instead, morality should be understood as the solution to a practical problem that arises for self-interested human beings. We all want to live as well as possible; but in order to flourish, we need a peaceful, cooperative social order. And we cannot have one without rules. Those rules *are* the moral rules; morality consists of the precepts we need to follow in order to get the benefits of social living. That—not God, inherent purposes, or altruism—is the key to understanding ethics.

Hobbes begins by asking what it would be like if there were no way to enforce social rules. Suppose there were no government institutions—no laws, no police, and no courts. In this situation, each of us would be free to do as we pleased. Hobbes called this "the state of nature." What would it be like? Hobbes thought it would be dreadful. In the state of nature, he says,

> there would be no place for industry, because the fruit thereof is uncertain: and consequently no culture of

the earth; no navigation, nor use of the commodities that may be imported by sea; no commodious building; no instruments of moving, and removing, such things as require much force; no knowledge of the face of the earth; no account of time; no arts; no letters; no society; and which is worst of all, continual fear, and danger of violent death; and the life of man, solitary, poor, nasty, brutish, and short.

The state of nature would be awful, Hobbes thought, due to four basic facts about human life:

- There is *equality of need*. Each of us needs the same basic things in order to survive—food, clothing, shelter, and so on. Although we may differ in some of our needs (diabetics need insulin, others don't), we are all essentially alike.
- There is *scarcity*. We do not live in the Garden of Eden, where milk flows in streams and every tree hangs heavy with fruit. The world is a hard, inhospitable place, where the things we need do not come in abundance. We have to work hard to produce them, and even then they may be in short supply.
- There is *the essential equality of human power*. Who will get the scarce goods? No one can simply take what she wants. Even though some people are smarter and tougher than others, even the strongest can be brought down when those who are less strong act together.
- Finally, there is *limited altruism*. If we cannot prevail by our own strength, what hope do we have? Can we rely on the goodwill of others? We cannot. Even if people are not wholly selfish, they care most about themselves, and we cannot assume that they will step aside when their interests conflict with ours.

Together, these facts paint a grim picture. We all need the same basic things, and there aren't enough of them to go around. Therefore, we will have to compete for them. But no one can prevail in this competition, and no one—or almost no one—will look after the needs of his neighbors. The result, as Hobbes puts it, is a "constant state of war, of one with all." And it is a war no one can win. Whoever wants to survive will try to seize what he needs and prepare to defend it from attack.

Meanwhile, others will be doing the same thing. Life in the state of nature would be intolerable.

Hobbes did not think this was mere speculation. He pointed out that this is what actually happens when governments collapse during civil uprisings. People hoard food, arm themselves, and lock out their neighbors. Moreover, nations themselves behave like this when international law is weak. Without a strong, overarching authority to maintain the peace, countries guard their borders, build up their armies, and feed their own people first.

To escape the state of nature, we must find a way to work together. In a stable and cooperative society, we can produce more essential goods and distribute them in a rational way. But establishing such a society is not easy. People must agree on rules to govern their interactions. They must agree, for example, not to harm one another and not to break their promises. Hobbes calls such an agreement "the social contract." As a society, we follow certain rules, and we have ways to enforce them. Some of those ways involve the law—if you assault someone, the police may arrest you. Other ways involve "the court of public opinion"—if you get a reputation for lying, then people may turn their backs on you. All of these rules, taken together, form the social contract.

It is only within the context of the social contract that we can become beneficent beings, because the contract creates the conditions under which we can afford to care about others. In the state of nature, it is every man for himself; it would be foolish for anyone to look out for others and put his own interests in jeopardy. But in society, altruism becomes possible. By releasing us from "the continual fear of violent death," the social contract frees us to take heed of others. Jean-Jacques Rousseau (1712–1778) went so far as to say that we become different kinds of creatures when we enter civilized relations with others. In *The Social Contract* (1762), he writes:

> The passage from the state of nature to the civil state produces a very remarkable change in man. . . . Then only, when the voice of duty takes the place of physical impulses . . . does man, who so far had considered only himself, find that he is forced to act on different principles, and to consult his reason before listening to his inclinations. . . . His faculties are so stimulated and

developed, . . . his feelings so ennobled, and his whole soul
so uplifted, that, did not the abuses of this new condition
often degrade him below that which he left, he would be
bound to bless continually the happy moment which took
him from it forever, and, instead of a stupid and unimagi-
native animal, made him an intelligent being and a man.

And what does the "voice of duty" require this new man
to do? It requires him to set aside his self-centered designs in
favor of rules that benefit everyone. But he is able to do this
only because others have agreed to do the same thing—that is
the essence of the "contract."

The Social Contract Theory explains the purpose of both
morality and government. The purpose of morality is to make
social living possible; the purpose of government is to enforce
vital moral rules. We can summarize the social contract conception of morality as follows: *Morality consists in the set of rules, governing behavior, that rational people will accept, on the condition that
others accept them as well.* And rational people will accept a rule
only if they can expect to gain from it. Thus, morality is about
mutual benefit; you and I are morally bound to follow a rule
only if we would be better off living in a society in which that
rule were usually followed.

6.2. The Prisoner's Dilemma

Hobbes's argument is one way of arriving at the Social Con-
tract Theory. Another argument makes use of the Prisoner's
Dilemma—a problem invented by Merrill M. Flood and Melvin
Dresher around 1950. Here's how the problem goes.

Suppose you live in a totalitarian society, and one day, to
your astonishment, you are arrested and charged with treason.
The police say that you have been plotting against the government with a man named Smith, who has also been arrested and
is being held in a separate cell. The interrogator demands that
you confess. You protest your innocence; you don't even know
Smith. But this does you no good. It soon becomes clear that
your captors are not interested in the truth; they merely want to
convict someone. They offer you the following deal:

- If Smith does not confess, but you confess and testify
  against him, then they will release you. You will go free,
  while Smith will be put away for 10 years.

- If Smith confesses and you do not, the situation will be reversed—he will go free while you get 10 years.
- If you both confess, you will each be sentenced to 5 years.
- If neither of you confesses, then there won't be enough evidence to convict either of you. They can hold you for a year, but then they will have to let both of you go.

Finally, you are told that Smith is being offered the same deal; but you cannot communicate with him, and you have no way of knowing what he will do.

The problem is this: Assuming that your only goal is to spend as little time in jail as possible, what should you do? Confess or not confess? For the purposes of this problem, you should forget about maintaining your dignity and standing up for your rights. That is not what this problem is about. You should also forget about trying to help Smith. This problem is strictly about calculating what is in your own best interests. What will get you free the quickest?

At first glance, it may seem that the question cannot be answered unless you know what Smith will do. But that is an illusion. The problem has a perfectly clear solution: No matter what Smith does, you should confess. This can be shown as follows:

(1) Either Smith will confess or he won't.

(2) Suppose Smith confesses. Then, if you confess you will get 5 years, whereas if you do not confess you will get 10 years. Therefore, if he confesses, you are better off confessing.

(3) On the other hand, suppose Smith does not confess. Then, if you confess you will go free, whereas if you do not confess you get one year. Therefore, if Smith does not confess, you will still be better off confessing.

(4) Therefore, you should confess. That will get you out of jail the soonest, no matter what Smith does.

So far, so good. But remember that Smith is being offered the same deal. Thus, he will also confess. The result will be that you both get 5-year sentences. *But if you had both done the opposite, you both could have gotten out in only one year.* It's a curious situation: Because you and Smith both act selfishly, you both wind up worse off.

Now suppose you can communicate with Smith. In that case, you could make a deal with him. You could agree that neither of you will confess; then you will both get the 1-year detention. By cooperating, you will both be better off than if you act independently. Cooperating will not get either of you the optimum result—immediate freedom—but it will get both of you a better result than you would have gotten alone.

It is vital, however, that any agreement between you and Smith be enforceable, because if he reneges and confesses while you keep the bargain, you will end up serving the maximum 10 years while he goes free. Thus, in order for you to rationally participate in such a deal, you need to be sure that Smith will keep up his end.

Morality as the Solution to Prisoner's-Dilemma-Type Problems. The Prisoner's Dilemma is not just a clever puzzle. Although the story it tells is fictitious, the pattern it exemplifies comes up often in real life. Consider, for example, the choice between two general strategies of living. You could pursue your own interests exclusively—in every situation, you could do whatever will benefit yourself, taking no notice of anyone else. Let us call this "acting selfishly." Alternatively, you could care about others, balancing their interests against your own, and sometimes forgoing your own interests for their sake. Let us call this strategy "acting benevolently."

But it is not only you who has to decide how to live. Other people also have to choose which strategy to adopt. There are four possibilities: (a) You could be selfish while other people are benevolent; (b) others could be selfish while you are benevolent; (c) everyone could be selfish; and (d) everyone could be benevolent. How would you fare in each of these situations? Purely from the standpoint of your own welfare, you might assess the possibilities like this:

- You would be best off if you were selfish while other people were benevolent. You would get the benefit of their generosity without having to return the favor. (In this situation, you would be a "free rider.")
- Second-best would be if everyone were benevolent. You would no longer have the advantages that come from ignoring other people's interests, but you would be

treated well by others. (This is the situation of "ordinary morality.")

- A bad situation, but not the worst, would be one in which everyone was selfish. You would try to protect your own interests, but you would get little help from others. (This is Hobbes's "state of nature.")
- You would be worst off if you were benevolent while others were selfish. Other people could stab you in the back whenever they saw fit, but you would never do the same. You would come out on the short end every time. (This is the "sucker's payoff.")

This situation has the same structure as the Prisoner's Dilemma. In fact, it *is* a Prisoner's Dilemma, even though it involves no prisoners. Again, we can prove that you should adopt the selfish strategy:

(1) Either other people will respect your interests or they won't.

(2) If they do respect your interests, you will be better off not respecting theirs, at least whenever that would be to your advantage. This will be the optimum situation—you get to be a free rider.

(3) If they do not respect your interests, then it will be foolish for you to respect theirs. That will land you in the worst possible situation—you get the sucker's payoff.

(4) Therefore, regardless of what other people do, you are better off adopting the policy of looking out for yourself. You should be selfish.

And now we come to the catch: Other people, of course, can reason in the same way, and the result will be that we end up in Hobbes's state of nature. Everyone will be selfish, willing to knife anyone who gets in their way. In that situation, each of us would be worse off than if we all cooperated.

To escape the dilemma, we need another enforceable agreement, this time to obey the rules of mutually respectful social living. As before, cooperation will not yield the optimum outcome for each individual, but it will lead to a better result than noncooperation. We need, in David Gauthier's words, to "bargain our way into morality." We can do that by establishing laws and social customs that protect the interests of everyone involved.

6.3. Some Advantages of the Social Contract Theory

Morality, on this theory, consists in the rules that rational people will accept, on the condition that others accept them as well. The strength of this theory is due, in large part, to the fact that it provides plausible answers to some difficult questions.

1. *What moral rules are we bound to follow, and how are those rules justified?* The morally binding rules are the ones that facilitate harmonious social living. We could not live together in peace if we allowed murder, assault, theft, lying, promise breaking, and so on. The rules forbidding those acts are therefore justified by their tendency to promote harmony and cooperation. On the other hand, "moral rules" that condemn prostitution, sodomy, and sexual promiscuity cannot be justified on these grounds. How is social living hampered by private, voluntary sexual activity? How would it benefit us to agree to such rules? What people do behind closed doors is outside the scope of the social contract. Such rules, therefore, have no claim on us.

2. *Why is it rational for us to follow the moral rules?* We *agree* to follow the moral rules because we benefit from living in a place where the rules are accepted. However, we *actually do* follow the rules—we keep our end of the bargain—because the rules will be enforced, and it is rational for us to avoid punishment. Why don't you kidnap your boss? Because you might get caught.

But what if you think you won't get caught? Why follow the rules then? To answer this question, first note that you don't want *other* people to break the rules when they think they can avoid punishment—you don't want other people to commit murder, assault, and so on, just because they think they can get away with it. After all, they might be murdering or assaulting *you.* For this reason, we want others to accept the contract in more than a frivolous or lighthearted way. We want them to form a *firm intention* to hold up their end of the bargain; we want them to become the sort of people who won't be tempted to stray. And, of course, they will demand the same of us, as part of the agreement. But once we have this firm intention, it is rational to act on it. Why don't you kidnap your boss, when you think you can get away with it? Because you've made a firm decision not to be that sort of person.

3. *Under what circumstances is it rational to break the rules?* We agree to obey the rules on the condition that others obey them as well. But when someone else breaks the rules, he releases us from our obligations toward him. For example, suppose someone refuses to help you in circumstances in which he clearly should. If later on he needs your help, you may rightly feel that you have no duty to help him.

The same point explains why punishing criminals is acceptable. Lawbreakers are treated differently from other citizens—in punishing them, we treat them in ways that are normally forbidden. Why can we do this? Remember that the rules apply to you only if other people also follow them. So, you may disregard those rules when dealing with someone who doesn't follow them. In breaking the rules, the criminal thus leaves himself open to retaliation. This explains why it is legitimate for the government to enforce the law.

4. *How much can morality demand of us?* Morality seems to require that we be impartial, that is, that we give no greater weight to our own interests than to the interests of others. But suppose you face a situation in which you must choose between your own death and the deaths of five other people. Impartiality, it seems, would require you to choose your own death; after all, there are five of them and only one of you. Are you morally bound to sacrifice yourself?

Philosophers have often felt uneasy about this sort of example; they have felt instinctively that somehow there are limits to what morality can demand of us. Therefore, they have traditionally said that such heroic actions are *supererogatory*— that is, above and beyond the call of duty, admirable when they occur but not morally required. Yet it is hard to explain why such actions are not required. If morality demands impartial behavior, and it is better that one person die rather than five, then you should be required to sacrifice yourself.

What does the Social Contract Theory say about this? Suppose the question is whether to have the rule "If you can save many lives by sacrificing your own life, then you must do so." Would it be rational to accept this rule, on the condition that everyone else accepts it? Presumably, it would be. After all, each of us is more likely to benefit from this rule than to be harmed by it—you're more likely to be among those saved than to be the one and only person who gives up her life. Thus, it may seem that the Social Contract Theory does require moral heroism.

But this is not so. On the Social Contract Theory, morality consists in the rules that rational people will accept *on the condition that others accept them as well.* However, it would not be rational to make an agreement that we don't expect others to follow. Can we expect other people to follow this rule of self-sacrifice—can we expect strangers to give up their lives for us? We cannot. Most people won't be that benevolent, even if they have promised to be. Can we expect the threat of punishment to *make them* that benevolent? Again, we cannot; people's fear of death is likely to overwhelm any fear they have of punishment. Thus, there is a natural limit to the amount of self-sacrifice that the social contract can require: Rational people will not agree to rules so demanding that others won't follow them. In this way, the Social Contract Theory explains a feature of morality that other theories may remain silent on.

6.4. The Problem of Civil Disobedience

Moral theories should help us understand concrete moral issues. The Social Contract Theory in particular should help us understand issues about social institutions—after all, explaining the proper function of those institutions is one of the main goals of the theory. So let's consider again our obligation to obey the law. Are we ever justified in breaking the law? If so, when?

The great modern examples of civil disobedience are taken from the Indian independence movement led by Mohandas K. Gandhi (1869–1948) and the American civil rights movement led by Martin Luther King Jr. (1929–1968). Both movements were characterized by public, conscientious, nonviolent refusal to comply with the law. In 1930, Gandhi and his followers marched to the coastal village of Dandi, where they defied British law by distilling salt from saltwater. The British had been controlling salt production so they could force the Indian peasants to buy it at high prices. In America, Dr. King led the Montgomery Bus Boycott, which began after Rosa Parks was arrested on December 1, 1955, for refusing to give up her bus seat to a white man. Parks was defying one of the "Jim Crow" laws designed to enforce racial segregation in the South.

Gandhi and King, the two greatest proponents of nonviolence in the 20th century, were both murdered by gunfire.

Their movements had importantly different goals. Gandhi and his followers did not recognize the right of the British to govern India; they wanted to replace British rule with an entirely different system. King and his followers, however, did not question the legitimacy of the American government. Rather, they objected only to particular laws and social policies that they felt were unjust—so unjust, in fact, that they refused to comply with them.

In his "Letter from the Birmingham City Jail" (1963), King describes the frustration and anger that arise

> when you have seen vicious mobs lynch your mothers and fathers at will and drown your sisters and brothers at whim; when you have seen hate-filled policemen curse, kick, brutalize and even kill your black brothers and sisters with impunity; when you see the vast majority of your twenty million Negro brothers smothering in an airtight cage of poverty in the midst of an affluent society; when you suddenly find your tongue twisted and your speech stammering as you seek to explain to your six-year-old daughter why she can't go to the public amusement park that has just been advertised on television, and see tears welling up in her little eyes when she is told that Funtown is closed to colored children, and see the depressing clouds of inferiority begin to form in her little mental sky.

The problem was not only that racial segregation, with all its attendant evils, was enforced by social custom; it was a matter of *law* as well, law that black citizens were denied a voice in formulating. When urged to rely on ordinary democratic processes, King pointed out that all attempts to use these processes had failed. And as for "democracy," he said, that word had no meaning to southern blacks: "Throughout the state of Alabama all types of conniving methods are used to prevent Negroes from becoming registered voters and there are some counties without a single Negro registered to vote despite the fact that the Negro constitutes a majority of the population." King believed, therefore, that blacks had no choice but to defy the unjust laws and to accept the consequences by going to jail.

Today we remember King as a great moral leader. At the time, however, his strategy of civil disobedience was highly controversial. Many liberals expressed sympathy for his goals but didn't agree with his tactic of breaking the law. An article in the *New York State Bar Journal* in 1965 expressed the typical worries. After assuring his readers that "long before Dr. King was born, I espoused, and still espouse, the cause of civil rights for all people," Louis Waldman, a prominent New York lawyer, argues:

> Those who assert rights under the Constitution and the laws made thereunder must abide by that Constitution and the law, if that Constitution is to survive. They cannot pick and choose; they cannot say they will abide by those laws which they think are just and refuse to abide by those laws which they think are unjust. . . .
>
> The country, therefore, cannot accept Dr. King's doctrine that he and his followers will pick and choose, knowing that it is illegal to do so. I say, such doctrine is not only illegal and for that reason alone should be abandoned, but that it is also immoral, destructive of the principles of democratic government, and a danger to the very civil rights Dr. King seeks to promote.

Waldman had a point: If our legal system is basically decent, then defying the law is on its face a bad thing, because open defiance of particular laws might weaken people's respect for the law generally. To meet this objection, King sometimes said that the evils he opposed were so serious, so numerous, and so difficult to fight that civil disobedience was justified as a last resort. The end justifies the means, though the means are regrettable. This argument may be enough to answer Waldman's objections. But there is a more profound reply available.

According to the Social Contract Theory, we are obligated to obey the law because we each participate in a social system that promises more benefits than burdens. The benefits are the benefits of social living: We escape the state of nature and live in a society in which we are secure and enjoy basic rights. To gain these benefits, we agree to uphold the institutions that make them possible. This means that we must obey the law, pay our taxes, and so forth—these are the burdens we accept in return.

But what if some citizens are denied their basic rights? What if the police, instead of protecting them, "curse, kick, brutalize and even kill [them] with impunity"? What if some groups of people are denied a decent education while they and their families are "smothering in an airtight cage of poverty"? Under such circumstances, the social contract is not being honored. By asking the disadvantaged group to obey the law and respect society's institutions, we are asking them to accept the burdens of social living while being denied its benefits.

This line of reasoning suggests that civil disobedience is not an undesirable "last resort" for socially disenfranchised groups. Rather, it is the most natural and reasonable means of expressing protest. For when the disadvantaged are denied the benefits of social living, they are released from the contract that would otherwise require them to follow society's rules. This is the deepest argument for civil disobedience, and the Social Contract Theory presents it clearly and forcefully.

6.5. Difficulties for the Theory

The Social Contract Theory is one of the major options in contemporary moral philosophy, along with Utilitarianism, Kantianism, and Virtue Ethics. It is easy to see why; the theory seems to explain a great deal about moral life. Two important objections, however, have been made against it.

First, it is said that the Social Contract Theory is based on a historical fiction. We are asked to imagine that people once lived in isolation from one another, that they found this intolerable, and that they eventually banded together, agreeing to follow social rules of mutual benefit. But none of this ever happened. It is just a fantasy. So of what relevance is it? To be sure, if people *had* come together in this way, we could explain their obligations to one another as the theory suggests: They would be obligated to obey the rules that they had agreed to obey. But even then, there would be problems. Was the agreement unanimous? If not, what about the people who didn't sign up—are they *not* required to act morally? And if the contract was made a long time ago by our ancestors, why should we be bound to it? But anyway, there never was such a contract, and so nothing can be explained by appealing to it. As one critic wisecracked, the social contract "isn't worth the paper it's not written on."

To be sure, none of us ever signed a "real" contract—there is no piece of paper bearing our signatures. Immigrants, who promise to obey the law when they are granted citizenship, are the exception. The contract theorist might say, however, that a social arrangement like the one described does exist, for all of us: There is a set of rules that everyone recognizes as binding on them, and we all benefit from the fact that these rules are generally followed. Each of us accepts the benefits conferred by this arrangement; and, more than that, we expect and encourage other people to observe the rules. This is a description of the actual world; it is not fictitious. And, by accepting the benefits of this arrangement, we incur an obligation to do our part—which at least means that we should follow the rules. We are thus bound by an *implicit* social contract. It is "implicit" because we become a party to it not by explicitly making a promise, but by accepting the benefits of social living.

Thus, the story of the "social contract" need not be intended as a description of historical events. Rather, it is a useful analytical tool, based on the idea that we may understand our moral obligations *as if* they had arisen in this way. Consider the following situation: Suppose you come upon a group of people playing an elaborate game. It looks like fun, and you join in. After a while, however, you begin to break some of the rules, because that looks like more fun. When the other players protest, you say that you never promised to follow the rules. However, your remark is irrelevant. Perhaps nobody promised to obey; but, by joining the game, each person implicitly agreed to abide by the rules that make the game possible. It is *as though* they had all agreed. Morality is like this. The "game" is social living; the rules, which make the game possible, are the rules of morality.

That response to the first objection, however, is ineffective. When a game is in progress, and you join in, it is obvious that you *choose* to join in, because you could have just walked away. For that reason, you must respect the game's rules, or you will rightly be regarded as a nuisance. By contrast, somebody born into today's big cooperative world does not choose to join it; nobody chooses to be born. And then, once a person has grown up, the costs of leaving that world are severe. How could you opt out? You might become a survivalist and never use electricity, roads, the water service, and so on. But that would be a great burden. Alternatively, you might leave the country. But what if you don't like the social rules that exist in any of the other countries, either? Moreover, as David Hume

(1711–1776) observed, many people are not "free to leave their country" in any meaningful sense:

> Can we seriously say that a poor peasant . . . has a free choice to leave his country, when he knows no foreign language or manners, and lives from day to day by the small wages which he acquires? We may as well assert that a man, by remaining [on a ship], freely consents to the dominion of the master, though he was carried on board while asleep, and must leap into the ocean and perish the moment he leaves.

Thus, life is not like joining a game, whose rules you may reject by walking away. Rather, life is like being thrust into a game you can't walk away from. The contract theorist has not explained why one must obey the rules of such a game.

Does the first objection therefore refute the Social Contract Theory? I don't think so. The contract theorist may say this: Participating in a sensible social scheme is rational; it really is in one's best interest. *This is why the rules are valid*—because they benefit those who live under them. If someone doesn't agree to the rules, the rules still apply to him; he's just being irrational. Suppose, for example, that a survivalist forgoes the benefits of social living. May he then refuse to pay his taxes? He may not, because even he would be better off paying his taxes *and* enjoying the benefits of clean water, paved roads, indoor plumbing, and so on. The survivalist might not want to play the game, but the rules still apply to him, because it would really and truly be in his interest to join in.

This defense of the Social Contract Theory abandons the idea that morality is based on an agreement. However, it holds fast to the idea that morality consists in rules of mutual benefit. It also accords with the definition of the theory we gave earlier: *Morality consists in the set of rules, governing behavior, that rational people will accept, on the condition that others accept them as well.* Rational people will agree to the mutually beneficial rules.

The second objection is more troubling. Some individuals cannot benefit us. Thus, according to the Social Contract Theory, these individuals have no claim on us, and we may ignore their interests when we're writing up the rules of society. The moral rules will therefore let us treat these individuals in any way whatsoever. This implication of the theory is unacceptable.

There would be at least four vulnerable groups:

- Human infants
- Nonhuman animals
- Future generations
- Oppressed populations

Suppose, for example, that a sadist wanted to torment a cat or a small child. *He* would not benefit from a system of rules forbidding the torture of infants and animals; after all, the infant and the cat cannot benefit him, and he wants to practice his cruel behavior. Of course, the infant's parents, and the cat's owners, would be indirectly harmed under such a system, and they might want to retaliate against the sadist. In such a situation, it is hard to know what moral rules would be valid. But suppose the sadist found some abandoned children or some stray cats out in the woods. Now the Social Contract Theory cannot condemn him even if he commits acts of the greatest cruelty.

Or consider future generations. They cannot benefit us; we'll be dead before they are even born. But we can profit at their expense. Why shouldn't we run up the national debt? Why shouldn't we pollute the lakes and coat the skies with carbon dioxide? Why shouldn't we bury toxic waste in containers that will fall apart in a hundred years? It would not be against *our* interests to allow such actions; it would only harm our descendants. So, we may do so. Or consider oppressed populations. When the Europeans colonized new lands, why weren't they morally allowed to enslave the native inhabitants? After all, the native inhabitants did not have the weapons to put up a good fight. The Europeans could benefit most by creating a society in which the native inhabitants would be their slaves.

This objection does not concern some minor aspect of the theory; it goes right to the root of the tree. The Social Contract Theory is grounded in self-interest and reciprocity; thus, it seems unable to recognize the moral duties we have to individuals who cannot benefit us.

CHAPTER 7

The Utilitarian Approach

The greatest happiness of the greatest number is the foundation of morals and legislation.

JEREMY BENTHAM, *COLLECTED WORKS* (1843)

7.1. The Revolution in Ethics

The late 18th and 19th centuries witnessed an astonishing series of upheavals: The modern nation-state emerged from the French Revolution and the wreckage of the Napoleonic empire; the revolutions of 1848 showed the transforming power of the ideas of "liberty, equality, and fraternity"; in the New World, America was born, sporting a new kind of constitution; and the American Civil War (1861–1865) would finish off slavery in Western civilization. All the while, the Industrial Revolution was bringing about a complete restructuring of society.

It is not surprising that new ideas about ethics emerged during this era. In particular, Jeremy Bentham (1748–1832) made a powerful argument for a novel conception of morality. Morality, he urged, is not about pleasing God, nor is it about being faithful to abstract rules. Rather, morality is about making the world as happy as possible. Bentham believed in one ultimate moral principle, namely, the Principle of Utility. This principle requires us, in all circumstances, to produce the most happiness that we can.

Bentham was the leader of a group of philosophical radicals whose aim was to reform the laws and institutions of England along utilitarian lines. One of his followers was James Mill, the distinguished Scottish philosopher, historian, and economist. James Mill's son, John Stuart Mill (1806–1873), would become the leading advocate of utilitarian moral theory.

John Stuart's advocacy was even more elegant and persuasive than Bentham's. Mill's short book *Utilitarianism* (1861) is still required reading for serious students of ethics.

At first glance, the Principle of Utility may not seem like such a radical idea; in fact, it may seem too obvious to mention. Who *doesn't* believe that we should oppose suffering and promote happiness? Yet, in their own way, Bentham and Mill were as revolutionary as the other two great intellectual innovators of the 19th century, Darwin and Marx.

To understand why the Principle of Utility was so radical, consider what it *leaves out* of morality: Gone are all references to God or to abstract moral rules "written in the heavens." Morality is no longer conceived of as faithfulness to some divinely given code or some set of inflexible rules. As Peter Singer (1946–) would later put it, morality is not "a system of nasty puritanical prohibitions . . . designed to stop people [from] having fun." Rather, the point of morality is the happiness of beings in this world, and nothing more; and we are permitted—even required—to do whatever is necessary to promote that happiness. This was a revolutionary idea.

As I said, the utilitarians were social reformers as well as philosophers. They intended their doctrine to make a difference, not only in thought but in practice. To illustrate this, we will briefly examine the implications of their ideas for three practical issues: euthanasia, marijuana, and the treatment of nonhuman animals. These issues do not exhaust the practical applications of Utilitarianism; nor are they necessarily the ones that utilitarians would find most pressing. But they do give us a good sense of how utilitarians approach moral issues.

7.2. First Example: Euthanasia

Sigmund Freud (1856–1939), the legendary psychologist, was diagnosed with oral cancer after a lifetime of cigar smoking. During his final years, Freud's health went up and down, but in early 1939 a large swelling formed in the back of his mouth, and he would have no more good days. Freud's cancer was active and inoperable, and he was also suffering from heart failure. As his bones decayed, they cast off a foul smell, driving away his favorite dog. Mosquito netting had to be draped over his bed to keep flies away.

On September 21, at the age of 83, Freud took his friend and personal physician, Max Schur, by the hand and said, "My dear Schur, you certainly remember our first talk. You promised me then not to forsake me when my time comes. Now it's nothing but torture and makes no sense any more." Forty years earlier Freud had written, "What has the individual come to . . . if one no longer dares to disclose that it is this or that man's turn to die?" Dr. Schur said he understood Freud's request. He injected Freud with a drug in order to end his life. "He soon felt relief," Dr. Schur wrote, "and fell into a peaceful sleep."

Did Max Schur do anything wrong? On the one hand, he was motivated by noble sentiments—he loved his friend and wanted to relieve his misery. Moreover, Freud had asked to die. All this argues for a lenient judgment. On the other hand, what Schur did was morally wrong, according to the dominant moral tradition in our culture.

That tradition is Christianity. Christianity holds that human life is a gift from God, and only God may decide to end it. The early church prohibited all killing, believing that Jesus's teachings permitted no exceptions to the rule. Later, the church recognized some exceptions, such as capital punishment and killing in war. But suicide and euthanasia remained forbidden. To summarize the church's doctrine, theologians formulated the rule: *the intentional killing of innocent people is always wrong*. This idea, more than any other, has shaped Western attitudes about the morality of killing. Thus we may be reluctant to excuse Max Schur, even though he acted from noble motives. He intentionally killed an innocent person; therefore, according to our tradition, what he did was wrong.

Utilitarianism takes a very different approach. It asks: which action available to Max Schur would have produced the greatest balance of happiness over unhappiness? The person whose happiness was most at stake was Sigmund Freud. If Schur had not killed him, Freud would have lived on, in wretched pain. How much unhappiness would this have involved? It is hard to say precisely; but Freud's condition was so bad that he preferred death. Killing him ended his agony. Therefore, utilitarians have concluded that euthanasia, in such a case, is morally right.

Although this argument is very different from arguments in the Christian tradition, the classical utilitarians did not think they were advocating an atheistic or antireligious philosophy.

Bentham thought that the faithful would endorse the utilitarian standpoint if only they viewed God as *benevolent*. He writes:

> The dictates of religion would coincide, in all cases, with those of utility, were the Being, who is the object of religion, universally supposed to be as benevolent as he is supposed to be wise and powerful. . . . But among the [advocates] of religion . . . there seem to be but few . . . who are real believers in his benevolence. They call him benevolent in words, but they do not mean that he is so in reality.

The morality of mercy killing might be a case in point. How, Bentham might ask, could a benevolent God forbid the killing of Sigmund Freud? If someone were to say, "God is caring and loving—but He forbids us from putting Freud out of his misery," this would be exactly what Bentham means by "calling him benevolent in words, but not meaning that he is so in reality."

The majority of religious people disagree with Bentham, and not only our moral tradition but our legal tradition has evolved under the influence of Christianity. Among Western nations, euthanasia is legal in only a handful of countries. In the United States, it is simply murder, and a doctor who intentionally kills her patient could spend the rest of her life in prison. What would Utilitarianism say about this? If euthanasia is moral, on the utilitarian view, should it also be legal?

In general, we don't want to outlaw morally acceptable behavior. Bentham was trained in the law, and he thought of the Principle of Utility as a guide for both legislators and ordinary people. The purpose of the law, he thought, is to promote the welfare of all citizens. In order to serve this purpose, the law should restrict people's freedom as little as possible. In particular, no activity should be outlawed unless that activity is harmful or dangerous to others. Bentham opposed, for example, laws regulating the sexual conduct of consenting adults. But it was Mill who gave this principle its most eloquent expression, in his book *On Liberty* (1859):

> The only purpose for which power can be rightfully exercised over any member of a civilized community, against his will, is to prevent harm to others. His own good, either physical or moral, is not a sufficient warrant. . . . Over himself, over his own body and mind, the individual is sovereign.

Thus, for the classical utilitarians, laws against euthanasia are unjustified restrictions on people's ability to control their own lives. When Max Schur killed Sigmund Freud, he was helping Freud end his life in the manner that Freud had chosen. No harm was caused to anyone else, and so it was no one else's business. Bentham himself is said to have requested euthanasia in his final days. However, we do not know whether his request was granted.

7.3. Second Example: Marijuana

William Bennett was America's first "drug czar." From 1989 to 1991, as President George H. W. Bush's top advisor on drug policy, he advocated the aggressive enforcement of U.S. drug laws. Bennett, who holds a Ph.D. in philosophy, said, "The simple fact is that drug use is wrong. And the moral argument, in the end, is the most compelling argument." Bennett's "moral argument," it seems, is just the assertion that drug use is wrong, by its very nature. What would utilitarians think about this? For them, there is no "simple fact" as to whether drug use is immoral. Rather, the moral argument must address the complex question of whether drug use increases or decreases happiness. Let's think about one drug in particular: marijuana. What would a utilitarian say about the ethics of pot?

People have strong feelings on this topic. Younger people who use drugs might be defensive and deny that pot causes any harm at all; older people who don't use drugs might be judgmental while failing to distinguish marijuana from harder drugs like cocaine and methamphetamine. A good utilitarian will ignore such feelings. What are the pros and cons of marijuana, according to Utilitarianism?

The main benefit of pot is the pleasure it brings. Not only is marijuana enormously relaxing, but marijuana can greatly enhance the pleasure of sensory activities, such as eating, listening to music, and having sex. This fact is almost never mentioned in public discussion; people seem to assume that enjoyment is irrelevant to morality. Utilitarians, however, disagree. For them, the whole issue is whether pot increases or decreases happiness. And utilitarians do not believe in "bad pleasures." If something feels good, then it is good, at least to that extent.

How pleasurable is marijuana? Some people love it; some people don't like it; and a lot depends on whether it is used in a comfortable setting. Thus, it is hard to generalize. But the facts suggest that many people enjoy getting high. Marijuana is the most popular illicit drug in America: One-third of Americans have tried it; 6% have used it in the past month; and Americans spend more than $10 billion per year on it, despite the threat of prison.

What unhappiness does marijuana cause? Some of the charges made against it are unfounded. First, marijuana does not cause violence; pot tends to make people passive, not aggressive. Second, marijuana is not a "gateway drug" that causes people to crave and use harder drugs. Often, people do use pot before using harder drugs, but that is because pot is so widely available. In neighborhoods where crack cocaine is easier to get, people usually try crack first. Third, marijuana is not highly addictive. According to the experts, it is less addictive than caffeine. Utilitarians do not want to base their assessment on false information.

Marijuana, however, does have some real disadvantages, which the utilitarian must weigh against the benefits. First, some people do get addicted to pot. Although marijuana withdrawal is not as traumatic as, say, heroin withdrawal, quitting is unpleasant for the addict. Second, long-term heavy use can cause mild cognitive damage, which may decrease happiness. Third, getting high all the time would make a person unproductive. Fourth, *smoking* pot is bad for your respiratory system; one joint may be as bad for your lungs as about six cigarettes. However, ingesting marijuana in other ways—for example, by baking it into brownies—should not be bad for your lungs at all.

What do utilitarians conclude from all this? When we look at the harms and benefits, the occasional use of pot hardly seems to be a moral issue at all; there are no known disadvantages to it. Thus, utilitarians consider casual use to be a matter of personal preference. Heavy marijuana use raises more complex issues. Does the pleasure one gets from long-term, heavy use outweigh the disadvantages? It probably depends on the person. Anyway, the question is so difficult that utilitarians may disagree on the answer.

So far we've been discussing the individual's decision of whether to use marijuana. What about the law—should pot be illegal, according to Utilitarianism? The fact that many people enjoy getting high is a strong reason to legalize the drug, according to Utilitarianism. What other factors are relevant?

If marijuana were legal, more people would use it, and several worries arise from that fact: society as a whole might become less productive; taxpayers might get stuck with the medical bills of heavy users; and more people might drive while high. It should be noted, however, that marijuana impairs driving ability only slightly, because people who are stoned drive cautiously and defensively.

On the other hand, society would be better off insofar as marijuana replaced alcohol as a drug of abuse: stoned citizens are unproductive, but alcoholics miss even more work because of the bad morning-after hangover; alcoholism is especially expensive in terms of health care; alcohol impairs driving ability much more than pot does; and, finally, drunks are far more violent than potheads. Thus, one benefit of legalizing pot would be fewer alcoholics, even if there would be more potheads.

Also, there are two big costs to maintaining the current laws. The first is the lost revenue for society. With marijuana illegal, society spends money on criminal enforcement; with marijuana legal, society collects money from taxing pot. Legalizing marijuana in the United States would save about $7.7 billion per year in enforcement costs, and it would generate between $2.4 and $6.2 billion in tax revenue, depending on whether pot was taxed normally or at the higher rate at which alcohol and tobacco are now taxed.

But the greatest cost is the harm done to the offenders. In the United States, over 700,000 people are arrested each year for possession of marijuana, and more than 44,000 people are currently in prison for marijuana offenses. Not only is being arrested and incarcerated horrible, but ex-cons have trouble finding decent jobs. Utilitarians care about these harms, even though the harms are inflicted on lawbreakers who knew they might be punished.

Thus, almost all utilitarians favor the legalization of marijuana. On the whole, marijuana is less harmful than alcohol or cigarettes, which Western societies already tolerate. However, utilitarians must be flexible; if new evidence emerges, showing marijuana to be more harmful than was previously thought, then the utilitarian view might change.

7.4. Third Example: Nonhuman Animals

The treatment of animals has traditionally been regarded as a trivial matter. Christians believe that man alone is made in God's image and that animals do not have souls. Thus, by the natural order of things, we can treat animals in any way we like. Saint Thomas Aquinas (1225–1274) summed up the traditional view when he wrote:

> Hereby is refuted the error of those who said it is sinful for a man to kill brute animals; for by the divine providence they are intended for man's use in the natural order. Hence it is not wrong for man to make use of them, either by killing them or in any other way whatever.

But isn't it wrong to be *cruel* to animals? Aquinas concedes that it is, but he says the reason has to do with human welfare, not the welfare of the animals:

> And if any passages of Holy Scripture seem to forbid us to be cruel to brute animals, for instance to kill a bird with its young, this is either to remove man's thoughts from being cruel to other men, lest through being cruel to animals one becomes cruel to human beings; or because injury to an animal leads to the temporal hurt of man, either of the doer of the deed, or of another.

Thus, people and animals are in separate moral categories. Animals have no moral standing of their own; we are free to treat them in any way we please.

Put so bluntly, the traditional doctrine might make us a little nervous: It seems extreme in its lack of concern for nonhuman animals, many of which are, after all, intelligent and sensitive creatures. Yet only a little reflection is needed to see how much of our conduct is actually guided by this doctrine. We eat animals; we use them as experimental subjects in our laboratories; we use their skins for clothing and their heads as wall ornaments; we make them the objects of our amusement in circuses and rodeos; and we track them down and kill them for sport.

If one is uncomfortable with the theological "justification" of these practices, Western philosophers have offered plenty of secular ones. Philosophers have said that animals are not *rational*, that they lack the ability to *speak*, or that they are simply not *human*—and all these are given as reasons why their interests lie outside the sphere of moral concern.

The utilitarians, however, would have none of this. On their view, what matters is not whether an animal has a soul, is rational, or any of the rest. All that matters is whether it can experience happiness and unhappiness. If an animal can suffer, then we have a duty to take that into account when deciding what to do. In fact, Bentham argues that whether an animal is human or nonhuman is just as irrelevant as whether the animal is black or white. He writes:

> The day *may* come when the rest of the animal creation may acquire those rights which never could have been withholden from them but by the hand of tyranny. The French have already discovered that the blackness of the skin is no reason why a human being should be abandoned without redress to the caprice of a tormentor. It may one day come to be recognized that the number of the legs, the villosity of the skin, or the termination of the *os sacrum* are reasons equally insufficient for abandoning a sensitive being to the same fate. What else is it that should trace the insuperable line? Is it the faculty of reason, or perhaps the faculty of discourse? But a full-grown horse or dog is beyond comparison a more rational, as well as a more conversable animal, than an infant of a day or a week or even a month old. But suppose they were otherwise, what would it avail? The question is not, Can they *reason?* nor Can they *talk?* but, Can they *suffer?*

If a human is tormented, why is it wrong? Because that person suffers. Similarly, if a nonhuman is tormented, it also suffers. Whether it is a *human* or an *animal* that suffers is simply irrelevant. To Bentham and Mill, this line of reasoning was conclusive. Humans and nonhumans are equally entitled to moral concern.

This view may seem as extreme, in the opposite direction, as the traditional view that grants animals no moral standing at all. Are animals really to be regarded as the equals of humans? In some sense, Bentham and Mill thought so, but they did not believe that animals and humans must always be treated in the same way. There are factual differences between them that will often justify differences in treatment. For example, because of their intellectual capacities, humans can take pleasure in things that nonhumans cannot enjoy—mathematics, literature, strategy games, and so on. And, similarly, humans' superior capacities make them capable of frustrations and disappointments that other animals cannot experience. Thus, our duty to promote happiness entails a duty to promote those special enjoyments for humans, as well as to prevent any special harms they might suffer. At the same time, however, we have a moral duty to take into account the suffering of animals, and their suffering counts equally with any similar suffering experienced by a human.

In 1970 the British psychologist Richard D. Ryder coined the term "speciesism" to refer to the idea that animal interests matter less than human interests. Utilitarians believe that speciesism is discrimination against other species, just as racism is discrimination against other races. Ryder wonders how we can possibly justify allowing experiments such as these:

- In Maryland in 1996, scientists used beagle dogs to study septic shock. They cut holes in the dogs' throats and placed *E. coli*-infected clots into their stomachs. Within three weeks, most of the dogs had died.
- In Taiwan in 1997, scientists dropped weights onto rats' spines in order to study spinal injury. The researchers found that greater injuries were caused by dropping the weights from greater heights.
- Since the 1990s, chimpanzees, monkeys, dogs, cats, and rodents have been used to study alcoholism. After addicting the animals to alcohol, scientists have observed such symptoms as vomiting, tremor, anxiety, and seizures. When the animals are in alcoholic withdrawal, scientists have induced convulsions by lifting them by their tails, by giving them electric shocks, and by injecting chemicals into their brains.

The utilitarian argument is simple enough. We should judge actions right or wrong depending on whether they cause more happiness or unhappiness. The animals in these experiments were obviously caused terrible suffering. Was there any compensating gain in happiness that justified it? Was greater unhappiness being prevented, for other animals or for humans? If not, the experiments were morally unacceptable.

This style of argument does not imply that all animal experiments are immoral. Rather, it suggests judging each one on its own merits. The utilitarian principle does, however, imply that experiments that cause a lot of pain require significant justification. We cannot simply assume that, in dealing with nonhumans, anything goes.

But criticizing animal experiments is too easy for most of us. We may feel self-righteous or superior because we do not do such research ourselves. All of us, however, are involved in cruelty when we eat meat. The facts about meat production are more disturbing than any facts about animal experimentation.

Most people believe, in a vague way, that slaughterhouses are unpleasant, but that animals raised for food are otherwise treated humanely. In fact, farm animals live in abhorrent conditions before being taken off to slaughter. Veal calves, for example, spend 24 hours per day in pens so small that they cannot turn around, lie down comfortably, or even twist their heads around to get rid of parasites. The producers put them in tiny pens to save money and to keep their meat tender. The cows clearly miss their mothers, and like human infants, they want something to suck, so they try in vain to suck the sides of their wooden stalls. The calves are also fed a diet deficient in iron and roughage, in order to keep their meat pale and tasty. Their craving for iron becomes so strong that they will lick at their own urine, if they're allowed to turn around—which normally they would never do. Without roughage, the calves cannot form a cud to chew. For this reason, they cannot be given straw bedding, because they would eat it, in an attempt to consume roughage. So, for these animals, the slaughterhouse is not an unpleasant end to an otherwise contented existence.

The veal calf is just one example. Chickens, turkeys, pigs, and adult cows all live in horrible conditions before being slaughtered. The utilitarian argument on these matters is simple enough. The system of meat production causes enormous suffering for the animals with no compensating benefits. Therefore, we should abandon that system. We should either become vegetarians or else treat our animals humanely before killing them.

What is most revolutionary in all this is simply the idea that the interests of nonhuman animals *count*. We normally assume that human beings alone are worthy of moral consideration.

Utilitarianism challenges that assumption and insists that the moral community must be expanded to include all creatures whose interests can be affected by what we do. Human beings are in many ways special, and an adequate morality must acknowledge that. But we are not the only animals on this planet, and an adequate morality must acknowledge that fact as well.

CHAPTER 8

*T*he Debate over Utilitarianism

The creed which accepts . . . the Greatest Happiness
Principle . . . holds that actions are right . . . as they tend to promote
happiness, wrong as they tend to produce the reverse of happiness.
JOHN STUART MILL, *UTILITARIANISM* (1861)

Man does not strive after happiness; only the Englishman does that.
FRIEDRICH NIETZSCHE, *TWILIGHT OF THE IDOLS* (1889)

8.1. The Classical Version of the Theory

Classical Utilitarianism can be summed up in three propositions: (a) The morality of an action depends solely on the consequences of the action; nothing else matters. (b) An action's
consequences matter only insofar as they involve the greater
or lesser happiness of individuals. (c) In the assessment of
consequences, each individual's happiness gets "equal consideration." This means that equal amounts of happiness always
count equally; nobody's well-being matters more just because
he is rich, let's say, or powerful, or handsome. Morally, everyone counts the same. According to Classical Utilitarianism, an
action is right if it produces the greatest overall balance of happiness over unhappiness.

Classical Utilitarianism was developed and defended by
three of the greatest philosophers in 19th-century England:
Jeremy Bentham (1748–1832), John Stuart Mill (1806–1873),
and Henry Sidgwick (1838–1900). Thanks in part to their work,
Utilitarianism has had a profound influence on modern thinking. Most moral philosophers, however, reject the theory. In what
follows, we will discuss some of the objections that have made the
theory unpopular. In examining these arguments, we will also be
pondering some of the deepest questions in ethical theory.

8.2. Is Pleasure All That Matters?

The question *What things are good?* is different from the question *What actions are right?* and Utilitarianism answers the second question by reference to the first. Right actions are the ones that produce the most good. But what is good? The utilitarian reply is: happiness. As Mill puts it, "The utilitarian doctrine is that happiness is desirable, and the only thing desirable, as an end; all other things being only desirable as means to that end."

But what is happiness? According to the classical utilitarians, happiness is pleasure. Utilitarians understand "pleasure" broadly, to include all mental states that feel good. A sense of accomplishment, a delicious taste, and the heightened awareness that comes at the climax of a suspenseful movie are all examples of pleasure. The thesis that pleasure is the one ultimate good—and pain the one ultimate evil—has been known since antiquity as Hedonism. The idea that things are good or bad because of how they make us *feel* has always had a following in philosophy. Yet a little reflection seems to reveal flaws in this theory.

Consider these two examples:

- *You think someone is your friend, but he ridicules you behind your back.* No one tells you, so you never know. Is this unfortunate for you? Hedonists would have to say it is not, because you are never caused any pain. Yet we believe that there is something bad going on. You are being mistreated, even though you are unaware of it and suffer no unhappiness.

- *A promising young pianist's hands are injured in a car accident so that she can no longer play.* Why is this bad for her? Hedonists would say it is bad because it causes her pain and eliminates a source of joy for her. But suppose she finds something else that she enjoys just as much— suppose, for example, she gets as much pleasure from watching hockey on TV as she once got from playing the piano. Why is her accident now a tragedy? The hedonist can only say that she will feel frustrated and upset whenever she thinks of what might have been, and *that* is her misfortune. But this explanation gets things backward. It is not as though, by feeling upset, she has turned a neutral situation into a bad one. On the contrary, the bad situation is what made her unhappy. She might have become a great pianist, and now she will not. We cannot eliminate the tragedy by getting her to cheer up and watch hockey.

Both of these examples rely on the same idea: We value things other than pleasure. For example, we value artistic creativity and friendship. These things make us happy, but that's not the only reason we value them. It seems like a misfortune to lose them, even if there is no loss of happiness.

For this reason, most present-day utilitarians reject the classical assumption of Hedonism. Some of them bypass the question of what's good, saying only that right actions are the ones that have the best results, however that is measured. Other utilitarians, such as the English philosopher G. E. Moore (1873–1958), have compiled short lists of things to be regarded as valuable in themselves. Moore suggested that there are three obvious intrinsic goods—pleasure, friendship, and aesthetic enjoyment—and so right actions are those actions that increase the world's supply of these things. Still others say that we should act so as to maximize the satisfaction of people's *preferences.* We won't discuss the merits and demerits of these theories of the good. I mention them only to note that, although Hedonism has largely been rejected, contemporary utilitarians have not found it difficult to carry on.

8.3. Are Consequences All That Matter?

To determine whether an action is right, utilitarians believe that we should look at *what will happen as a result of doing it.* This idea is central to the theory. If things other than consequences are important in determining what is right, then Utilitarianism is incorrect. Here are three arguments that attack the theory at just this point.

Justice. In 1965, writing in the racially charged climate of the American civil rights movement, H. J. McCloskey asks us to consider the following case:

> Suppose a utilitarian were visiting an area in which there was racial strife, and that, during his visit, a Negro rapes a white woman, and that race riots occur as a result of

the crime. . . . Suppose too that our utilitarian is in the area of the crime when it is committed such that his testimony would bring about the conviction of [whomever he accuses]. If he knows that a quick arrest will stop the riots and lynchings, surely, as a utilitarian, he must conclude that he has a duty to bear false witness in order to bring about the punishment of an innocent person.

Such an accusation would have bad consequences—the innocent man would be convicted—but there would be enough good consequences to outweigh them: The riots and lynchings would be stopped, and many lives would be saved. The best outcome would thus be achieved by bearing false witness; therefore, according to Utilitarianism, lying is the thing to do. But, the argument continues, it would be wrong to bring about the conviction of an innocent person. Therefore, Utilitarianism must be incorrect.

According to the critics of Utilitarianism, this argument illustrates one of the theory's most serious shortcomings, namely, that it is incompatible with the ideal of justice. Justice requires that we treat people fairly, according to the merits of their particular situations. In McCloskey's example, Utilitarianism requires that we treat someone unfairly. Therefore, Utilitarianism cannot be right.

Rights. Here is an example from the U.S. Court of Appeals. In the case of *York v. Story* (1963), arising out of California:

> In October, 1958, appellant [Ms. Angelynn York] went to the police department of Chino for the purpose of filing charges in connection with an assault upon her. Appellee Ron Story, an officer of that police department, then acting under color of his authority as such, advised appellant that it was necessary to take photographs of her. Story then took appellant to a room in the police station, locked the door, and directed her to undress, which she did. Story then directed appellant to assume various indecent positions, and photographed her in those positions. These photographs were not made for any lawful or legitimate purpose.
>
> Appellant objected to undressing. She stated to Story that there was no need to take photographs of her in the nude, or in the positions she was directed to take, because the bruises would not show in any photograph. . . .

Later that month, Story advised appellant that the pictures did not come out and that he had destroyed them. Instead, Story circulated these photographs among the personnel of the Chino police department. In April, 1960, two other officers of that police department, appellee Louis Moreno and defendant Henry Grote, acting under color of their authority as such, and using police photographic equipment located at the police station, made additional prints of the photographs taken by Story. Moreno and Grote then circulated these prints among the personnel of the Chino police department.

Ms. York brought suit against these officers and won. Her legal rights had clearly been violated. But what about the *morality* of the officers' behavior? Utilitarianism says that actions are defensible if they produce a favorable balance of happiness over unhappiness. This suggests that we compare the amount of unhappiness caused to York with the amount of pleasure the photographs gave to Officer Story and the others. And it is at least possible that more happiness than unhappiness was created. In that case, the utilitarian conclusion would be that their actions were morally acceptable. But this seems perverse. Why should the pleasure of Story and his friends matter at all? They had no right to treat York in this way, and the fact that they enjoyed doing so hardly seems relevant.

Consider a related case. Suppose a Peeping Tom spied on a woman through her bedroom window and secretly took pictures of her undressed. Suppose he is never caught, and he never shows the pictures to anyone. Under these circumstances, the only consequence of his action seems to be an increase in his own happiness. No one else, including the woman, is caused any unhappiness at all. How, then, could a utilitarian deny that the Peeping Tom's actions are right? Utilitarianism again appears to be unacceptable.

The key point is that Utilitarianism is at odds with the idea that people have *rights* that may not be trampled on merely because one anticipates good results. In these examples, the woman's right to privacy is violated. But we could think of similar cases in which other rights are at issue—the right to worship freely, the right to speak one's mind, or even the right to live. On Utilitarianism, an individual's rights may always be trampled upon if enough people benefit from the trampling. Utilitarianism has thus been accused of supporting the "tyranny of the majority": if the majority of people would take pleasure in someone's rights being abused, then those rights should be abused, because the pleasure of the majority outweighs the suffering of the one. However, we do not think that our individual rights should mean so little, morally. The notion of an individual right is not a utilitarian notion. Quite the opposite: It is a notion that places limits on how an individual may be treated, regardless of the good that might be accomplished.

Backward-Looking Reasons. Suppose you have promised to do something—say, you promised to meet your friend at a coffee shop this afternoon. But when the time comes to go, you don't want to do it; you need to catch up on some work and you would rather stay home. You try to call her up to cancel, but she isn't answering her cell phone. What should you do? Suppose you judge that the utility of getting your work done slightly outweighs the irritation your friend would experience from being stood up. Applying the utilitarian standard, you might conclude that staying home is better than keeping your promise. However, this does not seem correct. The fact that you *promised* imposes an obligation on you that you cannot escape so easily. Of course, if a great deal were at stake—if, for example, you had to rush your mother to the hospital—you would be justified in breaking the promise. But a *small* gain in happiness cannot overcome the obligation created by your promise; the obligation should mean something, morally. Thus, Utilitarianism once again seems mistaken.

This criticism is possible because Utilitarianism cares only about the *consequences* of our actions. However, we normally think that considerations about the past are important, too. You made a promise to your friend, and that's a fact about the past. Utilitarianism seems faulty because it excludes such backward-looking reasons.

Once we understand this point, we can think of other examples of backward-looking reasons. The fact that someone committed a crime is a reason to punish him. The fact that someone did you a favor last week is a reason for you to do her a favor next week. The fact that you hurt someone yesterday is a reason to make it up to him today. These are all facts about the past that are relevant to determining our obligations. But Utilitarianism makes the past irrelevant, and so it seems flawed.

8.4. Should We Be Equally Concerned for Everyone?

The last part of Utilitarianism says that we must treat each person's happiness as equally important—or as Mill put it, we must be "as strictly impartial as a disinterested and benevolent spectator." Stated abstractly, this sounds plausible, but it has troubling implications. One problem is that the requirement of "equal concern" places too great a demand on us; another problem is that it disrupts our personal relationships.

The Charge That Utilitarianism Is Too Demanding. Suppose you are on your way to the movies when someone points out that the money you are about to spend could be used to feed the starving or to provide inoculations for third-world children. Surely, those people need food and medicine more than you need to see Brad Pitt and Angelina Jolie. So you forgo your entertainment and donate your money to charity. But that is not the end of it. By the same reasoning, you cannot buy new clothes, a car, an iPhone, or a PlayStation. Probably you should move into a cheaper apartment. After all, what's more important—that you have these luxuries, or that children have food?

In fact, faithful adherence to the utilitarian standard would require you to give away your wealth until you've made yourself as poor as the people you're helping. Or rather, you'd need to leave yourself just enough to maintain your job, so that you can keep on giving. Although we would admire someone who did this, we would not think that such a person was merely "doing his duty." Rather, we would regard him as a saint, as someone whose generosity went *beyond* the call of duty. Philosophers call such actions *supererogatory*. But Utilitarianism seems unable to recognize this moral category.

The problem is not merely that Utilitarianism would require us to give away most of our things. It would also prevent us from carrying on our lives. We all have goals and projects that make our lives meaningful. But an ethic that requires us to promote the general welfare would force us to abandon those endeavors. Suppose you are a Web designer, not getting rich but making a decent living; you have two children whom you love; and on weekends, you like to perform with an amateur theater group. In addition, you enjoy reading history. How could there be anything wrong with this? But judged by the utilitarian standard, you are leading an immoral life. After all, you could be doing a lot more good if you spent your time in other ways.

The Charge That Utilitarianism Disrupts Our Personal Relationships. In practice, none of us is willing to treat everyone equally, because that would require giving up our special ties to friends and family. We are all deeply partial where our family and friends are concerned. We love them, and we go to great lengths to help them. To us, they are not just members of the great crowd of humanity—they are special. But all this is inconsistent with impartiality. When you are impartial, you miss out on intimacy, love, affection, and friendship.

At this point, Utilitarianism seems to have lost all touch with reality. What would it be like to care about one's spouse no more than one cares about complete strangers? The very idea is absurd; not only is it profoundly contrary to normal human emotions, but loving relationships could not even exist apart from special responsibilities and obligations. Again, what would it be like to treat one's children with no greater love than one has for strangers? As John Cottingham puts it, "A parent who leaves his child to burn" because "the building contains someone else whose future contribution to the general welfare promises to be greater, is not a hero; he is (rightly) an object of moral contempt, a moral leper."

8.5. The Defense of Utilitarianism

Together, these objections appear to be decisive. Utilitarianism seems unconcerned with both justice and individual rights. Moreover, it cannot account for backward-looking reasons. If we lived by the theory, we would become poor, and we would have to stop loving our family and our friends.

Most philosophers have therefore abandoned Utilitarianism. Some philosophers, however, continue to defend it. They do so in three different ways.

The First Defense: Contesting the Consequences. Most of the arguments against Utilitarianism go like this: a situation is described; then it is said that some particular (vile!) action would have the best consequences under those circumstances; then Utilitarianism is faulted for advocating that action. These arguments, however, succeed only if the actions they describe really would have the best consequences. Would they? According to the first defense, they would not.

Consider, for example, McClosky's argument, in which Utilitarianism is supposed to support framing an innocent man in order to stop a race riot. In the real world, would bearing false witness in this way actually have good consequences? Probably not. The liar might be discovered, and then the situation would be worse than before. And even if the lie succeeded, the real culprit would remain at large and might commit more crimes, to be followed by more riots. Moreover, if the guilty party were later caught, which is always possible, the liar would be in deep trouble, and confidence in the criminal justice system would erode. The moral is that although one might *think* that one can bring about the best consequences by such behavior, experience in fact teaches the opposite: Utility is not served by framing innocent people.

The same goes for the other arguments. Lying, violating people's rights, breaking one's promises, and severing one's intimate relationships all have bad consequences. Only in philosophers' imaginations is it otherwise. In the real world, Peeping Toms are caught, just as Officer Story was caught, and their victims pay the price. In the real world, when people lie, their reputations suffer and other people get hurt; and when people break their promises and fail to return favors, they lose their friends.

So that is the first defense. Unfortunately, it is not very effective. While it is true that *most* acts of false witness and the like have bad consequences, it cannot be said that *all* such acts have bad consequences. At least once in a while, one can bring about a good result by doing something repugnant to moral common sense. Therefore, in at least some real-life cases, Utilitarianism will conflict with common sense. Moreover, even if the anti-utilitarian arguments had to rely on fictitious examples, those arguments would retain their power. Theories like Utilitarianism are supposed to apply to *all* situations, including situations that are merely hypothetical. Thus, showing that Utilitarianism has unacceptable implications in made-up cases is a valid way of critiquing it. The first defense, then, is weak.

The Second Defense: The Principle of Utility Is a Guide for Choosing Rules, Not Acts. Revising a theory is a two-step process: first, you identify which feature of the theory needs work; second, you change only that feature, leaving the rest of the theory intact. What feature of Classical Utilitarianism is causing the trouble?

The troublesome assumption is that *each individual action* should be judged by the utilitarian standard. Whether it would be wrong to tell a particular lie depends on the consequences of *telling that particular lie;* whether you should keep a particular promise depends on the consequences of *keeping that particular promise;* and so on for each of the examples we have considered. If what we care about is the consequences of particular actions, then we can always dream up circumstances in which a horrific action will have the best consequences.

Therefore, the new version of Utilitarianism modifies the theory so that individual actions are no longer judged by the Principle of Utility. Instead, we first ask what *set of rules* is optimal, from a utilitarian viewpoint. In other words, what rules should we follow in order to maximize happiness? Individual acts are then assessed according to whether they abide by these rules. This new version of the theory is called "Rule-Utilitarianism," to distinguish it from the original theory, now commonly called "Act-Utilitarianism."

Rule-Utilitarianism has an easy answer to the anti-utilitarian arguments. An act-utilitarian would incriminate the innocent man in McCloskey's example because the consequences of *that particular act* would be good. But the rule-utilitarian would not reason in that way. She would first ask, What rules of conduct tend to promote the most happiness? And one good rule is "Don't bear false witness against the innocent." That rule is simple and easy to remember, and following it will almost always increase happiness. By appealing to it, the rule-utilitarian can conclude that in McCloskey's example we should not testify against the innocent man.

Similar reasoning can be used to establish rules against violating people's rights, breaking promises, lying, betraying one's friends, and so on. We should accept such rules because following them, as a regular practice, promotes the general happiness. So we no longer judge acts by their utility but by their conformity with these rules. Thus, Rule-Utilitarianism cannot be convicted of violating our moral common sense. In shifting emphasis from the justification of acts to the justification of rules, Utilitarianism has been brought into line with our intuitive judgments.

However, a serious problem with Rule-Utilitarianism arises when we ask whether the ideal rules have *exceptions*. Must the rules be followed no matter what? What if a "forbidden" act would greatly increase the overall good? The rule-utilitarian might give any one of three answers.

First, if she says that in such cases we may violate the rules, then it looks like she wants to assess actions on a case-by-case basis. This is Act-Utilitarianism, not Rule-Utilitarianism.

Second, she might suggest that we formulate the rules so that violating them never will increase happiness. For example, instead of using the rule "Don't bear false witness against the innocent," we might use the rule "Don't bear false witness against the innocent, unless doing so would achieve some great good." If we change all of the rules in this way, then Rule-Utilitarianism will be exactly like Act-Utilitarianism in practice; the rules we follow will always tell us to choose the act that promotes the most happiness. But now Rule-Utilitarianism does not provide a response to the anti-utilitarian arguments; like Act-Utilitarianism, Rule-Utilitarianism tells us to incriminate the innocent, break our promises, spy on people in their homes, and so on.

Finally, the rule-utilitarian might stand her ground and say that we should never break the rules, even to promote happiness. J. J. C. Smart (1920–) says that such a person suffers from an irrational "rule worship." Whatever one thinks of that, this version of Rule-Utilitarianism is not really a utilitarian theory. Utilitarians care solely about happiness and about consequences; but this theory, in addition, cares about following rules. The theory is thus a mix of Utilitarianism and something else entirely. To paraphrase one writer, this type of Rule-Utilitarianism is like a rubber duck: just as a rubber duck is not a kind of duck, this type of Rule-Utilitarianism is not a kind of Utilitarianism. And so, we cannot defend Utilitarianism by appealing to it.

The Third Defense: "Common Sense" Is Wrong. Finally, some utilitarians have offered a very different response to the objections. Upon being told that Utilitarianism conflicts with common sense, they respond, "So what?" Looking back at his own defense of Utilitarianism, J. J. C. Smart writes:

> Admittedly utilitarianism does have consequences which are incompatible with the common moral consciousness, but I tended to take the view "so much the worse for the common moral consciousness." That is, I was inclined to reject the common methodology of testing general ethical principles by seeing how they square with our feelings in particular instances.

This breed of utilitarian—hard-nosed and unapologetic— can offer three responses to the anti-utilitarian arguments.

The First Response: All Values Have a Utilitarian Basis. Critics of Utilitarianism say that the theory can't make sense of some of our most important values—such as the value we attach to truth telling, promise keeping, respecting others' privacy, and loving our children. Consider, for example, lying. The main reason not to lie, the critics say, has nothing to do with bad consequences. The reason is that lying is dishonest; it betrays people's trust. That fact has nothing to do with the utilitarian calculation of benefits. Honesty has a value over and above any value that the utilitarian can acknowledge. And the same is true of promise keeping, respecting others' privacy, and loving our children.

But according to philosophers such as Smart, we should think about these values one at a time and consider why they're important. When people lie, the lies are often discovered, and those betrayed feel hurt and angry. When people break their promises, they irritate their neighbors and alienate their friends. Someone whose privacy is violated may feel humiliated and want to withdraw from others. When people don't care more about their own children than they do about strangers, their children feel unloved, and one day they too may become unloving parents. All these things reduce happiness. Far from being at odds with the idea that we should be honest, dependable, respectful, and loving to our children, Utilitarianism explains why those things are good.

Moreover, apart from the utilitarian explanation, these duties would seem inexplicable. What could be stranger than saying that lying is wrong "in itself," apart from any harm it causes? And how could people have a "right to privacy" unless respecting that right brought them some benefit? On this way of thinking, Utilitarianism is not incompatible with common sense; on the contrary, Utilitarianism justifies the common-sense values we have.

The Second Response: Our Gut Reactions Can't Be Trusted When Cases Are Exceptional. Although some cases of injustice serve the common good, those cases are exceptions. Lying, promise breaking, and violations of privacy usually lead to unhappiness, not happiness. This observation forms the basis of another utilitarian response.

Consider again McCloskey's example of the person tempted to bear false witness. Why do we immediately and instinctively believe it to be wrong to bear false witness against an innocent person? The reason, some say, is that throughout our lives we have seen lies lead to misery and misfortune. Thus, *we instinctively condemn all lies.* But when we condemn lies that are beneficial, our intuitive faculties are misfiring. Experience has taught us to condemn lies because they reduce happiness. Now, however, we are condemning lies that increase happiness. When confronting unusual cases, such as McCloskey's, perhaps we should trust the Principle of Utility more than our gut instincts.

The Third Response: We Should Focus on *All* the Consequences. When we're asked to consider a "despicable" action that maximizes happiness, the action is often presented in a way that encourages us to focus on its bad effects, rather than its good effects. If instead we focus on *all* the effects of the act, Utilitarianism seems more plausible.

Consider yet again the McCloskey example. McCloskey says it would be wrong to convict an innocent man because that would be unjust. But what about the *other* innocent people who will be hurt if the rioting and lynchings continue? What about the pain that will be endured by those who are beaten and tormented by the mob? What about the deaths that will occur if the man doesn't lie? Children will lose their parents, and parents will lose their children. Of course, we never want to face a situation like this. But if we must choose between securing the conviction of one innocent person and allowing the deaths of several innocent people, is it so unreasonable to think that the first option is preferable?

And consider again the objection that Utilitarianism is too demanding because it tells us to use our resources to feed starving children instead of using those resources on ourselves. If we focus our thoughts on those who would starve, do the demands of Utilitarianism seem so unreasonable? Isn't it self-serving of us to say that Utilitarianism is "too demanding," rather than saying that we should do more to help?

This strategy works better for some cases than for others. Consider the Peeping Tom. The unapologetic utilitarian will tell us to consider the pleasure *he* gets from spying on unsuspecting women. If he gets away with it, what harm has been done? Why should his action be condemned? Most people will condemn his behavior, despite the utilitarian arguments. Utilitarianism, as Smart suggests, cannot be fully reconciled with common sense. Whether the theory needs to be reconciled with common sense remains an open question.

8.6. Concluding Thoughts

If we consult what Smart calls our "common moral consciousness," many considerations other than utility seem morally important. But Smart is right to warn us that "common sense" cannot be trusted. That may turn out to be Utilitarianism's greatest contribution. The deficiencies of moral common sense become obvious if we think about it. Many white people once felt that there was an important difference between whites and blacks, so that the interests of whites were somehow more important. Trusting the "common sense" of their day, they might have insisted that an adequate moral theory should accommodate this "fact." Today, no one worth listening to would say such a thing, but who knows how many other irrational prejudices are still part of our moral common sense? At the end of his classic study of race relations, *An American Dilemma,* Nobel Laureate Gunnar Myrdal (1898–1987) reminds us:

> There must be still other countless errors of the same sort that no living man can yet detect, because of the fog within which our type of Western culture envelops us. Cultural influences have set up the assumptions about the mind, the body, and the universe with which we begin; pose the

questions we ask; influence the facts we seek; determine the interpretation we give these facts; and direct our reaction to these interpretations and conclusions.

Could it be, for example, that future generations will look back in disgust at the way affluent people in the 21st century enjoyed their comfortable lives while third-world children died of easily preventable diseases? Or at the way we confined and slaughtered helpless animals? If so, they might note that utilitarian philosophers were ahead of their time in condemning such things.

CHAPTER 9

*A*re There Absolute Moral Rules?

You may not do evil that good may come.
SAINT PAUL, *LETTER TO THE ROMANS* (ca. A.D. 50)

9.1. Harry Truman and Elizabeth Anscombe

Harry S. Truman will always be remembered as the man who made the decision to drop the atomic bombs on Hiroshima and Nagasaki. When he became president in 1945, following the death of Franklin D. Roosevelt, Truman knew nothing about the bomb; Roosevelt's advisors had to fill him in. The Allies were winning the war in the Pacific, they said, but at a terrible cost. Plans had been drawn up for an invasion of Japan, but that battle would be even bloodier than the D-Day assault on Normandy had been. Using the atomic bomb on one or two Japanese cities might bring the war to a speedy end, making the invasion unnecessary.

Truman was at first reluctant to use the new weapon. The problem was that each bomb would obliterate an entire city—not just the military targets, but the hospitals, schools, and homes. Women, children, old people, and other noncombatants would be wiped out along with the military personnel. The Allies had bombed cities before, but Truman sensed that the new weapon made the issue of noncombatants more acute. Moreover, the United States was on record as condemning attacks on civilian targets. In 1939, before America had entered the war, President Roosevelt had sent a message to the governments of France, Germany, Italy, Poland, and Great Britain, denouncing the bombardment of cities in the strongest terms. He had called it an "inhuman barbarism":

> The ruthless bombing from the air of civilians . . . which has resulted in the maiming and in the death of thousands of defenseless men, women, and children, has sickened the hearts of every civilized man and woman, and has profoundly shocked the conscience of humanity. If resort is had to this form of inhuman barbarism during the period of the tragic conflagration with which the world is now confronted, hundreds of thousands of innocent human beings who have no responsibility for, and who are not even remotely participating in, the hostilities which have now broken out, will lose their lives.

Truman expressed similar thoughts when he decided to authorize the bombings. He wrote in his diary that "I have told the Sec. of War, Mr. Stimson, to use it so that military objectives and soldiers and sailors are the target and not women and children. . . . The target will be a purely military one." It is hard to know what to make of this, since Truman knew that the bombs would destroy whole cities. Nonetheless, it is clear that he was worried about the issue of noncombatants.

It is also clear that Truman was sure of his decision. Winston Churchill, the wartime leader of Great Britain, met with Truman shortly before the bombs were dropped, and he later wrote, "The decision whether or not to use the atomic bomb to compel the surrender of Japan was never even an issue. There was unanimous, automatic, unquestioned agreement around our table." After signing the final order, thus sealing the fate of Hiroshima, Truman later said that he "slept like a baby."

Elizabeth Anscombe, who died in 2001, was a 20-year-old student at Oxford University when World War II began. At that time, she co-authored a controversial pamphlet arguing that Britain should not go to war because countries at war inevitably end up fighting by unjust means. "Miss Anscombe," as she was always known—despite her 59-year marriage and her seven children—would go on to become one of the 20th century's most distinguished philosophers, and the greatest woman philosopher in history.

Miss Anscombe was also a Catholic, and her religion was central to her life. Her ethical views reflected traditional Catholic teachings. In 1968, after Pope Paul VI affirmed the church's ban on contraception, she wrote a pamphlet explaining why artificial birth control is immoral. Late in her life, she was arrested while protesting outside a British abortion clinic. She also accepted the church's teaching about the ethical conduct of war, which brought her into conflict with Truman.

Harry Truman and Elizabeth Anscombe crossed paths in 1956. Oxford University was planning to give Truman an honorary degree in thanks for America's wartime help, and those proposing the honor thought it would be uncontroversial. But Anscombe and two other faculty members opposed the idea. Although they lost, they forced a vote on what would otherwise have been a rubber-stamp approval. Then, while the degree was being conferred, Anscombe knelt outside the hall, praying.

Anscombe wrote another pamphlet, this time explaining that Truman was a murderer because he had ordered the bombings of Hiroshima and Nagasaki. Truman, of course, thought the bombings were justified—they had shortened the war and saved lives. For Anscombe, this was not good enough. "For men to choose to kill the innocent as a means to their ends," she wrote, "is always murder." To the argument that the bombings saved more lives than they took, she replied, "Come now: if you had to choose between boiling one baby and letting some frightful disaster befall a thousand people—or a million people, if a thousand is not enough—what would you do?"

Anscombe's example was apt. The bomb blast at Hiroshima, which ignited birds in midair, did lead to babies being boiled: People died in rivers, reservoirs, and cisterns, trying in vain to escape the heat. Anscombe's point was that *some things may not be done, no matter what.* It does not matter if we could accomplish some great good by boiling a baby; it is simply wrong. Anscombe believed in a host of such rules. Under no circumstances, she said, may we intentionally kill innocent people; worship idols; make a false profession of faith; engage in sodomy or adultery; punish one person for the acts of another; or commit treachery, which she describes as "obtaining a man's confidence in a grave matter by promises of trustworthy friendship and then betraying him to his enemies."

Anscombe's husband, Peter Geach (1916–), agreed with this. Anscombe and Geach were the 20th century's foremost philosophical champions of the doctrine that moral rules are absolute.

9.2. The Categorical Imperative

The idea that moral rules have no exceptions is hard to defend. It is easy enough to explain why we *should* break a rule—we can simply point to cases in which following the rule would have terrible consequences. But how can we defend *not* breaking the rule in such cases? It is a daunting assignment. We might say that moral rules are God's inviolable commands. Apart from that, what can be said?

Before the 20th century, there was one major philosopher who believed that moral rules are absolute. Immanuel Kant (1724–1804) argued that lying is wrong under any circumstances. He did not appeal to theological considerations; he held, instead, that reason always forbids lying. To see how he reached this conclusion, we need to look at his general theory of ethics.

Kant observed that the word *ought* is often used nonmorally:

- If you want to become a better chess player, you *ought* to study the games of Garry Kasparov.
- If you want to go to college, you *ought* to take the SAT.

Much of our conduct is governed by such "oughts." The pattern is this: We have a certain desire (to become a better chess player, to go to college); we recognize that a certain course of action will help us get what we want (studying Kasparov's games, taking the SAT); and so we follow the indicated plan.

Kant called these "hypothetical imperatives" because they tell us what to do *provided that* we have the relevant desires. A person who did not want to improve her chess would have no reason to study Kasparov's games; someone who did not want to go to college would have no reason to take the SAT. Because the binding force of the "ought" depends on having the relevant desire, we can escape its force by letting go of the desire. So, for example, I can avoid taking the SAT by deciding that I don't want to go to college.

Moral obligations, by contrast, do not depend on having particular desires. The form of a moral obligation is not "*If* you want so-and-so, then you ought to do such-and-such." Instead, moral requirements are *categorical:* They have the form "You ought to do such-and-such, *period.*" The moral rule is not, for example, that you ought to help people *if* you care about them or *if* you want to be a good person. Instead, the rule is that you should help people *no matter what* your desires are. That is why moral requirements cannot be escaped simply by saying "But I don't care about that."

Hypothetical "oughts" are easy to understand. They merely tell us to do what is necessary to achieve our goals. Categorical "oughts," on the other hand, are mysterious. How can we be obligated to behave in a certain way regardless of our goals? Kant has an answer. Just as hypothetical "oughts" are possible because we have *desires,* categorical "oughts" are possible because we have *reason.* Categorical oughts, Kant says, are derived from a principle that every rational person must accept: the Categorical Imperative. In his *Foundations of the Metaphysics of Morals* (1785), Kant expresses the Categorical Imperative as follows:

> Act only according to that maxim by which you can at the same time will that it should become a universal law.

This principle provides a way to tell whether an act is morally permissible. When you are thinking about doing something, ask what rule you would be following if you actually did it. This rule will be the "maxim" of your act. Then ask whether you would be willing for your maxim to become a universal law. In other words, would you allow your rule to be followed by all people at all times? If so, then your maxim is sound, and your act is acceptable. But if not, then your act is forbidden.

Kant gives several examples of how this works. Suppose, he says, a man needs money, but no one will lend it to him unless he promises to pay it back—which he knows he won't be able to do. Should he make a false promise to get the loan? If he did, his maxim would be: *Whenever you need a loan, promise to repay it, even if you know you can't.* Now, could he will that this rule become a universal law? Obviously not, because it would be self-defeating. Once this rule became a universal practice, no one would believe such promises, and so no one would make loans based on them.

Kant gives another example, about giving aid. Suppose, he says, I refuse to help others in need, saying to myself, "What do I care? Let each person fend for himself." This, again, is a rule that I cannot will to be a universal law. For at some time in the future, I myself will need the help of others, and I will not want them to turn away.

9.3. Kant's Arguments on Lying

According to Kant, then, our behavior should be guided by universal laws, which are moral rules that hold true in all circumstances. Kant believed in many such exceptionless rules. We'll focus on the rule against lying, which Kant had especially strong feelings about. He said that lying under any circumstances is "the obliteration of one's dignity as a human being."

Kant offered two arguments for an absolute rule against lying.

1. His main argument relies on the Categorical Imperative. We could not will a universal law that allows us to lie, Kant said, because such a law would be self-defeating. As soon as lying became common, people would stop believing each other. Lying would then have no point, and in a sense would be impossible, because nobody would pay attention to what you say. Therefore, Kant reasoned, lying cannot be allowed. And so, it is forbidden under any circumstances.

This argument has a flaw, which will become clearer with an example. Suppose it was necessary to lie to save someone's life. Should you do it? Kant would have us reason as follows:

(1) We should do only those actions that conform to rules that we could will to be adopted universally.

(2) If you were to lie, you would be following the rule "It is okay to lie."

(3) This rule could not be adopted universally, because it would be self-defeating: People would stop believing one another, and then it would do no good to lie.

(4) Therefore, you should not lie.

Although Anscombe agreed with Kant's conclusion, she was quick to point out an error in his reasoning. The difficulty arises in step (2). Why should we say that, if you lied, you would be following the rule, "It is okay to lie"? Perhaps your maxim would be: "I will lie when doing so would save someone's life." *That* rule would not be self-defeating. It could become a universal law. And so, by Kant's own theory, it would be all right for you to lie. Thus, Kant's belief that lying is always wrong does not seem to be supported by his own moral theory.

2. Many of Kant's contemporaries thought that his insistence on absolute rules was strange, and they said so. One reviewer challenged him with this example: Imagine that some-one is fleeing from a murderer and tells you that he is going home to hide. Then the murderer comes by and asks you where the man is. You believe that, if you tell the truth, you will be aiding in a murder. Furthermore, the killer is already headed the right way, so if you simply remain silent, the worst result is likely. What should you do? Let's call this the Case of the Inquiring Murderer. Under these circumstances, most of us think, you should lie. After all, which is more important: tell-ing the truth or saving someone's life?

Kant responded in an essay with the charmingly old-fashioned title "On a Supposed Right to Lie from Altruistic Motives," in which he gives a second argument against lying. Perhaps, he says, the man on the run has actually left his home, and by telling the truth you would lead the killer to look in the wrong place. However, if you lie, the murderer may wander away and discover the man leaving the area, in which case you would be responsible for his death. Whoever lies, Kant says, "must answer for the consequences, however unforeseeable they were, and pay the penalty for them." Kant states his conclusion in the tone of a stern schoolmaster: "To be truthful . . . in all deliberations, therefore, is a sacred and absolutely commanding decree of reason, limited by no expediency."

This argument may be stated in a general form: We are tempted to make exceptions to the rule against lying because in some cases we think the consequences of honesty will be bad and the consequences of lying will be good. However, we can never be certain about what the consequences will be—we can-not *know* that good results will follow. The results of lying might be unexpectedly bad. Therefore, the best policy is to avoid the known evil—lying—and let the consequences come as they may. Even if the consequences are bad, they will not be our fault, for we will have done our duty.

A similar argument would apply to Truman's decision to drop the atomic bombs on Hiroshima and Nagasaki. The bombs were dropped in the hope that the war could be swiftly concluded. But Truman did not know for sure that this would happen. The Japanese might have hunkered down, and the invasion might still have been necessary. So, Truman was bet-ting hundreds of thousands of lives on the mere hope that good results might ensue.

The problems with this argument are obvious enough—so obvious, in fact, that it is surprising that a philosopher of Kant's caliber was not more sensitive to them. In the first place, the argument depends on an unreasonably pessimistic view of what we can know. Sometimes we can be quite confident of what the consequences of our actions will be, in which case we need not hesitate because of uncertainty. Moreover—and this is more significant, philosophically—Kant seems to assume that we would be morally responsible for any bad consequences of lying, but we would *not* be responsible for any bad consequences of telling the truth. Suppose, as a result of our telling the truth, the murderer found his victim and killed him. Kant seems to assume that we would be blameless. But can we escape responsibility so easily? After all, we aided the murderer. This argument, then, is not convincing.

Thus, Kant has failed to prove that lying is always wrong. The Case of the Inquiring Murderer shows what a tough row he chose to hoe. While Kant believes that any lie "obliterates one's dignity as a human being," common sense says that some lies are harmless. In fact, we have a name for them: white lies. Aren't white lies acceptable—or even required—when they can be used to save someone's life? This points to the main difficulty for the belief in absolute rules: shouldn't a rule be broken when following it would be disastrous?

9.4. Conflicts between Rules

Suppose it is held to be absolutely wrong to do X in any circumstances and also wrong to do Y in any circumstances. Then what about the case in which a person must choose between doing X and doing Y? This kind of conflict seems to show that moral rules can't be absolute.

Is there any way that this objection can be met? One way is to deny that such conflicts ever actually occur. Peter Geach took this view, appealing to God's providence. We can describe fictitious cases in which there is no way to avoid violating one of the absolute rules, he said, but God will not permit such circumstances to arise. Geach writes:

> If God is rational, he does not command the impossible; if God governs all events by his providence, he can see to it that circumstances in which a man is inculpably faced by

a choice between forbidden acts do not occur. Of course such circumstances . . . are consistently describable; but God's providence could ensure that they do not in fact arise. Contrary to what nonbelievers often say, belief in the existence of God does make a difference to what one expects to happen.

Do such cases actually occur? There is no doubt that serious moral rules sometimes clash. During World War II, Dutch fishermen smuggled Jewish refugees to England in their boats, and sometimes they would be stopped by Nazi patrols. The Nazi captain would call out and ask the Dutch captain where he was going, who was on board, and so forth. The fishermen would lie and be allowed to pass. Clearly, the fishermen had only two options: either they lie, or they let everyone on their boat be killed. No third alternative was available; they could not, for example, remain silent or outrun the Nazis. Thus, Geach appears to have been naïve. Terrible dilemmas do occur in the real world.

If such dilemmas occur, then doesn't this disprove the existence of absolute moral rules? Suppose, for example, the two rules "It is wrong to lie" and "It is wrong to facilitate the murder of innocent people" are both taken to be absolute. The Dutch fishermen would have to do one of these things; therefore, a moral view that absolutely prohibits both is incoherent.

This type of argument is impressive, but it is also limited. It can be levied only against *pairs* of absolute moral rules; two rules are needed to create the conflict. The argument won't stop someone from believing that there is just one absolute rule. And, in a way, everyone does. "Do what is right" is a moral principle we all believe in, which admits of no exceptions. We should always do what is right. However, this rule is so formal that it is trivial—we believe it because it doesn't really say anything. It is not the kind of absolute moral rule that Kant, Geach, and Anscombe wanted to argue for.

9.5. Kant's Insight

Few contemporary philosophers would defend Kant's Categorical Imperative. Yet it might be wrong to dismiss it too quickly. As Alasdair MacIntyre (1929–) observes, "For many who have never heard of philosophy, let alone of Kant, morality is roughly what Kant said it was"—that is, a system of rules that one must follow from a sense of duty. Is there some basic idea underlying the Categorical Imperative that we might accept, even if we don't believe in absolute moral rules? I think there is.

Remember that Kant viewed the Categorical Imperative as binding on rational agents simply because they are rational; in other words, a person who rejected this principle would be guilty not merely of being immoral but also of being irrational. This is a compelling idea. But what exactly does this mean? In what sense would it be irrational to reject the Categorical Imperative?

Note that a moral judgment must be backed by good reasons—if it is true that you ought (or ought not) to do such-and-such, then there must be a reason why you should (or should not) do it. For example, you may think that you ought not to set forest fires because property would be destroyed and people would be killed. The Kantian twist is to point out that *if you accept any considerations as reasons in one case, you must also accept them as reasons in other cases.* If there is another case in which property would be destroyed and people killed, you must accept this as a reason in that case, too. It is no good saying that you can accept reasons some of the time, but not all the time; or that other people must respect them, but not you. Moral reasons, if they are valid at all, are binding on all people at all times. This is a requirement of consistency, and Kant was right to think that no rational person may deny it.

This insight has some important implications. It implies that a person cannot regard herself as special, from a moral point of view: She cannot consistently think that she is permitted to act in ways that are forbidden to others, or that her interests are more important than other people's interests. As one commentator remarked, I cannot say that it is all right for me to drink your beer and then complain when you drink mine. Moreover, it implies that there are rational constraints on what we may do: We may want to do something—say, to drink someone else's beer—but recognize that we cannot consistently do it because we cannot at the same time accept the implication that he may drink our beer. If Kant was not the first to recognize this, he was the first to make it the cornerstone of a fully worked-out system of morals.

But Kant went one step further and said that consistency requires rules that have no exceptions. One can see how his insight pushed him in that direction; but the extra step was not necessary, and it has caused trouble for his theory. Rules, even within a Kantian framework, need not be absolute. All that Kant's basic idea requires is that when we violate a rule, we do so for a reason that we would be willing for anyone to accept. In the Case of the Inquiring Murderer, this means that we may violate the rule against lying only if we would be willing for anyone to lie in the same circumstances. And most of us would readily agree to that.

President Truman could also say that anyone in his position would have been justified in dropping the bomb. Thus, even if Truman was wrong, Kant's arguments do not prove it. One might say that dropping the bomb was wrong because Truman had better options. Perhaps he should have shown the Japanese the power of the bomb by dropping it onto an unpopulated area—negotiations might then have been successful. Or perhaps the Allies could have simply declared victory at that point in the war, even without a Japanese surrender. Saying things like that, however, is very different from saying that what Truman did violated an absolute rule.

CHAPTER 10

Kant and Respect for Persons

Are there any who would not admire man?
GIOVANNI PICO DELLA MIRANDOLA,
ORATION ON THE DIGNITY OF MAN (1486)

10.1. Kant's Core Ideas

Immanuel Kant thought that human beings occupy a special place in creation. Of course, he was not alone in thinking this. From ancient times, humans have considered themselves to be essentially different from all other creatures—and not just different, but better. In fact, humans have traditionally thought themselves to be quite fabulous. Kant certainly did. On his view, human beings have "an intrinsic worth" or "dignity" that makes them valuable "above all price."

Other animals, Kant thought, have value only insofar as they serve human purposes. In his *Lectures on Ethics* (1779), Kant writes, "But so far as animals are concerned, we have no direct duties. Animals . . . are there merely as means to an end. That end is man." We may, therefore, use animals in any way we please. We don't even have a "direct duty" to refrain from torturing them. Kant did condemn the abuse of animals, but not because the animals would be hurt. He worried, rather, about us: "He who is cruel to animals also becomes hard in his dealings with men."

When Kant said that human beings are valuable "above all price," this was not mere rhetoric. Kant meant that people are irreplaceable. If a child dies, this is a tragedy, and it remains tragic even if another child is born into the same family. On the other hand, "mere things" are replaceable. If your printer breaks, then everything is fine so long as you can get another printer. People, Kant believed, have a "dignity" that mere things lack.

136

Two facts about people, Kant thought, support this judgment.

First, because people have desires, things that satisfy those desires can have value *for* people. By contrast, "mere things" have value only insofar as they promote human ends. Thus, if you want to become a better poker player, a book about poker will have value for you; but apart from such ends, those books are worthless. Or, if you want to go somewhere, a car will have value for you; but apart from such desires, cars have no value.

Mere animals, Kant thought, are too primitive to have self-conscious desires and goals. Thus, they are "mere things." Kant did not believe, for example, that milk has value *for* the cat who wishes to drink it. But today we're more impressed with the mental life of animals than Kant was. We believe that animals do have desires and goals. So, perhaps there are Kantian grounds for saying that animals are not "mere things."

However, Kant's second reason would not apply to animals. People, Kant said, have "an intrinsic worth, i.e., dignity" because they are *rational agents,* that is, free agents capable of making their own decisions, setting their own goals, and guiding their conduct by reason. The only way that moral goodness can exist is for rational creatures *to act from a good will*—that is, to apprehend what they should do and act from a sense of duty. Human beings are the only rational agents that exist on earth; nonhuman animals lack free will, and they do not "guide their conduct by reason," because their rational capacities are too limited. If people disappeared, then so would the moral dimension of the world. This second fact about people is especially important for Kant.

Thus, Kant believed, human beings are not merely one valuable thing among others. Humans are the ones who do the valuing, and it is their conscientious actions that have moral worth. Human beings tower above the realm of things.

These thoughts are central to Kant's moral system. Kant believed that all of our duties can be derived from one ultimate principle, which he called the Categorical Imperative. Kant gave this principle different formulations, but at one point he expresses it like this:

> Act so that you treat humanity, whether in your own person or in that of another, always as an end and never as a means only.

Because people are so valuable, morality requires us to treat them "always as an end and never as a means only." What does this mean, and why should anyone believe it?

To treat people "as an end" means, on the most superficial level, treating them well. We must promote their welfare, respect their rights, avoid harming them, and generally "endeavor, so far as we can, to further the ends of others." But Kant's idea also has a deeper implication. To treat people as ends requires treating them with respect. Thus, we may not manipulate people, or "use" people to achieve our goals, no matter how good those goals may be. Kant gives this example: Suppose you need money, and you want a loan, but you know you cannot repay it. In desperation, you consider telling your friend you will repay it in order to get the money. May you do this? Perhaps you need the money for a good purpose— so good, in fact, that you might convince yourself that the lie would be justified. Nevertheless, you should not lie to your friend. If you did, you would be manipulating her and using her "merely as a means."

On the other hand, what would it be like to treat your friend "as an end"? Suppose you tell the truth—you tell her why you need the money, and you tell her you won't be able to pay her back. Then your friend can make up her own mind about whether to give you the loan. She can consult her own values and wishes, exercise her own powers of reasoning, and make a free choice. If she then decides to give you the money for your stated purpose, she will be choosing *to make that purpose her own.* Thus, you will not be using her as a mere means to achieving your goal, for it will be her goal, too. Thus, for Kant, to treat people as ends is to treat them "as beings who [can] contain in themselves the end of the very same action."

When you tell your friend the truth, and she gives you money, you are using her as a means to getting the money. However, Kant does not object to treating someone as a means; he objects to treating someone *only* as a means. Consider another example: Suppose your bathroom sink is stopped up. Would it be okay to call in a plumber—to "use" the plumber as a means to unclogging the drain? Kant would have no problem with this. The plumber, after all, understands the situation. You are not deceiving or manipulating him. He may freely choose to unclog your drain in exchange for payment. Although you are treating the plumber as a means, you are also treating him with dignity, as an "end-in-himself."

Treating people as ends, and respecting their rational capacities, has other implications. We should not force adults to do things against their will; instead, we should let them make their own decisions. We should therefore be wary of laws that aim to protect people from themselves—for example, laws requiring people to wear seat belts or motorcycle helmets. Also, we shouldn't forget that respecting *people* requires respecting *ourselves.* I should take good care of myself; I should develop my talents; I should do more than just slide by.

Kant's moral system is not easy to grasp. To understand it better, let's consider how Kant applied his ideas to the practice of criminal punishment. The rest of this chapter is devoted to that example.

10.2. Retribution and Utility in the Theory of Punishment

Jeremy Bentham (1748–1832) said that "all punishment is mischief: all punishment in itself is evil." Bentham had a point. Punishment, by its nature, always involves inflicting some harm on the person punished. As a society, we punish people by making them pay fines or go to prison, or even, sometimes, by killing them. How can it be right to treat people in these ways?

The traditional answer is that punishment is justified as a way of "paying back" the offender for his wicked deed. Those who have committed a crime deserve to be treated badly. It is a matter of justice: If you harm other people, justice requires that you be harmed, too. As the ancient saying has it, "An eye for an eye, and a tooth for a tooth." According to the doctrine of Retributivism, this is the main justification of punishment.

Retributivism was, on Bentham's view, a wholly unsatisfactory idea, because it advocates the infliction of suffering without any compensating gain in happiness. Retributivism would have us increase, not decrease, the amount of misery in the world. Kant was a retributivist, and he openly embraced this implication. In *The Critique of Practical Reason* (1788), he writes:

> When someone who delights in annoying and vexing peace-loving folk receives at last a right good beating, it is

certainly an ill, but everyone approves of it and considers it as good in itself even if nothing further results from it.

Thus, punishing people may increase the amount of misery in the world; but that is all right, for the extra suffering is borne by those who deserve it.

Utilitarianism takes a very different approach. According to Utilitarianism, our duty is to do whatever will increase the amount of happiness in the world. Punishment is, on its face, "an evil" because it makes the punished person unhappy. Thus, Bentham, a utilitarian, says, "If [punishment] ought at all to be admitted, it ought to be admitted in as far as it promises to exclude some greater evil." In other words, punishment can be justified only if it does enough good to outweigh the bad. And utilitarians have traditionally thought that it does. If someone breaks the law, then punishing that person can have several benefits.

First, punishment provides comfort and gratification to victims and their families. People feel very strongly that someone who mugged, raped, or robbed them should not go free. Victims also live in fear when they know that their attacker has not been caught. Philosophers sometimes ignore this justification of punishment, but it plays a prominent role in our legal system. Judges, lawyers, and juries often want to know what victims want. Indeed, whether the police will make an arrest, and whether the district attorney's office will prosecute a case, often depends on the wishes of the victims.

Second, by locking up criminals, or by executing them, we take them off the street. With fewer criminals on the street, there will be less crime. In this way, prisons protect society and thus reduce unhappiness. Of course, this justification does not apply to punishments in which the offender remains free, such as when a criminal is sentenced to probation with community service.

Third, punishment reduces crime by deterring would-be criminals. Someone who is tempted to commit a crime might not do so if he knows he might be punished. Obviously, the threat of punishment is not always effective; sometimes people break the law anyway. But there will be *less* misconduct if punishments are threatened. Imagine what would happen if the police stopped arresting thieves; surely there would be a lot more theft. Deterring crime thus prevents unhappiness.

Fourth, a well-designed system of punishment might help to rehabilitate wrongdoers. Criminals often have mental and emotional problems. Often, they are uneducated and illiterate and cannot hold down jobs. Why not respond to crime by attacking the problems that cause it? If someone is dangerous, we may imprison him. But while we have him behind bars, why not address his problems with psychological therapy, educational opportunities, and job training? If one day he can return to society as a productive citizen, then both he and society will benefit.

In America, the utilitarian view of punishment was once dominant. In 1954, the American Prison Association changed its name to "the American Correctional Association" and encouraged prisons to become "correctional facilities." Prisons were thus asked to "correct" inmates, not to "punish" them. Prison reform was common in the 1950s and 1960s. Prisons offered their inmates drug treatment programs, vocational training classes, and group counseling sessions, hoping to turn them into good citizens.

Those days, however, are long gone. In the 1970s, the newly announced "war on drugs" led to longer and longer prison sentences for drug offenders. This change in American justice was more retributive than utilitarian in nature, and it resulted in vastly more prisoners. Today the United States houses around 2.3 million inmates, giving it the highest incarceration rate of any country, by far. Most of those inmates are in state prisons, not federal prisons, and the states that must operate those facilities are strapped for cash. As a result, most of the programs aimed at rehabilitation were either scaled back or eliminated. The rehabilitation mentality of the 1960s has thus been replaced by a warehousing mentality, marked by prison overcrowding and plagued by underfunding. This new reality, which is less pleasant for the inmates themselves, suggests a victory for Retributivism.

10.3. Kant's Retributivism

The utilitarian theory of punishment has many opponents. Some critics say that prison reform does not work. California had the most vigorous program of reform in the United States, yet its prisoners were especially likely to commit crimes after being released. Most of the opposition, however, is based on theoretical considerations that go back at least to Kant.

Kant despised "the serpent-windings of Utilitarianism" because, he said, the theory is incompatible with human dignity. In the first place, it has us calculating how to use people as means to our ends. If we imprison the criminal in order to keep society safe, we are merely using him for the benefit of others. This violates Kant's belief that "one man ought never to be dealt with merely as a means subservient to the purpose of another."

Moreover, rehabilitation is really just the attempt to mold people into what *we* want them to be. As such, it violates their right to decide for themselves what sort of people they will be. We do have the right to respond to their wickedness by "paying them back" for it, but we do not have the right to violate their integrity by trying to manipulate their personalities.

Thus, Kant would have no part of utilitarian justifications. Instead, he argues that punishment should be governed by two principles. First, people should be punished simply because they have committed crimes, and for no other reason. Second, punishment should be *proportionate* to the seriousness of the crime. Small punishments may suffice for small crimes, but big punishments are necessary for big crimes:

> But what is the mode and measure of punishment which public justice takes as its principle and standard? It is just the principle of equality, by which the pointer of the scale of justice is made to incline no more to the one side than to the other. . . . Hence it may be said: "If you slander another, you slander yourself; if you steal from another, you steal from yourself; if you strike another, you strike yourself; if you kill another, you kill yourself." This is . . . the only principle which . . . can definitely assign both the quality and the quantity of a just penalty.

Kant's second principle leads him to endorse capital punishment; for in response to murder, only death is appropriate. In a famous passage, Kant says:

> Even if a civil society resolved to dissolve itself with the consent of all its members—as might be supposed in the case of a people inhabiting an island resolving to separate and scatter throughout the whole world—the last murderer lying in prison ought to be executed before the resolution was carried out. This ought to be done in order that

everyone may realize the desert of his deeds, and that blood-guiltiness may not remain on the people; for otherwise they will all be regarded as participants in the murder as a public violation of justice.

Although a Kantian must support the death penalty *in theory*, she might oppose it *in practice*. The worry, in practice, is that innocent people might be killed by mistake. In the United States, around 130 death row inmates have been released from prison after being proved innocent. None of those people were actually killed. But with so many close calls, it is almost certain that some innocent people have been put to death—and advocates of reform point to specific, troubling examples. Thus, in deciding whether to support a policy of capital punishment, Kantians must balance the injustice of the occasional, deadly mistake against the injustice of letting killers live.

Kant's two principles describe a general theory of punishment: Wrongdoers must be punished, and the punishment must fit the crime. This theory is deeply opposed to the Christian idea of turning the other cheek. In the Sermon on the Mount, Jesus avows, "You have heard that it was said, 'An eye for an eye and a tooth for a tooth.' But I say to you, Do not resist the one who is evil. If anyone slaps you on the right cheek, turn to him the other also." For Kant, such a response to evil is not only imprudent, but unjust.

What arguments can be given for Kant's Retributivism? We noted that Kant regards punishment as a matter of justice. He says that if the guilty are not punished, justice is not done. That is one argument. Also, we discussed why Kant rejects the utilitarian view of punishment. But he also provides another argument, based on his idea of treating people as "ends-in-themselves." This additional argument is Kant's contribution to the theory of Retributivism.

On the face of it, it seems unlikely that we could describe punishing someone as "respecting him as a person" or as "treating him as an end." How could sending someone to prison be a way of respecting him? Even more paradoxically, how could executing someone be a way of treating him with dignity? For Kant, treating someone "as an end" means treating him as a rational being, who is responsible for his behavior. So now we may ask: What does it mean to be a responsible being?

Consider, first, what it means *not* to be such a being. Mere animals, who lack reason, are not responsible for their actions; nor are people who are mentally ill and not in control of themselves. In such cases, it would be absurd to "hold them accountable." We could not properly feel gratitude or resentment toward them, because they are not responsible for any good or ill they cause. Moreover, we cannot expect them to understand *why* we treat them as we do, any more than they understand why they behave as they do. So we have no choice but to deal with them by manipulating them, rather than by treating them as rational individuals. When we scold a dog for eating off the table, for example, we are merely trying to "train" him.

On the other hand, a rational being can freely decide what to do, based on his own conception of what is best. Rational beings *are* responsible for their behavior, and so they are accountable for what they do. We may feel gratitude when they behave well and resentment when they behave badly. Reward and punishment—not "training" or other manipulation—are the natural expressions of gratitude and resentment. Thus, in punishing people, we are holding them responsible for their actions in a way in which we cannot hold mere animals responsible. We are responding to them not as people who are "sick" or who have no control over themselves, but as people who have freely chosen their evil deeds.

Furthermore, in dealing with responsible agents, we may properly allow their conduct to determine, at least in part, how we respond to them. If someone has been kind to you, you may respond by being generous; and if someone is nasty to you, you may take that into account in deciding how to respond. And why shouldn't you? Why should you treat everyone alike, regardless of how *they* have chosen to behave?

Kant gives this last point a distinctive twist. There is, on his view, a deep reason for responding to other people "in kind." When we choose to do something, after consulting our own values, we are in effect saying *this is the sort of thing that should be done.* In Kant's terminology, we are implying that our conduct be made into a "universal law." Therefore, when a rational being decides to treat people in a certain way, he decrees that in his judgment *this is the way people are to be treated.* Thus, if we treat him the same way in return, we are doing nothing more than treating him *as he has decided that people are to be treated.* If he treats others badly, and we treat him badly, we are complying with his own decision. We are, in a perfectly clear sense, respecting his judgment, by allowing it to control how we treat him. Thus, Kant says of the criminal, "His own evil deed draws the punishment upon himself."

This last argument can certainly be questioned. Why should we adopt the criminal's principle of action, rather than follow our own principles? Shouldn't we try to be "better than he is"? At the end of the day, what we think of Kant's theory may depend on our view of criminal behavior. If we see criminals as victims of circumstance, who do not ultimately control their own actions, then the utilitarian model will appeal to us. On the other hand, if we see criminals as rational agents who freely choose to do harm, then Kantian Retributivism will have great appeal for us. The resolution of this great debate might thus turn on whether we believe that human beings have free will, or whether we believe that outside forces impact human behavior so deeply that our freedom is an illusion. The debate about free will, however, is so complex, and so concerned with matters outside of ethics, that we will not discuss it here. This kind of dialectical situation is common in philosophy: when you study one matter deeply, you often come to realize that it depends on something else. And, unfortunately, that other thing often turns out to be as difficult as the set of problems you began with.

CHAPTER 11

Feminism and the Ethics of Care

> But it is obvious that the values of women differ very often from the values which have been made by the other sex; naturally, this is so. Yet it is the masculine values that prevail.
> VIRGINIA WOOLF, *A Room of One's Own* (1929)

11.1. Do Women and Men Think Differently about Ethics?

The idea that women and men think differently has traditionally been used to justify discrimination against women. Aristotle said that women are not as rational as men, and so they are naturally ruled by men. Immanuel Kant agreed, adding that women "lack civil personality" and should have no voice in public life. Jean-Jacques Rousseau tried to put a good face on this by emphasizing that women and men merely possess different virtues; but, of course, it turned out that men's virtues fit them for leadership, whereas women's virtues fit them for home and hearth.

Against this background, it is not surprising that the women's movement of the 1960s and 1970s denied that women and men differ psychologically. The conception of men as rational and women as emotional was dismissed as a mere stereotype. Nature makes no mental or moral distinction between the sexes, it was said; and when there seem to be differences, it is only because women have been conditioned by an oppressive system to behave in "feminine" ways.

These days, however, most feminists believe that women do think differently than men. But, they add, women's ways of thinking are not inferior to men's, nor do the differences justify

146

any kind of prejudice. On the contrary, female ways of thinking yield insights that have been missed in male-dominated areas. Thus, by attending to the distinctive approach of women, we can make progress in subjects that were stalled. Ethics is said to be a leading candidate for this treatment.

Kohlberg's Stages of Moral Development. Consider the following problem, devised by the educational psychologist Lawrence Kohlberg (1927–1987). Heinz's wife was near death, and her only hope was a drug that had been discovered by a pharmacist who was now selling it for an outrageously high price. The drug cost $200 to make, and the pharmacist was selling it for $2,000. Heinz could raise only half of that. The pharmacist said that half wasn't enough, and when Heinz promised to pay the rest later, the pharmacist still refused. In desperation, Heinz considered stealing the drug. Would that be wrong?

This problem, known as "Heinz's Dilemma," was used by Kohlberg in studying the moral development of children. Kohlberg interviewed children of various ages, presenting them with a series of dilemmas and asking them questions designed to reveal their thinking. Analyzing their responses, Kohlberg concluded that there are six stages of moral development. In these stages, the child or adult conceives of "right" in terms of

> obeying authority and avoiding punishment (stage 1);
>
> satisfying one's own desires and letting others do the same, through fair exchanges (stage 2);
>
> cultivating one's relationships and performing the duties of one's social roles (stage 3);
>
> obeying the law and maintaining the welfare of the group (stage 4);
>
> upholding the basic rights and values of one's society (stage 5);
>
> abiding by abstract, universal moral principles (stage 6).

So, if all goes well, we begin life with a self-centered desire to avoid punishment, and we end life with a set of abstract moral principles. Kohlberg, however, believed that only a small minority of adults make it to stage 5.

Heinz's Dilemma was presented to an 11-year-old boy named Jake, who thought it was obvious that Heinz should steal the drug. Jake explained:

> For one thing, a human life is worth more than money, and if the druggist only makes $1,000, he is still going to live, but if Heinz doesn't steal the drug, his wife is going to die.
> *(Why is life worth more than money?)*
> Because the druggist can get a thousand dollars later from rich people with cancer, but Heinz can't get his wife again.
> *(Why not?)*
> Because people are all different and so you couldn't get Heinz's wife again.

But Amy, also 11, saw the matter differently. Should Heinz steal the drug? Compared to Jake, Amy seems hesitant and evasive:

> Well, I don't think so. I think there might be other ways besides stealing it, like if he could borrow the money or make a loan or something, but he really shouldn't steal the drug—but his wife shouldn't die either. . . . If he stole the drug, he might save his wife then, but if he did, he might have to go to jail, and then his wife might get sicker again, and he couldn't get more of the drug, and it might not be good. So, they should really just talk it out and find some other way to make the money.

The interviewer asks Amy further questions, but she will not budge; she refuses to accept the terms in which the problem is posed. Instead, she recasts the issue as a conflict between Heinz and the pharmacist that must be resolved by further discussions.

In terms of Kohlberg's stages, Jake seems to have advanced beyond Amy. Amy's response is typical of people operating at stage 3, where personal relationships are paramount—Heinz and the pharmacist must work things out between them. Jake, on the other hand, appeals to impersonal principles—"a human life is worth more than money." Jake seems to be operating at one of the later stages.

Gilligan's Objection. Kohlberg began studying moral development in the 1950s. Back then, psychologists almost always studied behavior rather than thought processes, and psychological researchers were thought of as men in white coats who watched rats run through mazes. Kohlberg's humanistic, cognitive approach pursued knowledge in a more appealing way. However, his central idea was flawed. It is legitimate to study how people think at different ages—if children think differently at ages 5, 10, and 15, that is certainly worth knowing about. It is also worthwhile to identify the best ways of thinking. But these projects are different. One involves observing how children, in fact, think; the other involves assessing ways of thinking as better or worse. Different kinds of evidence are relevant to each investigation, and there is no reason to assume in advance that the results will match. Contrary to the opinion of older people, it *could* turn out that age does not bring wisdom.

Kohlberg's theory has also been criticized from a feminist perspective. In 1982, Carol Gilligan wrote a book called *In a Different Voice,* in which she objects to what Kohlberg says about Jake and Amy. The two children think differently, she says, but Amy's way of thinking is not inferior. When confronted with Heinz's Dilemma, Amy responds to the personal aspects of the situation, as females typically do, whereas Jake, thinking like a male, sees only "a conflict between life and property that can be resolved by a logical deduction." Jake's response will be judged "at a higher level" only if one assumes, as Kohlberg does, that an ethic of principle is superior to an ethic of intimacy and caring. But why should we assume that? Admittedly, most moral philosophers have favored an ethic of principle, but that may be because most moral philosophers have been men.

The "male way of thinking"—the appeal to impersonal principles—abstracts away the details that give each situation its special flavor. Women, Gilligan says, find it harder to ignore those details. Amy worries, "If [Heinz] stole the drug, he might save his wife then, but if he did, he might have to go to jail, and then his wife might get sicker again, and he couldn't get more of the drug." Jake, who reduces the situation to "a human life is worth more than money," ignores all this.

Gilligan suggests that women's basic moral orientation is one of caring: "taking care" of others in a personal way, not just being concerned for humanity in general. This explains why Amy's response seems, at first, confused and uncertain. Sensitivity to the needs of others leads women to "attend to voices other than their own and to include in their judgment other points of view." Thus, Amy could not simply reject the pharmacist's point of view; rather, she wanted to talk to him and try to accommodate him. According to Gilligan, "Women's moral weakness, manifest in an apparent diffusion and confusion of judgment, is thus inseparable from women's moral strength, an overriding concern with relationships and responsibilities."

Other feminists have taken these ideas and molded them into a distinctive view of ethics. Virginia Held (1929–) sums up the central idea: "Caring, empathy, feeling with others, being sensitive to each other's feelings, all may be better guides to what morality requires in actual contexts than may abstract rules of reason, or rational calculation, or at least they may be necessary components of an adequate morality."

Before discussing this idea, we may pause to consider how "feminine" it really is. *Do* women and men think differently about ethics? And if they do, why do they?

Is It True That Women and Men Think Differently? Since Gilligan's book appeared, psychologists have conducted hundreds of studies on gender, the emotions, and morality. These studies reveal some differences between women and men. Women tend to score higher than men on tests that measure empathy. Also, brain scans reveal that women have a lower tendency than men to enjoy seeing people punished who have treated them unfairly—perhaps because women empathize even with those who have wronged them. Finally, women seem to care more about close personal relationships, whereas men care more about larger networks of shallow relationships. As Roy Baumeister put it, "Women specialize in the narrow sphere of intimate relationships. Men specialize in the larger group."

Women and men probably do think differently about ethics. These differences, however, cannot be very great. It is not as though women make judgments that are incomprehensible to men, or vice versa. Men can understand the value of caring relationships, even if they have to be reminded sometimes; and they can agree with Amy that the happiest solution to Heinz's Dilemma would be for the two men to work it out. For their part, women will hardly disagree that human life is worth more than money. And when we look at individuals, we find that some men are especially caring, while some women rely heavily on abstract principles. Plainly, the two sexes do not inhabit different moral universes. One scholarly article reviewed 180 studies and found that women are only slightly more care-oriented than men, and men are only slightly more justice-oriented than women. Even this watered-down conclusion, however, invites the question: Why should women be, on average, more caring than men?

There seem to be two possibilities. First, we might look for a social explanation. Perhaps women care more because of the social roles they occupy. Traditionally, women have been expected to do the housework and take care of the kids. Even if this expectation is sexist, the fact remains that women have often performed these functions. And it is easy to see how taking care of a family could lead one to adopt an ethic of care. Thus, the care perspective could be part of the psychological conditioning that girls receive.

On the other hand, we might seek a genetic explanation. Some differences between males and females show up at a very early age. One-year-old girls will spend more time looking at a film of a face than a film of cars, whereas one-year-old boys prefer the cars. Even one-day-old girls, but not one-day-old boys, will spend more time looking at a friendly face than looking at a mechanical object of the same size. This suggests that females might naturally be more social than males. If this were true, why would it be true?

Charles Darwin's theory of evolution might provide some insight. We may think of the Darwinian "struggle for survival" as a competition to get the maximum number of one's genes into the next generation. Traits that help accomplish this will be preserved in future generations, while traits that work against this goal will tend to disappear. In the 1970s, researchers in the field of Evolutionary Psychology began applying these ideas to human psychology. The idea is that people today have the emotions and behavioral tendencies that enabled their ancestors to survive and reproduce in the distant past.

From this point of view, the key difference between males and females is that men can father thousands of children, while women can give birth only once every nine and a half months, until menopause. This means that males and females have different reproductive strategies. For men, the optimum strategy is to impregnate as many women as possible. Having done that, the man cannot devote much time to any particular child. For women, the optimum strategy is to invest heavily in each child and to have sex only with those men who are willing to stick around. This creates a tension between men and women, and it might explain why the sexes have evolved different attitudes. It explains, notoriously, why men have a greater sex drive than women. It also explains why women might be more attracted than men to the values of the nuclear family—in particular, to the value of caring.

This kind of explanation is often misunderstood. The point is not that people consciously calculate how to propagate their genes; no one does that. Nor is the point that people *should* calculate in this way; from an ethical point of view, they should not. The point is just to explain what we observe.

11.2. Implications for Moral Judgment

Not all female philosophers are feminists, and not all feminists embrace the ethics of care. Nonetheless, the ethics of care is closely identified with modern feminist philosophy. As Annette Baier (1929–) puts it, "'Care' is the new buzzword."

One way of understanding an ethical view is to ask what difference it would make in practice. Does an ethic of care have different implications than a "male" approach to ethics? Here are three examples.

Family and Friends. Traditional theories of obligation are notoriously ill-suited to describing life among family and friends. Those theories take the notion of *what we should do* as morally fundamental. But, as Baier observes, when we try to construe "being a loving parent" as a duty, we encounter problems. A loving parent is motivated by love, not by duty. If parents care for their children only because they feel it is their duty, the children will sense it and realize they are unloved.

Moreover, the ideas of equality and impartiality that pervade theories of obligation seem deeply antagonistic to the values of love and friendship. John Stuart Mill (1806–1873) said that a moral agent must be "as strictly impartial as a disinterested and benevolent spectator." But that is not the standpoint of a parent or friend. We do not regard our family and friends merely as members of the great crowd of humanity; we think of them as special.

The ethics of care, on the other hand, is perfectly suited to describe such relations. The ethics of care does not take "obligation" or "duty" as fundamental; nor does it require that we impartially promote the interests of everyone alike. Instead, it begins with a conception of moral life as a network of relationships with specific people, and it sees "living well" as caring for those people, attending to their needs, and maintaining their trust.

These outlooks lead to different judgments about what we may do. May I devote my time and resources to caring for my friends and family, even if this means ignoring the needs of other people? From an impartial point of view, our duty is to promote the interests of everyone alike. But few of us accept that view. The ethics of care affirms the priority that we naturally give to our family and friends, and so it seems more plausible than an ethic of principle. Of course, it is not surprising that the ethics of care appears to do a good job of explaining the nature of our moral relations with friends and family. After all, those relationships are its primary inspiration.

Children with HIV. Around the world, about 2.5 million children under the age of 15 have HIV, the virus that can cause AIDS. Right now only one-fourth of those children get decent medical care, while only half of pregnant women who have HIV are taking steps to protect their unborn children from the virus. Organizations such as UNICEF work to improve these numbers, but they never have enough money. By contributing to their work, we could save lives.

A traditional ethic of principle, such as Utilitarianism, would conclude from this that we have a substantial duty to support UNICEF. The reasoning is straightforward: Almost all of us spend money on luxuries. Luxuries are not as important as protecting children from AIDS. Therefore, we should give at least some of our money to UNICEF. Of course, this argument would become complicated if we tried to fill in all the details. But the basic idea is clear enough.

One might think that an ethic of care would reach a similar conclusion—after all, shouldn't we care for those disadvantaged children? But that misses the point. An ethic of care focuses on small-scale, personal relationships. If there is no such relationship, "caring" cannot take place. Nel Noddings (1929–) explains that the caring relation can exist only if the "cared-for" can interact with the "one-caring." At a minimum, the cared-for must be able to receive and acknowledge the care in a personal, one-to-one encounter. Otherwise, there is no obligation: "We are not obliged to act as one-caring if there is no possibility of completion in the other." Thus, Noddings concludes that we have no obligation to help "the needy in the far regions of the earth."

Many feminists regard Noddings's view as too extreme. Making personal relationships the whole of ethics, as she does, seems as wrong-headed as ignoring them altogether. A better approach might be to say that the ethical life includes both caring relationships *and* a benevolent concern for people generally. Our obligation to support UNICEF might then be seen as arising from our obligations of benevolence. If we take this approach, we may interpret the ethics of care as *supplementing* traditional theories rather than replacing them. Annette Baier seems to have this in mind when she writes that, eventually, "women theorists will need to connect their ethics of love with what has been the men theorists' preoccupation, namely, obligation."

Animals. Do we have obligations to nonhuman animals? Should we, for example, refrain from eating them? One argument from an ethic of principle says that how we raise animals for food causes them great suffering, and so we should nourish ourselves without the cruelty. Since the modern animal rights movement began in the 1970s, this sort of argument has persuaded many people to become vegetarians.

Noddings suggests that this is a good issue "to test the basic notions on which an ethic of caring rests." What are those basic notions? First, such an ethic appeals to intuition and feeling rather than to principle. This leads to a different conclusion about vegetarianism, for most people do not feel that eating meat is wrong or that the suffering of livestock is important. Noddings observes that our emotional responses to humans are different from our responses to animals.

A second "basic notion on which an ethic of caring rests" is the primacy of personal relationships. These relationships, as we have noted, always involve the cared-for interacting with the one-caring. Noddings believes that people do have this sort of relationship with their pets:

> When one is familiar with a particular animal family, one comes to recognize its characteristic form of address. Cats, for example, lift their heads and stretch toward the one they are addressing. . . . When I enter my kitchen in the morning and my cat greets me from her favorite spot on the counter, I understand her request. This is the spot where she sits and "speaks" in her squeaky attempt to communicate her desire for a dish of milk.

A relationship is established, and the attitude of care must be summoned. But one has no such relationship with the cow in the slaughterhouse, and so, Noddings concludes, we have no obligation not to eat it.

What are we to make of this? If we use this issue "to test the basic notions on which an ethic of caring rests," does the ethic pass or fail the test? The opposing arguments are impressive. First, intuition and feeling are not reliable guides—at one time, people's intuitions told them that slavery was acceptable and that the subordination of women to men was God's plan. And second, whether the animal is in a position to respond "personally" to you may have a lot to do with the satisfaction you get from helping, but it has nothing to do with the animal's needs. Similarly, whether a faraway child would suffer from being HIV+ has nothing to do with whether she can thank you personally for helping her avoid infection. These arguments, of course, appeal to principles that are said to be typical of male reasoning. Therefore, if the ethic of care is taken to be the whole of morality, such arguments will be ignored. On the other hand, if caring is only one part of morality, the arguments from principle will have considerable force. Livestock might come within the sphere of moral concern, not because of our caring relation with them, but for other reasons.

11.3. Implications for Ethical Theory

It is easy to see the influence of men's experience in the ethical theories they have created. Historically, men have dominated public life, where relationships are often impersonal and contractual. In politics and business, relationships can even be adversarial when interests collide. So we negotiate; we bargain and make deals. Moreover, in public life our decisions may affect large numbers of people we do not know. So we may try to calculate which decisions will have the best overall outcome for the most people. And what do men's theories emphasize? Impersonal duty, contracts, the balancing of competing interests, and the calculation of costs and benefits.

Little wonder, then, that feminists accuse moral philosophy of having a male bias. The concerns of private life are almost wholly absent, and the "different voice" of which Carol Gilligan speaks is silent. A moral theory tailored to women's concerns would look very different. In the small-scale world of friends and family, bargaining and calculating play a much smaller role, while love and caring dominate. Once this point is made, there is no denying that morality must find a place for it.

Private life, however, is not easy to accommodate within the traditional theories. As we noted, "being a loving parent" is not about calculating how one should behave. The same might be said about being a loyal friend or a dependable coworker. To be loving, loyal, and dependable is to be *a certain kind of person,* which is very different from impartially "doing your duty."

The contrast between "being a certain kind of person" and "doing your duty" lies at the heart of a larger conflict between two kinds of ethical theory. Virtue Ethics sees being a moral person as having certain traits of character: being kind, generous, courageous, just, prudent, and so on. Theories of obligation, on the other hand, emphasize impartial duty: They portray the moral agent as someone who listens to reason, figures out the right thing to do, and does it. One of the chief arguments for Virtue Ethics is that it seems well suited to accommodate the values of both public and private life. The two spheres simply require different virtues. Public life requires justice and beneficence, while private life requires love and caring.

The ethics of care, therefore, may be best understood as one part of the ethics of virtue. Many feminist philosophers view it in this light. Although Virtue Ethics is not an exclusively feminist project, it is so closely tied to feminist ideas that Annette Baier dubs its male promoters "honorary women." The verdict on the ethics of care may depend, ultimately, on the viability of a broader theory of the virtues.

CHAPTER 12

Virtue Ethics

The excellency of hogs is fatness, of men virtue.
                    BENJAMIN FRANKLIN, *POOR RICHARD'S ALMANACK* (1736)

12.1. The Ethics of Virtue and the Ethics of Right Action

In thinking about any subject, it matters greatly what questions we start with. In Aristotle's *Nicomachean Ethics* (ca. 325 B.C.), the central questions are about *character*. Aristotle begins by asking "What is the good of man?" and his answer is "an activity of the soul in conformity with virtue." He then discusses such virtues as courage, self-control, generosity, and truthfulness. Most of the ancient thinkers came to ethics by asking *What traits of character make someone a good person?* As a result, "the virtues" occupied center stage in their discussions.

As time passed, however, this way of thinking became neglected. With the coming of Christianity, a new set of ideas emerged. The Christians, like the Jews, viewed God as a lawgiver, and so they saw obedience to those laws as the key to righteous living. For the Greeks, the life of virtue was inseparable from the life of reason. But Saint Augustine, the influential fourth-century Christian thinker, distrusted reason and believed that moral goodness depends on subordinating oneself to the will of God. Thus, when medieval philosophers discussed the virtues, it was in the context of Divine Law, and the "theological virtues" of faith, hope, charity, and obedience occupied the spotlight.

After the Renaissance period (1400–1650), moral philosophy again became more secular, but philosophers did not return to the Greek way of thinking. Instead, the Divine Law was replaced by something called the "Moral Law." The Moral Law, which was said to spring from human reason rather than from God, was a system of rules specifying which actions are right. Our duty as moral persons, it was said, is to follow those rules. Thus, modern moral philosophers approached their subject by asking a question fundamentally different from the one asked by the ancients. Instead of asking *What traits of character make someone a good person?* they asked *What is the right thing to do?* This led them in a different direction. They went on to develop theories, not of virtue, but of rightness and obligation:

- *Ethical Egoism:* Each person ought to do whatever will best promote his or her own interests.
- *The Social Contract Theory:* The right thing to do is to follow the rules that rational, self-interested people would agree to follow for their mutual benefit.
- *Utilitarianism:* One ought to do whatever will lead to the most happiness.
- *Kant's theory:* Our duty is to follow rules that we could accept as universal laws—that is, rules that we would be willing for everyone to follow in all circumstances.

And these are the theories that have dominated moral philosophy from the 17th century on.

Should We Return to Virtue Ethics? Recently, however, a number of philosophers have advanced a radical idea. Moral philosophy, they say, is bankrupt, and we should return to Aristotle's way of thinking.

This was suggested by Elizabeth Anscombe in her article "Modern Moral Philosophy" (1958). Anscombe believes that modern moral philosophy is misguided because it rests on the incoherent notion of a "law" without a lawgiver. The very concepts of obligation, duty, and rightness, she says, are inseparable from this self-contradictory notion. Therefore, we should stop thinking about obligation, duty, and rightness, and return to Aristotle's approach. The virtues should once again take center stage.

In the wake of Anscombe's article, a flood of books and essays appeared discussing the virtues, and Virtue Ethics soon became a major option again. In what follows, we will first take a look at what Virtue Ethics is like. Then we will consider some reasons for preferring this theory to other, more modern ways of approaching the subject. Finally, we will consider whether a return to Virtue Ethics would be desirable.

12.2. The Virtues

A theory of virtue should have several components: a statement of what a virtue is, a list of the virtues, an account of what these virtues consist in, and an explanation of why these qualities are good. In addition, the theory should tell us whether the virtues are the same for all people or whether they differ from person to person or from culture to culture.

What Is a Virtue? Aristotle said that a virtue is a trait of character manifested in habitual action. The word "habitual" here is important. The virtue of honesty, for example, is not possessed by someone who tells the truth only occasionally or only when it benefits her. The honest person is truthful as a matter of course; her actions "spring from a firm and unchangeable character."

But this does not distinguish virtues from vices, for vices are also traits of character manifested in habitual action. The other part of the definition is evaluative: virtues are good, whereas vices are bad. Thus, a virtue is a *commendable* trait of character manifested in habitual action. Saying this, of course, doesn't tell us which traits of character are good or bad. Later we will flesh this out by discussing the ways in which some particular virtues are good. For now, we may note that virtuous qualities are those qualities that will make us seek out someone's company. As Edmund L. Pincoffs (1919–1991) put it, "Some sorts of persons we prefer; others we avoid. The properties on our list [of virtues and vices] can serve as reasons for preference or avoidance."

We seek out people for different purposes, and this affects which virtues are relevant. In looking for an auto mechanic, we want someone who is skillful, honest, and conscientious; in looking for a teacher, we want someone who is knowledgeable, articulate, and patient. Thus, the virtues of auto repair are different from the virtues of teaching. But we also assess people *as people,* in a more general way, so we also have the concept of a good person. The moral virtues are the virtues of persons as such. Thus, we may define a moral virtue as *a trait of character, manifested in habitual action, that it is good for anyone to have.*

What Are the Virtues? What, then, are the virtues? Which traits of character should be fostered in human beings? There is no short answer, but the following is a partial list:

benevolence	fairness	patience
civility	friendliness	prudence
compassion	generosity	reasonableness
conscientiousness	honesty	self-discipline
cooperativeness	industriousness	self-reliance
courage	justice	tactfulness
courteousness	loyalty	thoughtfulness
dependability	moderation	tolerance

This list could be expanded, of course.

What Do These Virtues Consist In? It is one thing to say, in general, that we should be conscientious, compassionate, and tolerant; it is another thing to say exactly what these character traits are. Each of the virtues has its own distinctive features and raises its own distinctive problems. Let's consider four examples.

1. *Courage.* According to Aristotle, virtues are midpoints between extremes: A virtue is "the mean by reference to two vices: the one of excess and the other of deficiency." Courage is a mean between the extremes of cowardice and foolhardiness—it is cowardly to run away from all danger, yet it is foolhardy to risk too much.

Courage is sometimes said to be a military virtue because soldiers so obviously need to have it. But soldiers are not the only ones who need courage. We all need courage, and not just when we face a preexisting danger, such as an enemy soldier or a grizzly bear. Sometimes we need the courage to *create* a situation that will be unpleasant for us. It takes courage to apologize. If a friend is grieving, it takes courage to ask her directly how she is doing. It takes courage to volunteer to do something nice that you don't really want to do.

If we consider only ordinary cases, the nature of courage seems unproblematic. But unusual circumstances present more troublesome cases. Consider the 19 hijackers who murdered almost 3,000 people on September 11, 2001. They faced certain death, evidently without flinching, but in the service of an evil cause. Were they courageous? The American political commentator Bill Maher implied that they were—and so he lost his television show, *Politically Incorrect*. But was Maher correct? The philosopher Peter Geach wouldn't think so. "Courage in an unworthy cause," he says, "is no virtue; still less is courage in an evil cause. Indeed I prefer not to call this nonvirtuous facing of danger 'courage.'"

It is easy to see Geach's point. Calling a terrorist "courageous" seems to praise his performance, and we do not want to do that. But, on the other hand, it doesn't seem quite right to say that he is *not* courageous—after all, look at how he behaves in the face of danger. To resolve this dilemma, perhaps we should just say that he displays two qualities of character, one admirable (steadfastness in facing danger) and one detestable (a willingness to kill innocent people). He is courageous, as Maher suggested, and courage is a good thing; but because his courage is deployed in such an evil cause, his behavior is *on the whole* extremely wicked.

2. *Generosity.* Generosity is the willingness to give to others. One can be generous with any of one's resources—with one's time, for example, or one's money or one's knowledge. Aristotle says that generosity, like courage, is a mean between extremes: It falls between stinginess and extravagance. The stingy person gives too little; the extravagant person gives too much; the generous person gives just the right amount. But what amount is just right?

Another ancient teacher, Jesus of Nazareth, said that we must give everything we have to the poor. Jesus considered it wrong to possess riches while other people are dying of starvation. Those who heard Jesus speak found his teaching too demanding, and they generally rejected it. Human nature has not changed much in the last 2,000 years: today, few people follow Jesus's advice, even among those who claim to admire him.

On this issue, the modern utilitarians are Jesus's moral descendants. They hold that in every circumstance it is our duty to do whatever will have the best overall consequences for everyone concerned. This means that we should be generous with our money until further giving would harm us as much as it would help others. In other words, we should give until we ourselves become the most worthy recipients of whatever money remains in our hands. If we did this, then we would become poor.

Why do people resist this idea? The main reason may be self-interest; we do not want to become destitute. But this is about more than money; it is also about time and energy. Adopting such a policy would prevent us from living normal lives. Our lives consist of projects and relationships that require a considerable investment of money, time, and effort. An ideal of "generosity" that demands too much of us would require us to abandon our everyday lives. We'd have to live like saints.

A reasonable interpretation of generosity might therefore be something like this: We should be as generous with our resources as we can be while still carrying on our normal lives. But even this interpretation leaves us with an awkward question. Some people's "normal lives" are quite extravagant—think of a rich person who has grown accustomed to great luxuries. Surely such a person can't be generous unless he is willing to sell his yacht to feed the hungry. The virtue of generosity, it would seem, cannot exist in the context of a life that is too opulent. So, to make this interpretation of generosity "reasonable," our conception of normal life must not be too extravagant.

3. *Honesty.* The honest person is someone who, first of all, does not lie. But is that enough? Lying is not the only way of misleading people. Geach tells the story of Saint Athanasius, who "was rowing on a river when the persecutors came rowing in the opposite direction: 'Where is the traitor Athanasius?' 'Not far away,' the Saint gaily replied, and rowed past them unsuspected."

Geach approves of the saint's deception, even though he would disapprove of the saint's telling an outright lie. Lying, according to Geach, is always forbidden: someone possessing the virtue of honesty will never even consider it. Honest people do not lie; so, they must find other ways of attaining their goals. Athanasius found such a way, even in his predicament. He did not lie to his pursuers; he "merely" deceived them. But isn't deception dishonest? Why should some ways of misleading people be dishonest, and others not?

To answer that question, let's think about why honesty is a virtue to begin with. Why is honesty good? Part of the reason is large-scale: Civilization depends on it. Our ability to live together in communities depends on our ability to communicate. We talk to one another, read each other's writing, exchange information and opinions, express our desires to one another, make promises, ask and answer questions, and much more. Without these sorts of exchanges, social living would be impossible. But people must be honest for such exchanges to work.

On a smaller scale, when we take people at their word, we make ourselves vulnerable to them. By accepting what they say and modifying our behavior accordingly, we place our well-being in their hands. If they speak truthfully, all is well. But if they lie, then we end up with false beliefs; and if we act on those beliefs, then we do foolish things. We trusted them, and they betrayed our trust. Dishonesty is manipulative. By contrast, honest people treat others with respect.

If these ideas account for why honesty is a virtue, then lies and "deceptive truths" are both dishonest. After all, both types of deceit are objectionable for the same reasons. Both have the same goal: the point of lying *and* deceiving is to make the listener acquire a false belief. In Geach's example, Athanasius got his persecutors to believe that he was not in fact Athanasius. Had Athanasius lied to his pursuers, rather than merely deceiving them, then his words would have served the same purpose. Because both actions aim at false beliefs, both can disrupt the smooth functioning of society, and both violate trust. If you accuse someone of lying to you, and she responds by saying that she did not lie—she "merely" deceived you—then you would not be impressed. Either way, she took advantage of your trust and manipulated you into believing something false. The honest person will neither lie nor deceive.

But will the honest person *never* lie? Geach's example raises the question of whether virtue requires adherence to absolute rules. Let's distinguish two views:

1. An honest person will never lie or deceive.
2. An honest person will never lie or deceive except in rare circumstances when there are compelling reasons to do so.

Despite Geach's protest, there are good reasons to favor the second view, even with regard to lying.

First, remember that honesty is not the only thing we value. In a specific situation, some other value might get priority—for example, the value of self-preservation. Suppose Saint Athanasius had lied and said, "I don't know where that traitor is," and as a result, his pursuers went off on a wild-goose chase. Now the saint would get to live another day. If this had occurred, most of us would continue to regard Saint Athanasius as honest. We would merely say that he valued his own life more than the telling of one lie.

Moreover, if we consider why honesty is good, then we can see that Athanasius would have been justified in lying to his pursuers. Obviously, that particular lie would not have disrupted the smooth functioning of society. But wouldn't it at least have violated the trust of the people who were pursuing him? The response is that, if lying is a violation of trust, then for lying to be immoral, the person you're lying to must *deserve* your trust. But in this case, the saint's pursuers did not deserve his trust, because they were persecuting him unjustly. Thus, even an honest person may sometimes lie or deceive with full justification.

4. *Loyalty to friends and family.* Friendship is essential to the good life. As Aristotle says, "No one would choose to live without friends, even if he had all other goods":

> How could prosperity be safeguarded and preserved without friends? The greater our prosperity is, the greater are the risks it brings with it. Also, in poverty and all other kinds of misfortune men believe that their only refuge consists in their friends. Friends help young men avoid error; to older people they give the care and help needed to supplement the failing powers of action which infirmity brings.

The benefits of friendship, of course, go far beyond material assistance. Psychologically, we would be lost without our friends. Our triumphs seem hollow without friends to share them with, and we need our friends even more when we fail. Our self-esteem depends in large measure on the assurances of friends: By returning our affection, they confirm our worth as human beings.

If we need friends, then we need the qualities that enable us to *be* a friend. Near the top of the list is loyalty. Friends can be counted on. You stick by your friends even when things are going badly and even when, objectively speaking, you should abandon them. Friends make allowances for one another; they forgive offenses and refrain from harsh judgments. There are limits, of course—sometimes only a friend can tell us the hard truth about ourselves. But criticism is acceptable from friends because we know that they are not rejecting us.

None of this is to deny that we have duties to other people, even to strangers. But those duties are associated with different virtues. Generalized beneficence is a virtue, and it may demand a great deal, but it does not require the same level of concern for strangers as for friends. Justice is another such virtue; it requires impartial treatment for all. But friends are loyal to one another, so the demands of justice are weaker when friends are involved.

We are even closer to family members than we are to friends, so we may show family members even more loyalty and partiality. In Plato's *Euthyphro*, Socrates learns that Euthyphro has come to the courthouse to prosecute his own father for murder. Socrates expresses surprise at this and wonders whether a son should bring charges against his father. Euthyphro sees no impropriety: For him, a murder is a murder. Euthyphro has a point, but we might still be shocked that someone could take the same attitude toward his father that he would take toward a stranger. A close family member, we might think, need not be involved in such a legal matter. This point is recognized in American law: In the United States, one cannot be compelled to testify in court against one's husband or wife.

Why Are the Virtues Important? We said that virtues are traits of character that are good for people to have. This raises the question of why the virtues are good. Why should a person be courageous, generous, honest, or loyal? The answer may depend on the virtue in question. Thus:

- Courage is good because we need it to cope with danger.
- Generosity is desirable because there will always be people who need help.
- Honesty is needed because without it relations between people would go wrong in all sorts of ways.
- Loyalty is essential to friendship; friends stand by one another even when others would turn away.

This list suggests that each virtue is valuable for a different reason. However, Aristotle offers a general answer to our question—he says that the virtues are important because the virtuous person will fare better in life. The point is not that the virtuous will always be richer; the point is that we need the virtues in order to flourish.

To see what Aristotle is getting at, consider who we are and how we live. On the most general level, we are social creatures who want the company of others. So we live in communities among family, friends, and fellow citizens. In this setting, such qualities as loyalty, fairness, and honesty are needed to interact success-fully with others. On a more individual level, we might have a job and pursue particular interests. Those endeavors might call for other virtues, such as perseverance and industriousness. Finally, it is part of our common human condition that we must some-times face danger or temptation, so courage and self-control are needed. Thus, the virtues all have the same general sort of value: They are all qualities needed for successful living.

Are the Virtues the Same for Everyone? Finally, we may ask whether a single set of traits is desirable for all people. Should we speak of *the* good person, as though all good people come from one mold? Friedrich Nietzsche (1844–1900) thought not. In his flamboyant way, Nietzsche observes:

> How naive it is altogether to say: "Man *ought* to be such-and-such!" Reality shows us an enchanting wealth of types, the abundance of a lavish play and change of forms—and some wretched loafer of a moralist comments: "No! Man ought to be different." He even knows what man should be like, this wretched bigot and prig: he paints himself on the wall and comments, *"Ecce homo!"* ["Behold the man!"]

There is obviously something to this. The scholar who devotes his life to understanding medieval literature and the profes-sional soldier are very different kinds of people. A Victorian woman who would never expose a leg in public and a woman who sunbathes on a nude beach have very different standards of modesty. And yet all may be admirable in their own ways.

There is, then, an obvious sense in which the virtues may differ from person to person. Because people lead different kinds of lives, have different sorts of personalities, and occupy different social roles, the qualities of character that help them flourish may differ.

It is tempting to go even further and say that the virtues differ from society to society. After all, the kind of life that is pos-sible will depend on the values and institutions that dominate a region. A scholar's life is possible only where there are institu-tions, such as universities, that make intellectual investigation possible. Much the same could be said about being an athlete, a priest, a geisha, or a samurai warrior. The character traits that are needed to occupy those roles will differ, and so the traits needed to live successfully will differ. Thus, the virtues will be different.

To this, it may be answered that *certain virtues will be needed by all people in all times*. This was Aristotle's view, and he was probably right. Aristotle believed that we all have a great deal in common, despite our differences. "One may observe," he says, "in one's travels to distant countries the feelings of recognition and affiliation that link every human being to every other human being." Even in the most disparate societies, people face the same basic problems and have the same basic needs. Thus:

- Everyone needs courage, because no one (not even the scholar) can always avoid danger. Also, everyone needs the courage to take the occasional risk.
- In every society, there will be some people who are worse off than others; so, generosity will always be prized.
- Honesty is always a virtue because no society can exist without dependable communication.
- Everyone needs friends, and to have friends one must be a friend; so, everyone needs loyalty.

This sort of list could—and in Aristotle's hands it does—go on and on.

To summarize, then, it may be true that in different societies the virtues are given different interpretations, and different actions may be counted as satisfying them; and it may be true that the value of a character trait will vary from person to person and from society to society. But it cannot be right to say that social customs determine whether any particular character trait is a virtue. The major virtues flow from our common human condition.

12.3. Two Advantages of Virtue Ethics

Virtue Ethics is often said to have two selling points.

1. *Moral motivation.* Virtue Ethics is appealing because it provides a natural and attractive account of moral motivation. Consider the following:

You are in the hospital recovering from a long illness. You are bored and restless, and so you are delighted when Smith comes to visit. You have a good time talking to him; his visit really cheers you up. After a while, you tell Smith how much you enjoy seeing him—he really is a good friend to take the trouble to come see you. But, Smith says, he is merely doing his duty. At first you think he is only being modest, but the more you talk, the clearer it becomes that he is speaking the literal truth. He is not visiting you because he wants to or because he likes you, but only because he thinks he should "do the right thing." He feels it is his duty to visit you, perhaps because you are worse off than anyone else he knows.

This example was suggested by the American philosopher Michael Stocker (1940–). As Stocker points out, you'd be very disappointed to learn Smith's motive; now his visit seems cold and calculating. You thought he was your friend, but now you know otherwise. Commenting on Smith's behavior, Stocker says, "Surely there is something lacking here—and lacking in moral merit or value."

Of course, there is nothing wrong with *what* Smith did. The problem is *why* he did it. We value friendship, love, and respect, and we want our relationships to be based on mutual regard. Acting from an abstract sense of duty or from a desire to "do the right thing" is not the same. We would not want to live in a community of people who acted only from such motives, nor would we want to be such a person ourselves. Therefore, the argument goes, theories that focus on right action cannot provide a completely satisfactory account of the moral life. For that, we need a theory that emphasizes personal qualities such as friendship, love, and loyalty—in other words, a theory of the virtues.

2. *Doubts about the "ideal" of impartiality.* A dominant theme in modern moral philosophy has been impartiality—the idea that all persons are morally equal, and that we should treat everyone's interests as equally important. The utilitarian theory is typical. "Utilitarianism," John Stuart Mill writes, "requires [the moral agent] to be as strictly impartial as a disinterested and benevolent spectator." The book you are now reading also treats impartiality as a fundamental ethical requirement: In the first chapter, impartiality was included in the "minimum conception" of morality.

It may be doubted, though, whether impartiality is really such a noble ideal. Consider our relationships with family and friends. Should we be impartial where their interests are concerned? A mother loves her children and cares for them in a way that she does not care for other children. She is partial to them through and through. But is anything wrong with that? Isn't that exactly the way a mother should be? Again, we love our friends, and we are willing to do things for them that we would not do for others. What's wrong with that? Loving relationships are essential to the good life. But any theory that emphasizes impartiality will have a hard time accounting for this.

A moral theory that emphasizes the virtues, however, can easily account for all this. Some virtues are partial and some are not. Loyalty involves partiality toward loved ones and friends; beneficence involves equal regard for everyone. What is needed is not some general requirement of impartiality, but an understanding of how these virtues relate to one another.

12.4. Virtue and Conduct

As we have seen, theories that emphasize right action seem incomplete because they neglect the question of character. Virtue Ethics remedies this problem by making character its central concern. But as a result, Virtue Ethics runs the risk of being incomplete in the other direction. Moral problems are frequently problems about what to *do*. What can a theory of virtue tell us about the assessment, not of character, but of action?

The answer will depend on the spirit in which Virtue Ethics is offered. On the one hand, we might combine the best features of the right-action approach with insights drawn from the virtues approach—we might try to improve Utilitarianism or Kantianism, for example, by supplementing them with a theory of moral character. This seems sensible. If so, then we can assess right action simply by relying on Utilitarianism or Kantianism.

On the other hand, some writers believe that Virtue Ethics should be understood as an *alternative* to the other theories. These writers believe that Virtue Ethics is a complete moral theory in itself. We might call this *Radical Virtue Ethics*. What would such a theory say about right action? Either it will need to dispense with the notion of "right action" altogether, or it will have to give some account of the idea derived from the conception of virtuous character.

It might sound crazy, but some philosophers have argued that we should get rid of such concepts as "morally right action." Anscombe says that "it would be a great improvement" if we stopped using such notions. We could still assess conduct as better or worse, she says, but we would do so in other terms. Instead of saying that an action was "morally wrong," we would say that it was "intolerant" or "unjust" or "cowardly"—terms derived from the vocabulary of virtue. On her view, such terms allow us to say everything that we need to say.

But advocates of Radical Virtue Ethics need not reject notions such as "morally right." These ideas can be retained but given a new interpretation within the virtue framework. We could still assess actions based on the reasons that can be given for or against them. However, *the reasons cited will all be reasons connected with the virtues.* Thus, the reasons for doing some particular action might be that it is honest, or generous, or fair; while the reasons against doing it might be that it is dishonest, or stingy, or unfair. On this approach, the right thing to do is whatever a virtuous person would do.

12.5. The Problem of Incompleteness

The main objection to Radical Virtue Ethics is that it is incomplete. It seems to be incomplete in three ways.

First, Radical Virtue Ethics cannot explain everything it should explain. Consider a typical virtue, such as dependability. Why should I be dependable? Plainly, we need an answer to this question that goes beyond the simple observation that being dependable is a virtue. We want to know *why* dependability is a virtue; we want to know why it is good. Possible explanations might be that being dependable is to one's own advantage, or being dependable promotes the general welfare, or dependability is needed by those who must live together and rely on one another. The first explanation looks suspiciously like Ethical Egoism; the second is utilitarian; and the third recalls the Social Contract Theory. But none of these explanations are couched in terms of the virtues. Any explanation of why a particular virtue is good, it seems, would have to take us beyond the narrow confines of Radical Virtue Ethics.

If Radical Virtue Ethics doesn't explain *why* something is a virtue, then it won't be able to tell us whether the virtues apply in difficult cases. Consider the virtue of being beneficent, or being kind. Suppose I hear some news that would upset you to know about. Maybe I've learned that someone you used to know died in a car accident. If I don't tell you this, you might never find out. Suppose, also, that you're the sort of person who would want to be told. If I know all this, should I tell you the news? What would be the *kind* thing to do? It's a hard question, because what you would prefer—being told—conflicts with what would make you feel good—not being told. Would a kind person care more about what you want, or more about what makes you feel good? Radical Virtue Ethics cannot answer this question. To be kind is to look out for someone's best interests; but Radical Virtue Ethics does not tell us what someone's best interests are. So, the second way in which the theory is incomplete is that it cannot give a full interpretation of the virtues. It cannot say exactly when they apply.

Finally, Radical Virtue Ethics is incomplete because it cannot help us deal with cases of moral conflict. Suppose I just got a haircut—a mullet the likes of which have not been seen since 1992—and I put you on the spot by asking you what you think. You can either tell me the truth, or you can say I look just fine. Honesty and kindness are both virtues, and so there are reasons both for and against each alternative. But you must do one or the other—you must either tell the truth and be unkind, or not tell the truth and be kind. Which should you do? If someone told you, "Well, you should act virtuously in this situation," that wouldn't help you decide what to do; it would only leave you wondering which virtue to follow. Clearly, we need guidance beyond the resources of Radical Virtue Ethics.

By itself, it seems, Radical Virtue Ethics is limited to platitudes: be kind, be honest, be patient, be generous, and so on. Platitudes are vague, and when they conflict, we must look beyond them for guidance. Radical Virtue Ethics needs the resources of a larger theory.

12.6. Conclusion

It seems best to regard Virtue Ethics as part of our overall theory of ethics rather than as being a complete theory in itself. The total theory would include an account of all the considerations that figure in practical decision making, together with their underlying rationales. The question is whether such a theory can accommodate both an adequate conception of right action and a related conception of virtuous character.

I don't see why not. Suppose, for example, that we accept a utilitarian theory of right action—we believe that one ought to do whatever will lead to the most happiness. From a moral point of view, we would want a society in which everyone leads happy and satisfying lives. We could then ask which actions, which social policies, *and which qualities of character* would most likely lead to that result. An inquiry into the nature of virtue could then be conducted from within that larger framework.

CHAPTER 13

*W*hat Would a Satisfactory Moral Theory Be Like?

Some people believe that there cannot be progress in
Ethics, since everything has already been said. . . . I believe
the opposite. . . . Compared with the other sciences,
Non-Religious Ethics is the youngest and least advanced.
DEREK PARFIT, *REASONS AND PERSONS* (1984)

13.1. Morality without Hubris

Moral philosophy has a rich and fascinating history. Scholars
have approached the subject from many different perspectives,
producing theories that both attract and repel the thoughtful
reader. Almost all the classical theories contain plausible elements, which is hardly surprising, since they were devised by
philosophers of undoubted genius. Yet the various theories
conflict with each other, and most of them are vulnerable to
crippling objections. One is left wondering what to believe.
What, in the final analysis, is the truth? Of course, different philosophers would answer this question in different ways. Some
might refuse to give an answer, on the grounds that we do
not know enough to have reached the "final analysis." In this
respect, moral philosophy is not much worse off than any other
subject—we do not know the final truth about most things. But
we do know a lot, and it might not be rash to say something
about what a satisfactory moral theory might be like.

A Modest Conception of Human Beings. A satisfactory theory
would be realistic about where human beings fit in the grand
scheme of things. The "big bang" occurred some 13.7 billion
years ago, and the earth was formed around 4.5 billion years

173

ago. Life on earth evolved slowly, mostly according to the principles of natural selection. When the dinosaurs went extinct
65 million years ago, this left more room for the evolution of
mammals, and a few hundred thousand years ago, one line of
that evolution produced us. In geological time, we arrived only
yesterday.

But no sooner did our ancestors arrive than they began
to think of themselves as the crown of creation. Some of them
even imagined that the whole universe had been made for their
benefit. Thus, when they began to develop theories of right
and wrong, they held that the protection of their own interests
had a kind of ultimate and objective value. The rest of creation,
they reasoned, was intended for their use. But now we know
better. We now know that we exist by evolutionary accident, as
one species among millions, on one small speck of an unimag-
inably vast cosmos. The details of this picture are revised each
year, as more is discovered, but the main outlines are well
established. Some of the old story remains: human beings are
still the smartest animals we know and the only ones that use
language. Those facts, however, cannot justify an entire worldview that places us at the center.

How Reason Gives Rise to Ethics.   Human beings have evolved
as rational beings. Because we are rational, we are able to take
some facts as reasons for behaving one way rather than another.
We can articulate those reasons and think about them. Thus, if
an action would help satisfy our desires, needs, and so on—in
short, if it would *promote our interests*—then we take that as a
reason to do it.

The origin of our concept of "ought" may be found in
these facts. If we were incapable of considering reasons, we
would have no use for such a notion. Like the other animals,
we would act from instinct or habit. But the examination of
reasons introduces a new factor. Now we find ourselves driven
to act in certain ways as a result of deliberation—as a result of
thinking about our behavior and its consequences. We use the
word *ought* to mark this new element of the situation: We ought
to do what there are the strongest reasons for doing.

Once we see morality as a matter of acting on reason,
another important point emerges. In reasoning about what
to do, we can be consistent or inconsistent. One way of being

inconsistent is to accept a fact as a reason on one occasion but to reject it as a reason on a similar occasion. This happens when one places the interests of one's own race above the interests of other races, despite the absence of any reason to do so. Racism is an offense against morality because it is an offense against reason. Similar remarks apply to other doctrines that divide humanity into the morally favored and disfavored, such as nationalism, sexism, and classism. The upshot is that reason requires impartiality: We ought to act so as to promote the interests of everyone alike.

If Psychological Egoism were true—if we could care only about ourselves—this would mean that reason demands more of us than we can manage. But Psychological Egoism is not true; it presents a false picture of human nature and the human condition. We have evolved as social creatures, living together in groups, wanting one another's company, needing one another's cooperation, and capable of caring about one another's welfare. So there is a pleasing "fit" between (a) what reason requires, namely, impartiality; (b) the requirements of social living, namely, adherence to rules that serve everyone's interests, if fairly applied; and (c) our natural inclination to care about others, at least to a modest degree. All three work together to make morality not only possible but *natural* for us.

13.2. Treating People as They Deserve

The idea that we should "promote the interests of everyone alike" is appealing when it is used to refute bigotry. However, sometimes there is good reason to treat people differently— sometimes people *deserve* to be treated better or worse than others. Human beings are rational agents who can make free choices. Those who choose to treat others well deserve good treatment; those who choose to treat others badly deserve ill treatment.

This sounds harsh until we consider examples. Suppose Smith has always been generous, helping you whenever she could, and now she is in trouble and needs your help. You now have a special reason to help her, beyond the general obligation you have to be helpful to everyone. She is not just a member of the great crowd of humanity; she has earned your respect and gratitude through her conduct.

By contrast, consider someone with the opposite history. Your neighbor Jones has always refused to help you out. One day, for example, your car wouldn't start, and he wouldn't give you a ride to work—he just couldn't be bothered. Some time later, though, *he* has car trouble and asks *you* for a ride. Now Jones deserves to have to fend for himself. If you gave him a ride despite his past behavior, you would be choosing to treat him better than he deserves.

Treating people as they have chosen to treat others is not just a matter of rewarding friends and holding grudges against enemies. It is a matter of treating people as responsible agents who merit particular responses, based on their past conduct. There is an important difference between Smith and Jones: one of them deserves our gratitude; the other deserves our resentment. What would it be like if we did not care about such things?

For one thing, we would be denying people the ability to earn good treatment at the hands of others. This is important. Because we live in communities, how each of us fares depends not only on what we do but on what others do as well. If we are to flourish, we need others to treat us well. A social system in which deserts are acknowledged gives us a way of doing that; it is a way of granting people the power to determine their own fates.

Absent this, what are we to do? We might imagine a system in which a person can get good treatment only by force, or by luck, or as a matter of charity. But the practice of acknowledging deserts is different. It gives people control over whether others will treat them well or badly. It says to them, "If you behave well, you will be *entitled* to good treatment from others. You will have earned it." Acknowledging deserts is ultimately about treating other people with respect.

13.3. A Variety of Motives

There are other ways in which the idea of "promoting the interests of everyone alike" apparently fails to capture the whole of moral life. (I say "apparently" because I will ask later whether it really does.) Certainly, people should sometimes be motivated by an impartial concern for others. But there are other morally praiseworthy motives:

- A mother loves and cares for her children. She does not want to "promote their interests" simply because they are people she can help. Her attitude toward them is entirely different from her attitude toward other children. While she might want to help other children when she can, that vaguely benevolent feeling is nothing like the love she has for her own.
- A man is loyal to his friends. Again, he is not concerned with their interests only as part of his concern for people generally. They are his friends, and so they are special to him.

Only a philosophical fool would want to eliminate love, loyalty, and the like from our understanding of the moral life. If such motives were eliminated, and instead people simply calculated what was best, we would all be much worse off. Anyway, who would want to live in a world without love and friendship?

Of course, people may have many other valuable motives:

- A composer is concerned, above all else, to finish her symphony. She pursues this even though she might do "more good" by doing something else.
- A teacher devotes great effort to preparing his classes, even though more good might be done by directing his energy elsewhere.

While these motives are not usually considered "moral," we should not want to eliminate them from human life. Taking pride in one's job, wanting to create something of value, and many other noble intentions contribute to both personal happiness and the general welfare. We should no more want to eliminate them than to eliminate love and friendship.

13.4. Multiple-Strategies Utilitarianism

Above, I gave a sketchy justification of the principle that "we ought to act so as to promote the interests of everyone alike." But then I noted that this cannot be the whole story about our moral obligations because sometimes we should treat people differently, according to their individual deserts. And then I discussed some morally important motives that seem unrelated to the impartial promotion of interests.

Yet it may be possible to see these diverse concerns as interrelated. At first blush, it seems that treating people according to their individual deserts is quite different from seeking to promote the interests of everyone alike. But when we asked why deserts are important, the answer turned out to be that *we would all be much worse off* if acknowledging deserts was not part of our social scheme. And when we ask why love, friendship, artistic creativity, and pride in one's work are important, the answer is that *our lives would be so much poorer* without such things. This suggests that there is a single standard at work in our assessments.

Perhaps, then, the single moral standard is human welfare. What is important is that people be as happy as possible. This standard can be used to assess a wide variety of things, including actions, policies, social customs, laws, rules, motives, and character traits. But this does not mean that we should always think in terms of making people as happy as possible. Our day-to-day lives will go better if, instead, we simply love our children, enjoy our friends, take pride in our work, keep our promises, and so on. An ethic that values "the interests of everyone alike" will endorse this conclusion.

This is not a new idea. Henry Sidgwick (1838–1900), the great utilitarian theorist of the Victorian era, made the same point:

> The doctrine that Universal Happiness is the ultimate *standard* must not be understood to imply that Universal Benevolence is the only right or always best *motive* of action . . . it is not necessary that the end which gives the criterion of rightness should always be the end at which we consciously aim: and if experience shows that the general happiness will be more satisfactorily attained if men frequently act from other motives than pure universal philanthropy, it is obvious that these other motives are reasonably to be preferred on Utilitarian principles.

This passage has been cited in support of a view called "Motive Utilitarianism." According to that view, we should act from the motives that best promote the general welfare.

Yet the most plausible view of this type does not focus exclusively on motives; nor does it focus entirely on acts or rules, as other theories have done. The most plausible theory might be called *Multiple-Strategies Utilitarianism*. This theory is utilitarian, because the ultimate goal is to maximize the general welfare.

However, the theory recognizes that we may use diverse strategies to pursue that goal. Sometimes we aim directly at it. For example, a senator may support a bill because she believes that it would raise the standard of living for everyone, or an individual may send money to the International Red Cross because he believes that this would do more good than any other action he might perform. But usually we don't think of the general welfare at all; instead, we simply care for our children, work at our jobs, obey the law, keep our promises, and so on.

Right Action as Living According to the Best Plan. We can make the idea behind Multiple-Strategies Utilitarianism a little more specific.

Suppose we had a fully specified list of the virtues, motives, and methods of decision making that would enable a person to be happy and to contribute to the welfare of others. And suppose, further, that this is the *optimum* list for that person; there is no other combination of virtues, motives, and methods of decision making that would do a better job. The list would include at least the following:

- The virtues that are needed to make one's life go well
- The motives on which to act
- The commitments that one will have to friends, family, and others
- The social roles that one will occupy, with the responsibilities and demands that go with them
- The duties and concerns associated with the projects one will undertake, such as becoming a DJ or a soldier or an undertaker
- The everyday rules that one will usually follow without even thinking
- A strategy, or group of strategies, about when to consider making exceptions to the rules, and the grounds on which those exceptions can be made

The list would also specify the relations between the different items on the list—what takes priority over what, how to adjudicate conflicts, and so on. It would be very hard to construct such a list. As a practical matter, it might even be impossible. But we can be fairly sure that it would include endorsements of friendship, honesty, and other familiar virtues. It would tell us to keep our promises, but not always, and to refrain from harming people, but not always; and so on. And it would probably tell us to stop living in luxury while millions of children die of preventable diseases.

At any rate, there is some combination of virtues, motives, and methods of decision making that is best *for me*, given my circumstances, personality, and talents—"best" in the sense that it will optimize the chances of my having a good life, while optimizing the chances of other people having good lives, too. Call this optimum combination *my best plan*. The right thing for me to do is to act in accordance with my best plan.

My best plan may have a lot in common with yours. Presumably, they will both include rules against lying, stealing, and killing, together with an understanding about when to make exceptions to those rules. They will both include virtues such as patience, kindness, and self-control. They may both contain instructions for raising children, including what virtues to foster in them.

But our best plans need not be identical. People have different personalities and talents. One person may find fulfillment as a priest while another could never live like that. Thus, our lives might include different sorts of personal relationships, and we might need to cultivate different virtues. People also live in different circumstances and have access to different resources—some are rich; some are poor; some are privileged; some are persecuted. Thus, the optimum strategies for living will differ.

In each case, however, the identification of a plan as the best plan will be a matter of assessing how well it promotes the interests of everyone alike. So the overall theory is utilitarian, even though it may frequently endorse motives that do not look utilitarian at all.

13.5. The Moral Community

As moral agents, we should be concerned with everyone whose welfare might be affected by what we do. This may seem like a pious platitude, but in reality it can be a hard doctrine. Around the world, one child in five fails to get essential vaccinations, resulting in about two million unnecessary deaths each year. Citizens in the affluent countries could easily cut this number in half, but they won't. People would no doubt do more if children in their own neighborhoods were dying, but the location of the children shouldn't matter: Everyone is included in the community of moral concern. If the interests of all children, no matter where they lived, were taken seriously, it would force us to change our ways.

If the moral community is not limited to people in one *place*, neither is it limited to people at any one *time*. Whether people will be affected by our actions now or in the future is irrelevant. Our obligation is to consider all their interests equally. One consequence of this pertains to nuclear weapons. Such weapons not only have the power to maim and kill innocent people, but they can also poison the environment for thousands of years. If the welfare of future generations is given proper weight, it is difficult to imagine any circumstance in which such weapons should be used. Climate change is another issue that affects the interests of our descendants. If we fail to reverse the effects of global warming, our children will suffer even more than we will.

There is one other way in which our conception of the moral community must be expanded. Humans are not alone on this planet. Other sentient animals—that is, animals capable of feeling pleasure and pain—also have interests. When we abuse them or kill them, they are harmed, just as humans can be harmed in those ways. Bentham and Mill were right to insist that the interests of nonhuman animals must be included in our moral calculations. As Bentham pointed out, excluding creatures from moral consideration because of their species is no more justified than excluding them because of their race, nationality, or sex. So, the single moral standard is not human welfare, but sentient welfare.

13.6. Justice and Fairness

Utilitarianism has been criticized as unfair and unjust. Can the complications we have introduced help?

One criticism concerns punishment. We can imagine cases in which it would promote the general welfare to frame an innocent person. Such an act would be blatantly unjust, yet Utilitarianism would seem to require it. More generally, as Kant pointed out, utilitarians are happy to "use" criminals for the achievement of society's ends. Even if those ends are worthwhile—such as the reduction of future crime—we might be uncomfortable with a theory that endorsed manipulation as a legitimate moral strategy.

However, our theory takes a different view of punishment than utilitarians have usually taken. In fact, our view is close to Kant's. In punishing someone, we are treating him worse than we treat others. But this is justified by the person's own past deeds: It is a response to what he has done. That is why it is not right to frame an innocent person; the innocent person has done nothing to deserve such treatment.

The theory of punishment, however, is only one aspect of justice. Questions of justice arise any time one person is treated differently from another. Suppose an employer must choose which of two employees to promote. The first candidate has worked hard, taking on extra work, giving up vacation time, and so on. The second candidate, on the other hand, has never done more than he had to. Obviously, the two employees will be treated very differently: One will get the promotion; the other will not. But this is all right, according to our theory. The first employee has earned the promotion; the second has not.

A person's voluntary actions can justify a departure from the policy of "equal treatment," but nothing else can. This goes against a common view of the matter. Often, people think it is right for individuals to be rewarded for physical beauty, superior intelligence, and other qualities that are due, in large part, to having the right DNA and being raised by the right parents. And in practice, people often have better jobs and more money just because they were born with greater natural gifts into wealthier families. But on reflection, this does not seem right. People do not deserve their native endowments; they have them only as a result of what John Rawls (1921–2002) calls "the natural lottery." Suppose the first employee in our example was passed over for the promotion, despite her hard work, because the second employee had some natural ability that was more useful in the new position. Even if the employer could justify this decision in terms of the company's needs, the first employee would rightly feel cheated. She has worked harder, yet he is getting the promotion, and the benefits that go with it, because of something he did nothing to earn. That is not fair. In a just society, people could improve their circumstances through hard work, but they would not benefit from a lucky birth.

13.7. Conclusion

What would a satisfactory moral theory look like? I have out-lined the possibility that seems most plausible to me: According to Multiple-Strategies Utilitarianism, we should maximize the interests of all sentient beings by living according to our best plan. Modesty, however, is required when making such a proposal. Over the centuries, philosophers have articulated and defended a wide variety of moral theories, and history has always found flaws in their conceptions. Still, there is hope, if not for my suggestion, then for some other proposal down the road. Civilization is only a few thousand years old. If we do not destroy it, then the study of ethics has a bright future.

Notes on Sources

Chapter 1: What Is Morality?

The ethicists' comments about Baby Theresa are from an Associated Press report by David Briggs, "Baby Theresa Case Raises Ethics Questions," *Champaign-Urbana News-Gazette*, March 31, 1992, p. A-6.

The poll about separating conjoined twins is from the *Ladies' Home Journal*, March 2001. The judges' comments about Jodie and Mary are from the *Daily Telegraph*, September 23, 2000.

Information about the Tracy Latimer case is from *The New York Times*, December 1, 1997, National Edition, p. A-3. The quotation is from the Canadian Broadcasting Corporation, January 19, 2001.

Chapter 2: The Challenge of Cultural Relativism

The story of the Greeks and the Callatians is from Herodotus, *The Histories*, translated by Aubrey de Selincourt, revised by A. R. Burn (Harmondsworth, Middlesex: Penguin Books, 1972), pp. 219–220. The quotation from Herodotus toward the end of the chapter is from the same source.

The information about the Eskimos is from Peter Freuchen, *Book of the Eskimos* (New York: Fawcett, 1961), and E. Adamson Hoebel, *The Law of Primitive Man* (Cambridge, MA: Harvard University Press, 1954), chapter 5. The estimate of how female infanticide affects the male/female ratio in the Eskimo population is from Hoebel's work.

The William Graham Sumner quotation is from his *Folkways* (Boston: Ginn, 1906), p. 28.

The New York Times series on female genital mutilation included articles (mainly by Celia W. Dugger) published in 1996 on April 15, April 25, May 2, May 3, July 8, September 11, October 5, October 12, and December 28. I also learned about Fauziya Kassindja from her interview on PBS; see http://www.pbs.org/speaktruthtopower/fauziya.html. The figures of "28 African nations" and "about 135 million" come from the World Health Organization's "An Update on WHO's Work on Female Genital Mutilation" (2011), p. 1.

The story about the Nigerian woman sentenced to death comes from Associated Press articles on August 20, 2002, and September 25, 2003. The story about the Australian woman convicted on drug charges comes from a May 27, 2005, article in *The New York Times*. The story about the Saudi woman who was sentenced to being lashed comes from *The New York Times* (articles on November 16 and December 18, 2007).

The Dan Savage quotation about monogamy is from Mark Oppenheimer, "Married, with Infidelities," *The New York Times Magazine*, July 3, 2011, pp. 22–27, 46 (quotation on p. 23).

Chapter 3: Subjectivism in Ethics

The quotation from Matt Foreman is from *The New York Times*, June 25, 2001.

The Gallup Poll information is from www.gallup.com.

"If you're involved in the gay and lesbian lifestyle, it's bondage." Michele Bachmann, speaking at *EdWatch National Education Conference*, November 6, 2004. I learned about the Bachmanns' clinic from *Anderson Cooper 360*, "Keeping Them Honest" (July 13, 2011), http://ac360.blogs.cnn.com/2011/07/13/video-ex-patient-speaks-about-clinics-therapy/.

The Catholic view about homosexuality is quoted from *Catechism of the Catholic Church* (Mahwah, NJ: Paulist Press, 1994), p. 566.

Charles L. Stevenson, *Ethics and Language* (New Haven, CT: Yale University Press, 1944). Disagreement in belief/disagreement in attitude, pp. 2–4; "*Any* statement about *any* matter of fact . . . ," p. 114.

The story about Katie Shelton and Mark Friedrich is from the Carnegie Hero Fund Commission's website: www.carnegiehero.org.

"This is a very serious matter. . . .": Michele Bachmann, on the radio program "Prophetic Views Behind the News" (hosted by Jan Markell), KKMS 980-AM, March 20, 2004.

The quotation by James Dobson is from the April 2004 *Focus on the Family Newsletter*, which he read on the radio on March 24, 2004.

Nanette Gartrell and Henny Bos, "U.S. National Longitudinal Lesbian Family Study: Psychological Adjustment of 17-Year-Old Adolescents," *Pediatrics* 126, no. 1 (July 2010), pp. 1–9.

The General Accounting Office (which later became the Government Accountability Office) estimated in 2004 that the Defense of Marriage Act (DOMA) affects the implementation of 1,138 federal laws (source: General Accounting Office, *Defense of Marriage Act: Update to Prior Report*, GAO-04-353R [January 23, 2004]). These laws typically affect employee benefits. Gays who got married under state law are ineligible because DOMA defines marriage as being between a man and a woman, and federal law in America takes precedence over state law.

Gay sex is illegal in 76 countries: see the November 2010 "Harper's Index" in *Harper's Magazine* (source: International Lesbian, Gay, Bisexual, Trans and Intersex Association).

Heather Elise Murphy, *Suicide Risk among Gay, Lesbian, and Bisexual College Youth* (PhD Dissertation, University of Washington, 2007).

Chapter 4: Does Morality Depend on Religion?

77% of Americans support Judge Roy Moore: Gallup Poll, September 2003. 80% of Americans believe in God, and another 12% in a higher power: Gallup Poll, May 2010. 41% believe that Jesus Christ will return to earth by 2050: Pew Research Center for the People & the Press, June 2010. I learned about the clergy's role in assigning movie ratings from the documentary *This Film Is Not Yet Rated* (2006).

The Bertrand Russell quotation is from his essay "A Free Man's Worship," in *Mysticism and Logic* (Garden City, NY: Doubleday, Anchor Books, n.d.), pp. 45–46.

Antony Flew makes the remark about philosophical talent in his *God and Philosophy* (New York: Dell, 1966), p. 109.

Hamlet's exact words were "Why, then 'tis none to you; for there is nothing either good or bad, but thinking makes it so: to me it is a prison" (act 2, scene 2, lines 254–256 of *The Tragedy of Hamlet, Prince of Denmark,* in *The Complete Works of William Shakespeare* [USA: Octopus Books, 1985, p. 844]).

The quotations from Aristotle are from *The Basic Works of Aristotle,* edited by Richard McKeon (New York: Random House, 1941), p. 249, and *The Politics,* translated by T. A. Sinclair (Harmondsworth, Middlesex: Penguin Books, 1962), p. 40.

The quotation from Saint Thomas Aquinas is from the *Summa Theologica,* III *Quodlibet,* 27, translated by Thomas Gilby in *St. Thomas Aquinas: Philosophical Texts* (New York: Oxford University Press, 1960).

The passage supposedly about abortion is Jeremiah 1:4–8. I quoted the "English Standard Version" translation of *The Holy Bible* (2001).

On the history of Catholic thought, see John Connery, SJ, *Abortion: The Development of the Roman Catholic Perspective* (Chicago: Loyola University Press, 1977) (the Church has never said that the fetus acquires a soul at conception: p. 308). I am grateful to Steve Sverdlik for tutoring me in this area.

Pope Benedict XVI's acceptance of evolution and the Big Bang Theory is confirmed by many sources; for example: Lorenzago di Cadore, "Pope: Creation vs. Evolution Clash an 'Absurdity'" (msnbc.

com news services, July 25, 2007), http://www.msnbc.msn.com/id/
19956961/ns/world_news-europe/t/pope-creation-vs-evolution-clash-
absurdity/#.TjoyRb8sU50; and "Pope: God behind Big Bang" (CBS
News, January 7, 2011), http://www.cbsnews.com/8301-501465_
162-20027781-501465.html.

Chapter 5: Ethical Egoism

Each day 22,000 children under five die: *2010 Annual Report*, UNICEF/
United States Fund, p. 1.

For information about Raoul Wallenberg, see John Bierman,
The Righteous Gentile (New York: Viking Press, 1981). For information
about Gentiles who risked their lives to protect Jews, see http://www
.yadvashem.org.

The information about Zell Kravinsky comes from "The Gift," an
article by Ian Parker in the *New Yorker* (August 2, 2004). The information about Oseola McCarty comes from Bill Clinton, *Giving: How Each
of Us Can Change the World* (New York: Alfred A. Knopf, 2007), p. 26.

Dale Carnegie, *How to Win Friends and Influence People* (New York:
Simon and Schuster, 1981; first published in 1936), p. 31.

The story about Abraham Lincoln is from the Springfield *Monitor*, quoted by Frank Sharp in his *Ethics* (New York: Appleton Century,
1928), p. 75.

The story about the man who leapt onto the train tracks is from
the January 3, 2007, edition of *The New York Times*.

The quotations from Ayn Rand are from her book *The Virtue of
Selfishness* (New York: Signet, 1964), pp. 27, 32, 80, and 81.

The newspaper stories are from *The Baltimore Sun*, August 28, 2001;
The Miami Herald, August 28, 1993, October 6, 1994, and June 2, 1989;
The New York Times, April 28, 2008; and the *Macon Telegraph*, July 15, 2005.

For Kurt Baier's argument, see his book *The Moral Point of View*
(Ithaca, NY: Cornell University Press, 1958), pp. 189–190.

Chapter 6: The Social Contract Theory

The chapter-opening quote is from chapter 18, section 202, of
Locke's *Second Treatise*. The full sentence reveals a different meaning
than the partial passage: "Wherever law ends, tyranny begins if the
law be transgressed to another's harm."

Hobbes's estimate of the state of nature is from his *Leviathan*,
Oakeshott edition (Oxford: Blackwell, 1960), chapter 13. See p. 82.

The Rousseau quotation is from *The Social Contract and Discourses,* translated by G. D. H. Cole (New York: Dutton, 1959), pp. 18–19.

That Flood and Dresher first formulated the Prisoner's Dilemma around 1950 is mentioned in Richmond Campbell, "Background for the Uninitiated," *Paradoxes of Rationality and Cooperation,* edited by Richmond Campbell and Lanning Sowden (Vancouver: University of British Columbia Press, 1985), p. 3.

The quotations from King and Waldman may be found in *Civil Disobedience: Theory and Practice,* edited by Hugo Adam Bedau (New York: Pegasus Books, 1967), pp. 76–77, 78, 106, and 107.

The Hume quotation is from "Of the Original Contract," reprinted in *Hume's Moral and Political Philosophy,* edited by Henry D. Aiken (New York: Hafner, 1948), p. 363.

Chapter 7: The Utilitarian Approach

"Priestley was the first (unless it was Beccaria) who taught my lips to pronounce this sacred truth:—That the greatest happiness of the greatest number is the foundation of morals and legislation" (Jeremy Bentham, "Extracts from Bentham's Commonplace Book," *Collected Works,* vol. 10 [Edinburgh: published under the superintendence of John Bowring and printed by William Tait, 1843], p. 142).

Peter Singer says that morality is not a system of nasty puritanical prohibitions in *Practical Ethics,* 2nd ed. (Cambridge: Cambridge University Press, 1993), p. 1.

The account of Freud's death was taken from Ronald W. Clark, *Freud: The Man and the Cause* (New York: Random House, 1980), pp. 525–527; and Paul Ferris, *Dr. Freud: A Life* (Washington, DC: Counterpoint, 1997), pp. 395–397.

The quotations from Bentham are from his book *An Introduction to the Principles of Morals and Legislation,* 1st ed. (printed in 1780; published in 1789), p. 125 (on God) and p. 311 (on animals), available in many reprintings. Bentham discusses sexual ethics in "Offences Against One's Self," written around 1785 and published posthumously.

The quotation from Mill's *On Liberty* (1859) is from paragraph 9 of chap. 1, "Introductory."

Much of the information on marijuana comes from *Pot Politics: Marijuana and the Costs of Prohibition,* edited by Mitch Earleywine (Oxford: Oxford University Press, 2007). The essays cited below are from that book, unless otherwise indicated.

From Mitch Earleywine, "Thinking Clearly about Marijuana Policy," pp. 3–16: One-third of Americans have tried pot (p. 4); on the Gateway Theory (pp. 7–8); when crack is more widely available

(p. 8); the William Bennett quotation (p. 9); marijuana does not cause violence (p. 10). Marijuana does not cause crime: see Eric Blumenson and Eva Nilsen, "Liberty Lost: The Moral Case for Marijuana Law Reform," *Indiana Law Journal* 85 (Winter 2010), pp. 279–300 (p. 284).

In 2007, 5.8% of Americans aged 12 and older had used pot in the past month: "Results from the 2007 National Survey on Drug Use and Health: National Findings," http://oas.samhsa.gov/nsduh/2k7nsduh/2k7results.cfm, p. 1.

Americans spend more than $10 billion per year on marijuana: the Office of National Drug Control Policy's *2008 Marijuana Sourcebook* gives only the old figure that Americans spent $10.5 billion in 2000 (p. 11).

From Robert Gore and Mitch Earleywine, "Marijuana's Perceived Addictiveness: A Survey of Clinicians and Researchers," pp. 176–186: Pot is less addictive than caffeine (p. 179). Gore and Earleywine surveyed 746 drug-abuse counselors, mental health specialists, and academic researchers.

From Wayne Hall, "A Cautious Case for Cannabis Depenalization," pp. 91–112: on driving (p. 92); on the respiratory system (pp. 92–93); on cognitive damage (p. 95); on the Gateway Theory (pp. 96–97); on the difficulties ex-cons face finding jobs (p. 102). Also, according to the Pew Charitable Trusts, the odds of an American rising out of the bottom 20% economic bracket within 20 years depends heavily on whether he is an ex-con: if he is, then the odds are 1 in 50; if he isn't, then the odds are 1 in 7 (*Harper's Magazine*, "Harper's Index," August 2011).

From Kevin A. Sabet, "The (Often Unheard) Case against Marijuana Leniency," pp. 325–352: One joint is like six cigarettes (p. 328, citing the British Lung Foundation from 2002).

From Anthony Liguori, "Marijuana and Driving: Trends, Design Issues, and Future Recommendations," pp. 71–90: See especially p. 83.

From Daniel Egan and Jeffrey A. Miron, "The Budgetary Implications of Marijuana Prohibition," pp. 17–39: on enforcement costs and possible tax gains (p. 29).

Over 700,000 people are arrested each year for possession of marijuana: Blumenson and Nilsen, "Liberty Lost," p. 280. In 2007, there were around 872,720 (total) marijuana arrests: *Crime in the United States, 2007* (Department of Justice/Federal Bureau of Investigation), combining information from the "Persons Arrested" page (http://www.fbi.gov/ucr/cius2007/arrests/index.html) and "Table 29" (http://www.fbi.gov/ucr/cius2007/data/table_29.html). The 44,000+ figure is based on the government's reporting of the number of drug offenders in prison and the percentage of such offenders serving time for marijuana crimes.

Being arrested on marijuana charges is horrible, even if one is not imprisoned: Blumenson and Nilsen, "Liberty Lost," pp. 289–291.

The quotations from Aquinas about animals are from *Summa Contra Gentiles*, book 3, chap. 112. See *Basic Writings of St. Thomas Aquinas*, edited by Anton C. Pegis (New York: Random House, 1945), vol. 2, p. 222.

Richard D. Ryder, "Speciesism in the Laboratory," in *In Defense of Animals: The Second Wave*, edited by Peter Singer (Oxford: Blackwell, 2006). Ryder coined "speciesism": p. ix; the experiments: pp. 91–92.

Chapter 8: The Debate over Utilitarianism

"The utilitarian doctrine is that happiness is desirable . . .": John Stuart Mill, *Utilitarianism* (1861; available in various reprintings), chap. 4, para. 2.

G. E. Moore discusses what has intrinsic value in the last chapter of *Principia Ethica* (Cambridge: Cambridge University Press, 1903).

McCloskey's example of the utilitarian tempted to bear false witness is from his paper "A Non-Utilitarian Approach to Punishment," *Inquiry* 8 (1965), pp. 239–255.

"As strictly impartial as a disinterested and benevolent spectator": John Stuart Mill, *Utilitarianism* (1861; available in various reprintings), chap. 2, para. 18.

The quotation from John Cottingham is from his article "Partialism, Favouritism and Morality," *Philosophical Quarterly* 36 (1986), p. 357.

The Smart quotation is from J. J. C. Smart and Bernard Williams, *Utilitarianism: For and Against* (Cambridge: Cambridge University Press, 1973), p. 68. "Rule worship" is discussed on p. 10.

Frances Howard-Snyder, "Rule Consequentialism Is a Rubber Duck," *American Philosophical Quarterly* 30 (1993), pp. 271–278.

See Gunnar Myrdal, *An American Dilemma: The Negro Problem and American Democracy* (1944; available in various reprintings).

Chapter 9: Are There Absolute Moral Rules?

The quotation from Franklin Roosevelt is from his communication *The President of the United States to the Governments of France, Germany, Italy, Poland and His Britannic Majesty*, September 1, 1939.

The excerpts from Truman's diary are from Robert H. Ferrell, *Off the Record: The Private Papers of Harry S. Truman* (New York: Harper and Row, 1980), pp. 55–56.

The Churchill quote is from Winston S. Churchill, *The Second World War*, vol. 6: *Triumph and Tragedy* (New York: Houghton Mifflin Company, 1953), p. 553.

Anscombe's 1939 pamphlet "The Justice of the Present War Examined," as well as her 1956 pamphlet "Mr Truman's Degree," can be found in G. E. M. Anscombe, *Ethics, Religion and Politics: Collected Philosophical Papers*, vol. 3 (Minneapolis: University of Minnesota Press, 1981). See pp. 64, 65. Also in that volume is her "Modern Moral Philosophy," pp. 26–42 (originally published in *Philosophy* 33, no. 124 [January 1958], pp. 1–19). See p. 27 (critique of Kant) and p. 34 (examples of absolute moral rules).

The grisly details about Hiroshima are from Richard Rhodes, *The Making of the Atomic Bomb* (New York: Simon and Schuster, 1986), p. 715 (birds igniting in midair), and pp. 725–726 (people dying in water).

Kant's statement of the Categorical Imperative is from his *Foundations of the Metaphysics of Morals*, translated by Lewis White Beck (Indianapolis: Bobbs-Merrill, 1959), p. 39.

Kant's "On a Supposed Right to Lie from Altruistic Motives" can be found in *Critique of Practical Reason and Other Writings in Moral Philosophy*, translated by Lewis White Beck (Chicago: University of Chicago Press, 1949). The quotation is from p. 348.

The Peter Geach quotation is from his *God and the Soul* (London: Routledge and Kegan Paul, 1969), p. 128.

MacIntyre's remark is at the beginning of the chapter on Kant in his *A Short History of Ethics* (New York: Macmillan, 1966).

Chapter 10: Kant and Respect for Persons

Kant's remarks on animals are from his *Lectures on Ethics*, translated by Louis Infield (New York: Harper and Row, 1963), pp. 239–240. I altered one sentence without changing its meaning: "he who is cruel to animals also becomes hard in his dealings with men" (not "becomes hard also").

The second formulation of the Categorical Imperative, in terms of treating persons as ends, is in *Foundations of the Metaphysics of Morals*, translated by Lewis White Beck (Indianapolis: Bobbs-Merrill, 1959), p. 47. The remarks about "dignity" and "price" are on p. 53.

Bentham's statement "All punishment is mischief" is from *The Principles of Morals and Legislation* (New York: Hafner, 1948), p. 170.

The quotations from Kant on punishment are from *The Metaphysical Elements of Justice*, translated by John Ladd (Indianapolis: Bobbs-Merrill, 1965), pp. 99–107, except for the quotation about the "right good beating," which is from *Critique of Practical Reason*, translated by Lewis White Beck (Chicago: University of Chicago Press, 1949), p. 170.

On the change in terminology from "prisons" to "correctional facilities," see Blake McKelvey, *American Prisons: A History of Good Intentions* (Montclair, NJ: Patterson Smith, 1977), p. 357.

The United States has about 2.3 million inmates: Bureau of Justice Statistics website, http://bjs.ojp.usdoj.gov/index.cfm?ty=pbdetail&iid=2200. Highest incarceration rate in the world: *Pocket World in Figures, 2011 Edition* (The Economist) (London: Profile Books, 2010), p. 101; and the International Centre for Prison Studies website, http://www.prisonstudies.org/info/worldbrief/wpb_stats.php?area=all&category=wb_poprate. On changes in the American prison system between the 1960s and 1990s, see Eric Schlosser, "The Prison-Industrial Complex," *Atlantic Monthly*, December 1998.

On December 22, 2006, a story on National Public Radio cited California officials as saying that California has the highest recidivism rate in the country.

Jesus talks about "turning the other cheek" in Matthew 5:38–39. I have used the "English Standard Version" translation of *The Holy Bible* (2001).

Chapter 11: Feminism and the Ethics of Care

Heinz's Dilemma is explained in Lawrence Kohlberg, *Essays on Moral Development*, vol. 1: *The Philosophy of Moral Development* (New York: Harper and Row, 1981), p. 12. For the six stages of moral development, see the same work, pp. 409–412.

Amy and Jake are quoted by Carol Gilligan in her *In a Different Voice: Psychological Theory and Women's Development* (Cambridge, MA: Harvard University Press, 1982), pp. 26, 28. The other quotations from Gilligan are from pp. 16–17, 31.

The Virginia Held quotation is from her "Feminist Transformations of Moral Theory," *Philosophy and Phenomenological Research* 50 (1990), p. 344.

Women score higher than men on empathy tests: M. H. Davis, "Measuring Individual Differences in Empathy: Evidence for a Multidimensional Approach," *Journal of Personality and Social Psychology* 44, no. 1 (January 1983), pp. 113–126; and P. E. Jose, "The Role of Gender and Gender Role Similarity in Readers' Identification with Story Characters," *Sex Roles* 21, nos. 9–10 (November 1989), pp. 697–713.

Brain scans and punishment: Tania Singer et al., "Empathetic Neural Responses Are Modulated by the Perceived Fairness of Others," *Nature*, January 26, 2006, pp. 466–469.

Roy F. Baumeister, "Is There Anything Good about Men?" American Psychological Association, invited address, 2007 (quotation from p. 9).

Women are only slightly more care-oriented than men: Sara Jaffee and Janet Shibley Hyde, "Gender Differences in Moral Orientation: A Meta-Analysis," *Psychological Bulletin* 126, no. 5 (2000), pp. 703–726.

Male/female differences appear at an early age: Larry Cahill, "His Brain, Her Brain," *Scientific American*, April 25, 2005 (8 pages), citing the work of Simon Baron-Cohen and Svetlana Lutchmaya.

"'Care' is the new buzzword": Annette Baier, *Moral Prejudices* (Cambridge, MA: Harvard University Press, 1994), p. 19. The other quotations from Baier are from p. 4 ("connect their ethics of love") and p. 2 ("honorary women").

The figures about HIV are from *Global Report: UNAIDS Report on the Global AIDS Epidemic/2010:* 2.5 million children have HIV (p. 23); around one-fourth get decent medical care (pp. 97–98); around half of pregnant women are protecting their children (p. 78).

The quotations from Nel Noddings are from her book *Caring: A Feminine Approach to Ethics and Moral Education* (Berkeley: University of California Press, 1984), pp. 149–155.

Chapter 12: Virtue Ethics

The quotations from Aristotle are from book 2 of the *Nicomachean Ethics*, translated by Martin Ostwald (Indianapolis: Bobbs-Merrill, 1962), except for the quotation about friendship, which is from book 8, and the quotation about visiting foreign lands, which is Martha C. Nussbaum's translation in her article "Non-Relative Virtues: An Aristotelian Approach," in *Midwest Studies in Philosophy*, vol. 13: *Ethical Theory: Character and Virtue*, edited by Peter A. French, Theodore E. Uehling Jr., and Howard K. Wettstein (Notre Dame, IN: University of Notre Dame Press, 1988), pp. 32–53.

Pincoffs's suggestion about the nature of virtue appears in his book *Quandaries and Virtues: Against Reductivism in Ethics* (Lawrence: University of Kansas Press, 1986), p. 78.

Peter Geach's remark about courage is from his book *The Virtues* (Cambridge: Cambridge University Press, 1977), p. xxx. The story about Saint Athanasius is on p. 114.

Jesus says that we should give all we have to help the poor in Matthew 19:21–24, Mark 10:21–25, and Luke 18:22–25.

Plato's *Euthyphro* is available in several translations, including Hugh Tredennick and Harold Tarrant's in *Plato: The Last Days of Socrates* (New York: Penguin Books, 2003).

The Nietzsche quotation is from *Twilight of the Idols*, "Morality as Anti-Nature," pt. 6, translated by Walter Kaufmann in *The Portable Nietzsche* (New York: Viking Press, 1954), p. 491.

Michael Stocker's example is from his article "The Schizophrenia of Modern Ethical Theories," *Journal of Philosophy* 73 (1976), pp. 453–466.

The John Stuart Mill quote is from chapter 2 of his *Utilitarianism* (1861; available in various reprintings).

Elizabeth Anscombe rejects the notion of "morally right" in her article "Modern Moral Philosophy," *Philosophy* 33 (1958), pp. 1–19, reprinted in *Ethics, Religion and Politics: The Collected Philosophical Papers of G. E. M. Anscombe*, vol. 3 (Minneapolis: University of Minnesota Press, 1981), pp. 26–42 ("it would be a great improvement": p. 33).

Chapter 13: What Would a Satisfactory Moral Theory Be Like?

The age of the universe is taken from the "WMAP" data as presented on NASA's website. "WMAP" is the Wilkinson Microwave Anisotropy Probe, which was launched in 2001 and collected data until 2010.

The Sidgwick quotation is from Henry Sidgwick, *The Methods of Ethics*, 7th ed. (London: Macmillan, 1907), p. 413.

One-fifth of children miss their vaccinations, resulting in two million annual deaths: *2010 Annual Report*, UNICEF/United States Fund, p. 15.

John Rawls discusses the "natural lottery" on p. 74 of *A Theory of Justice* (Cambridge, MA: Harvard University Press, 1971), and on p. 64 of the revised edition of that book, published in 1999.

*I*ndex

A Pra<
Exercises 1

Third edition

A Practical English Grammar
Exercises 1

A. J. Thomson
A. V. Martinet

Oxford University Press

Oxford University Press
Walton Street, Oxford OX2 6DP

Oxford New York Toronto
Delhi Bombay Calcutta Madras Karachi
Petaling Jaya Singapore Hong Kong Tokyo
Nairobi Dar es Salaam Cape Town
Melbourne Auckland

and associated companies in
Berlin Ibadan

Oxford and *Oxford English* are trade marks of
Oxford University Press

ISBN 0 19 431343 3

© Oxford University Press 1961, 1962, 1964,
1972, 1975, 1980, 1986

Exercises 1 and *2* were originally published between 1961 and
1972 as ten individual books of exercises.

Exercises 1 first published as *Combined Exercises Volume 1* 1975
Second edition 1980 (reprinted seven times)
Third edition 1986
Ninth impression 1990

Typeset in Great Britain by
VAP Group, Kidlington, Oxford.
Printed in Hong Kong

Preface to the third edition

This is one of two books of exercises designed to accompany *A Practical English Grammar*.

To coincide with the publication of the fourth edition of the *Grammar* the books have been altered in the following ways:

1 Some exercises have been transferred from Book 1 to Book 2 and some from Book 2 to Book 1. Where exercises on similar structures appear in both books, those in Book 2 are slightly more difficult than those in Book 1.

2 The sequence of the exercises in both books has been rearranged to conform to the order of chapters in the *Grammar*.

3 Four exercises have been added to Book 1, bringing the total to 100, and one to Book 2, bringing the total to 90.

4 Changes have been made to the text of some of the exercises, chiefly in Book 1.

5 The grading of the exercises has now been extended to both books. ■ means difficult, ▨ means moderately difficult and ☐ means easy. The gradings are printed at the head of each exercise.

6 The numbers printed after 'PEG' at the head of each exercise now refer to paragraphs in the fourth edition of the *Grammar*.

Answers have been supplied to most of the exercises. They are to be found in the key at the end of each book.

Some of the exercises are in the form of a dialogue between two people. Where the speakers are not named, a change of speaker is shown by the symbol ' ~ '.

Contents

1 Articles

PEG chapter 1

2 Auxiliary verbs

PEG chapters 10–16

7

Contents

3 Present and past tenses
PEG chapters 17–18

4 Future forms
PEG chapter 19

5 Conditionals
PEG chapter 21

6 Infinitive
PEG chapter 23

7 Gerund, infinitive and participles
PEG chapters 23–6

8 Passive
PEG chapter 30

Contents

9 Indirect speech
PEG chapter 31

10 Purpose
PEG chapter 33

Key

1 Articles

1 Articles: a/an

◾ PEG 1–4

Insert **a** or **an** if necessary.

1 My neighbour is . . . photographer; let's ask him for . . . advice about colour films.
2 We had . . . fish and . . . chips for . . . lunch. ~
   That doesn't sound . . . very interesting lunch.
3 I had . . . very bad night; I didn't sleep . . . wink.
4 He is . . . vegetarian; you won't get . . . meat at his house. He'll give you . . . nut cutlet. ~
   Last time I had . . . nut cutlet I had . . . indigestion.
5 . . . travel agent would give you . . . information about . . . hotels.
6 We'd better go by . . . taxi—if we can get . . . taxi at such . . . hour as 2 a.m.
7 . . . person who suffers from . . . claustrophobia has . . . dread of being confined in . . . small space, and would always prefer . . . stairs to . . . lift.
8 Do you take . . . sugar in . . . coffee? ~
   I used to, but now I'm on . . . diet. I'm trying to lose . . . weight.
9 . . . man suffering from . . . shock should not be given anything to drink.
10 You'll get . . . shock if you touch . . . live wire with that screwdriver. Why don't you get . . . screwdriver with . . . insulated handle?
11 It costs fifty-five and . . . half pence and I've only got . . . fifty pence piece. ~
   You can pay by . . . cheque here. ~
   But can I write . . . cheque for . . . fifty-five and . . . half pence?
12 . . . Mr Smith is . . . old customer and . . . honest man. ~
   Why do you say that? Has he been accused of . . . dishonesty?
13 I'm not . . . wage-earner; I'm . . . self-employed man. I have . . . business of my own. ~
   Then you're not . . . worker; you're . . . capitalist!
14 When he was charged with . . . murder he said he had . . . alibi.
15 . . . friend of mine is expecting . . . baby. If it's . . . girl she's going to be called Etheldreda. ~
   What . . . name to give . . . girl!

16 I have . . . hour and . . . half for lunch. ~
I only have . . . half . . . hour—barely . . . time for . . . smoke and . . .
cup of coffee.

17 I hope you have . . . lovely time and . . . good weather. ~
But I'm not going for . . . holiday; I'm going on . . . business.

18 He looked at me with . . . horror when I explained that I was . . .
double agent.

19 I wouldn't climb . . . mountain for £1,000! I have . . . horror of . . .
heights.

X 20 I have . . . headache and . . . sore throat. I think I've got . . . cold. ~
I think you're getting . . . flu.

21 . . . Mr Jones called while you were out (*neither of us knows this
man*). He wants to make . . . complaint about . . . article in the
paper. He was in . . . very bad temper.

22 If you go by . . . train you can have quite . . . comfortable journey,
but make sure you get . . . express, not . . . train that stops at all the
stations.

23 . . . few people know (*hardly anyone knows*) that there is . . . secret
passage from this house to . . . old smugglers' cave in the cliffs.

24 I'm having . . . few friends in to . . . coffee tomorrow evening.
Would you like to come? ~
I'd love to, but I'm afraid I'm going to . . . concert.

25 It's time you had . . . holiday. You haven't had . . . day off for . . .
month.

26 He broke . . . leg in . . . skiing accident. It's still in . . . plaster.

X 27 I want . . . assistant with . . . knowledge of French and . . .
experience of . . . office routine.

28 I see that your house is built of . . . wood. Are you insured against
. . . fire?

29 The escaping prisoner camped in . . . wood but he didn't light . . .
fire because . . . smoke rising from the wood might attract . . .
attention.

30 I had . . . amazing experience last night. I saw . . . dinosaur eating
. . . meat pie in . . . London park. ~
You mean you had . . . nightmare. Anyway, dinosaurs didn't eat . . .
meat.

31 I'll pay you . . . hundred . . . week. It's not . . . enormous salary but
after all you are . . . completely unskilled man.

X 32 If you kept . . . graph you could see at . . . glance whether you were
making . . . profit or . . . loss.

33 . . . little (*hardly anything*) is known about the effect of this drug; yet
. . . chemist will sell it to you without . . . prescription.

34 I have . . . little money left; let's have dinner in . . . restaurant.

X 35 Would it be . . . trouble to you to buy me . . . newspaper on your
way home?

36 . . . man is . . . reasoning animal.

2 Articles: the

☑ PEG 6-8

Insert **the** if necessary.

1 . . . youngest boy has just started going to . . . school; . . . eldest boy is at . . . college.

2 She lives on . . . top floor of an old house. When . . . wind blows, all . . . windows rattle.

3 . . . darkness doesn't worry . . . cats; . . . cats can see in . . . dark.

4 My little boys say that they want to be . . . spacemen, but most of them will probably end up in . . . less dramatic jobs.

5 Do you know . . . time? ~
Yes, . . . clock in . . . hall has just struck nine. ~
Then it isn't . . . time to go yet.

6 He was sent to . . . prison for . . . six months for . . . shop-lifting. When . . . six months are over he'll be released; . . . difficulty then will be to find . . . work. ~
Do you go to . . . prison to visit him?

7 I went to . . . school to talk to . . . headmistress. I persuaded her to let Ann give up . . . gymnastics and take . . . ballet lessons instead.

8 . . . ballet isn't much use for . . . girls; it is much better to be able to play . . . piano.

9 I am on . . . night duty. When you go to . . . bed, I go to . . . work.

0 Peter's at . . . office but you could get him on . . . phone. There's a telephone box just round . . . corner

1 He got . . . bronchitis and was taken to . . . hospital. I expect they'll send him home at . . . end of . . . week. ~
Have you rung . . . hospital to ask how he is?

2 Ann's habit of riding a motorcycle up and down . . . road early in . . . morning annoyed . . . neighbours and in . . . end they took her to . . . court.

3 He first went to . . . sea in a Swedish ship, so as well as learning . . . navigation he had to learn . . . Swedish.

4 . . . family hotels are . . . hotels which welcome . . . parents and . . . children.

5 On . . . Sundays my father stays in . . . bed till ten o'clock, reading . . . Sunday papers.

6 Then he gets up, puts on . . . old clothes, has . . . breakfast and starts . . . work in . . . garden.

7 My mother goes to . . . church in . . . morning, and in . . . afternoon goes to visit . . . friends.

8 Like many women, she loves . . . tea parties and . . . gossip.

9 My parents have . . . cold meat and . . . salad for . . . supper, . . . winter and . . . summer.

0 During . . . meal he talks about . . . garden and she tells him . . . village gossip.

Articles

21 We have a very good train service from here to . . . city centre and
most people go to . . . work by train. You can go by . . . bus too, of
course, but you can't get a season ticket on . . . bus.

22 . . . dead no longer need . . . help. We must concern ourselves with
. . . living. We must build . . . houses and . . . schools and . . .
playgrounds.

23 I'd like to see . . . Mr Smith please. ~
Do you mean . . . Mr Smith who works in . . . box office or . . . other
Mr Smith?

24 Did you come by . . . air? ~
No, I came by . . . sea. I had a lovely voyage on . . . Queen
Elizabeth II.

25 . . . most of . . . stories that . . . people tell about . . . Irish aren't
true.

26 . . . married couples with . . . children often rent . . . cottages by . . .
seaside for . . . summer holidays.
. . . men hire boats and go for . . . trips along . . . coast; . . . children
spend . . . day on . . . beach and . . . poor mothers spend . . . most of
. . . time doing . . . cooking and cleaning.

27 It's usually safe to walk on . . . sand, but here, when . . . tide is
coming in, . . . sand becomes dangerously soft. . . . people have been
swallowed up by it.

28 When . . . Titanic was crossing . . . Atlantic she struck an iceberg
which tore a huge hole in her bow. . . . captain ordered . . . crew to
help . . . passengers into . . . boats.

29 Everywhere . . . man has cut down . . . forests in order to cultivate
. . . ground, or to use . . . wood as . . . fuel or as . . . building
material.

30 But . . . interference with . . . nature often brings . . . disaster. . . .
tree-felling sometimes turns . . . fertile land into a dustbowl.

31 . . . people think that . . . lead is . . . heaviest metal, but . . . gold is
heavier.

32 Our air hostess said, '. . . rack is only for . . . light articles. . . .
heavy things such as . . . bottles must be put on . . . floor.'

33 . . . windows are supposed to let in . . . light; but . . . windows of this
house are so small that we have to have . . . electric light on all . . .
time.

34 There'll always be a conflict between . . . old and . . . young. . . .
young people want . . . change but . . . old people want . . . things to
stay . . . same.

35 . . . power tends to corrupt and . . . absolute power corrupts
absolutely.

36 You can fool some of . . . people all . . . time, and all . . . people
some of . . . time; but you cannot fool all . . . people all . . . time.

14

3 Articles: a/an, the

☑ PEG 1–8

Insert **a, an** or **the** if necessary.

1 There was . . . knock on . . . door. I opened it and found . . . small dark man in . . . blue overcoat and . . . woollen cap.
2 He said he was . . . employee of . . . gas company and had come to read . . . meter.
3 But I had . . . suspicion that he wasn't speaking . . . truth because . . . meter readers usually wear . . . peaked caps.
4 However, I took him to . . . meter, which is in . . . dark corner under . . . stairs (. . . meters are usually in . . . dark corners under . . . stairs).
5 I asked if he had . . . torch; he said he disliked torches and always read . . . meters by . . . light of . . . match.
6 I remarked that if there was . . . leak in . . . gaspipe there might be . . . explosion while he was reading . . . meter.
7 He said, 'As . . . matter of . . . fact, there was . . . explosion in . . . last house I visited; and Mr Smith, . . . owner of . . . house, was burnt in . . . face.'
8 'Mr Smith was holding . . . lighted match at . . . time of . . . explosion.'
9 To prevent . . . possible repetition of this accident, I lent him . . . torch.
10 He switched on . . . torch, read . . . meter and wrote . . . reading down on . . . back of . . . envelope.
11 I said in . . . surprise that . . . meter readers usually put . . . readings down in . . . book.
12 He said that he had had . . . book but that it had been burnt in . . . fire in . . . Mr Smith's house.
13 By this time I had come to . . . conclusion that he wasn't . . . genuine meter reader; and . . . moment he left . . . house I rang . . . police.
14 Are John and Mary . . . cousins? ~
No, they aren't . . . cousins; they are . . . brother and . . . sister.
15 . . . fog was so thick that we couldn't see . . . side of . . . road. We followed . . . car in front of us and hoped that we were going . . . right way.
16 I can't remember . . . exact date of . . . storm, but I know it was . . . Sunday because everybody was at . . . church. On . . . Monday . . . post didn't come because . . . roads were blocked by . . . fallen trees.
17 Peter thinks that this is quite . . . cheap restaurant.
18 There's been . . . murder here. ~
Where's . . . body? ~
There isn't . . . body. ~
Then how do you know there's been . . . murder?

Articles

19 Number . . . hundred and two, . . . house next door to us, is for sale.
It's quite . . . nice house with . . . big rooms. . . . back windows look
out on . . . park.

20 I don't know what . . . price . . . owners are asking. But Dry and Rot
are . . . agents. You could give them . . . ring and make them . . .
offer.

21 . . . postman's little boy says that he'd rather be . . . dentist than . . .
doctor, because . . . dentists don't get called out at . . . night.

22 Just as . . . air hostess (*there was only one on the plane*) was handing
me . . . cup of . . . coffee . . . plane gave . . . lurch and . . . coffee
went all over . . . person on . . . other side of . . . gangway.

23 There was . . . collision between . . . car and . . . cyclist at . . .
crossroads near . . . my house early in . . . morning. . . . cyclist was
taken to . . . hospital with . . . concussion. . . . driver of . . . car was
treated for . . . shock. . . . witnesses say that . . . car was going at
. . . seventy miles . . . hour.

24 Professor Jones, . . . man who discovered . . . new drug that
everyone is talking about, refused to give . . . press conference.

25 Peter Piper, . . . student in . . . professor's college, asked him why
he refused to talk to . . . press.

26 We're going to . . . tea with . . . Smiths today, aren't we? Shall we
take . . . car? ~
We can go by . . . car if you wash . . . car first. We can't go to . . .
Mrs Smith's in . . . car all covered with . . . mud.

27 He got . . . job in . . . south and spent . . . next two years doing . . .
work he really enjoyed.

28 It is . . . pleasure to do . . . business with such . . . efficient
organization.

29 . . . day after . . . day passed without . . . news, and we began to lose
. . . hope.

30 Would you like to hear . . . story about . . . Englishman, . . .
Irishman and . . . Scotsman? ~
No. I've heard . . . stories about . . . Englishmen, . . . Irishmen and
. . . Scotsmen before and they are all . . . same.

31 But mine is not . . . typical story. In my story . . . Scotsman is
generous, . . . Irishman is logical and . . . Englishman is romantic. ~
Oh, if it's . . . fantastic story I'll listen with . . . pleasure.

32 My aunt lived on . . . ground floor of . . . old house on . . . River
Thames. She was very much afraid of . . . burglars and always
locked up . . . house very carefully before she went to . . . bed. She
also took . . . precaution of looking under . . . bed to see if . . .
burglar was hiding there.

33 '. . . modern burglars don't hide under . . . beds,' said her daughter.
'I'll go on looking just . . . same,' said my aunt.

34 One morning she rang her daughter in . . . triumph. 'I found . . .
burglar under . . . bed . . . last night,' she said, 'and he was quite . . .
young man.'

16

35 . . . apples are sold by . . . pound. These are forty pence . . . pound.
36 It was . . . windy morning but they hired . . . boat and went for . . .
sail along . . . coast. In . . . afternoon . . . wind increased and they
soon found themselves in . . . difficulties.

4 Articles and possessive adjectives

■ PEG 1–8, 62–3

Insert **a, an, the**, or **my, his, her, our, your, their** if necessary.

1 He took off . . . coat and set to work.
2 Why are you standing there with . . . hands in . . . pockets?
3 At most meetings . . . people vote by raising . . . right hands.
4 The bullet struck him in . . . foot.
5 They tied . . . hands behind . . . back and locked him in a cellar.
6 He took . . . shoes off and entered on . . . tiptoe.
7 Someone threw . . . egg which struck the speaker on . . . shoulder.
8 I have . . . headache.
9 I have . . . pain in . . . shoulder.
10 The windscreen was smashed and the driver was cut in . . . face by
broken glass.
11 He was . . . very tall man with . . . dark hair and . . . small beard,
but I couldn't see . . . eyes because he was wearing . . . dark glasses.
12 He tore . . . trousers getting over a barbed wire fence.
13 Brother and sister were quite unlike each other. He had . . . fair
wavy hair; . . . hair was dark and straight.
14 She pulled . . . sleeve to attract his attention.
15 She pulled him by . . . sleeve.
16 'Hands up!' said the masked man, and we all put . . . hands up.
17 Ask . . . woman in front of you to take off . . . hat.
18 He stroked . . . chin thoughtfully.
19 If you're too hot why don't you take off . . . coat?
20 I saw him raise . . . right hand and take . . . oath.
21 The lioness bit him in . . . leg.
22 You should change . . . wet shoes, or you'll catch another cold.
23 There was a shot and a policeman came out with . . . blood running
down . . . face.
24 We shook . . . hands with . . . host.
25 He fell off his horse and injured . . . back.
26 The barman seized the drunk by . . . collar.
27 Leave . . . coats in . . . cloakroom; don't bring them into . . . theatre.
28 He fell down a flight of stairs and broke . . . rib.
29 He pointed to a woman in . . . green dress.
30 He is . . . thoroughly selfish man; he wouldn't lift . . . finger to help
anyone.
31 You'll strain . . . eyes if you read in . . . bad light.

Articles

32 She was on . . . knees, scrubbing . . . kitchen floor.
33 He has . . . horrible job; I wouldn't like to be in . . . shoes.
34 You've got . . . shirt on inside out.
35 'Pull up . . . socks,' said his mother.
36 I hit . . . thumb with a hammer when I was hanging the picture.

5 a/an and one

■ PEG 4

Insert **a/an** or **one** if necessary.

1 . . . of my friends advised me to take . . . taxi; another said that
   there was quite . . . good bus service.
2 . . . friend of mine lent me . . . book by Meredith. I've only . . . more
   chapter to read. Would you like . . . loan of it afterwards? ~
   No, thanks. I read . . . of his books . . . few years ago and didn't like
   it. Besides I have . . . library book to finish. If I don't take it back
   tomorrow I'll have to pay . . . fine.
3 . . . man I met on the train told me . . . rather unusual story.
4 Most people like . . . rest after . . . hard day's work, but Tom
   seemed to have . . . inexhaustible supply of energy.
5 I've told you . . . hundred times not to come into . . . room with . . .
   hat on.
6 It's unlucky to light three cigarettes with . . . match. ~
   That's only . . . superstition. Only . . . idiot believes in superstitions.
7 He says . . . caravan is no good; he needs . . . cottage.
8 . . . plate is no good; we need . . . dozen.
9 Last time there was . . . fog here . . . plane crash-landed in . . . field
   near the airport. The crew had . . . lucky escape. . . . man broke his
   leg; the rest were unhurt.
10 You've been . . . great help to me; . . . day I will repay you.
11 My car broke down near . . . bus stop. There was . . . man waiting
   for . . . bus so I asked him for . . . advice.
12 He took . . . quick look at my car and said, 'Buy . . . new . . . .'
13 There was . . . woman there. The rest were men. ~
   There shouldn't have been even . . . woman. It was meant to be . . .
   stag party.
14 Don't tell . . . soul! Not even your wife! ~
   Of course not! I'd never tell . . . secret to . . . woman.
15 Most of the staff had been there for only . . . very short time, but
   . . . man had been there . . . year and . . . half, so he knew . . . little
   more than the rest.
16 Could you lend me . . . dictionary, please? I'm trying to do . . .
   crossword puzzle. ~
   I'm afraid I've only got . . . dictionary, and Tom's borrowed it.

18

17 . . . chop won't be enough for Tom; he'll want two; he's . . . small
man but he's got . . . big appetite.
18 'I want . . . volunteers for . . . dangerous job,' said the captain.
There was . . . long silence.
'Isn't there even . . . man who will take . . . risk?' he asked.
. . . voice called out from the back, 'Will there be . . . reward?'
19 I have . . . flat on the top floor. You get . . . lovely view from there.
20 . . . day a new director arrived. He was . . . ambitious, bad-tempered
man, and the staff took . . . instant dislike to him.
21 Suddenly . . . bullet struck . . . street lamp . . . little to Bill's left. He
looked up and saw . . . man with . . . gun standing at . . . open
window.
22 Bill fired back twice. . . . bullet hit the wall, the other broke . . .
pane of . . . glass. He heard . . . angry shout.
23 . . . day—it was . . . dry day with . . . good visibility—Tom was
driving along . . . country road in . . . borrowed car.
24 You're making . . . mistake after another. Have you . . . hangover,
or something? ~
No, but I had . . . very bad night last night. The people next door
were having . . . party. ~
. . . bad night shouldn't have such . . . effect on your work. I often
have three bad nights in succession. I live in . . . very noisy street.

2 Auxiliary verbs

6 Auxiliary verbs

☐ PEG 106-7

Auxiliaries here are used both alone and as part of various tenses of ordinary verbs.
Read the following (a) in the negative (b) in the interrogative. These sentences, except for nos. 1 and 13, could also be used for question tag exercises (see Exercise 13).

Note:

1 **may** for possibility rarely begins a sentence. Instead we use **do you think (that)** + present/future or **is** + subject + **likely** + infinitive:

    Tom may know.
    Do you think (that) Tom knows?
    Is Tom likely to know?

2 Use **needn't** as the negative of **must**.

1 It may cost £100.
2 Men should help with the housework.
3 Tom would pay her.
4 They could play the guitar.
5 We're seeing Mary tomorrow.
6 She ought to keep it in the fridge.
7 You can understand it.
8 The police were watching the house.
9 You can go with him.
10 They've got a house.
11 Your boss will be angry.
12 Tom should pay the fine.
13 They may come tonight.
14 They were cleaning their shoes.
15 He must write in French.
16 You have read the instructions.
17 These pearls are made by oysters.
18 The ice was thick enough to walk on.
19 This will take a long time.
20 They may (*permission*) take the car.
21 You've made a mistake.
22 Ann would like a skiing holiday.

3 We must do it at once.
4 Tom could come.
5 They were in a hurry.
6 There is enough salt in it.
7 You could see the sea from the house.
8 Ann will be able to drive you.
9 They had written to him.
0 We must cook it in butter.
1 It is freezing.
2 She ought to accept the offer.
3 There'll be time for tea.
4 I'm right.
5 He may be at home.
6 He used to live here.

7 Auxiliaries conjugated with do/does/did

□ PEG 106–7, 123, 126 (see also Exercise 17)

Some auxiliaries when used in certain ways make their negative and
interrogative according to the rule for ordinary verbs, i.e. with **do**.
Sometimes either form is possible.

Make the sentences (a) negative and (b) interrogative, using
do/does/did.

1 They have eggs for breakfast.
2 He needs a new coat.
3 He used to sell fruit.
4 They have to work hard.
5 She does the housework.
6 He needs more money.
7 He had a row with his boss.
8 She had a heart attack.
9 Her hair needed cutting.
0 He does his homework after supper.
1 She has a singing lesson every week.
2 She had to make a speech.
3 He does his best.
4 He has to get up at six every day.
5 The children have dinner at school.
6 She dared him to climb it.
7 You did it on purpose.
8 He has his piano tuned regularly. (*see 119*)
9 He dares to say that!
0 They had a good time.
1 The drink did him good.

21

22 My watch needs cleaning.
23 He had an accident.
24 You had your house painted.
25 She used to make her own clothes.
26 You do the exercises.
27 He had difficulty (in) getting a job.
28 He dared to interrupt the president, did he? (*Omit final* did he?)

8 Auxiliary verbs

☐ PEG 106-7

Put the following verbs into the past tense. (Auxiliaries are used both by themselves and as part of certain forms and tenses of ordinary verbs.)
Use **had to** as the past tense of **must** and **didn't need** as a past tense of **needn't**.

1 He isn't working hard.
2 She doesn't like cats.
3 I can't say anything.
4 We must read it carefully.
5 He won't help us.
6 He can lift it easily.
7 It isn't far from London.
8 Isn't it too heavy to carry?
9 He needn't pay at once.
10 He hopes that Tom will be there. (He hoped . . .)
11 How much does this cost?
12 He says that Ann may be there. (He said . . .)
13 How old is he?
14 Do you see any difference?
15 I do what I can.
16 How far can you swim?
17 I must change my shoes.
18 Tom dares not complain.
19 I don't dare (to) touch it.
20 Have you time to do it?
21 Are you frightened?
22 Must you pay for it yourself?
23 The letter needn't be typed.
24 We hope that he'll come. (We hoped. . .)
25 He says that she may not be in time. (He said that she . . .)
26 Do you understand what he is saying? I don't.
27 There are accidents every day at these crossroads.
28 She thinks that it may cost £100. (She thought that it . . .)
29 Doesn't Mr Pitt know your address?

30 They aren't expecting me, are they?
31 He thinks that the snakes may be dangerous. (*see 28*)
32 She wants to know if she can borrow the car. (She wanted to know if . . .)
33 Can't you manage on £100 a week?
34 Tom is certain that he will win.
35 Can you read the notice? No, I can't.
36 I don't think that the bull will attack us.

9 Auxiliary verbs

☐ PEG 108

Answer the following questions (a) in the affirmative (b) in the negative, in each case repeating the auxiliary and using a pronoun as subject.
>   Do you need this? ~ *Yes, I do/No, I don't.*
>   Can Tom swim? ~ *Yes, he can/No, he can't.*

Note also:
>   Is that Bill? ~ *Yes, it is/No, it isn't.*
>   Will there be time? ~ *Yes, there will/No, there won't.*

Use **needn't** in 7 and 15. Use **must** in 26 and 35.

1 Is the water deep?
2 Do you know the way?
3 Can you swim?
4 Does he come every day?
5 Is that Tom over there?
6 Are you Tom's brother?
7 Must you go?
8 Are you enjoying yourselves?
9 Did he see you?
10 Would £10 be enough?
11 May I borrow your car?
12 Is this the front of the queue?
13 Will she be there?
14 Do you play cards?
15 Should I tell the police?
16 Can you cook?
17 Are you ready?
18 Could women join the club?
19 Is your name Pitt?
20 Were they frightened?
21 Will his mother be there?
22 Ought I to get a new one?
23 Should I tell him the truth?

24 Was the driver killed?
25 Have you any money?
26 Need we finish the exercise?
27 Used he to ride in races?
28 Would you like to see him?
29 Is this yours?
30 Do you want it?
31 Can I take it?
32 Will you bring it back tomorrow?
33 Are you free this evening?
34 Am I in your way?
35 Need I wear a tie?
36 Was that Bill on the phone?

10 Additions to remarks, using auxiliary verbs

□ PEG 112

Part 1 Add to the following remarks using (**and**) **so** + the
noun/pronoun in brackets + the auxiliary. If there is an auxiliary in
the first remark repeat this; if not use **do/does/did**.
    He lives in London. (I) He lives in London *and so do I*.
    He had to wait. (you) He had to wait *and so had you*.

1 I have read it. (John)
2 He is a writer. (she)
3 Tom can speak Welsh. (his wife)
4 She ought to get up. (you)
5 I should be wearing a seat belt. (you)
6 John will be there. (Tom)
7 The first bus was full. (the second)
8 I bought a ticket. (my brother)
9 You must come. (your son)
10 This bus goes to Piccadilly. (that)
11 I'm getting out at the next stop. (my friend)
12 He used to work in a restaurant. (I)

Part 2 Add to the following remarks using (**and**) **neither/nor** + the
auxiliary + the noun/pronoun in brackets.
    He isn't back. (she) He isn't back *and neither is she*.

13 I haven't seen it. (Tom)
14 You shouldn't be watching TV. (Tom)
15 You mustn't be late. (I)
16 He can't come. (his sister)
17 I don't believe it. (Ann)
18 Alice couldn't understand. (Andrew)

19 I'm not going. (you)
20 This telephone doesn't work. (that)
21 Tom's car won't start. (mine)
22 I hadn't any change. (the taxi driver)
23 He didn't know the way. (anyone else)
24 My father wouldn't mind. (my mother)

Part 3 Contrary additions.
Add to the following remarks using **but** + noun/pronoun + the auxiliary or **do/does/did**. Make a negative addition to an affirmative remark:
  She thanked me. (he) She thanked me *but he didn't*.
Make an affirmative addition to a negative remark:
  She can't eat oysters. (I) She can't eat oysters *but I can*.

Use **needn't** as the negative of **must**, and **must** as the affirmative of **needn't**.

25 John was seasick. (Mary)
26 He wasn't there. (she)
27 You must go. (your brother)
28 My sister can speak German. (I)
29 Alexander didn't want to wait. (James)
30 Bill needn't stay. (Stanley)
31 A cat wouldn't eat it. (a dog)
32 He will enjoy it. (his wife)
33 I haven't got a computer. (my neighbour)
34 This beach is safe for bathing. (that beach)
35 I must leave early. (you)
36 You don't have to pay tax. (I)

11 Agreements and disagreements with remarks, using auxiliary verbs

☐ PEG 109

Part 1 Agreements with affirmative remarks.
Agree with the following remarks, using **yes/so** + pronoun + the auxiliary or **do/does/did**. To express surprise, use **Oh, so . . .**
  He has a good influence on her. ~ *Yes, he has.*

1 We must have a large room.
2 I was very rude.
3 She always wears dark glasses.
4 She may be a spy.
5 Tom could tell us where to go.
6 There's a snake in that basket.

7 He needs six bottles.
8 This boat is leaking!
9 His revolver was loaded.
10 This restaurant might be expensive.
11 They used to have a parrot.
12 The fog is getting thicker.

Part 2 Agreements with negative remarks.
Agree with the following remarks, using **no** + pronoun + the auxiliary.
Elephants never forget. ~ *No, they don't.*

13 Cuckoos don't build nests.
14 He didn't complain.
15 It isn't worth keeping.
16 He can't help coughing.
17 The ice wasn't thick enough.
18 The lift wouldn't come down.
19 This flat hasn't got very thick walls.
20 They don't have earthquakes there.
21 The oranges didn't look very good.
22 It hasn't been a bad summer.
23 I don't look my age.
24 He mightn't like that colour.

Part 3 Disagreements with affirmative or negative remarks.
Disagree with the following remarks, using **oh no/but** + pronoun + auxiliary. Use a negative auxiliary if the first verb is affirmative and an affirmative auxiliary if the first verb is negative.
He won't be any use. ~ *(Oh) yes, he will.*
She worked here for a year. ~ *(Oh) no, she didn't.*

25 You're drunk.
26 I didn't do it on purpose.
27 They weren't in your way.
28 I wasn't born then.
29 She'd rather live alone.
30 You gave him my address.
31 I can use your bicycle.
32 That five pound note belongs to me.
33 He didn't mean to be rude.
34 Children get too much pocket money.
35 Exams should be abolished.
36 She promised to obey him.

12 Question tags after negative statements

☐ PEG 110

Add question tags to the following statements.
Bill doesn't know Ann.
Bill doesn't know Ann, does he?
Ann hasn't got a phone.
Ann hasn't got a phone, has she?
this/that (subject) becomes **it** in the tag. **there** remains unchanged:
That isn't Tom, is it?
There won't be time, will there?
All the tags, except the tag for no. 30, should be spoken in the usual way with a statement intonation. But they could also be practised with a question intonation. The important word in the statement must then be stressed.

1 You aren't afraid of snakes.
2 Ann isn't at home.
3 You don't know French.
4 Tom didn't see her.
5 This isn't yours.
6 Mary wasn't angry.
7 Bill hasn't had breakfast.
8 You won't tell anyone.
9 I didn't wake you up.
10 Tom doesn't like oysters.
11 You don't want to sell the house.
12 It doesn't hurt.
13 People shouldn't drink and drive.
14 You aren't going alone.
15 They couldn't pay the rent.
16 You don't agree with Bill.
17 There wasn't a lot to do.
18 I needn't say anything.
19 That wasn't Ann on the phone.
20 You didn't do it on purpose.
21 This won't take long.
22 She doesn't believe you.
23 It didn't matter very much.
24 He shouldn't put so much salt in it.
25 Mary couldn't leave the children alone.
26 You aren't doing anything tonight.
27 You wouldn't mind helping me with this.
28 George hadn't been there before.
29 The children weren't surprised.
30 You wouldn't like another drink.

31 Tom doesn't have to go to lectures.
32 Bill hasn't got a car.
33 Bill couldn't have prevented it.
34 I needn't wait any longer.
35 There weren't any mosquitoes.
36 The fire wasn't started deliberately.

13 Question tags after affirmative statements

☑ PEG 110

Add question tags to the following statements:
   Tom goes to Bath quite often, *doesn't he?*
   He told you about his last trip, *didn't he?*
   It was very cold last night, *wasn't it?*

Be careful of the contractions **'s** and **'d**:
   He's ready, *isn't he?*   He's finished, *hasn't he?*
   He'd seen it, *hadn't he?* He'd like it, *wouldn't he?*

These should be practised mainly with a statement intonation, but they could also be said with a question intonation. See notes to previous exercise.

1 The children can read French.
2 He's ten years old.
3 Bill came on a bicycle.
4 The Smiths have got two cars.
5 Your grandfather was a millionaire.
6 Tom should try again.
7 It could be done.
8 Your brother's here.
9 That's him over there.
10 George can leave his case here.
11 This will fit in your pocket.
12 His wife has headaches quite often.
13 She's got lovely blue eyes.
14 The twins arrived last night.
15 Mary paints portraits.
16 Bill puts the money in the bank.
17 Bill put the money in the bank.
18 Prices keep going up.
19 I've seen you before.
20 Bill's written a novel.
21 His mother's very proud of him.
22 The twins used to play rugby.
23 Tom might be at home now.
24 We must hurry.

25 You'd been there before.
26 You'd like a drink.
27 The boys prefer a cooked breakfast.
28 Mary ought to cook it for them.
29 That was Ann on the phone.
30 The Smiths need two cars.
31 You'll help me.
32 He used to eat raw fish.
33 There'll be plenty for everyone.
34 You'd better wait for Bill.
35 You'd come if I needed help.
36 You could come at short notice.

4 Question tags: mixed

◪ PEG 110

See notes to Exercises 12 and 13.
Note that a statement containing words such as **none**, **nobody**,
hardly/hardly any etc. is treated as a negative statement:
  He hardly ever makes a mistake, does he?

When the subject is **nobody/anybody/everybody** etc., the pronoun
they is used in the tag:
  Nobody liked the play, did they?

Add question tags to the following statements.

1 You take sugar in tea.
2 But you don't take it in coffee.
3 The lift isn't working today.
4 It never works very well.
5 The area was evacuated at once.
6 There was no panic.
7 Though everybody realized the danger.
8 There was a lot of noise.
9 But nobody complained.
10 Mary hardly ever cooks.
11 She buys convenience foods.
12 She'd save money if she bought fresh food.
13 Mr Smith usually remembered his wife's birthdays.
14 But he didn't remember this one.
15 And his wife was very disappointed.
16 He ought to have made a note of it.
17 Neither of them offered to help you.
18 They don't allow pet dogs in this shop.
19 But guide dogs can come in.
20 He hardly ever leaves the house.

21 That isn't Bill driving.
22 Nothing went wrong.
23 Lions are loose in this reserve.
24 So we'd better get back in the car.
25 It'd be unpleasant to be attacked by a lion.
26 And it wouldn't be any use running away.
27 It is a pity Ann didn't come with us.
28 She'd have enjoyed it.
29 They should have planned the expedition more carefully.
30 Lives were lost unnecessarily.
31 She warned him not to ride the stallion.
32 But he never takes advice.
33 There used to be trees here.
34 There isn't any point in waiting.
35 He'll hardly come now.
36 Your central heating doesn't work very well.

15 Auxiliaries followed by full or bare infinitive

☐ PEG 246

Put **to** where necessary before the infinitives in brackets.

1 You needn't (come) tomorrow.
2 People used (travel) on horseback.
3 I'll have (hurry).
4 You ought (take) a holiday.
5 I'll (lend) him some money.
6 You are (go) at once.
7 We didn't have (pay) anything.
8 There won't (be) enough room for everyone.
9 You can (see) the windmill from here.
10 He was able (explain).
11 We may have (stay) here all night.
12 He used (spend) a lot of time in his library.
13 He didn't dare (say) anything.
14 Don't (move).
15 We'll (look) for a hotel.
16 You needn't (look) for a hotel; I'll be able (put) you up.
17 The doctor said that I ought (give up) smoking.
18 He used (drink) quite a lot.
19 He should (be) ready by now.
20 May I (ask) you a question?
21 I shan't be able (do) it till after the holidays.
22 I didn't need (say) anything.
23 How dare you (open) my letters!
24 They ought (warn) people about the dangerous currents.

25 I should (say) nothing about it if I were you.
26 You are not (mention) this to anyone.
27 Why do they (obey) him? ~
   They don't dare (refuse).
28 You must (look) both ways before crossing the road.
29 Your map may (have been) out of date.
30 You ought (have finished) it last night.
31 I must (say) I think you behaved very badly.
32 I will have (carry) a tent.
33 We've got (get out).
34 It might (kill) somebody.
35 Ought you (be) watching TV?
36 Shouldn't you (be) doing your homework?

6 Auxiliaries: mixed

◢ PEG chapters 11–16

Fill each of the following gaps with a suitable auxiliary or auxiliary form.

1 Schoolboy to friend: I left my book at home. . . . I share yours?
2 I'm taking swimming lessons. I hope to . . . to swim by the end of the month.
3 You . . . better take off your wet shoes.
4 I'm sorry I'm late. I . . . to wait ages for a bus.
5 Teacher: You . . . (obligation) read the play, but you . . . (no obligation) read the preface.
6 I knew he was wrong but I . . . (hadn't the courage) to tell him so.
7 You're getting fat. You . . . to cut down on your beer drinking.
8 He . . . to smoke very heavily. Now he hardly smokes at all.
9 The new motorway . . . opened this afternoon. (plan)
10 I've come without any money. . . . you possibly lend me £5?
11 Ann: . . . we meet at Piccadilly Circus?
12 Tom: It . . . be better to meet at the theatre. We . . . miss one another at Piccadilly.
13 . . . you like to come canoeing with me next weekend?
14 Mary: I . . . to pay 20p. for this little chap on the bus yesterday.
15 Ann: My little boy's under three so I . . . (No obligation. Use present tense.) to pay for him.
16 The plane . . . landed (unfulfilled plan) at Heathrow, but it has been diverted to Gatwick.
17 You've spelt it wrong. There . . . be another 's'.
18 You . . . told me! (I'm disappointed that you didn't tell me.)
19 We . . . to take a taxi. Otherwise we'll be late.

20 At the holiday camp we . . . to get up at six and bathe in the river. Then we . . . come back and cook an enormous breakfast. (*routine actions*)
21 Tom . . . know the address. (*Tom probably knows.*)
22 Tom . . . know the address. (*I'm sure that Tom knows.*)
23 I've lost my umbrella! I . . . left it on the bus! (*deduction*)
24 Theatre regulations: At the end of the performance the public . . . (*are permitted to*) leave by all exit doors.
25 If I . . . you I'd get a taxi.
26 Did you paint it yourself or did you . . . it painted?
27 You . . . (*negative*) to be driving so fast. There's a speed limit here.
28 You . . . (*request*) get me some aspirin when you're at the chemist's.

17 have: possessive

◪ PEG 122

In British English, **have** meaning **possess** is not normally conjugated with **do** except when there is an idea of habit.

I haven't (got) a watch.   (present possession)
How many corners *has* a   (a characteristic rather than a habit
cube?
He *doesn't* usually *have* time   (habit)
to study.

In the past, **did** is used for habit; otherwise either form is possible:
Did you have/Had you an umbrella when you left the house?

In other English-speaking countries, however, the **do** forms are used almost exclusively. It would therefore be possible to use **do/did** forms throughout the following exercises (except in no. 27), but students are asked to use **have not/have you** forms where they could be used. Where both are equally usual this will be noted in the key.

Fill the spaces with the correct forms of **have**, adding **got** where possible. Only one space will be left in each clause, but note that **got** may be separated from **have** by another word. When a negative form is required '(*negative*)' will be placed at the end of the example.

1 He is standing there in the rain and . . . even the sense to put up his umbrella. (*negative*)
2 He . . . a cold in the head. ~
  That's nothing new; he always . . . a cold.
3 I . . . brainwaves very often, but I . . . one now. (*1st verb negative*)
4 It is no good arguing with someone who . . . a bee in his bonnet.
5 Why don't you say something? You . . . an excuse? (*negative*)
6 You . . . this toothache yesterday?
7 How many letters . . . the alphabet?

8 The houses in your country . . . flat roofs?
9 You . . . the time? (= Do you know the time?) ~
No, I . . . a watch. (*negative*)
10 You ever . . . an impulse to smash something?
11 He . . . £1,000 a year when his father dies.
12 Air passengers usually . . . much luggage. (*negative*)
13 You . . . any objection to sitting with your back to the engine?
14 Oysters . . . always pearls in them. (*negative*)
15 Your door . . . a little hole through which you can peep at callers?
(*negative*)
16 You . . . a match on you? ~
No, I don't smoke so I never . . . matches.
17 What is your opinion? ~
I . . . an opinion. (*negative*)
18 That cup . . . a crack in it.
19 You . . . any suspicion who did it?
20 This desk . . . a secret drawer? ~
No, modern desks ever . . . secret drawers. (*negative*)
21 When you go to a place for the first time, you ever . . . a feeling that
you've been there before?
22 Babies . . . teeth when they're born?
23 How many sides . . . a pentagon?
24 Our cat . . . kittens every year. ~
How many she . . . each time?
25 They say that if children . . . complete freedom when they are
young, they . . . inhibitions when they grow up. (*2nd verb negative*)
26 You . . . mosquitoes in your country in summer?
27 You . . . children? ~
Yes, I . . . two, a boy and a girl.
28 You . . . a motor cycle? ~
No, I only . . . an ordinary bicycle, but I . . . a motor cycle next year.
29 Why do you suddenly want to back out? You . . . cold feet?
30 Customer: You . . . any mushrooms today?
Shopkeeper: We usually . . . them but I'm afraid we . . . any at the
moment. (*last verb negative*)
31 I think I know the man you mean. He . . . one blue eye and one
brown one? (*negative*)
32 Children nowadays . . . far too much pocket money. I . . . any when I
was at school. (*2nd verb negative*)
33 We were always getting lost in the desert. ~
You . . . compasses? (*negative*)
34 Red-haired people always . . . bad tempers?
35 Do you think we should eat this meat? It . . . a very nice smell.
(*negative*)
36 The stairs are on fire! You . . . a long rope?

18 have: various uses

☑ PEG 123

have can mean **take** (a meal/lesson/bath, etc.), **entertain** (guests), **encounter** (difficulty, etc.), **enjoy** (a time/journey, etc.). When used in these ways:
(a) **have** usually forms its negative and interrogative with **do**.
(b) **have** can be used in the continuous tenses.

Put the correct form of **have** into the following sentences. Use **am having, is having**, etc., as a future form.

1 We . . . some friends in for dinner tomorrow night.
2 You . . . a good journey yesterday?
3 Don't disturb him; he . . . a rest.
4 We . . . lunch early tomorrow.
5 How many lessons he . . . a week? ~
   He usually . . . four.
6 You . . . earthquakes in your country?
7 What time you . . . breakfast? ~
   We usually . . . it at 8.00.
8 What you . . . for breakfast? ~
   We . . . toast and coffee.
9 Why you . . . a cooked breakfast? (*negative*) ~
   It's too much trouble.
10 Why were they making such a noise? ~
   They . . . an argument.
11 You . . . a thunderstorm yesterday?
12 Come in, we . . . a debate.
13 You . . . a cup of coffee? ~
   Yes, please.
14 We . . . a meeting tomorrow to discuss safety precautions.
15 The tree just missed the roof, we . . . a very lucky escape.
16 How did you damage your car? You . . . an accident?
17 I . . . a look at that house tomorrow. If I like it I'll buy it.
18 We . . . very bad weather just now.
19 I . . . a very interesting conversation with the milkman when my
   neighbour interrupted me.
20 English people always . . . roast beef for lunch on Sundays?
21 It is difficult to learn a foreign language when you . . . an
   opportunity of speaking it. (*negative*)
22 The farmers . . . a lot of trouble with foxes at present.
23 On the whole women drivers . . . so many accidents as men drivers.
   (*negative*)
24 You . . . anything to eat before you left home? ~
   Oh yes, I . . . bacon and eggs.
25 You . . . any difficulty getting into your flat last night?

26 Are you enjoying yourself? ~
   Yes, I , . . a wonderful time.
27 How often he . . . a singing lesson?
28 You . . . a good night? ~
   No, I slept very badly.
29 Why were they late? ~
   They . . . a puncture.
30 We . . . a party here next week. Would you like to come?
31 Why didn't you speak to her? ~
   I . . . a chance. (*negative*)
32 We . . . a lecture next Monday.
33 I . . . tea with her tomorrow.
34 He . . . an operation next week.
35 He ever . . . nightmares?
36 When he got tired of it I . . . a try. ~
   You . . . any luck? ~
   Yes, I caught a great big fish.

19 The **have** + object + past participle construction

☑ PEG 119

Part 1 Fill in the spaces by inserting the correct form of **have**. Use
am/is/are having as a future form. (**get** can be used instead of **have**,
but is more colloquial.)

1 I . . . my house painted. That is why there is all this mess.
2 My hair looks dreadful; I think I . . . it set tomorrow.
3 The attic was dark so last year we . . . skylight put in.
4 That dead tree is dangerous. I . . . it cut down tomorrow.
5 We . . . just . . . central heating installed. The house is warm!
6 I can't read Greek so I . . . the documents translated. My nephew is
   helping with the translation.
7 . . . you . . . the film developed or did you develop it yourself?
8 Why . . . he . . . all his shoes specially made?
   He says that he has to because his feet are different sizes.
9 . . . you . . . your milk delivered or do you go to the shop for it?
10 If you hate cleaning fish why . . . you . . . them cleaned at the
   fishmonger's? (*negative*)
11 How often . . . you . . . your brakes tested?
12 I'm afraid it's rather draughty here but I . . . that broken pane
   replaced tomorrow.

Part 2 Fill in the spaces by inserting the correct form of **have**, the past participle of the verb in brackets and, where necessary, a pronoun.

13 Your ankle is very swollen. You'd better . . . it . . . (x-ray)
14 Your roof is leaking, you should . . . it . . . (repair)
15 The trousers are too long; I must . . . (shorten)
16 No one will be able to read your notes. ~
   I know; I . . . them . . . (type)
17 That's a good piano but you should . . . it . . . (tune)
18 Why don't you . . . the document . . . ? (photocopy)
19 He didn't like the colour of the curtains so he . . . (dye)
20 He went to a garage to . . . the puncture . . . (mend)
21 His arm was broken so he had to go to hospital to . . . (set)
22 The battery is all right now. I . . . just . . . it . . . (recharge)
23 It's a beautiful photo. I'm going to . . . (enlarge)
24 Be careful of those knives. I . . . just . . . (sharpen)

Part 3 Rewrite the sentences using a **have** + object + past participle construction and omitting the words in bold type.
   I **employed a plumber** to examine my boiler.
   I had my boiler examined.

25 I **pay a garage** to service my car.
26 The tap keeps dripping so I must **send for a plumber** to see to it.
27 I **paid a watchmaker** to clean my watch.
28 **An artist** is painting her portrait. She . . .
29 They **arranged for the police** to arrest the man.
30 He **paid a lorry** driver to tow the car to a garage.
31 They are **employing builders** to build a garage.
32 I **pay a window cleaner** to clean my windows every month.
33 I **went to an oculist and** he tested my eyes for me.
34 **The old gypsy** is telling Tom's fortune. Tom . . .
35 I **asked the fishmonger** to open the oysters **for me**.
36 I **went to a jeweller and** he pierced my ears **for me**.

20 be

■ PEG 113–17, 290, 293, 300, 302

This is a general exercise which includes infinitives, subjunctives, conditionals, and some examples of the **be** + infinitive construction When this last construction or a passive construction is required the second verb is given in brackets at the end of the sentence.
   Why are all those dogs wearing harness? ~
   They . . . as guide dogs for the blind. (train)
   They are being trained as guide dogs for the blind.

Fill the spaces in the following sentences by inserting the correct form of **be** with, where necessary, the past participle or present or perfect infinitive of the verb in brackets.

Remember that, in the passive, **be** can be used in the continuous tenses.

1 They are cutting down all the trees. The countryside . . . (ruin)
2 The Prime Minister . . . a speech tonight. (make)
3 If I . . . you I'd go on to the next exercise.
4 . . . late once is excusable but . . . late every day is not.
5 He ordered that all lights . . . (extinguish)
6 How long you . . . here?
7 My flat was full of dust because the old house just opposite . . . (pull down)
8 He asked where he . . . it. (put)
   I told him to put it on the mantelpiece.
9 It . . . difficult to read a newspaper upside down? (*Use negative.*)
10 You . . . here till I return. That is an order. (stay)
11 He suggests that prominent people . . . to contribute. (ask)
12 Even if you . . . to go on your knees to him I don't think it would make him change his mind.
13 I . . . on a catering course when I leave school. My parents have arranged it. (go)
14 What is happening now? ~
   The injured man . . . out of the arena. (carry)
15 It's better . . . too early than too late.
16 I wish you . . . here. I miss you very much.
17 Why did you leave him behind? You . . . him with you. (*Those were your instructions.*) (take)
18 She is learning Italian. She . . . by a professor from Milan. (teach)
19 I know I . . . half an hour late yesterday but I . . . half an hour early tomorrow. ~
   I'd rather you . . . punctual every day. (*see 297*)
20 It is impossible . . . right every time.
21 He . . . here by seven but now it's nine and there's no sign of him. (be)
22 They decided that voting papers . . . to all members. (send)
23 There . . . eggs for breakfast tomorrow?
24 If only I . . . there! (But I wasn't.)
25 The Queen . . . the new hospital next week. (open)
26 I couldn't see the man who was guiding us and I didn't know where we . . . (take)
27 It . . . a trilogy but in the end the author found that he had only enough material for two volumes. (be)
28 You . . . very angry if I refused?
29 The matter . . . discussed in tomorrow's debate.

30 His mare . . . in tomorrow's race but he said this morning that she was sick and wouldn't be running after all. (run)
31 The house wasn't ready; it still . . . and there were pots of paint an¹ ladders everywhere. (paint)
32 They decided that an expurgated edition . . . for use in schools. (print)
33 His works are immensely popular; they . . . into all the major European languages. (translate)
34 It is high time you . . . in bed.
35 I had my instructions and I knew exactly what I . . . (do)
36 If this report . . . believed, we are going to have a very severe drought.

21 it is/there is

☑ PEG 67, 116–17

Insert **it is/there is** in the spaces. In some sentences, contracted plural, negative and interrogative forms, or the past or future tense are required.

1 What's the time? ~ . . . . . . 3.30. ~
And what's the date? ~ . . . . . . the 24th.
2 How far . . . . . . to York? ~
. . . . . . 50 miles.
3 . . . . . . very stormy last night. ~
Yes, ... storms all over the country.
4 . . . . . . freezing very hard. . . . . ice on the lake tomorrow.
5 As . . . . . . sunny she decided to take the children to the sea.
6 Why don't you go for a walk? . . . . . . a pity to stay in when . . . . so nice outside.
7 . . . . . . not any shadows because . . . . . . not any sun.
8 . . . . . . going to be a bus strike tomorrow. ~
. . . . all right if . . . . . . a fine day; but if . . . . . . wet
. . . . long queues on the Underground.
9 . . . . . . not any glass in the windows; that is why . . . . . . so cold ¹ the room.
10 . . . . . . very wet yesterday; . . . . . . impossible to go out.
11 . . . . . . a lot of rain last week. . . . . . . floods everywhere.
12 . . . . . . a thick fog last night. . . . . . . several accidents on the motorway.
13 . . . . . . foolish to drive fast when . . . . . . foggy.
14 . . . . . . difficult to find your way round this town. . . . . . . so man¹ streets all looking exactly alike.
15 Come on, children! . . . . . . time to get up! . . . . . . nearly breakfa¹ time.

16 . . . . lunch time when we get to York, so let's have lunch
there. ~
No, ... not be time for lunch because our train to Edinburgh
leaves York at 13.15.
17 . . . . . . a funny smell here. . . . . . . turpentine?
18 . . . . . . all sorts of stories about Robin Hood, but . . . . . . not
known exactly who he was or what he did.
19 . . . . . . said that if you break a mirror you'll be unlucky for seven
years.
20 As he had very bad sight . . . . . . difficult for him to recognize
people.
21 'Can I have a *Telegraph*, please?' said the customer.
'I'm afraid . . . . . . not any left,' said the newsagent. 'But . . . . . . a
Guardian on the rack beside you. Why not take that? . . . . . . just as
good.'
22 . . . . . . not necessary to carry your passport everywhere with you
but . . . . . . advisable to carry some document of identity.
23 . . . . . . a guard outside the door and . . . . . . bars on the windows.
. . . . . . impossible to escape.
24 . . . . . . a garage behind the hotel? ~
Yes, but . . . . . . rather full. I don't think . . . . . . room for your
car.
25 One night . . . . . . a heavy fall of snow which blocked all the roads.
Luckily . . . . . . plenty of food in the house.
26 . . . . . . a hotel in the village, so we decided to stay there.
. . . . . . a charming village and I was very happy there, but my
children were bored because . . . . . . nothing to do in the evenings.
27 . . . . . . five flats in the building—one on each floor. Mine's on the
top floor. . . . . . . no lift but . . . . . . supposed to be good for the
figure to run up and down stairs, ...?
28 . . . . . . a pity you haven't another bedroom. ~
Yes, but . . . . . . quite a big loft, which I am thinking of turning into
a bedroom. . . . . . . a skylight so . . . . . . not . . . a ventilation
problem.
29 . . . . . . all sorts of legends about these caves. . . . . . . said that
smugglers hid their goods here and that . . . . . . an underground
passage leading to the village inn.
30 Tell me something about *King Lear*. ~
. . . . . . the story of a king who divided his kingdom between his
daughters. . . . . . . foolish to give away your property like that. . . .
. . . never certain that your family will behave generously to you in
return.
31 Has Tom any more children? ~
Yes. . . . . . . a daughter, Ann. ~
Oh yes, ... Ann who opened the door to us yesterday, ...?
32 He thought that . . . . . . better to say nothing about his change of
plan.

33 . . . . . . a long time before I got an answer. Then one day a letter arrived—well, ... not really a letter, for . . . . . . only one sentence on the paper.
34 . . . . . . a pond beside your house? ~ Yes, ... ~ How deep . . . . . .?
35 We've done all we can. . . . . . . nothing to do now but wait.
36 Just cross out that word and go on. . . . . . . not necessary to begin again. (or . . . . . . no need to begin again.)

22 can and be able

■ PEG 136–8

Part 1   can, used to express ability with **could, shall/will be able**
Fill the following spaces, using **can** for present, **could** for past and **shall/will be able** for future. There is no need to use other **able** form in this section. Put **to** where necessary before the infinitives.

1 . . . you stand on your head? ~
   I . . . when I was at school but I . . . now. (*2nd verb negative*)
2 When I've passed my driving test I . . . hire a car from our local garage.
3 At the end of the month the Post Office will send him an enormous telephone bill which he . . . pay. (*negative*)
4 I . . . remember the address. (*negative*) ~
   . . . you even remember the street? (*negative*)
5 When the fog lifts we . . . see where we are.
6 You've put too much in your rucksack; you never . . . carry all that.
7 When I was a child I . . . understand adults, and now that I am an adult I . . . understand children. (*negative, negative*)
8 When you have taken your degree you . . . put letters after your name?
9 Don't try to look at all the pictures in the gallery. Otherwise when you get home you . . . remember any of them. (*negative*)
10 When I first went to Spain I . . . read Spanish but I . . . speak it. (*2nd verb negative*)
11 . . . you type? ~
   Yes, I . . . type but I . . . do shorthand. (*2nd verb negative*)
12 I'm locked in. I . . . get out! (*negative*) ~
   . . . you squeeze between the bars? (*negative*) ~
   No! I . . .; I'm too fat. (*negative*)

Part 2 could and was able

In some of the following sentences either **could** or **was able** could be used. In others only **was/were able** is possible. Fill the spaces and put **to** where necessary before the infinitives.

13 He was very strong; he . . . ski all day and dance all night.
14 The car plunged into the river. The driver . . . get out but the passengers were drowned.
15 I was a long way from the stage. I . . . see all right but I . . . hear very well. (*2nd verb negative*)
16 We . . . borrow umbrellas; so we didn't get wet.
17 . . . you walk or did they have to carry you?
18 I had no key so I . . . lock the door. (*negative*)
19 I knew the town so I . . . advise him where to go.
20 When the garage had repaired our car we . . . continue our journey.
21 At five years old he . . . read quite well.
22 When I arrived everyone was asleep. Fortunately I . . . wake my sister and she let me in.
23 The swimmer was very tired but he . . . reach the shore before he collapsed.
24 The police were suspicious at first but I . . . convince them that we were innocent.

Part 3 PEG 222 C, 223 B, 283–4

This section includes examples of **could** used for polite requests and as a conditional.

25 . . . I speak to Mr Pitt, please? ~
    I'm afraid he's out at the moment. . . . you ring back later?
26 If you stood on my shoulders . . . you reach the top of the wall? ~
    No, I'm afraid I . . . (*negative*)
27 If I sang . . . you accompany me on the piano? ~
    No, I . . ., I . . . play the piano! (*negative, negative*)
28 If a letter comes for me . . . you please forward it to this address?
29 She made the wall very high so that boys . . . climb over it. (*negative*)
30 They took his passport so that he . . . leave the country. (*negative*)
31 . . . you tell me the time, please? ~
    I'm afraid I. . . . I haven't got a watch. (*negative*)
32 If you had to, . . . you go without food for a week? ~
    I suppose I . . . if I had plenty of water.
33 . . . you lend me £5? ~
    No, I . . . (*negative*)
34 They used to chain valuable books to library desks so that people . . . take them away. (*negative*)
35 He says that he saw Clementine drowning but . . . help her as he . . . swim. (*negative, negative*)
36 If you had had the right tools . . . you have repaired the engine?

41

Auxiliary verbs

23 may

☐ PEG 127-33, 285, 288, 340

Insert the correct form of **may/might** except in 10 and 36, where a **be allowed** form is necessary.

1 It . . . rain, you'd better take a coat.
2 He said that it . . . rain.
3 We . . . as well stay here till the weather improves.
4 . . . I borrow your umbrella?
5 You . . . tell me! (*I think I have a right to know.*)
6 Candidates . . . not bring textbooks into the examination room.
7 People convicted of an offence . . . (*have a right to*) appeal.
8 If he knew our address he . . . come and see us.
9 . . . I come in? ~
   Please do.
10 When he was a child he . . . (*they let him*) do exactly as he liked.
11 I think I left my glasses in your office. You . . . ask your secretary t
    look for them for me. (*request*)
12 He . . . be my brother (*I admit that he is*) but I don't trust him.
13 I . . . never see you again.
14 He . . . be on the next train. We . . . as well wait.
15 If we got there early we . . . get a good seat.
16 The police . . . (*have a right to*) ask a driver to take a breath test.
17 You ought to buy now; prices . . . go up.
18 I'll wait a week so that he . . . have time to think it over.
19 He isn't going to eat it; I . . . as well give it to the dog.
20 You . . . at least read the letter. (*I think you should.*)
21 You . . . have written. (*I am annoyed/disappointed that you didn't.*)
22 We'd better be early; there . . . be a crowd.
23 Nobody knows how people first came to these islands. They . . .
    have sailed from South America on rafts.
24 You . . . (*have permission to*) use my office.
25 He said that we . . . use his office whenever we liked.
26 I don't think I'll succeed but I . . . as well try.
27 You ought to go to his lectures, you . . . learn something.
28 If we can give him a blood transfusion we . . . be able to save his
    life.
29 Two parallel white lines in the middle of the road mean that you . . .
    not overtake.
30 If I bought a lottery ticket I . . . win £1,000.
31 If you said that, he . . . be very offended.
32 I wonder why they didn't go. ~
    The weather . . . have been too bad.
33 Warning: No part of this book . . . be reproduced without the
    publisher's permission.
34 He has refused, but he . . . change his mind if you asked him again.

35 . . . I see your passport, please?
36 He . . . (*negative*) drive since his accident. (*They haven't let him drive*.)

34 must and have to

◢ PEG 144-5

Fill the spaces in the following sentences by inserting **must** or the present, future, or past form of **have to**.

1 She . . . leave home at eight every morning at present.
2 Notice in a picture gallery: Cameras, sticks and umbrellas . . . be left at the desk.
3 He sees very badly; he . . . wear glasses all the time.
4 I . . . do all the typing at my office.
5 You . . . read this book. It's really excellent.
6 The children . . . play in the streets till their mothers get home from work.
7 She felt ill and . . . leave early.
8 Mr Pitt . . . cook his own meals. His wife is away.
9 I hadn't enough money and I . . . pay by cheque.
10 I never remember his address; I always . . . look it up.
11 Employer: You . . . come to work in time.
12 If you go to a dentist with a private practice you . . . pay him quite a lot of money.
13 Father to small son: You . . . do what Mummy says.
14 My neighbour's child . . . practise the piano for three hours a day.
15 Doctor: I can't come now.
   Caller: You . . . come; he's terribly ill.
16 English children . . . stay at school till the age of 16.
17 In my district there is no gas laid on. People . . . use electricity for everything.
18 Notice above petrol pump: All engines . . . be switched off.
19 Mother to daughter: You . . . come in earlier at night.
20 The shops here don't deliver. We . . . carry everything home ourselves.
21 The buses were all full; I . . . get a taxi.
22 Notice beside escalators: Dogs and push chairs . . . be carried.
23 'Au pair' girls usually . . . do quite a lot of housework.
24 Tell her that she . . . be here by six. I insist on it.
25 When a tyre is punctured the driver . . . change the wheel.
26 Park notice: All dogs . . . be kept on leads.
27 She . . . learn how to drive when her local railway station is closed.
28 Railway notice: Passengers . . . cross the line by the footbridge.
29 I got lost and . . . ask a policeman the way.
30 Farmers . . . get up early.

Auxiliary verbs

31 If you buy that television set you . . . buy a licence for it.
32 When I changed my job I . . . move to another flat.
33 Waiters . . . pay tax on the tips that they receive.
34 Father to son: I can't support you any longer; you . . . earn your ow
   living from now on.
35 Railway notice: Passengers . . . be in possession of a ticket.
36 Whenever the dog wants to go out I . . . get up and open the door.

25 must not and need not

☐ PEG 146

Use **must not** or **need not** to fill the spaces in the following
sentences.

1 You . . . ring the bell; I have a key.
2 Notice in cinema: Exit doors . . . be locked during performances.
3 You . . . drink this: it is poison.
4 We . . . drive fast; we have plenty of time.
5 You . . . drive fast; there is a speed limit here.
6 Candidates . . . bring books into the examination room.
7 You . . . write to him for he will be here tomorrow.
8 We . . . make any noise or we'll wake the baby.
9 You . . . bring an umbrella. It isn't going to rain.
10 You . . . do all the exercise. Ten sentences will be enough.
11 We . . . reheat the pie. We can eat it cold.
12 Mother to child: You . . . tell lies.
13 You . . . turn on the light; I can see quite well.
14 You . . . strike a match; the room is full of gas.
15 You . . . talk to other candidates during the exam.
16 We . . . make any more sandwiches; we have plenty now.
17 You . . . put salt in any of his dishes. Salt is very bad for him.
18 You . . . take anything out of a shop without paying for it.
19 You . . . carry that parcel home yourself; the shop will send it.
20 You . . . clean the windows. The window-cleaner is coming
   tomorrow.
21 Mother to child: You . . . play with matches.
22 Church notice: Visitors . . . walk about the church during a service.
23 I . . . go to the shops today. There is plenty of food in the house.
24 You . . . smoke in a non-smoking compartment.
25 Police notice: Cars . . . be parked here.
26 We . . . open the lion's cage. It is contrary to Zoo regulations.
27 You . . . make your bed. The maid will do it.
28 I want this letter typed but you . . . do it today. Tomorrow will do.

29 I'll lend you the money and you . . . pay me back till next month.
30 We . . . climb any higher; we can see very well from here.
31 You . . . look under the bed. There isn't anybody there.
32 You . . . ask a woman her age. It's not polite.
33 You've given me too much. ~
   You . . . eat it all.
34 We . . . forget to shut the lift gates.
35 Mother to child: You . . . interrupt when I am speaking.
36 If you want the time, pick up the receiver and dial 8081; you . . . say
   anything.

26 need not and don't have to etc.

■ PEG 148–50

Replace the words in bold type by **need not/need I?** etc., or a
negative or interrogative **have to** form.
   I've been invited to a wedding; but I can't go. **Will it be
   necessary for me** to send a present?
   Shall I have to send a present?

1 **It isn't necessary for him to** go on working. He has already reached
   retiring age. (*He . . .*)
2 **Was it necessary for you to** wait a long time for your bus?
3 **It isn't necessary for me to** water my tomato plants every day.
4 **It will be necessary for them to** get up early when they go out to
   work every day.
5 We had to stop at the frontier but we **were not required to** open our
   cases.
6 **It wasn't necessary to** walk. He took us in his car. (*We . . .*)
7 My employer said, '**I shan't require** you tomorrow.' (*You . . . come.*)
8 **It is never necessary for me to** work on Saturdays.
9 When I am eighteen I'll be of age. Then **it won't be necessary to** live
   at home if I don't want to.
10 New teacher to his class: **It isn't necessary for you to** call me 'Sir';
   call me 'Bill'.
11 **Will it be necessary for us to** report this accident to the police?
12 When you buy something on the instalment system you **are not
   required to** pay the whole price at once.
13 Did you know enough English to ask for your ticket?
   It wasn't necessary to say anything. I bought my ticket at a machine.
14 **It isn't necessary to** buy a licence for a bicycle in England. (*We . . .*)
15 **Is it essential for you to** finish tonight?
16 **Is it necessary for people to** go everywhere by boat in Venice?
17 **Will it be necessary for me to** sleep under a mosquito net?

18 Most people think that civil servants **are not required to** work very hard.
19 **It wasn't necessary to swim.** We were able to wade across.
20 **It isn't necessary for you to** drive me to the station. I can get a taxi.
21 Our plane was delayed so we had lunch at the airport. But **it wasn't necessary to** pay for the lunch. The airline gave it to us.
22 **Is it obligatory for us to** vote?
23 When you were a child **were you required to** practise the piano?
24 I saw the accident but fortunately **it wasn't necessary for me to** give evidence as there were plenty of other witnesses.
25 Small boy to friend: **It won't be necessary for you to** work hard when you come to my school. The teachers aren't very strict.
26 They had plenty of time. **It wasn't necessary for them to** hurry.
27 **Is it necessary for you to** take your dog with you everywhere?
28 What time **was it necessary for you to** leave home?
29 I brought my passport but I **wasn't required to** show it to anyone.
30 I missed one day of the exam. **Will it be necessary for me to** take the whole exam again?
31 **Is it really necessary for you to** practise the violin at 3 a.m.?
32 Everything was done for me. **It wasn't necessary for me to** do anything.
33 **Are** French children **obliged to** go to school on Saturdays?
34 I was late for the opera. ~
Was it necessary for you to wait till the end of the first act before finding your seat?
35 He repaired my old watch so **it wasn't necessary for me to** buy a new one after all.
36 **Were you required to** make a speech?

27 must, can't and needn't with the perfect infinitive

■ PEG 152, 156, 159

must + perfect infinitive is used for affirmative deductions.
can't/couldn't + infinitive is used for negative deductions.
needn't + perfect infinitive is used for a past action which was unnecessary but was performed.

Fill the spaces in the following sentences by using one of these forms + the perfect infinitive of the verbs in brackets.

1 Did you hear me come in last night? ~
No, I . . . (be) asleep.
2 I wonder who broke the wineglass; it . . . (be) the cat for she was out all day.
3 You . . . (help) him. (*You helped him but he didn't need help.*)

4 I had my umbrella when I came out but I haven't got it now. ~
   You . . . (leave) it on the bus.
5 He . . . (escape) by this window because it is barred.
6 I . . . (give) £10. £5 would have been enough.
7 I saw a rattlesnake near the river yesterday. ~
   You . . . (see) a rattlesnake. There aren't any rattlesnakes in this
   country.
8 He is back already. ~
   He . . . (start) very early.
9 He returned home with a tiger cub. ~
   His wife (be) very pleased about that.
10 I bought two bottles of milk. ~
   You . . . (buy) milk; we have heaps in the house.
11 I phoned you at nine this morning but got no answer. ~
   I'm sorry. I . . . (be) in the garden.
12 I left my bicycle here and now it's gone. ~
   Someone . . . (borrow) it.
13 When she woke up her watch had vanished. ~
   Someone . . . (steal) it while she slept.
14 I've opened another bottle. ~
   You . . . (do) that. We've only just started this one.
15 The machine said, 'You weigh 65 kilos,' and I said, 'Thank you.' ~
   You . . . (say) anything.
16 I told him to turn left and he immediately turned right! ~
   He . . . (understand) you.
17 Perhaps he swam across. ~
   No, he . . . (do) that; he can't swim.
18 Do you remember reading about it in the newspapers? ~
   No, I . . . (be) abroad at the time.
19 He . . . (walk) from here to London in two hours. It isn't possible.
20 He was very sick last night. ~
   The meat we had for supper . . . (be) good.
21 There was a dock strike and the liner couldn't leave port. ~
   The passengers . . . (be) furious.
22 We went to a restaurant and had a very good dinner for £3. ~
   You . . . (have) a very good dinner if you only paid £3.
23 I have just watered the roses. ~
   You . . . (water) them. Look, it's raining now!
24 That carpet was made entirely by hand. ~
   It . . . (take) a long time.
25 The door was open. ~
   It . . . (be) open. I had locked it myself and the key was in my
   pocket.
26 He said that he watered the plants every day. ~
   He . . . (water) them. If he had they wouldn't have died.
27 He came out of the water with little red spots all over his back. ~
   He . . . (be) stung by a jelly-fish.

28 We've sent for a doctor. ~
   You . . . (send) for him. I am perfectly well.
29 I've made two copies. ~
   You . . . (make) two. One would have been enough.
30 There was a terrible crash at 3 a.m. ~
   That . . . (be) Tom coming in from his party.
31 I had to get down the mountain in a thick fog. ~
   That . . . (be) very difficult.
32 I saw Ann in the library yesterday. ~
   You . . . (see) her; she is still abroad.
33 How did he get out of the house? He . . . (come) down the stairs for
   they were blazing.
34 You . . . (lend) him your map. He has one of his own.
35 I spoke in English, very slowly. ~
   You . . . (speak) slowly. He speaks English very fluently.
36 He was found unconscious at the foot of the cliff. He . . . (fall) 200
   metres.

3 Present and past tenses

28 The simple present tense

☐ PEG 172

Read the following in the third person singular. Do not change the object if it is plural. Note that after certain consonants a final **es** is pronounced as a separate syllable. See PEG 12 B: *kiss, kisses* /kɪs, kɪsɪz/.

1 They wish to speak to you. (He)
2 Buses pass my house every hour.
3 They help their father. (He)
4 We change planes at Heathrow.
5 You watch too much TV. (He)
6 They worry too much. (He)
7 I cash a cheque every month. (He)
8 I always carry an umbrella. (She)
9 They wash the floor every week. (She)
10 His sons go to the local school.
11 These hens lay brown eggs.
12 Rubber balls bounce.
13 These figures astonish me.
14 Do you like boiled eggs? (he)
15 These seats cost £10.
16 They fish in the lake. (He)
17 Elephants never forget.
18 They usually catch the 8.10 bus.
19 They sometimes miss the bus.
20 I mix the ingredients together.
21 The rivers freeze in winter.
22 They fly from London to Edinburgh.
23 The carpets match the curtains.
24 They realize the danger.
25 I use a computer.
26 What do they do on their days off? ~
   They do nothing. They lie in bed all day.
27 The boys hurry home after school.
28 They push the door open.
29 They kiss their mother.
30 They box in the gymnasium.
31 They dress well.
32 Your children rely on you.

33 They snatch ladies' handbags.
34 You fry everything.
35 The taxes rise every year.
36 They do exercises every morning.

29 The simple present tense

☐ PEG 172

Read the following (a) in the negative (b) in the interrogative.

In Nos. 2 and 14, **have** is used as an ordinary verb and should be treated as one.

1 You know the answer.
2 He has breakfast at 8.00.
3 He loves her.
4 Some schoolgirls wear uniforms.
5 He trusts you.
6 He tries hard.
7 The park closes at dusk.
8 He misses his mother.
9 The children like sweets.
10 He finishes work at 6.00.
11 He lives beside the sea.
12 He bullies his sisters.
13 This stove heats the water.
14 She has a cooked breakfast.
15 She carries a sleeping bag.
16 He usually believes you.
17 She dances in competitions.
18 You remember the address.
19 She plays chess very well.
20 He worries about her.
21 These thieves work at night.
22 He leaves home at 8.00 every day.
23 Ann arranges everything.
24 She agrees with you.
25 Their dogs bark all night.
26 Their neighbours often complain.
27 Tom enjoys driving at night.
28 He engages new staff every Spring.
29 Tom looks very well.
30 They sell fresh grape juice here.
31 He charges more than other photographers.
32 She cuts her husband's hair.
33 They pick the apples in October.
34 The last train leaves at midnight.

35 He relaxes at weekends.
36 She refuses to discuss it.

30 The present continuous tense

☐ PEG 164-7

Put the verbs in brackets into the present continuous tense. In No.
25, **have** is used as an ordinary verb and can therefore be used in the
continuous tense.

1 She (not work), she (swim) in the river.
2 He (teach) his boy to ride.
3 Why Ann (not wear) her new dress?
4 The aeroplane (fly) at 2,000 metres.
5 What Tom (do) now? He (clean) his shoes.
6 This fire (go) out. Somebody (bring) more coal?
7 It (rain)? ~
   Yes, it (rain) very hard. You can't go out yet.
8 Why you (mend) that old shirt?
9 You (not tell) the truth. ~
   How do you know that I (not tell) the truth?
10 Who (move) the furniture about upstairs? ~
   It's Tom. He (paint) the front bedroom.
11 Mrs Jones (sweep) the steps outside her house.
12 What you (read) now? I (read) *Crime and Punishment*.
13 It is a lovely day. The sun (shine) and the birds (sing).
14 Someone (knock) at the door. Shall I answer it? ~
   I (come) in a minute. I just (wash) my hands.
15 She always (ring) up and (ask) questions.
16 Why you (make) a cake? Someone (come) to tea?
17 Where is Tom? ~
   He (lie) under the car.
18 Can I borrow your pen or you (use) it at the moment?
19 You (do) anything this evening? ~
   No, I'm not. ~
   Well, I (go) to the cinema. Would you like to come with me?
20 We (have) breakfast at 8.00 tomorrow as Tom (catch) an early train.
21 Ann usually does the shopping, but I (do) it today as she isn't well.
22 Why you (type) so fast? You (make) a lot of mistakes.
23 Mother (rest) now. She always rests after lunch.
24 They (dig) an enormous hole just outside my gate. ~
   What they (do) that for? ~
   I don't know. Perhaps they (look) for oil.
25 What (make) that terrible noise? ~
   It's the pneumatic drill. They (repair) the road.

26 The children are very quiet. Go and see what they (do). ~
They (cut) up some £5 notes.
27 What you (wait) for? ~
I (wait) for my change; the boy just (get) it.
28 I can't hear what you (say); the traffic (make) too much noise.
29 She always (lose) her glasses and (ask) me to look for them.
30 Mother: What you (look) at? Something (happen) in the street?
31 Child: Yes. The house opposite is on fire! Come and look.
Mother: I can't. I (bath) the babies. Is the Fire Brigade here?
32 Child: Yes. Fire engines (rush) up and the firemen (jump) out and
(unroll) their hoses.
33 Smoke (pour) from the windows! People (stop) to watch.
A policeman (try) to move them on.
34 An old man (climb) out of a first floor window!
A fireman (help) him! Two boys (slide) down a rope!
35 A woman (wave) from the attic and a fireman (go) up a ladder to
help her!
36 Now he (come) down again! He (carry) a baby! The crowd (cheer!)

31 The simple present and the present continuous

■ PEG 164–74

Put the verbs in brackets into the simple present or the present
continuous tense.

1 Cuckoos (not build) nests. They (use) the nests of other birds.
2 You can't see Tom now: he (have) a bath.
3 He usually (drink) coffee but today he (drink) tea.
4 What she (do) in the evenings? ~
She usually (play) cards or (watch) TV.
5 I won't go out now as it (rain) and I (not have) an umbrella.
6 The last train (leave) the station at 11.30.
7 He usually (speak) so quickly that I (not understand) him.
8 Ann (make) a dress for herself at the moment. She (make) all her
own clothes.
9 Hardly anyone (wear) a hat nowadays.
10 I'm afraid I've broken one of your coffee cups. ~
Don't worry. I (not like) that set anyway.
11 I (wear) my sunglasses today because the sun is very strong.
12 Tom can't have the newspaper now because his aunt (read) it.
13 I'm busy at the moment. I (redecorate) the sitting room.
14 The kettle (boil) now. Shall I make the tea?
15 You (enjoy) yourself or would you like to leave now? ~
I (enjoy) myself very much. I (want) to stay to the end.
16 How you (get) to work as a rule? ~
I usually (go) by bus but tomorrow I (go) in Tom's car.

17 Why you (put) on your coat? ~
   I (go) for a walk. You (come) with me? ~
   Yes, I'd love to come. You (mind) if I bring my dog?
18 How much you (owe) him? ~
   I (owe) him £5. ~
   You (intend) to pay him?
19 You (belong) to your local library? ~
   Yes, I do. ~
   You (read) a lot? ~
   Yes, quite a lot. ~
   How often you (change) your books? ~
   I (change) one every day.
20 Mary usually (learn) languages very quickly but she (not seem) able
   to learn modern Greek.
21 I always (buy) lottery tickets but I never (win) anything.
22 You (like) this necklace? I (give) it to my daughter for her birthday
   tomorrow.
23 I won't tell you my secret unless you (promise) not to tell anyone. ~
   I (promise).
24 You always (write) with your left hand?
25 You (love) him? ~
   No, I (like) him very much but I (not love) him.
26 You (dream) at night? ~
   Yes, I always (dream) and if I (eat) too much supper I (have)
   nightmares.
27 The milk (smell) sour. You (keep) milk a long time?
28 These workmen are never satisfied; they always (complain).
29 We (use) this room today because the window in the other room is
   broken.
30 He always (say) that he will mend the window but he never (do) it.
31 You (know) why an apple (fall) down and not up?
32 You (write) to him tonight? ~
   Yes, I always (write) to him on his birthday. You (want) to send any
   message?
33 Tom and Mr Pitt (have) a long conversation. I (wonder) what they
   (talk) about.
34 You (believe) all that the newspapers say? ~
   No, I (not believe) any of it. ~
   Then why you (read) newspapers?
35 This car (make) a very strange noise. You (think) it is all right? ~
   Oh, that noise (not matter). It always (make) a noise like that.
36 The fire (smoke) horribly. I can't see across the room. ~
   I (expect) that birds (build) a nest in the chimney. ~
   Why you (not put) wire across the tops of your chimneys? ~
   Tom (do) that sometimes but it (not seem) to make any difference.

32 The simple present and the present continuous

■ PEG 164-74

Put the verbs in brackets into the simple present or present continuous tense.

1 What Tom (think) of the Budget? ~
He (think) it most unfair. ~
I (agree) with him.
2 What this one (cost)? ~
It (cost) forty pence.
3 You (hear) the wind? It (blow) very strongly tonight.
4 You (see) my car keys anywhere? ~
No, I (look) for them but I (not see) them.
5 He never (listen) to what you say. He always (think) about
something else.
6 This book is about a man who (desert) his family and (go) to live on
a Pacific island.
7 You (understand) what the lecturer is saying? ~
No, I (not understand) him at all.
8 What you (have) for breakfast usually? ~
I usually (eat) a carrot and (drink) a glass of cold water.
9 When the curtain (rise) we (see) a group of workers. They (picket) a
factory gate.
10 Why you (walk) so fast today? You usually (walk) quite slowly. ~
I (hurry) because I (meet) my mother at 4 o'clock and she (not like)
to be kept waiting.
11 I (wish) that dog would lie down. He (keep) jumping up on my lap. ~
I (think) he (want) to go for a walk.
12 You (recognize) that man? ~
I (think) that I have seen him before but I (not remember) his name.
13 Look at that crowd. I (wonder) what they (wait) for.
14 This message has just arrived and the man (wait) in case you (want)
to send a reply.
15 Stop! You (not see) the notice? ~
I (see) it but I can't read it because I (not wear) my glasses. What it
(say)? ~
It (say) 'These premises are patrolled by guard dogs'.
16 She always (borrow) from me and she never (remember) to pay me
back.
17 You (need) another blanket or you (feel) warm enough?
18 It (save) time if you (take) the path through the wood? ~
No, it (not matter) which path you take.
19 I (save) up because I (go) abroad in July.
20 I (think) it is a pity you don't take more exercise. You (get) fat.
21 The plane that you (look) at now just (take) off for Paris.
22 Tom never (do) any work in the garden; he always (work) on his car

23 What he (do) to his car now? ~
   I (think) he (polish) it.
24 That film (come) to the local cinema next week. You (want) to see it?
25 How Peter (get) on at school? ~
   Very well. He (seem) to like the life.
26 Why Mrs Pitt (look) so angry? ~
   Mr Pitt (smoke) a cigarette and (drop) the ash on the carpet.
27 This is our itinerary. We (leave) home on the 8th, (arrive) in Paris on
   the 9th, (spend) the day in Paris, and (set) out that night for
   Venice. ~
   That (sound) most interesting. You must tell me all about it when
   you (get) back.
28 This story is about a boy who (make) friends with a snake which he
   (find) in his garden. Then he (go) away but he (not forget) the snake
   and some years later he (return) and (look) for it.
29 He (find) the snake who (recognize) its old friend and (coil) round
   him affectionately. But, unfortunately, the snake is by now a full-
   grown boa-constrictor and its embrace (kill) the poor boy.
30 The snake (feel) sorry about this? ~
   I (not know). The story (end) there.
31 How you (end) a letter that (begin), 'Dear Sir'? ~
   I always (put), 'Yours truly', but Tom (prefer) 'Yours faithfully'.
32 What the word 'catastrophe' (mean)? ~
   It (mean) 'disaster'.
33 What you (wait) for? ~
   I (wait) for the shop to open. ~
   But it (not open) till 9.00. ~
   I (know) but I (want) to be early, as their sale (start) today.
34 Why you (smoke) a cigar, Mrs Pitt? You (not smoke) cigars as a
   rule. ~
   I (smoke) it because I (want) the ash. This book (say) that cigar ash
   mixed with oil (remove) heat stains from wood.
35 Who (own) this umbrella? ~
   I (not know). Everybody (use) it but nobody (know) who (own) it.
36 You (mind) if I (ask) you a question? ~
   That (depend) on the question. ~
   It (concern) your brother. ~
   I (refuse) to answer any question about my brother.

33 The simple past tense

☐ PEG 175-6

Put the verbs in the following sentences into the simple past tense.

1 I go to work by bus.
2 I meet her on Tuesdays.

3 He always wears black.
4 I make cakes every week.
5 She gets up at 6.30.
6 He understands me.
7 He shuts the shop at 6.00.
8 She speaks slowly.
9 He leaves the house at 9.00.
10 I read a chapter every night.
11 You eat too much.
12 I see him every day.
13 Tom sings in the choir.
14 He cries when he is hurt.
15 Who knows the answer?
16 I think I know it.
17 The curtain rises at 8.00.
18 He takes the dog out twice a day.
19 We buy them here.
20 I dream every night.
21 Bluetits often lay eggs in that nesting box.
22 He often feels ill.
23 I know what he wants.
24 I usually pay him £5.
25 His dog always bites me.
26 It smells odd.
27 It costs 30p.
28 My back hurts.
29 I lie down after lunch.
30 We drink water.
31 His roses grow well.
32 He rides every day.
33 He often falls off.
34 These dogs fight whenever they meet.
35 He puts up his prices every year.
36 He sleeps badly.

34 The simple past tense

☐ PEG 175-6

Put the verbs in the following sentences into (a) the negative (b) the interrogative.

1 She saw your brother.
2 We heard a terrible noise.
3 He slept till 10.00.
4 He looked at the picture.
5 They drank all the wine.

6 They set out early enough.
7 She thought about it.
8 The police caught the thief.
9 He hid the letter.
10 She found her watch.
11 His nose bled.
12 My mother chose this hotel.
13 She lent you enough money.
14 Keiko taught Japanese.
15 Tom hurt his foot.
16 He broke his arm.
17 His wife came at 8.00.
18 He lost his wallet.
19 His son wrote a novel.
20 They flew to New York.
21 Ann drew you a map.
22 Tom laid the table.
23 Mr Pitt fell downstairs.
24 She lost her way.
25 He forbade her to leave.
26 I sent it to the laundry.
27 Jack kept the money.
28 He rode slowly.
29 They spent it all.
30 She sold the car.
31 Jean rang the bell.
32 The sun rose at 6.00.
33 The boys ran home.
34 He shook the bottle.
35 He forgave her.
36 They broadcast an appeal for money.

35 The past continuous tense

☐ PEG 178

Put the verbs in brackets into the past continuous tense.

1 Detective: I'm afraid I must ask you both what you (do) yesterday at 10.20 p.m.
Mr X: I (play) chess with my wife.
Mr Y: I (listen) to a play on the radio.
2 The children were frightened because it (get) dark.
3 It was a fine day and the roads were crowded because a lot of people (rush) to the seaside.
4 The aeroplane in which the football team (travel) crashed soon after taking off.

57

5   He usually wears sandals but when I last saw him he (wear) boots.
6   The house was in great disorder because he (redecorate) it.
7   The director didn't allow the actors to travel by air while they (work on the film.
8   The car had nobody in it but the engine (run).
9   Two children (play) on the sand and two fishermen (lean) against an upturned boat.
10 I was alone in the house at that time because Mr Jones (work) in the garage and Mrs Jones (shop).
11 He said that he was the captain of a ship which (sail) that night for Marseilles.
12 Are you going to Rome? I thought that you (go) to Milan.
13 My wife and I (talk) about you the other day.
14 When I first met him he (study) painting.
15 There was a strong smell and the sound of frying. Obviously Mrs Jones (cook) fish.
16 Tom ate nothing for lunch because he (diet). He said that he (try) to lose 10 kilos.
17 Who you (talk) to on the telephone as I came in?
    I (talk) to Mr Pitt.
18 As she (climb) the ladder it slipped sideways and she fell off it.
19 When I first met him he (work) in a restaurant.
20 He watched the children for a moment. Some of them (bathe) in the sea, others (look) for shells, others (play) in the sand.
21 Where he (live) when you saw him last?
22 She (stand) at the bus stop. I asked her what bus she (wait) for.
23 From the sounds it was clear that Mary (practise) the piano.
24 There had been an accident and men (carry) the injured people to an ambulance.
25 Two men (fight) at a street corner and a policeman (try) to stop them. ~
    What they (fight) about? ~
    Nobody seemed to know.
26 Tom (sit) in a corner with a book. I told him that he (read) in very bad light.
27 I went into the garden to see what the boys (do). James (weed) and Alexander (cut) the grass.
28 They had taken off the wheel of the car and (mend) the puncture. I asked when it would be ready.
29 When I arrived at the meeting the first speaker had just finished speaking and the audience (clap).
30 The traffic (make) so much noise that I couldn't hear what he (say).
31 While he (learn) to drive he had twenty-five accidents.
32 He had a bad fall while he (repair) his roof.
33 He was a little mad. He always (try) to prove that the earth was flat.
34 While we (fish) someone came to the house and left this note.

35 The exam had just begun and the candidates (write) their names at the top of their papers.
36 Just as I (wonder) what to do next, the phone rang.

36 The simple past and the past continuous

☐ PEG 175–81

Put the verbs in brackets into the simple past or the past continuous tense.

1 I lit the fire at 6.00 and it (burn) brightly when Tom came in at 7.00.
2 When I arrived the lecture had already started and the professor (write) on the overhead projector.
3 I (make) a cake when the light went out. I had to finish it in the dark.
4 I didn't want to meet Paul so when he entered the room I (leave).
5 Unfortunately when I arrived Ann just (leave), so we only had time for a few words.
6 He (watch) TV when the phone rang. Very unwillingly he (turn) down the sound and (go) to answer it.
7 He was very polite. Whenever his wife entered the room he (stand) up.
8 The admiral (play) bowls when he received news of the invasion. He (insist) on finishing the game.
9 My dog (walk) along quietly when Mr Pitt's Pekinese attacked him.
10 When I arrived she (have) lunch. She apologized for starting without me but said that she always (lunch) at 12.30.
11 He always (wear) a raincoat and (carry) an umbrella when he walked to the office.
12 What you (think) of his last book? ~
   I (like) it very much.
13 I (share) a flat with him when we were students. He always (complain) about my untidiness.
14 He suddenly (realize) that he (travel) in the wrong direction.
15 He (play) the guitar outside her house when someone opened the window and (throw) out a bucket of water.
16 I just (open) the letter when the wind (blow) it out of my hand.
17 The burglar (open) the safe when he (hear) footsteps. He immediately (put) out his torch and (crawl) under the bed.
18 When I (look) for my passport I (find) this old photograph.
19 You looked very busy when I (see) you last night. What you (do)?
20 The boys (play) cards when they (hear) their father's step. They immediately (hide) the cards and (take) out their lesson books.
21 He (clean) his gun when it accidentally (go) off and (kill) him.
22 He (not allow) us to go out in the boat yesterday as a strong wind (blow).

23 As I (cross) the road I (step) on a banana skin and (fall) heavily.
24 I still (lie) on the road when I (see) a lorry approaching.
25 Luckily the driver (see) me and (stop) the lorry in time.
26 How you (damage) your car so badly? ~
    I (run) into a lamp-post yesterday. ~
    I suppose you (drive) too quickly or were not looking where you (go)
27 As he (get) into the bus it (start) suddenly and he (fall) backwards o
    to the road.
28 I (call) Paul at 7.00 but it wasn't necessary because he already (get)
    up.
29 When he (mend) the fuse he (get) a very bad shock.
30 When I (hear) his knock I (go) to the door and (open) it, but I (not
    recognize) him at first because I (not wear) my glasses.
31 When I came in they (sit) round the fire. Mr Pitt (do) a crossword
    puzzle, Mrs Pitt (knit), the others (read). Mrs Pitt (smile) at me and
    (say), 'Come and sit down.'
32 While the guests (dance) thieves (break) into the house and (steal) a
    lot of fur coats.
33 The next day, as they (know) that the police (look) for them, they
    (hide) the coats in a wood and (go) off in different directions.
34 She was very extravagant. She always (buy) herself new clothes.
35 Her mother often (tell) her that she (spend) too much money but sh
    never (listen).
36 Whenever the drummer (begin) practising, the people in the next fl
    (bang) on the wall.

37 The simple past and the past continuous

◼ PEG 175–81

Put the verbs in brackets into the simple past or past continuous
tense.

1 Mr Smith never (wake) up in time in the mornings and always (get)
   into trouble for being late; so one day he (go) to town and (buy) an
   alarm clock.
2 To get home he (have to) go through a field where a bad-tempered
   bull usually (graze).
3 This bull normally (not chase) people unless something (make) him
   angry. Unfortunately, as Mr Smith (cross) the field, his alarm clock
   (go) off.
4 This (annoy) the bull, who immediately (begin) to chase Mr Smith.
5 Mr Smith (carry) an open umbrella as it (rain) slightly. He (throw)
   the umbrella to the ground and (run) away as fast as he could.
6 The bull (stop) and (begin) to attack the umbrella. While he (do) thi
   Mr Smith escaped.

7 When he (awake) she (sit) by the window. She (look) at something in the street, but when he (call) her she (turn) and (smile) at him.

8 Why you (interrupt) me just now? I (have) a very interesting conversation with Mr Pitt.

9 The murderer (carry) the corpse down the stairs when he (hear) a knock on the door.

10 When I (look) through your books I (notice) that you have a copy of *Murder in the Cathedral.*

11 As they (walk) along the road they (hear) a car coming from behind them. Tom (turn) round and (hold) up his hand. The car (stop).

12 When I (arrive) at the station Mary (wait) for me. She (wear) a blue dress and (look) very pretty. As soon as she (see) me she (wave) and (shout) something, but I couldn't hear what she (say) because everybody (make) such a noise.

13 The prisoner (escape) by climbing the wall of the garden where he (work). He (wear) blue overalls and black shoes.

14 She said that the car (travel) at 40 k.p.h. when it (begin) to skid.

15 She said that she (not like) her present flat and (try) to find another.

16 While he (make) his speech the minister suddenly (feel) faint. But someone (bring) him a glass of water and after a few minutes he (be able) to continue.

17 When I (see) him he (paint) a portrait of his wife. ~
You (like) it? ~
He only just (start) when I (see) it, so I couldn't judge.

18 I (take) my friend to a murder trial the other day. ~
Who (be) tried? ~
A man called Bill Sykes. ~
Was he acquitted? ~
I don't know. They still (listen) to the evidence when we (leave).

19 I (be) sorry that I (have to) leave the party early, because I (enjoy) myself.

20 As we (come) here a policeman (stop) us. He (say) that he (look) for some stolen property and (ask) if he could search the car.

21 I (see) you yesterday from the bus. Why you (use) a stick? ~
I (use) a stick because I had hurt my leg that morning falling off a horse. ~
Whose horse you (ride)?

22 The floor was covered with balls of wool. Obviously Mrs Pitt (knit) something.

23 Ann said that she (be) on holiday. I (say) that I (hope) that she (enjoy) herself.

24 While he (water) the flowers it (begin) to rain. He (put) up his umbrella and (go) on watering.

25 I just (write) a cheque when I (remember) that I (have) nothing in the bank.

26 I (find) this ring as I (dig) in the garden. It looks very old. I wonder who it (belong) to?

27 When I last (see) her she (hurry) along the road to the station. I (ask) her where she (go) and she (say), 'London', but I don't think she (speak) the truth because there (not be) any train for London at that time.

28 The tailor said, 'Your suit will be ready on Monday.' But when I (call) on Monday he still (work) on it.

29 The teacher (come) into the classroom unusually early and one of the boys, who (smoke) a cigarette, (have) no time to put it out. So he (throw) it into the desk and (hope) for the best.

30 A little later the teacher (notice) that smoke (rise) from this desk. 'You (smoke) when I (come) in?' he (ask).

31 While I (swim) someone (steal) my clothes and I (have to) walk home in my swimsuit.

32 The men (say) that they (work) on the road outside my house and that they (want) some water to make tea.

33 He (say) that he (build) himself a house and that he (think) it would be ready in two years.

34 At 3 a.m. Mrs Pitt (wake) her husband and (say) that she (think) that someone (try) to get into the house.

35 Why you (lend) him that book? I still (read) it. ~
I'm sorry. I (not know) that you still (read) it.

36 I (come) in very late last night and unfortunately the dog (wake) up and (start) to bark. This (wake) my mother who (come) to the top of the stairs and (say), 'Who is there?'
I (say), 'It is me,' but she (not hear) me because the dog (bark) so loudly, so she (go) back to her room and (telephone) the police.

38 The present perfect tense

☐ PEG 182–9

Put the verbs in brackets into the present perfect tense, and fill the spaces by repeating the auxiliary.

> You (wash) the plates? ~
> Yes, I . . .
> *Have you washed the plates?* ~
> *Yes, I have.*
>
> You (see) him lately? ~
> No, I . . .
> *Have you seen him lately?* ~
> *No, I haven't.*

1 Where you (be)? ~
I (be) to the dentist.

2 You (have) breakfast? ~
Yes, I . . .

3 The post (come)? ~
  Yes, it . . .
4 You (see) my watch anywhere? ~
  No, I'm afraid I . . .
5 Someone (wind) the clock? ~
  Yes, Tom . . .
6 I (not finish) my letter yet.
7 He just (go) out.
8 Someone (take) my bicycle.
9 The phone (stop) ringing.
10 You (hear) from her lately? ~
   No, I . . .
11 I just (wash) that floor.
12 The cat (steal) the fish.
13 You (explain) the exercise? ~
   Yes, I . . .
14 There aren't any buses because the drivers (go) on strike.
15 You (have) enough to eat? ~
   Yes, I (have) plenty, thank you.
16 Charles (pass) his exam? ~
   Yes, he . . .
17 How many bottles the milkman (leave)? ~
   He (leave) six.
18 I (live) here for ten years.
19 How long you (know) Mr Pitt? ~
   I (know) him for ten years.
20 Would you like some coffee? I just (make) some.
21 Mary (water) the tomatoes? ~
   Yes, I think she . . .
22 You (not make) a mistake? ~
   No, I'm sure I . . .
23 Why you (not mend) the fuse? ~
   I (not have) time.
24 You (dive) from the ten-metre board yet? ~
   No, I . . .
25 You ever (leave) a restaurant without paying the bill? ~
   No, I . . .
26 I (ask) him to dinner several times.
27 He always (refuse).
28 You ever (ride) a camel?
29 I (buy) a new carpet. Come and look at it.
30 He (post) the letter?
31 Why he (not finish)? He (have) plenty of time.
32 I often (see) him but I never (speak) to him.
33 You ever (eat) caviar? ~
   No, I . . .
34 We just (hear) the most extraordinary news.

35 The police (recapture) the prisoners who escaped yesterday.
36 I (not pay) the telephone bill yet.

39 The present perfect and the simple past

☐ PEG 175–7, 182–9

(a) Fill the spaces by repeating the auxiliary used in the question, putting it into the negative where necessary.
(b) Put the verb in brackets into the present perfect or the simple past tense.

Have you seen that play? (a) Yes, I . . .
Yes, I have.
(b) Yes, I (be) there last night.
Yes, I was there last night.

1 Have you wound the clock?
   (a) Yes, I . . .
   (b) Yes, I (wind) it on Monday

2 Have you ever eaten snails?
   (a) No, I . . .
   (b) Yes, I (eat) some at Tom's party last week.

3 Has she fed the dog?
   (a) Yes, I think she . . .
   (b) Yes, she (feed) him before lunch.

4 Have they repaired the road?
   (a) No, they . . .
   (b) They only (repair) part of i so far.

5 Have they done their homework?
   (a) Yes, they (do) it all.
   (b) Yes, they (do) it before the left school.

6 Have you found the matches?
   (a) No, I . . .
   (b) No, I (not find) them yet.

7 Have you made the coffee?
   (a) Yes, I . . .
   (b) I (make) some yesterday: v can use that.

8 Have you been here before?
   (a) No, I . . .
   (b) Yes, I (be) here several times.

9 Have you seen him lately?
   (a) No, I . . .
   (b) No, I (not see) him since Christmas.

10 Have you been to the opera this week?
   (a) Yes, I . . .
   (b) Yes, I (go) to *Faust* on Friday.

11 Have you ever driven this car?
    (a) Yes, I (drive) it once or twice.
    (b) Yes, I (drive) it when you were away.

12 Has he missed his train?
    (a) No, he . . . .
    (b) Yes, he . . . It (go) five minutes ago.

13 Have they been through Customs?
    (a) Yes, they . . .
    (b) Yes, their luggage (be) examined at Dover.

14 Has he spoken to her?
    (a) Yes, he . . .
    (b) Yes, he (speak) to her on Friday.

15 Have you spent all your money?
    (a) No, I only (spend) half of it.
    (b) Yes, I . . .

16 How much have you saved since Christmas?
    (a) I (not save) anything.
    (b) I (save) £3.

17 Has his temperature gone down?
    (a) No, it . . .
    (b) Yes, it (go) down last night.

18 Have you seen his garden?
    (a) No, I (not see) it yet.
    (b) I (see) the house on Monday but I (not see) the garden.

19 Have you paid the bill?
    (a) Yes, I . . .
    (b) Yes, I (pay) it while you were away.

20 Have you ever flown a plane?
    (a) No, I . . .
    (b) Yes, I (fly) when I was at university.

21 Has your dog ever bitten anyone?
    (a) Yes, he (bite) a policeman last week.
    (b) Yes, he (bite) me twice.

22 Have you planted your peas?
    (a) Yes, I (plant) them on Tuesday.
    (b) No, I . . . yet.

23 Has he written to the paper?
    (a) Yes, he . . .
    (b) Yes, he (write) at once.

24 Have you ever drunk vodka?
    (a) No, I . . .
    (b) I (drink) it once in Russia but I (not drink) it since.

40 The present perfect and the simple past

■ PEG 175–7, 182–9

Put the verbs in brackets into the present perfect or the simple past tense. In some sentences the present perfect continuous (PEG 190) is also possible.

1 This is my house. ~
   How long you (live) here? ~
   I (live) here since 1970.
2 He (live) in London for two years and then (go) to Edinburgh.
3 You (wear) your hair long when you were at school? ~
   Yes, my mother (insist) on it.
4 But when I (leave) school I (cut) my hair and (wear) it short ever since.
5 Shakespeare (write) a lot of plays.
6 My brother (write) several plays. He just (finish) his second tragedy
7 I (fly) over Loch Ness last week. ~
   You (see) the Loch Ness monster?
8 I (not see) him for three years. I wonder where he is.
9 He (not smoke) for two weeks. He is trying to give it up.
10 Chopin (compose) some of his music in Majorca.
11 When he (arrive)? ~
   He (arrive) at 2.00.
12 You (lock) the door before you left the house?
13 I (read) his books when I was at school. I (enjoy) them very much.
14 I can't go out because I (not finish) my work.
15 I never (drink) whisky. ~
   Well, have some now.
16 I (write) the letter but I can't find a stamp.
17 The clock is slow. ~
   It isn't slow, it (stop).
18 Here are your shoes; I just (clean) them.
19 I (leave) home at 8.00 and (get) here at twelve.
20 I (do) this sort of work when I (be) an apprentice.
21 He just (go) out.
22 He (go) out ten minutes ago.
23 You (have) breakfast yet? ~
   Yes, I (have) it at 8.00.
24 I (meet) him last June.
25 You (see) the moon last night?
26 The concert (begin) at 2.30 and (last) for two hours. Everyone (enjoy) it very much.
27 The play just (begin). You are a little late.
28 The newspaper (come)? ~
   Yes, Ann is reading it.

29 The actors (arrive) yesterday and (start) rehearsals early this morning.
30 It (be) very cold this year. I wonder when it is going to get warmer.
31 Cervantes (write) *Don Quixote.*
32 We (miss) the bus. Now we'll have to walk.
33 He (break) his leg in a skiing accident last year.
34 Mr Pound is the bank manager. He (be) here for five years.
35 Mr Count (work) as a cashier for twenty-five years. Then he (retire) and (go) to live in the country.
36 You (be) here before? ~
   Yes, I (spend) my holidays here last year. ~
   You (have) a good time? ~
   No, it never (stop) raining.

41 The present perfect and the simple past

■ PEG 175-7, 182-9

Put the verbs in brackets into the present perfect or simple past tense. Fill the spaces by repeating the auxiliary used in the preceding verb.
   You (see) Mary on Monday? ~
   Yes, I . . .
   Did you see Mary on Monday? ~
   Yes, I did.

1 Where is Tom? ~
   I (not see) him today, but he (tell) Mary that he'd be in for dinner.
2 I (buy) this in Bond Street. ~
   How much you (pay) for it? ~
   I (pay) £100.
3 Where you (find) this knife? ~
   I (find) it in the garden. ~
   Why you (not leave) it there?
4 I (lose) my black gloves. You (see) them anywhere? ~
   No, I'm afraid I . . . . When you last (wear) them? ~
   I (wear) them at the theatre last night. ~
   Perhaps you (leave) them at the theatre.
5 Do you know that lady who just (leave) the shop? ~
   Yes, that is Miss Thrift. Is she a customer of yours? ~
   Not exactly. She (be) in here several times but she never (buy) anything.
6 He (leave) the house at 8.00. ~
   Where he (go)? ~
   I (not see) where he (go).

7 He (serve) in the First World War. ~
When that war (begin)? ~
It (begin) in 1914 and (last) for four years.
8 Who you (vote) for at the last election? ~
I (vote) for Mr Pitt. ~
He (not be) elected, (be) he? ~
No, he (lose) his deposit.
9 You (like) your last job? ~
I (like) it at first but then I (quarrel) with my employer and he
(dismiss) me. ~
How long you (be) there? ~
I (be) there for two weeks.
10 I (not know) that you (know) Mrs Pitt. How long you (know) her? ~
I (know) her for ten years.
11 That is Mr Minus, who teaches me mathematics, but he (not have)
time to teach me much. I only (be) in his class for a week.
12 You (hear) his speech on the radio last night? ~
Yes, I . . . ~
What you (think) of it?
13 I (not know) that you (be) here. You (be) here long? ~
Yes, I (be) here two months. ~
You (be) to the Cathedral? ~
Yes, I (go) there last Sunday.
14 You ever (try) to give up smoking? ~
Yes, I (try) last year, but then I (find) that I was getting fat so I
(start) again.
15 You (see) today's paper? ~
No, anything interesting (happen)?
Yes, two convicted murderers (escape) from the prison down the
road.
16 Mary (feed) the cat? ~
Yes, she (feed) him before lunch. ~
What she (give) him? ~
She (give) him some fish.
17 How long you (know) your new assistant? ~
I (know) him for two years. ~
What he (do) before he (come) here? ~
I think he (be) in prison.
18 I (not see) your aunt recently. ~
No. She (not be) out of her house since she (buy) her colour TV.
19 The plumber (be) here yet? ~
Yes, but he only (stay) for an hour. ~
What he (do) in that time? ~
He (turn) off the water and (empty) the tank.

0 Where you (be)?
I (be) out in a yacht. ~
You (enjoy) it? ~
Yes, very much. We (take) part in a race. ~
You (win)? ~
No, we (come) in last.
1 How long that horrible monument (be) there? ~
It (be) there six months. Lots of people (write) to the Town Council
asking them to take it away but so far nothing (be) done.
2 I just (be) to the film *War and Peace*. You (see) it? ~
No, I . . . . Is it like the book? ~
I (not read) the book. ~
I (read) it when I (be) at school. ~
When Tolstoy (write) it? ~
He (write) it in 1868. ~
He (write) anything else?
3 Hannibal (bring) elephants across the Alps. ~
Why he (do) that? ~
He (want) to use them in battle.
4 Where you (be)? ~
I (be) to the dentist. ~
He (take) out your bad tooth? ~
Yes, he . . . ~
It (hurt)? ~
Yes, horribly.
5 She (say) that she'd phone me this morning, but it is now 12.30 and
she (not phone) yet.
6 I just (receive) a letter saying that we (not pay) this quarter's
electricity bill. I (not give) you the money for that last week? ~
Yes, you . . . but I'm afraid I (spend) it on something else.
7 How long you (be) out of work? ~
I'm not out of work now. I just (start) a new job. ~
How you (find) the job? ~
I (answer) an advertisement in the paper.
8 You (finish) checking the accounts? ~
No, not quite. I (do) about half so far.
9 I (cut) my hand rather badly. Have you a bandage? ~
I'll get you one. How it (happen)? ~
I was chopping some wood and the axe (slip).
0 How you (get) that scar? ~
I (get) it in a car accident a year ago.
1 You (meet) my brother at the lecture yesterday? ~
Yes, I . . . . We (have) coffee together afterwards.
2 He (lose) his job last month and since then he (be) out of work. ~
Why he (lose) his job? ~
He (be) very rude to Mr Pitt.

33 What are all those people looking at? ~
   There (be) an accident. ~
   You (see) what (happen)? ~
   Yes, a motor cycle (run) into a lorry.
34 I (phone) you twice yesterday and (get) no answer.
35 Originally horses used in bull fights (not wear) any protection, but
   for some time now they (wear) special padding.
36 That house (be) empty for a year. But they just (take) down the 'Fo
   Sale' sign, so I suppose someone (buy) it.

42 The present perfect continuous tense

☐ PEG 190-1

Put the verbs in brackets into the present perfect continuous tense.

1 I (make) cakes. That is why my hands are all covered with flour.
2 Her phone (ring) for ten minutes. I wonder why she doesn't
   answer it.
3 He (overwork). That is why he looks so tired.
4 There is sawdust in your hair. ~
   I'm not surprised. I (cut) down a tree.
5 Have you seen my bag anywhere? I (look) for it for ages.
6 What you (do)? ~
   I (work) in the laboratory.
7 He (study) Russian for two years and doesn't even know the
   alphabet yet.
8 How long you (wait) for me? ~
   I (wait) about half an hour.
9 It (rain) for two days now. There'll be a flood soon.
10 We (argue) about this for two hours now. Perhaps we should stop!
11 I (bathe). That's why my hair is all wet.
12 You (drive) all day. Let me drive now.
13 How long you (wear) glasses?
14 The petrol gauge (say) 'Empty' for quite a long time now. Don't yo
   think we should get some petrol?
15 I'm sorry for keeping you waiting. I (try) to make a telephone call t
   Rome.
16 You (not eat) enough lately. That's why you feel irritable.
17 He (speak) for an hour now. I expect he'll soon be finished.
18 That helicopter (fly) round the house for the last hour; do you thin
   it's taking photographs?
19 The radio (play) since 7 a.m. I wish someone would turn it off.
20 I (shop) all day and I haven't a penny left.
21 We (live) here since 1977.
22 I'm on a diet. I (eat) nothing but bananas for the last month.
23 The children (look) forward to this holiday for months.

24 That pipe (leak) for ages. We must get it mended.
25 Tom (dig) in the garden all afternoon and I (help) him.
26 I (ask) you to mend that window for six weeks. When are you going to do it?
27 Someone (use) my bicycle. The chain's fallen off.
28 How long you (drive)? ~
   I (drive) for ten years.
29 The trial (go) on for a long time. I wonder what the verdict will be.
30 It (snow) for three days now. The roads will be blocked if it doesn't stop soon.
31 Mary (cry)? ~
   No, she (not cry), she (peel) onions.
32 The car (make) a very curious noise ever since it ran out of oil.
33 He walked very unsteadily up the stairs and his wife said, 'You (drink)!'
34 Your fingers are very brown. You (smoke) too much.
35 You usually know when someone (eat) garlic.
36 Ever since he came to us that man (try) to make trouble.

43 The present perfect and the present perfect continuous

☑ PEG 191–2

Put the verbs in brackets into the present perfect or the present perfect continuous tense. (In some cases either could be used.)

1 We (walk) ten kilometres.
2 We (walk) for three hours.
3 You (walk) too fast. That's why you are tired.
4 I (make) sausage rolls for the party all the morning.
5 How many you (make)? ~
   I (make) 200.
6 That boy (eat) seven ice-creams.
7 He (not stop) eating since he arrived.
8 The driver (drink). I think someone else ought to drive.
9 I (pull) up 100 dandelions.
10 I (pull) up dandelions all day.
11 What you (do)? ~
   We (pick) apples.
12 How many you (pick)? ~
   We (pick) ten basketfuls.
13 I (sleep) on every bed in this house and I don't like any of them.
14 He (sleep) since ten o'clock. It's time he woke up.
15 He (ride); that's why he is wearing breeches.
16 I (ride) all the horses in this stable.
17 What a lovely smell! ~
   Mary (make) jam.

18 The students (work) very well this term.
19 I only (hear) from him twice since he went away.
20 I (hear) from her regularly. She is a very good correspondent.
21 I (grease) my car. That's why my hands are so dirty.
22 I (polish) this table all the morning and she isn't satisfied with it yet.
23 I (work) for him for ten years and he never once (say) 'Good morning' to me.
24 He (teach) in this school for five years.
25 I (teach) hundreds of students but I never (meet) such a hopeless class as this.
26 Why you (be) so long in the garage? ~
   The tyres were flat; I (pump) them up.
27 I (pump) up three tyres. Would you like to do the fourth?
28 I (look) for mushrooms but I (not find) any.
29 He (cough) a lot lately. He ought to give up smoking.
30 You (hear) the news? Tom and Ann are engaged! ~
   That's not new; I (know) it for ages!
31 I (try) to finish this letter for the last half-hour. I wish you'd go away or stop talking. ~
   I hardly (say) anything.
32 The driver of that car (sound) his horn for the last ten minutes.
33 It (rain) for two hours and the ground is too wet to play on, so the match (be) postponed.
34 He (hope) for a rise in salary for six months but he (not dare) to ask for it yet.
35 Mr Smith, you (whisper) to the student on your right for the last five minutes. You (help) him with his exam paper or he (help) you?
36 Why you (make) such a horrible noise? ~
   I (lose) my key and I (try) to wake my wife by throwing stones at her window. ~
   You (throw) stones at the wrong window. You live next door.

44 **for** and **since**

☐ PEG 187

Fill the spaces in the following sentences by using **for** or **since**.

1 We've been fishing . . . two hours.
2 I've been working in this office . . . a month.
3 They've been living in France . . . 1970.
4 He has been in prison . . . a year.
5 I've known that . . . a long time.
6 That man has been standing there . . . six o'clock.
7 She has driven the same car . . . 1975.
8 Things have changed . . . I was a girl.
9 The kettle has been boiling . . . a quarter of an hour.

10 The central heating has been on . . . October.
11 That trunk has been in the hall . . . a year.
12 He has been very ill . . . the last month.
13 I've been using this machine . . . twelve years.
14 We've been waiting . . . half an hour.
15 Mr Pitt has been in hospital . . . his accident.
16 He hasn't spoken to me . . . the last committee meeting.
17 I have been very patient with you . . . several years.
18 They have been on strike . . . November.
19 The strike has lasted . . . six months.
20 It has been very foggy . . . early morning.
21 They have been quarrelling ever . . . they got married.
22 I've been awake . . . four o'clock.
23 I've been awake . . . a long time.
24 We've had no gas . . . the strike began.
25 I've earned my own living . . . I left school.
26 Nobody has seen him . . . last week.
27 The police have been looking for me . . . four days.
28 I haven't worn low-heeled shoes . . . I was at school.
29 He had a bad fall last week and . . . then he hasn't left the house.
30 He has been under water . . . half an hour.
31 That tree has been there . . . 2,000 years.
32 He has been Minister of Education . . . 1983.
33 I've been trying to open this door . . . forty-five minutes.
34 He hasn't eaten anything . . . twenty-four hours.
35 We've had terrible weather . . . the last month.
36 Nobody has come to see us . . . we bought these bloodhounds.

4 Future forms

45 The present continuous tense as a future form

☐ PEG 202

Put the verbs in brackets into the present continuous tense.

1 They are going to drill for oil here. They (start) on Monday.
2 My uncle (make) a speech on Friday.
3 I (take) my sister to the ballet tomorrow.
4 She (call) for me at six.
5 He (play) at Wimbledon next summer.
6 I (meet) her at the station at ten.
7 The sales (not start) till Monday.
8 How you (get) to the party tomorrow? ~
   I (go) by car. ~
   Who (drive)?
9 The piano tuner (come) this afternoon.
10 You (give) him anything for his birthday? ~
   Yes, I (give) him a dictionary.
11 The windows (be) cleaned today. Then we'll be able to see out.
12 She (come) out of hospital next week.
13 We (have) dinner early tonight as we (go) to the theatre.
14 Where you (go) for your holidays this year? ~
   I (go) to Holland.
15 He (not give) a lecture tonight.
16 I (have) my photograph taken tomorrow.
17 I (buy) her a burglar alarm for a wedding present.
18 The elections (be) held next week.
19 I (have) lunch with my aunt on Thursday.
20 The committee (meet) next Wednesday.
21 My grandparents (celebrate) their golden wedding next week.
22 I (lend) him my car for his holidays.
23 The strikers (return) to work next week.
24 Smith's (open) a new branch in this street in July.
25 We've bought a new house and (move) in very soon.
26 I (not take) up judo next winter.
27 They (get) married next week.
28 You (do) anything tonight? ~
   Yes, I (go) to my carpentry class.
29 The Prime Minister (fly) to America tomorrow.
30 He (start) a new job on Friday.

31 The Queen (give) a garden party next week. You (go)?
32 My brother (be) released on Tuesday. I (meet) him outside the prison.
33 I (catch) the 6.30 plane tomorrow. ~
   Where you (leave) your car? ~
   I (not take) the car.
34 Her mother (send) her to France next year.
35 I (go) to the dentist tomorrow. Miss Pitt (take) my class.
36 I (lend) my flat to my American cousins next year.

46 The **be going to** form

☐ PEG 203, 206

Put the verbs in brackets into the **be going to** form.

1 You (miss) your train.
2 The pressure cooker (explode).
3 When you (pay) the bill?
4 She (dye) the old curtains blue.
5 We (make) this whisky bottle into a lamp.
6 What you (do) with this room? ~
   I (paint) the walls in black and white stripes.
7 The umpire (blow) his whistle.
8 You (eat) all that?
9 That man with the tomato in his hand (throw) it at the speaker.
10 That door (slam).
11 The bull (attack) us.
12 It (rain). Look at those clouds.
13 The cat (have) kittens.
14 The men in the helicopter (try) to rescue the man in the water.
15 That rider (fall) off.
16 These two men (cycle) across Africa.
17 The Lord Mayor is standing up. He (make) a speech.
18 He (grow) a beard when he leaves school.
19 This aeroplane (crash).
20 I (stop) here for a moment to get some petrol.
21 You (ask) him to help you?
22 I've lent you my car once. I (not do) it again.
23 I have seen the play. Now I (read) the book.
24 Small boy: I (be) a frogman when I grow up.
25 I (not sleep) in this room. It is haunted.
26 We (buy) a metal detector and look for buried treasure.
27 You (reserve) a seat?
28 I (plant) an oak tree here.
29 The dog (bury) the bone.
30 I (have) a bath.

Future forms

31 I (smuggle) this out of the country.
32 There was very little blossom this spring. Apples (be) scarce.
33 I don't like this macaroni. I (not finish) it.
34 I (not stay) here another minute.
35 They (try) him for manslaughter when he comes out of hospital.
36 We (make) a lot of money out of this.

47 The present continuous and the **be going to** form

☑ PEG 202-6

Planned future actions can be expressed by the present continuous
tense with a time expression or by the **be going to** form with or
without a time expression. The present continuous is mainly used
for very definite arrangements in the near future. The **be going to**
form can be used more widely.

Use the present continuous where possible in the following
sentences and put the remaining verbs into the **be going to** form.

1   I (play) bridge tonight with Tom and Ann.
2   He (have) an operation next week.
3   It's very cold. I (light) a fire.
4   We (have) some friends to lunch tomorrow.
5   I've bought a piano; it (be) delivered this afternoon. ~
    Where you (put) it? ~
    I (put) it in the dining room.
6   You (go) to the auction tomorrow? ~
    Yes, I (go) but I (not buy) anything.
7   I've reminded you once; I (not do) it again.
8   I (have) my hair cut this afternoon.
9   My nephew (come) to stay with me next weekend. ~
    Where you (put) him? ~
    I (put) him in the room in the tower.
10 Our class (start) German next term.
11 I (spend) a few days in London next week.
12 The Town Council (build) a new school here.
13 What you (tell) the police? ~
    I (tell) them the truth.
14 He (start) tomorrow.
15 The Queen (open) Parliament next month.
16 The Prime Minister (speak) on TV tonight.
17 This shop (close) down next week.
18 When you (have) your next lesson? ~
    I (have) it on Monday.
19 I (collect) my new dress this afternoon.
20 We (take) the children to the seaside this summer.
21 I (give) him a football for his next birthday.

22 She (sing) in her first big concert next month.
23 He (go) to Spain for his holidays. ~
He (fly)? ~
No, he (go) by boat.
24 She (see) a specialist next week.
25 He (wash) the car?
26 He (ring) me up tonight.
27 The inspector (ask) you a few questions.
28 Her parents (give) a party for her next month. They (invite) sixty
guests.
29 Have you got a ticket for the big match on Saturday? ~
No, I don't even know who (play). ~
France (play) England.
30 They (launch) a ship this afternoon. You (come) to see it?
31 What you (do) with the money?
32 I (pick) you up at 6.30; don't forget.
33 Where you (go) tonight? ~
I (go) out with Peter. He (call) for me at eight.
34 I (compete) in the bicycle race tomorrow.
35 Mr Pitt has just phoned to say that he (not come) back till
Wednesday night.
36 I (read) you his answer to my letter of complaint.

48 The future simple

☐ PEG 207–9

Put the verbs in brackets into the future simple.

1 I (know) the result in a week.
2 You (be) in Rome tonight.
3 You (have) time to help me tomorrow?
4 It (matter) if I don't come home till morning?
5 You (be) able to drive after another five lessons.
6 Do you think that he (recognize) me?
7 Unless he runs he (not catch) the train.
8 He (lend) it to you if you ask him.
9 I hope I (find) it.
10 If petrol pump attendants go on strike we (not have) any petrol.
11 He (believe) whatever you tell him.
12 I (remember) this day all my life.
13 Perhaps he (arrive) in time for lunch.
14 If he works well I (pay) him £10.
15 I wonder how many of us still (be) here next year.
16 If you think it over you (see) that I am right.
17 If you learn another language you (get) a better job.
18 I am sure that you (like) our new house.

19 Newspaper announcement: The President (drive) along the High Street in an open carriage.
20 He (mind) if I bring my dog?
21 You (need) a visa if you are going to Spain.
22 If you open that trapdoor you (see) some steps.
23 You (feel) better when you've had a meal.
24 He (be) offended if you don't invite him.
25 She (have) £1000 a year when she is twenty-one.
26 If you put any more polish on that floor someone (slip) on it.
27 I wonder if he (succeed).
28 Papers (not be) delivered on the Bank Holiday.
29 I hope he (remember) to buy wine.
30 If you leave your roller skates on the path someone (fall) over them.
31 If they fall over them and hurt themselves they (sue) you.
32 Announcement: Mrs Pitt (present) the prizes.
33 If you want twenty cigarettes you (have) to give me more money.
34 Notice: The management (not be) responsible for articles left on the seats.
35 If I drop this it (explode).
36 What your father (say) when he hears about this accident? ~
   He (not say) much but he not (lend) me the car again.

49 The present continuous and the future simple

■ PEG 202, 207-9

Put the verbs in brackets into the present continuous or the future simple using the present continuous where possible.

(The **be going to** form could be used here instead of the present continuous, but for the sake of simplicity students are advised to use only the two tenses first mentioned.)

1 I am sure that I (recognize) him.
2 I (see) her tomorrow.
3 He (play) in a tennis match on Friday.
4 She (come) back on Monday.
5 I (go) again next year.
6 We (know) tonight.
7 You pay and I (owe) you the money.
8 I (believe) it when I see it.
9 I (have) my car repainted next week.
10 I hope that you (have) a good time tomorrow.
11 His speech (be) broadcast tonight.
12 The window-cleaner (come) at eight tomorrow.
13 Tom (catch) the 7.40 train.
14 Where you (meet) them? ~
   I (meet) them at midnight in the middle of the wood.

15 What horse you (ride) tomorrow?
16 Look! I've broken the teapot. What Mrs Pitt (say)? ~
   She (not mind); she never liked that one.
17 I've left the light on. It (matter)?
18 He (not forget) to come.
19 He (leave) in a few days.
20 I (remember) it.
21 If you drop that bottle it (break).
22 I never (forgive) him.
23 I'm sure that you (like) him.
24 They (lay) the foundations next week.
25 You (see) a signpost at the end of the road.
26 He has cut my hair too short. ~
   Don't worry; it (grow) again very quickly.
27 You (understand) when you are older.
28 The cat (scratch) you if you pull its tail.
29 I (be) back at 8.30.
30 If he doesn't work hard he (not pass) his exam.
31 She (go) on a cruise next summer.
32 I (move) to a new flat next week.
33 I am sorry that the child saw the accident. ~
   I don't think it matters. He soon (forget) all about it.
34 I (wait) here till he comes back.
35 He (not write) to you unless you write to him.
36 There (be) a big meeting here tomorrow.

50 will + infinitive and the be going to form

☑ PEG 201, 203–6

Future with intention can usually be expressed by **will** + infinitive
or the **be going to** form. Very often either of these can be used, but
when the intention is clearly premeditated the **be going to** form must
be used, and when the intention is clearly unpremeditated we must
use **will** + infinitive.

Put the verbs in brackets into one of these two forms. (In some of
the examples the present continuous could be used instead of the **be
going to** form.)

1 The fire has gone out! ~
  So it has. I (go) and get some sticks.
2 Did you remember to book seats? ~
  Oh no, I forgot. I (telephone) for them now.
3 He has just been taken to hospital with a broken leg. ~
  I'm sorry to hear that. I (send) him some grapes.
4 I've hired a typewriter and I (learn) to type.
5 I see that you have got a loom. You (do) some weaving?

Future forms

6 I can't understand this letter. ~
   I (call) my son. He (translate) it for you.
7 You (buy) meat? ~
   No, I (not eat) meat any more. I (eat) vegetables.
8 You've bought a lot of paint. You (redecorate) your kitchen?
9 Why are you getting out the jack? ~
   We have a puncture and I (change) the wheel. ~
   I (help) you.
10 Look what I've just bought at an auction! ~
   What an extraordinary thing! Where you (put) it?
11 Why are you peeling that bit of garlic? ~
   I (put) it in the stew.
12 What you (do) when you grow up? ~
   I (be) an acrobat in a circus.
13 What are you going to do with that dress? ~
   I (shorten) the skirt.
14 Will you lend me your season ticket? ~
   No, I (not lend) it to you. It is against the law.
15 That tree makes the house very dark. ~
   Very well, I (cut) it down.
16 I've just enrolled at the local technical college. I (attend) pottery
   classes next winter.
17 How do I get from here to London Bridge? ~
   I don't know, but I (ask) that policeman.
18 Why are you carrying a corkscrew? ~
   I (open) a bottle of wine.
19 Why's he putting the camera on a tripod? ~
   He (take) a group photo.
20 My brother has just returned from America. ~
   Oh good, we (ask) him to our next party.
21 Why have you set your alarm to go off at five-thirty? ~
   Because I (get) up then. I've got a lot to do.
22 I'm turning this cupboard into a darkroom. I (develop) my own films.
23 You look frozen. Sit down by the fire and I (make) you a cup of tea.
24 They've brought a rope and they (tow) the car to a garage.
25 I haven't bought any cigarettes because I (give) up smoking.
26 I have tried to explain but she doesn't understand English. ~
   I (say) it to her in Finnish: perhaps she'll understand that.
27 I've come out without any money. ~
   Never mind, I (lend) you some. How much do you want?
28 Do you see that car? They (raffle) it for charity.
29 They've hired a bulldozer. They (clear) away this rubble.
30 Child: I've torn my dress.
   Mother: I (mend) it for you.
31 I'm catching the 6.30 train. ~
   So am I. I (give) you a lift to the station.
32 I've bought some blue velvet and I (make) curtains for this room.

33 Why are you carrying that saw? ~
   I (shorten) the legs of the dining room table.
34 Why are you taking that big basket? ~
   I (buy) a lot of vegetables.
35 I've planned my future for the next ten years. ~
   That is very clever of you. What you (do) when you leave the
   university?
36 Why are you putting that old loaf into a paper bag? ~
   I (give) it to Mrs Pitt for her hens.

51 will + infinitive and the be going to form

☑ PEG 205

Both will you and are you going to can introduce questions about
future intentions. But will you very often introduces a request or
invitation. For this reason are you going to is more usual than will
you in questions about intentions. are you going to must of course be
used when the intention is obviously premeditated. (See also
Exercise 55.)

Put the verbs in brackets into one of these two forms. Where both
are possible it will be noted in the key. (In some examples the
present continuous tense could be used instead of the be going to
form.) The exercise contains requests, invitations, and questions
about intentions.

1 You (open) the door for me, please? ~
   Yes, certainly.
2 You (do) the washing-up tonight? ~
   No, I think it can wait till tomorrow.
3 I'm looking for my easel. ~
   You (paint) someone's portrait?
4 'You (read) this passage aloud, please,' said the examiner.
5 You (eat) any more of this, or shall I tell the waiter to take it away?
6 You aren't wearing your climbing boots. You (not climb) the
   mountain with the others?
7 'You (listen) to me!' said his mother angrily.
8 You (put) my car away from me, please? ~
   Yes, certainly.
9 You (have) another cup of coffee? ~
   No, thank you.
10 Why did you buy all these eggs? You (make) an enormous omelette?
11 There's the phone again. Take no notice. ~
   You (not answer) it?
12 You (come) and see me after the class? I want to discuss your work
   with you.
13 I see that you have ordered the *Guardian*. You really (read) it?

14 You (buy) stamps? ~
   Yes, I am. ~
   Then you (buy) some for me, please?
15 You (lend) me your fishing rod? ~
   Yes, of course. Where you (fish)?
16 You (finish) this book or shall I take it back to the library?
17 You (give) me 10p, please? ~
   Yes, here you are. You (make) a telephone call?
18 You (leave) that coil of barbed wire in the hall? Someone will fall
   over it if you do.
19 You (bath) your dog? ~
   Yes, you (help) me?
20 You (drive), please? I don't like driving at night.
21 You (ride) that horse? He looks very bad-tempered to me.
22 You (eat) it raw? You will be ill if you do.
23 You (have) some of this cake? I made it myself.
24 You really (call) the fire brigade? I don't think it is at all necessary.
25 You (paint) the whole room by yourself? It will take you ages.
26 You (be) ready in five minutes?
27 Hostess: John, you (sit) here at the end of the table?
28 You (do) something for me? ~
   Yes, of course; what is it?
29 You (be) angry if he refuses to help you?
30 Why have you brought your typewriter? You (work) this weekend?
31 You (call) me at six? I have to catch an early train.
32 You (walk) there in this rain? You'll get awfully wet.
33 You (sign) here, please?
34 What are all those notes for? You (give) a lecture?
35 Why do you want a candle? You (explore) the caves?
36 If I catch some fish, you (cook) them for me?

52 The future continuous tense

☐ PEG 211-13

This tense can be used

1 with a point in time to indicate that the action will begin before
this time and continue after it.

2 with or without a time to express a future without intention. In
this way it is very like the present continuous, but it is not, like the
present continuous, restricted in time and is a more detached and
casual way of expressing the future. It often implies that the action
will occur in the ordinary course of events or as a matter of routine.

(Except when used as in 1, above, this tense can usually be replaced
by one of the other future forms, though the exact shade of meaning
may then be lost.)

Put the verbs in brackets into the future continuous tense.

1 This time next month I (sit) on a beach.
2 When you arrive I probably (pick) fruit.
3 When we reach England it very likely (rain).
4 In a few days time we (fly) over the Pyrenees.
5 I'll call for her at eight. ~
  No, don't; she still (have) breakfast then.
6 I (wait) for you when you come out.
7 When you next see me I (wear) my new dress.
8 My son will be in the sixth form next year. ~
  That means that old Dr Adder (teach) him mathematics.
9 I'll give Jack your message. I can do it easily because I (see) him
  tomorrow. We go to work on the same train.
10 You (do) geometry next term.
11 I'll look out for you at the parade. ~
  Do, but I (wear) uniform so you may find it hard to recognize me.
12 We have to do night duty here. I (do) mine next week.
13 In a hundred years' time people (go) to Mars for their holidays.
14 He (use) the car this afternoon.
15 I (see) you again.
16 It's a serious injury but he (walk) again in six weeks.
17 I'll come at three o'clock. ~
  Good, I (expect) you.
18 They are pulling down all the old houses in this street. I expect they
  (pull) down mine in a few years' time.
19 I'd like to see your new flat. ~
  Well, come tomorrow, but it (not look) its best, for the painters still
  (work) on it.
20 Stand there, they (change) the guard in a minute and you'll get a
  good view.
21 You'd better go back now; your mother (wonder) where you are.
22 In fifty years' time we (live) entirely on pills.
23 What do you think the children (do) when we get home? ~
  I expect they (have) their supper.
24 The garden (look) its best next month.
25 It won't be easy to get out of the country. The police (watch) all the
  ports.
26 What the tide (do) at six tomorrow morning? ~
  It (come) in.
27 I've just remembered that I left the bathroom taps on. I expect the
  water (flow) down the stairs by now.
28 You (need) your camera tomorrow or can I borrow it?
29 We've just got to the top in time. The sun (rise) in a minute.
30 Air hostess: We (take off) in a few minutes. Please fasten your
  safety belts.
31 We'd better go out tomorrow because Mary (practise) the piano all
  day.

32 Don't ring her up at 6.00; she (put) the children to bed. Ring later.
33 We are making a house-to-house collection of things for the jumble sale. We (come) to your house next week.
34 That football club has lost some of its players. They (look out) for new men.
35 When I get home my dog (sit) at the door waiting for me.
36 Let's go down to the harbour; the fishing boats all (come) in because of the gale.

53 will + infinitive and the future continuous
☑ PEG 201, 211–14

See note for previous exercise.

Put the verbs in brackets into the appropriate future form, using will + infinitive or the future continuous. (Where alternative forms are possible they will be given in the key.)

1 There is going to be a bus strike. Everyone (walk) to work next week.
2 You've just missed the last train! ~
   Never mind, I (walk).
3 I'll ring you tomorrow at six. ~
   No, don't ring at six; I (bath) the baby then. Ring later.
4 Mother: Your face is dirty.
   Child: All right, I (wash) it.
5 Will you have lunch with me on the 24th? ~
   I'd love to, but I'm afraid I (do) my exam then.
6 I (work) for Mr Pitt next week as his own secretary will be away.
7 You (have) something to drink, won't you?
8 Why did you take his razor? He (look) for it everywhere tomorrow.
9 I hope you'll do well in the race tomorrow. I (think) of you.
10 Notice on board ship: In the event of an emergency all passengers (assemble) on the boat deck.
11 I don't feel well enough to go to the station to meet him. ~
   I (meet) him for you. But how I (recognize) him? ~
   He's small and fair, and he (wear) a black and white school cap.
12 I (leave) these flowers at the hospital for you. I (go) there anyway to visit my cousin.
13 You ought to try to get a ticket for the Spectators' Gallery next week; they (debate) international fishing rights.
14 You've left the light on. ~
   Oh, so I have. I (go) and turn it off.
15 I've just been appointed assistant at the local library. ~
   Then you (work) under my sister. She is head librarian there.

16 I want to post this letter but I don't want to go out in the rain. ~
   I (post) it for you. I (go) out anyway as I have to take the dog for a
   walk.
17 The prima ballerina is ill so I expect her understudy (dance) instead.
18 Today is Guy Fawkes' Day; this evening people (let) off fireworks
   and (make) bonfires in the streets.
19 Military order: Sentries (remain) on duty till they are relieved.
20 This time next Monday I (sit) in a Paris café reading *Le Figaro*. ~
   You (not read). You'll be looking at all the pretty girls.
21 Wages have gone up, so I suppose prices (go up) too.
22 It is nearly autumn; soon the leaves (change) colour.
23 Mother (on phone): My son has just burnt his hand very badly.
   Doctor: I (come) at once.
24 Customer in restaurant: Waiter, this plate is dirty.
   Waiter: I'm sorry, sir, I (bring) you another.
25 In a few years' time we all (live) in houses heated by solar energy.
26 It's beginning to get dark; the street lights (go on) in a few minutes.
27 We (not play) poker at the party tonight; our hostess doesn't approve
   of cards.
28 Let's wait here; the swing bridge (open) in a minute to let that ship
   through.
29 Guest: May I use your phone to ring for a taxi?
   Hostess: Oh, there's no need for that; my son (drive) you home.
30 Come on deck; we (enter) harbour in a few minutes.
31 Before you leave the office you (hand) the keys of the safe to Mr
   Pitt. Do you understand? ~
   Yes, sir.
32 Are you nearly ready? Our guests (arrive) any minute.
33 Loudspeaker announcement: The ship (leave) in a few minutes and
   all persons not travelling are asked to go ashore.
34 Now that the parking regulations have become stricter, more people
   (use) public transport and (leave) their cars at home.
35 I've got rats in my basement and I don't know how to get rid of
   them. ~
   I (bring) my dog round whenever you like. He (catch) them for you.
36 I'm afraid I've just broken your goldfish bowl. ~
   Never mind, I (put) the goldfish in the bath.

54 won't + infinitive and the future continuous negative
■ PEG 214

won't + infinitive (except when used as part of the ordinary future
simple, **shall/will**) usually implies that the subject refuses to perform
a certain action. The negative future continuous tense merely states
that a certain action will not take place.

Future forms

Put the verbs in brackets into the appropriate future form, using
won't + infinitive or the future continuous negative. (Where other
future forms are also possible this will be noted in the key.)

1 I don't like that man and I (not help) him.
2 He (not meet) her, because they will be in different places.
3 My husband (not cut) down the tree. He says that it is perfectly all
right as it is.
4 My husband (not cut) the hedge for some time, because he's got a lot
of other jobs to do first.
5 Tom (not come) to our party, because he will be away on that date.
6 Peter says that he (not come) to our party. He doesn't approve of
parties.
7 She says that she (not lend) me the book, because I never give books
back.
8 Mr Pitt (not speak) at the meeting tonight, because he has
unexpectedly had to go to hospital.
9 I'll work under anyone except my brother. I (not work) under him.
10 We'll be in the same firm, but we (not work) together, because we'll
be in different departments.
11 I (not have) that boy in my class. He is far too noisy.
12 I (not teach) you next week, as I have to go to Paris.
13 He is so angry with his sister that he (not speak) to her.
14 I'll give your message to my sister when I write; but I (not write) for
some time, as I only write once a month and I posted a letter to her
yesterday.
15 I (not feed) your dog again. He always tries to bite me when I come
near him.
16 They were very rude to me. I (not go) there again.
17 He said, 'I (not paint) you in that dress. It does not suit you.'
18 I (not take) any photographs for some time because my camera is
being repaired.
19 I (not borrow) his van again. The brakes don't work properly.
20 That boy (not wash) his face. He likes being dirty.
21 You can have the car tomorrow if you like. I (not use) it as I'll be far
too busy to go out.
22 She says that she (not send) the child to school, no matter what we
say. She thinks it is far better to educate children at home.
23 He says he (not play) for them again, because they aren't giving him
enough money.
24 She (not sing) at the next concert, because she has had to go home
suddenly.
25 I (not play) cards with you again. You always cheat.
26 She (not take) part in the bridge tournament, because she'll be away
then.
27 I (not eat) any more of this; I feel queer already.
28 I (not eat) curry again for a long time, because I am going to stay in
a house where no one knows how to cook it.

29 He says that he (not ride) that mare again, because she's dangerous.
30 Tom (not ride) in tomorrow's race, because he is too young. They don't allow riders under sixteen.
31 Whisky is absolutely necessary to me and I (not give) it up.
32 Jack (not drink) whisky this time next week, because he'll be in hospital and they won't give it to him there.
33 I (not open) the window. I dislike fresh air.
34 There is something on his mind, but he (not tell) me what it is.
35 The cat (not eat) fish so I have to buy meat for him.
36 He (not wear) uniform when you see him, because he'll be on leave then, and they don't wear uniform when they are on leave.

55 Second person interrogative: **will you** and other forms
■ PEG 215 B

will you? often introduces a request or invitation, and sometimes a command. It is often used also to introduce questions about intentions when the situation requires an unpremeditated decision.
> You can have either. Which will you have?
> You've missed the last train. What will you do now?

For other types of intention, however, it is usually safer to use one of the other future forms: **be going to**, the present continuous or the future continuous (which is considered the most polite form).

Put the verbs in brackets into one of the four forms. When more than one answer is possible, this will be noted in the key.

1 Why are you taking all that bread with you? You (feed) the swans?
2 You (let) your flat again next summer?
3 You (light) the fire for me, please? Here are the matches.
4 You (wear) a tie tomorrow? ~
   Oh no. Tom said, 'Come as you are.'
5 I know you don't like wearing ties, but (wear) one tomorrow, just to please me? ~
   Yes, of course.
6 Shop assistant: You (come) this way, please?
7 You (have) something more to eat? ~
   Yes, please, I'd like another sandwich.
8 You (have) anything more to eat? ~
   No, because I haven't any more money.
9 You (study) computer programming at college?
10 You (speak) to Tom at the meeting tomorrow, do you think?
11 You (turn) off the TV, please? No one is watching it.
12 You (take) your exam now or in December?
13 You (listen) in to the concert this evening?
14 You (help) me with this, please? I can't lift it.

15 Hotel receptionist: You (stay) for more than one night, Mrs Jones?
16 You (lend) me your typewriter for an hour? I want to type a letter.
17 You (meet) him at the station? ~
   No, we never meet him. He doesn't like being met.
18 You (come) sailing with me this afternoon? ~
   No, thank you, I don't like sailing.
19 You (have) some more wine? ~
   Yes, please.
20 I can't understand this letter. You (translate) it for me, Miss Pitt?
21 You (use) your camera this afternoon? ~
   No, you can borrow it if you like.
22 You (go) to the tobacconist's? ~
   Yes. ~
   Then you (get) me twenty cigarettes?
23 You (come) to the Motor Show with me next Wednesday? ~
   Thank you very much. I'd love to.
24 I'll be going abroad next week. Is there anything I can get you? ~
   You (pass) through Paris? ~
   Yes, I (spend) a few days there. ~
   Then you (get) me some scent?
25 I see that you are repairing your old henhouse. You (keep) hens?
26 I've just bought my tickets. ~
   You (travel) by sea or air?
27 What are all these slates for? You (repair) your roof?
28 You (hold) my parcels, please, while I put up my umbrella?
29 You (go) to Madeira as usual this summer?
30 You kindly (explain) why you didn't do what I told you?
31 You (recognize) him, do you think?
32 I've chosen a school for my son. ~
   You (send) him to a public school or to a State school?
33 Passenger to bus conductor: You (tell) me where to get off, please?
34 You (go) by car? If so, would you give my brother a lift?
35 You (type) all night again? Because if so I think I'll go to a hotel.
36 You (stop) interrupting! I'll never get finished if you don't keep
   quiet.

56 shall and will

⬛ PEG 201, 207–8, 233–4

shall is correct for the first person of the future simple (except when
this form is used to express intention), but in the affirmative and
negative will is very often used instead, i.e. we can say, 'I/we will'
and 'I/we won't' instead of 'I/we shall' and 'I/we shan't'. In the
interrogative will should not be used to replace shall.

There are some rather old-fashioned or formal constructions where **shall** is used with the second or third persons. Here **shall** cannot be replaced by **will**. Such constructions are usually avoided but a few examples have been given below.

Use **will** or **shall** to fill the spaces in the following sentences. Sometimes either could be used.

1 When you are in bed I . . . be at work.
2 Who'll help me? ~
  I . . .
3 We will unite to resist oppression, and tyrants . . . not triumph over us. (*We won't let them triumph.*)
4 What . . . we do now? ~
  Wait.
5 You've been a good child, and when we get home you . . . have a sweet. (*I'll give you a sweet.*)
6 Your father . . . hear of this. (*I'll certainly tell him.*)
7 . . . we go to the cinema? ~
  Yes, let's.
8 She . . . tell the same story over and over again. (*obstinate insistence*)
9 Club rule: Members . . . write the names of their guests in the book provided.
10 Theatre regulation: Persons . . . not be permitted to sit in the gangways.
11 Where . . . I be in six years' time, I wonder?
12 He . . . not come here again. (*He refuses.*)
13 He . . . not come here again. (*I won't let him come.*)
14 Clause in lease: The tenant . . . be responsible for all repairs.
15. This kind of snake . . . not bite unless it is startled.
16 . . . you have a cigarette? ~
  No, thanks, I don't smoke.
17 He . . . play his radio very loudly, which annoys me very much. (*obstinate insistence*)
18 By this time next year I . . . be earning my own living.
19 Who . . . take this letter to the post for me? ~
  I . . .
20 What . . . we do with all the food that's left over?
21 Do you know the way? No? Then I . . . show you.
22 Where . . . I put it? ~
  Put it behind the piano.
23 Police notice: . . . anyone who witnessed the accident please ring 2222.
24 Yachts . . . go round the course, passing the marks in the correct order. (*extract from Yacht Racing Rules*)
25 When . . . you hear the result? ~
  I . . . not hear for another week.
26 'I . . . not apologize', she said, stamping her foot.

27 Who . . . I say called? ~
   You needn't mention my name. He . . . know who I am.
28 She . . . never do anything you tell her.
29 I . . . not be here next week.
30 I . . . not have to do any cooking for a month. I'm going to an hotel.
31 . . . I put it on your desk? ~
   Please do.
32 I . . . fill up this form! The questions are impertinent. ~
   If you don't, madam, you . . . (*negative*) get your visa.
33 . . . you stand quite still for a moment, please?
34 . . . I put more salt in the stew?
35 A dog . . . obey his owner but a cat . . . not.
36 I . . . know whether you are telling the truth or not.

57 Time clauses

☐ PEG 342

The future simple is not used in time clauses, the simple present tense being used instead.

Put the verbs in brackets into the correct tense (present or future).

1 When he (return) I'll give him the key.
2 He'll be ready as soon as you (be).
3 I'll stay in bed till the clock (strike) seven.
4 She will be delighted when she (hear) this.
5 When the laundry comes I (have) some clean handkerchiefs.
6 I shan't buy tomatoes till the price (come) down.
7 Stay here till the lights (turn) green.
8 When it (get) cold I'll light the fire.
9 The lift (not start) until you press that button.
10 She'll have to behave better when she (go) to school.
11 When you look at yourself in the glass you (see) what I mean.
12 He (be) here before you go.
13 I (lend) you my cassette recorder whenever you want it.
14 He (wake) up when we turn the lights on.
15 He (ring) us up when he arrives in England?
16 He will wash up before he (go) to bed.
17 I won't come to London till the bus strike (be) over.
18 I (give) the childen their dinner before he (come) home.
19 They will be astonished when they (see) how slowly he works.
20 I'll pay you when I (get) my cheque.
21 I (go) on doing it until he tells me to stop.
22 I'll buy that house when I (have) enough money.
23 You (fall) rapidly through the air till your parachute opens.
24 We'll have to stay here till the tide (go) out.
25 When the Queen (arrive) the audience will stand up.

26 When the fog (lift) we'll be able to see where we are.
27 The refrigerator (go on) making that noise till we have it repaired.
28 As soon as the holidays begin this beach (become) very crowded.
29 The car (not move) till you take the brake off.
30 The alarm bell (go on) ringing till you press this button.
31 As soon as she (learn) to type I'll get her a job.
32 Look before you (leap). (*proverb*)
33 We (have) to stay on this desert island till we can repair our boat.
34 Don't count on a salary increase before you actually (get) it.
35 When winter (begin) the swallows will fly away to a warmer country.
36 We can't make any decision till he (arrive) here.

58 The future perfect tense

☐ PEG 216

Put the verbs in brackets into the future perfect tense.

1 In a fortnight's time we (take) our exam.
2 I (finish) this book by tomorrow evening.
3 By this time tomorrow we (have) our injections.
4 By the end of next year I (be) here twenty-five years.
5 I'll still be here next summer but Tom (leave).
6 I (finish) this job in twenty minutes.
7 By next winter they (build) four houses in that field.
8 When we reach Valparaiso we (sail) all round the world.
9 At the rate he is going he (spend) all his money by the time he is twenty-one.
10 By this time next year I (save) £250.
11 By the time we get to the party everything (be) eaten.
12 The train (leave) before we reach the station.
13 If I continue with my diet I (lose) 10 kilos by the end of the month.
14 By the end of my university course I (attend) 1,200 lectures.
15 By the end of this week my illness (cost) me £100.
16 By the time that he leaves school his parents (spend) £25,000 on his education.
17 By the end of the term I (read) all twelve volumes.
18 When you come back I (finish) all the housework.
19 The police (hear) of the theft by this time.
20 We (drink) all that wine by the end of the year.
21 On the fourth of next month he (be) in prison for ten years.
22 When we reach Crewe we (do) half of the journey.
23 At this rate you (break) all the wine glasses by the end of the month.
24 If we don't hurry the sun (rise) before we reach the top.
25 I'm going to Hyde Park to hear the people making speeches. ~
   You'll be too late. By the time you get there they (finish) their speeches and everybody (go) home.

26 By midnight he (be) unconscious for forty-eight hours.
27 By the end of the month 5,000 people (see) this exhibition.
28 By next April I (pay) £3,000 in income tax.
29 I suppose that when I come back in ten years' time all these old houses (be) pulled down.
30 On 21 October they (be) married for twenty-five years.
31 After this performance I (see) *Hamlet* twenty-two times.
32 The strike leader said, 'By midnight 500 men (come) out on strike.'
33 At your present rate you (burn) all that coal by the end of the month.
34 The treasurer said, 'By the end of the year all our debts (be paid) off.'
35 Tourist: We've only got five hours in Rome; we are leaving at six; but I'm sure that we (see) everything of importance by then.
36 Householder to Zoo: One of your elephants is in my garden eating my tomatoes.
   Zoo official: The elephant keeper will be with you in half an hour.
   Householder: Your elephant (eat) all my tomatoes by then.

59 Time clauses

◢ PEG 342

The future perfect tense is not used in time clauses, the present perfect being used instead.

Put the verbs in brackets into the correct tense, using the future, present, or present perfect. Compare 1 to 5 with 1 to 5 in Exercise 58.

1 When we (take) our exam we'll have a holiday.
2 When I (finish) the book I'll lend it to you.
3 When we (have) our injections I expect we'll feel awful.
4 When I (be) here for a year I'll ask for a rise.
5 When Tom (go) I'll tell you a secret.
6 By the time he (get) back from his holiday the milkman will have left twenty-one bottles of milk outside his door.
7 Don't drive at more than 50 k.p.h. till your car (do) 4,000 kilometres.
8 When you (do) 4,000 kilometres you can drive it at 70 k.p.h.
9 When you open the safe you (see) a small black box.
10 When we (have) lunch we'll go for a walk.
11 When the bell rings I (take) the meat out of the oven.
12 I'll bolt all the doors before I (go) to bed.
13 When we (see) the cathedral we'll go to the museum.
14 We'll have to stay up this tree till the bull (go) away.
15 He (not let) you out till you have finished your homework.
16 As soon as I hear from him I (let) you know.
17 My father will be furious when he (see) what you have done.

.8 You (not hear) the sound of the explosion till after you have seen the flash.
.9 These gates will remain shut until the train (pass).
:0 When he (sell) all his newspapers he'll go home.
:1 We can't have a fire here until we (sweep) the chimney.
:2 You (get) a shock when you open that box.
:3 When you are eighteen your father (give) you a latchkey.
:4 Don't jump out of the aeroplane until the pilot (say) 'Go!'
:5 I can't leave the country till the police (return) my passport.
:6 When a bottle of champagne (be) opened for twenty-four hours the wine is not fit to drink.
:7 Hotel receptionist: When you (sign) the hotel register the porter will show you your room.
:8 You (not know) how good oysters are till you have tasted one.
:9 That road will not be safe till the floods (subside).
:0 When everybody (leave) the park the park-keeper will lock the gates.
:1 When we have seen the Chamber of Horrors we (have) a cup of tea.
:2 When you (have) something to eat you'll feel better.
:3 I (stay) in court till the jury returns.
:4 You cannot become a member of this club until you (make) a parachute descent.
:5 When the boa constrictor (eat) the goat he will become very lethargic.
:6 As soon as everybody has gone to bed the mice (come) out of their holes.

0 **would** and **should**

■ PEG 140–1, 230–2, 235–7

Put **should** or **would** in the spaces in the following sentences.

1 . . . you mind opening the door?
2 . . . you like another cup of coffee?
3 He insisted that the newspaper . . . print an apology.
4 The old admiral . . . sit for hours watching the ships.
5 . . . you be so good as to keep an eye on my house while I am away?
6 I . . . say nothing about it if I were you.
7 That dress doesn't suit you; you . . . buy another.
8 If you pulled the communication cord the train . . . stop and you . . . be fined.
9 They went to the cinema at 2.30, so they . . . be back here by 6.00.
0 . . . you please help me with this?
1 It is very strange that he . . . think that.
2 I wish he . . . not play his radio so loudly.
3 . . . you be very kind and lend me your typewriter?

Future forms

14 I ... like to know where you have been.
15 It was decided that the matter . . . be referred to a special committee.
16 Perhaps you . . . be kind enough to let us know about this.
17 If the telephone . . . ring please say that I'll be back at six.
18 . . . you like to come or . . . you rather stay here?
19 There are too many accidents. Everyone . . . be much more careful
20 Their method was always the same; they . . . wait till their victim had left the bank and then go up to him and ask for a light.
21 What are you doing here? You . . . be in bed.
22 It is essential that this matter . . . be kept out of the newspapers.
23 He suggested that the money . . . be raised by public subscription.
24 If you . . . change your mind, this address will always find me.
25 If this machine . . . at any time fail to give complete satisfaction please post us the enclosed card.
26 He changed his name so that nobody . . . know what he had been before.
27 If he offered me money I . . . refuse.
28 I wish you . . . not ask so many questions.
29 He ordered that Tom . . . leave the house at once.
30 I . . . be most grateful if you . . . do this for me.
31 He is anxious that everyone . . . understand why he acted as he did
32 You . . . not argue with your father; you . . . obey him.
33 He was a very patient cat; he . . . sit for hours beside a mousehole.
34 . . . the pain return take one of these pills.
35 It is most important that I . . . see him at once.
36 He didn't dare (to) sell the ring in case someone . . . ask where he got it.

61 would and should

■ PEG 140–1, 230–2, 235–7

Put **should** or **would** in the spaces in the following sentences:

1 It is only fair that you . . . know the truth about your own father an it is better that you . . . hear it from me than from some stranger.
2 If you . . . kindly wait here a moment I'll ring the director's office.
3 . . . these measures fail to restore order harsher restrictions will have to be imposed.
4 The rocks were icy and he was terrified lest he . . . slip.
5 If Pierre liked any dish he . . . send for the chef and congratulate him, and if anything was wrong he . . . send for the manager and complain. ~
An Englishman . . . never dare to do that; he . . . be too shy.
6 I was just burying the bones in the garden when who . . . look over the hedge but the village policeman.

7 When he found out that the man had smallpox he urged that every effort . . . be made to contact his fellow passengers.

8 I wish you . . . go out or sit down. How . . . you like it if I kept tramping round when you were trying to work?

9 I've just received an anonymous threatening letter. What . . . I do about it? ~
I . . . take it to the police if I were you.

10 The committee thinks that you have been guilty of disloyalty. ~
I don't know why the committee . . . think that.

11 I can't repair it now but if you . . . like to leave it with me I'll see what can be done.

12 You complained to the manager, of course? ~
No, I asked to speak to him but he . . . not come to the phone. ~
You . . . have insisted.

13 Where will he be now? ~
Oh, he . . . be there by now; the flight only takes an hour.

14 If your main parachute . . . fail to open, your second one will open automatically.

15 I suggested that Tom . . . walk on and try to get help while I stayed with the injured man but he . . . not hear of this.

16 I am amazed that you . . . even suggest offering bribes.

17 This passage doesn't lead anywhere. It is odd that no one . . . have noticed this before.

18 . . . you mind not smoking; this is the petrol store. ~
Then there . . . be a 'No Smoking' notice.

19 Can't I trust you not to read my letters? It is ridiculous that I . . . have to lock things up in my own house.

20 He said he wished I . . . not come so often.

21 This train is entirely automatic; there is no driver; but a mechanic is always available in case anything . . . go wrong.

22 She had one rather boring habit; she . . . insist on telling people about her dreams.

23 He recommended that the trouble makers in the factory . . . be dismissed.

24 It is absurd that women . . . be paid less than men for doing the same work.

25 I . . . rather you asked him. Last time I tried to speak to him he . . . not listen.

26 When he went out he left the radio on so that his parents . . . think that he was still in his room.

27 He was determined that his children . . . go to the best schools available.

28 Tom says you are foolish to take such a risk. ~
He . . .! (*That is typical of him.*)

29 When four hours had passed and there was still no sign of him she began to be worried lest he . . . have met with some accident.

30 People are very fond of saying, 'This . . . be stopped', or,
'Something . . . be done about this', but if they were the governmen
they . . . not know how to stop it or what to do about it.
31 It is amazing that the Leaning Tower of Pisa . . . have stood for so
long.
32 He resigned from the government in order that everyone . . . know
that he disapproved of the new policy.
33 If I had had his education and he had had mine perhaps I . . . be
sitting at his desk and he . . . be out here sweeping the streets.
34 He was a terribly obstinate child, who . . . never obey the simplest
order, but . . . argue every point till she nearly went mad.
35 Robinson said, 'Why . . . Smith get all the credit when someone els
has done all the work?'
36 All day he . . . sit in his office immaculately dressed, but at night he
. . . put on dirty ragged clothing and roam about the streets with
disreputable companions.

5 Conditionals

52 Conditional sentences: type 1

☑ PEG 221

Put the verbs in brackets into the correct tenses.

1 If I see him I (give) him a lift.
2 The table will collapse if you (stand) on it.
3 If he (eat) all that he will be ill.
4 If I find your passport I (telephone) you at once.
5 The police (arrest) him if they catch him.
6 If he (read) in bad light he will ruin his eyes.
7 Someone (steal) your car if you leave it unlocked.
8 What will happen if my parachute (not open)?
9 If he (wash) my car I'll give him £10.
10 If she (need) a radio she can borrow mine.
11 If you (not go) away I'll send for the police.
12 I'll be very angry if he (make) any more mistakes.
13 If he (be) late we'll go without him.
14 She will be absolutely furious if she (hear) about this.
15 If you put on the kettle I (make) the tea.
16 If you give my dog a bone he (bury) it at once.
17 If we leave the car here it (not be) in anybody's way.
18 He'll be late for the train if he (not start) at once.
19 If you come late they (not let) you in.
20 If he (go) on telling lies nobody will believe a word he says.
21 Unless he (sell) more he won't get much commission.
22 If I lend you £10 when you (repay) me?
23 We'll have to move upstairs if the river (rise) any higher.
24 If he (work) hard today can he have a holiday tomorrow?
25 Ice (turn) to water if you heat it.
26 If the house (burn) down we can claim compensation.
27 If you (not like) this one I'll bring you another.
28 Unless you are more careful you (have) an accident.
29 Tell him to ring me up if you (see) him.
30 If I tell you a secret, you (promise) not to tell it to anyone else?
31 If you (not believe) what I say, ask your mother.
32 If he (like) the house will he buy it?
33 If you will kindly sit down I (make) enquiries for you.
34 Unless I have a quiet room I (not be able) to do any work.
35 She won't open the door unless she (know) who it is.
36 Should you require anything else please (ring) the bell for the attendant.

Conditionals

63 Conditional sentences: type 2

☑ PEG 222

Put the verbs in brackets into the correct tenses.

1 If I had a typewriter I (type) it myself.
2 If I (know) his address I'd give it to you.
3 He (look) a lot better if he shaved more often.
4 If you (play) for lower stakes you wouldn't lose so much.
5 If he worked more slowly he (not make) so many mistakes.
6 I shouldn't drink that wine if I (be) you.
7 More tourists would come to this country if it (have) a better climate.
8 If I were sent to prison you (visit) me?
9 If someone (give) you a helicopter what would you do with it?
10 I (buy) shares in that company if I had some money.
11 If he (clean) his windscreen he'd be able to see where he was going
12 If you drove your car into the river you (be able) to get out?
13 If you (not belong) to a union you couldn't get a job.
14 If I (win) a big prize in a lottery I'd give up my job.
15 What you (do) if you found a burglar in your house?
16 I could tell you what this means if I (know) Greek.
17 If everybody (give) £1 we would have enough.
18 He might get fat if he (stop) smoking.
19 If he knew that it was dangerous he (not come).
20 If you (see) someone drowning what would you do?
21 I (be) ruined if I bought her everything she asked for.
22 If you slept under a mosquito net you (not be) bitten so often.
23 I could get a job easily if I (have) a degree.
24 If she (do) her hair differently she might look quite nice.
25 If we had more rain our crops (grow) faster.
26 The whole machine would fall to pieces if you (remove) that screw.
27 I (keep) a horse if I could afford it.
28 I'd go and see him more often if he (live) on a bus route.
29 If they (ban) the sale of alcohol at football matches there might be less violence.
30 I (offer) to help if I thought I'd be any use.
31 What would you do if the lift (get) stuck between two floors?
32 If you (paint) the walls white the room would be much brighter.
33 If you (change) your job would it affect your pension?
34 If you knew you had only six weeks to live how you (spend) those six weeks?
35 You wouldn't have so much trouble with your car if you (have) it serviced regularly.
36 I'd climb over the wall if there (not be) so much broken glass on top of it.

4 Conditional sentences: type 3

☑ PEG 223

Put the verbs in brackets into the correct tenses.

1 If I had known that you were in hospital I (visit) you.
2 The ground was very soft. But for that, my horse (win).
3 If you (arrive) ten minutes earlier you would have got a seat.
4 You would have seen my garden at its best if you (be) here last week.
5 But for his quickness I (be) killed.
6 I shouldn't have believed it if I (not see) it with my own eyes.
7 If he had slipped he (fall) 500 metres.
8 If he had asked you, you (accept)?
9 If I (had) a map I would have been all right.
0 If I (know) that you were coming I'd have baked a cake.
1 I (offer) to help him if I had realized that he was ill.
2 If you had left that wasp alone it (not sting) you.
3 If I (realize) what a bad driver you were I wouldn't have come with you.
4 If I had realized that the traffic lights were red I (stop).
5 But for the fog we (reach) our destination ages ago.
6 If you had told me that he never paid his debts I (not lend) him the money.
7 If you (not sneeze) he wouldn't have known that we were there.
8 If you (put) some mustard in the sandwiches they would have tasted better.
9 The hens (not get) into the house if you had shut the door.
0 If he had known that the river was dangerous he (not try) to swim across it.
1 If you (speak) more slowly he might have understood you.
2 If he had known the whole story he (not be) so angry.
3 I shouldn't have eaten it if I (know) that there was ginger in it.
4 If I (try) again I think that I would have succeeded.
5 You (not get) into trouble if you had obeyed my instructions.
6 If you hadn't been in such a hurry you (not put) sugar into the sauce instead of salt.
7 If I (be) ready when he called he would have taken me with him.
8 She had a headache; otherwise she (come) with us.
9 If she had listened to my directions she (not turn) down the wrong street.
0 If you (look) at the engine for a moment you would have seen what was missing.
1 Rome (be captured) by her enemies if the geese hadn't cackled.
2 He would have been arrested if he (try) to leave the country.
3 I (take) a taxi if I had realized that it was such a long way.
4 You (save) me a lot of trouble if you had told me where you were going.

Conditionals

35 They would have forced their way into the house if I (not call) for help.
36 If he had put out his pipe before putting it in his pocket he (not burn) a hole in his coat.

65 Conditional sentences: mixed types
■ PEG 221–6

Put the verbs in brackets into the correct tenses.

1 If you (find) a skeleton in the cellar don't mention it to anyone.
2 If you pass your examination we (have) a celebration.
3 What (happen) if I press this button?
4 I should have voted for her if I (have) a vote then.
5 If you go to Paris where you (stay)?
6 If someone offered to buy you one of those rings, which you (choose)?
7 The flight may be cancelled if the fog (get) thick.
8 If the milkman (come) tell him to leave two pints.
9 Someone (sit) on your glasses if you leave them there.
10 You would play better bridge if you (not talk) so much.
11 What I (do) if I hear the burglar alarm?
12 If you (read) the instructions carefully you wouldn't have answered the wrong question.
13 I could repair the roof myself if I (have) a long ladder.
14 Unless they turn that radio off I (go) mad.
15 If you were made redundant what you (do)?
16 We'll have a long way to walk if we (run) out of petrol here.
17 If you shake that bottle of port it (not be) fit to drink.
18 I'll probably get lost unless he (come) with me.
19 You (not have) so many accidents if you drove more slowly.
20 If you (wear) a false beard nobody would have recognized you.
21 If she (leave) the fish there the car will get it.
22 Unless they leave a lamp beside that hole in the road somebody (fall) into it.
23 You'll get pneumonia if you (not change) your wet clothes.
24 If I had known that you couldn't eat octopus I (not buy) it.
25 If they (hang) that picture lower people would be able to see it.
26 She (be able) to walk faster if her shoes hadn't such high heels.
27 I (bring) you some beer if I had known that you were thirsty.
28 If you had touched that electric cable you (be) electrocuted.
29 If the story hadn't been true the newspaper (not print) it.
30 I (not buy) things on the instalment system if I were you.
31 Dial 999 if you (want) Police, Ambulance, or Fire Brigade.
32 You (not be) any use to me unless you learn to type.
33 If anyone attacked me, my dog (jump) at his throat.

100

34 If he were in he (answer) the phone.
35 The ship would have run aground if the pilot (make) one mistake.
36 I shouldn't have taken your umbrella if I (know) that it was the only one you had.

56 Conditional sentences: mixed types

■ PEG 221-6

Finish these sentences, taking care to use the correct tenses.

1 If he had taken my advice . . .
2 If you ate less . . .
3 We'll send for the doctor if . . .
4 If she practised more . . .
5 If there isn't enough wine in that bottle . . .
6 If you had checked the petrol before we started . . .
7 This clock wouldn't have run down if . . .
8 Try on the blue one if . . .
9 If these gates are locked . . .
10 If we leave before breakfast . . .
11 If the river rises any higher . . .
12 Her life might have been saved if . . .
13 If the volcano starts erupting . . .
14 The grass would look better if . . .
15 Unless it is a nice day . . .
16 If you don't put enough stamps on a letter, the person who gets it . . .
17 He would lend it to you if . . .
18 Unless this hotel gets another cook . . .
19 If the storm becomes worse . . .
20 If your uncle sees you . . .
21 If you tried to climb it without a guide . . .
22 If you didn't shake the camera so much, your photographs . . .
23 I'd have brought my coat . . .
24 If (= as) you don't like the picture . . .
25 He would have given her diamonds if . . .
26 If you had asked his permission . . .
27 If the fire had been noticed earlier . . .
28 If you had any sense . . .
29 You would have been angry if . . .
30 If he had put the flowers into water at once . . .
31 I should have ordered more coal if . . .
32 If you leave the gate open . . .
33 You will have to go to the dentist if . . .
34 He would have been drowned if . . .
35 If I'd had a car . . .
36 If Tom rings while I'm out . . .

Conditionals.

67 Mixed tenses and verb forms

■ PEG 221–6, 283–4

Conditional forms are used in requests.
Fill the gaps in the following dialogue with a suitable verb form.

Telephone conversation

1 Ann: . . . I . . . to Mr Wash, please?
2 Wash: Wash . . .
3 Ann: Good morning, Mr Wash. This is Ann Jones of 10 Cyprus Road.
   . . . you come and . . . my windows one Saturday this month?
4 Wash: I'm afraid I . . . (*negative*). The next six Saturdays are alread booked.
5 But I . . . . . . on Wednesday morning.
6 Ann: . . . you . . . very early on Wednesday? I leave at 8.15 on weekdays.
7 Wash: I . . . . . . to you by 8.30. . . . that be early enough?
8 Ann: No, it . . .! There . . . be nobody to let you in.
   I . . . the flat at 8.15.
9 Wash: Oh 8.15! I . . . you . . . 8.30!
10 Well, I suppose I . . . . . . to you by 8.00 as you're an old customer. But I . . . (*negative*) . . . a habit of it.
11 It means . . . breakfast at 6 and my wife . . . (*negative*) that.
12 She . . . always . . . to persuade me to give up window— . . . as it is She . . . it's dangerous.
13 Ann: What . . . she . . . you . . . instead?
14 Wash: Her father has a shop and she . . . . . . me . . . . . . in it.
15 She . . . it . . . be a nice steady job with regular hours.
16 And if I . . . in a shop she . . . . . . where I was.
17 Ann: And . . . you really . . . of giving it up?
18 Wash: No, I . . . the life. At least, I . . . it in summer.
19 Besides, I . . . . . . bored working in a shop.
20 Well, . . . Wednesday at 8.00 . . . you then, Miss Jones?
21 Ann: Yes, it . . . be splendid. It's very good of you . . . . . . so early
22 I . . . let you in and you can . . . yourself out.
23 You . . . shut the door carefully after you, . . . (*negative interrogative* you?
24 Wash: Yes, of course I . . . . I always . . . . Goodbye, Miss Jones.

6 Infinitive

68 Full or bare infinitive

☑ PEG 246

Insert **to** where necessary before the infinitives in brackets.

1 He made me (do) it all over again.
2 She can (sing) quite well.
3 He will be able (swim) very soon.
4 I used (live) in a caravan.
5 You ought (go) today. It may (rain) tomorrow.
6 You needn't (say) anything. Just nod your head and he will (understand).
7 I want (see) the house where our president was born.
8 He made her (repeat) the message.
9 May I (use) your phone?
10 You needn't (ask) for permission; you can (use) it whenever you like.
11 If you want (get) there before dark you should (start) at once.
12 I couldn't (remember) his address.
13 You'll be able (do) it yourself when you are older.
14 Would you like (go) now or shall we (wait) till the end?
15 They won't let us (leave) the Customs shed till our luggage has been examined.
16 How dare you (open) my letters!
17 He didn't dare (argue) with his boss.
18 I used (smoke) forty cigarettes a day.
19 Will you help me (move) the bookcase?
20 He wouldn't let my baby (play) with his gold watch.
21 They refused (accept) the bribe.
22 He is expected (arrive) in a few days.
23 Please let me (know) your decision as soon as possible.
24 He made us (wait) for hours.
25 Could you (tell) me the time, please?
26 We must (send) him a telegram.
27 I let him (go) early as he wanted (meet) his wife.
28 Where would you like (have) lunch?
29 You can (leave) your dog with us if you don't (want) (take) him with you.
30 I'd like him (go) to a university but I can't (make) him (go).
31 We could (go) to a concert, unless you'd prefer (visit) a museum.
32 You seem (know) this area very well. ~
   Yes, I used (live) here.

33 The kidnappers told the parents (not inform) the police, and the parents didn't dare (disobey).
34 Need I (come)? I'd much rather (stay) at home.
35 You can (take) a horse to water but you can't (make) him (drink). (*proverb*)
36 I'm sorry (disappoint) you but I can't (let) you (have) any more money till the end of the month.

69 Full or bare infinitive

◪ PEG 246

Insert **to** where necessary before the infinitives in brackets. (In som of the sentences a present participle could be used instead of an infinitive. These alternatives will be noted in the key.)

1 It is easy (be) wise after the event.
2 Do you (wish) (make) a complaint?
3 We don't (want) anybody (know) that we are here.
4 If you can't (remember) his number you'd better (look) it up.
5 I want her (learn) Esperanto; I think everybody ought to (know) it.
6 He is said (be) the best surgeon in the country.
7 Visitors are asked (not feed) the animals.
8 Could I (see) Mr Pitt, please? ~
I'm afraid Mr Pitt isn't in. Would you like (speak) to his secretary?
9 It's better (travel) hopefully than (arrive). (*proverb*)
10 He should (know) how (use) the film projector, but if he doesn't you had better (show) him.
11 He was made (sign) a paper admitting his guilt.
12 I heard the door (open) and saw a shadow (move) across the floor.
13 He tried (make) me (believe) that he was my stepbrother.
14 As we seem (have missed) the train we may as well (go) back to the house.
15 I felt the house (shake) with the explosion.
16 He told me (try) (come) early.
17 Before he let us (go) he made us (promise) (not tell) anyone what we had seen.
18 Would you (like) (come) in my car? ~
No, thanks, I'd rather (walk).
19 I advised him (ask) the bus conductor (tell) him where (get) off.
20 It is better (put) your money in a bank than (keep) it under your bed in an old stocking.
21 He doesn't even bother (read) letters, let alone (answer) them.
22 The bank robbers made the cashier (show) them how (open) the safe
23 If you knew he was wrong, why didn't you (say) something? ~
I didn't like (say) anything because he always gets angry if you contradict him.

24 It's better (be) sure than sorry.
25 What do you (want) me (tell) him? ~
    Tell him that any time he cares (call) I shall be delighted (discuss)
    the matter with him.
26 Did you remember (give) him the money? ~
    No, I didn't, I still have it in my pocket; but I'll (see) him tonight and
    I promise (not forget) this time.
27 I saw the driver (open) his window and (throw) a box into the
    bushes.
28 That is far too heavy for one person (carry); let me (help) you.
29 I was afraid (pick) up the revolver as I don't know how (handle)
    firearms.
30 I saw the plane (crash) into the hill and (burst) into flames.
31 There is nothing (do) but (wait) till somebody comes (let) us out.
32 He heard a cock (crow) in a neighbouring village.
33 You may as well (tell) us the truth. It will (be) easy (check) your
    story.
34 The American said he had seen nine presidents (come) and (go). ~
    He must (be) a very old man.
35 It is up to you (learn) the laws of your own country.
36 Would you rather (be) more stupid than you look or (look) more
    stupid than you are?

70 Infinitive represented by to

☑ PEG 247

In each of the following pairs of sentences an infinitive used in the
first sentence is repeated in the second. Read the sentences,
expressing this second infinitive by **to** only. Note that where the
second infinitive has an object, this word/phrase must be omitted.
    Why didn't you tell me the truth the first time? ~
    I meant to tell you the truth but I was too frightened.
    I meant to but I was too frightened.

1 Did you visit the Pyramids? ~
   No, I wanted to visit them but there wasn't time.
2 Why do you wear dark glasses? ~
   I have to wear them; I have weak eyes.
3 Do you smoke? ~
   No, I used to smoke but I don't now.
4 Would you like to go to the theatre tonight? ~
   Yes, I'd love to go to the theatre.
5 Why didn't you pay the bill for him? ~
   I offered to pay it but he refused.
6 Have you put the car in the garage? ~
   No, but I'm just going to put it there.

7 I want you two to apologize to each other. ~
   Well, I am willing to apologize if he apologizes first.
8 Did you reserve seats on the train? ~
   No, I tried to reserve them but they had all been booked already.
9 Did you answer the letter? ~
   No, I intended to answer it but I'm afraid I forgot
10 Why didn't you hit him? ~
   I was afraid to hit him.
11 I'd love to spend a night in a haunted room. ~
   I'd hate to spend a night in a haunted room.
12 Why didn't you ask your father for the money? ~
   I didn't like to ask him.
13 Did you get a chance to fly the aeroplane yourself? ~
   No, I wanted to fly it but the pilot wouldn't let me.
14 Why doesn't he punish his boys when they disobey him? ~
   He often threatens to punish them but he never actually does so.
15 Why didn't he repair the car himself? ~
   He wasn't able to repair it.
16 I used to drink whisky with my meals. ~
   I used to drink whisky with my meals also but I don't now.
17 Did you buy sausages? ~
   No, I meant to buy them but I forgot.
18 Why doesn't he try again? ~
   He doesn't want to try again.
19 You should visit the Prado when you are in Madrid. ~
   Yes, I intend to visit it.
20 Why doesn't he play games? ~
   His mother doesn't want him to play games.
21 You ought to stop work now. ~
   Yes, I am just going to stop.
22 Why do some jockeys carry extra weights? ~
   They are obliged to carry them by the regulations.
23 Did he help you? ~
   No, I asked him to help me but he said he hadn't time.
24 You should have thanked her before you left. ~
   I meant to thank her but when I was going I couldn't find her
   anywhere.
25 Why did she put parsley in the soup? ~
   I told her to put it in.
26 Why didn't he report it to the police? ~
   He was afraid to report it. He didn't think they'd believe him.
27 Why did he drive so fast? ~
   He had to drive fast; otherwise he'd have missed his train.
28 You used to like rice pudding. ~
   Yes, I know I used to like it but I don't now.
29 Why didn't you buy the car? ~
   I was advised not to buy it.

30 I hope the children won't go near the water. ~
I warned them not to go near it.
31 Why are we trying to get planning permission? ~
We have to get planning permission. It is the law.
32 I meant to work hard. ~
I know you meant to work hard but you didn't.
33 Do the boys tidy their own rooms? ~
They are supposed to tidy them but they don't always.
34 Why didn't he call the police. ~
He wasn't able to call them. His telephone line had been cut.
35 Why did you move your car? ~
The policeman told me to move it.
36 Why did you bring your mother-in-law? I particularly asked you not
to bring her.

1 too/enough/so ... as with infinitive

□ PEG 252

Combine each of the following pairs of sentences into one sentence
using too/enough with infinitive.
It is very cold. We can't go out.
It is too cold for us to go out.
He is strong. He can carry it.
He is strong enough to carry it.

Rewrite numbers 3, 20, and 35 using so ... as with infinitive.
(enough with infinitive could also be used here, while so ... as could
replace enough in numbers 9, 24, and 29. These alternatives are
given in the key.)

1 You are very young. You can't have a front-door key.
2 It is very cold. We can't bathe.
3 Would you be very kind and answer this letter by return?
4 I am rather old. I can't wear that kind of hat.
5 The ladder wasn't very long. It didn't reach the window.
6 He hadn't much money. He couldn't live on it. (*Omit* it.)
7 He was furious. He couldn't speak.
8 The fire isn't very hot. It won't boil a kettle.
9 Tom was very foolish. He told lies to the police.
10 You are quite thin. You could slip between the bars.
11 He is very ill. He can't eat anything.
12 Our new car is very wide. It won't get through those gates.
13 The floor wasn't strong. We couldn't dance on it. (*Omit* it.)
14 I was terrified. I couldn't move.
15 The bull isn't big. He couldn't harm you.
16 The coffee isn't strong. It won't keep us awake.
17 The river is deep. We can't wade it. (*Omit* it.)

18 He is lazy. He won't get up early.
19 He won't get up early so he never catches the fast train.
20 Would you be very good and forward my letters while I am away?
21 The ice is quite thick. We can walk on it. (*Omit* it.)
22 He was very drunk. He couldn't answer my question.
23 It is very cold. We can't have breakfast in the garden.
24 He was extremely rash. He set off up the mountain in a thick fog.
25 We aren't very high. We can't see the summit.
26 You aren't very old. You can't understand these things.
27 He was very snobbish. He wouldn't talk to any of us.
28 The package is very thick. I can't push it through the letterbox.
   (*Omit* it.)
29 She was very mean. She never gave to charity.
30 He is very impatient. He never listens to anyone.
31 I was very tired. I couldn't walk any further.
32 It's not very dark. We can't see the stars clearly.
33 It was very hot. You could fry an egg on the pavement.
34 The oranges were very bitter. We couldn't eat them. (*Omit* them.)
35 Would you be very kind and turn down the radio a little?
36 He is very selfish. He wouldn't put himself out for anyone.

72 Various infinitive constructions

■ PEG 26–7, 114, 239, 249–50

Replace the group of words in italics by an infinitive or an infinitive construction.
    It is important *that he should understand* this.
    It is important for him to understand this.
    He was the first man *who arrived.*
    He was the first man to arrive.

1 The captain was the last man *who left* the ship.
2 He got to the top *and was very disappointed when he found* that someone else had reached it first.
3 *The committee have decided to send you* to Paris. (You (go) to Paris, omit The committee have decided to send.)
4 Would you be *very* kind *and* lend me your umbrella?
5 There are a lot of sheets *that need mending.*
6 I was astonished *when I heard* that he had left the country.
7 It is better *that he should hear* it from you.
8 *I was rude* to him, *which was stupid.* (It was stupid . . .)
9 If he had another child *with whom he could play* he would be happier.
10 It is necessary *that everyone should know* the truth.
11 There was no place *where we could sit.*
12 He put his hand into his pocket *and was astonished when he found* that his wallet wasn't there.

13 *He rushed* into the burning house, *which* was very brave of him. (It was very brave . . .)
14 I can't go to the party; I have nothing *that I can wear.*
15 *It is expected that he will broadcast* a statement tonight. (He is expected . . .)
16 I want a kitchen *where* (= *in which*) *I can cook.*
17 He reached the station exhausted *and was very disappointed when he learnt* that the train had just left.
18 Haven't you anything *with which you could open it?*
19 *It seems that the crime was committed* by a left-handed man. (The crime seems . . . Use perfect infinitive passive.)
20 Is *it* likely *that he will arrive* before six? (Is he . . .)
21 I was *on the point of leaving* the house when the phone rang.
22 *This is the plan: someone will meet you* at the station . . . (You . . . (be met) at the station)
23 She is anxious *that they should have* every possible advantage.
24 *It is said that* he was a brilliant scientist. (He is said . . .)
25 The strikers decided *that the strike should continue.*
26 Would you be *very kind and translate* this for me?
27 It is advisable *that we should leave* the house separately.
28 *You signed* the document without reading it, *which was very stupid.* (It was stupid . . .)
29 *It is said that she has* a frightful temper. (She . . .)
30 He was the first man *who swam* the Channel.
31 *They believe that he is* honest. (He . . .)
32 *It appears that he was killed* with a blunt instrument. (He appears . . . Use passive infinitive.)
33 He was the only one *who realized* the danger.
34 *It is said that the earth was* originally part of the sun. (The earth . . .)
35 He took out his spare wheel and *was very disappointed when he discovered* that that tyre was also punctured.
36 *It is said that the murderer is hiding* in the woods near your house.

73 Perfect infinitive used with auxiliary verbs

■ PEG 255

Use the perfect infinitive of the verb in italics with the appropriate auxiliary verb. Phrases in bold type should not be repeated, but their meaning should be expressed by the auxiliary + perfect infinitive.

It is possible that he *telephoned* while we were out.
He may have telephoned while we were out.
You (*thank*) him for his present **but you didn't.**
You should have thanked him for his present.

1 I realized that my house was on fire. ~
That (*be*) a terrible moment.

Infinitive

2 I saw a ghost last night. ~
You (*not see*) a ghost; there aren't any ghosts. You (*dream*) it.
3 **It is possible that** a child *broke* the window.
4 You *carried* it yourself, **which was not necessary.**
5 I've had a toothache for two days. ~
You (*go*) to the dentist when it started.
6 There (*be*) motor-cycle races on the sands but as it is so wet they have been cancelled.
7 As I was standing in the hall your dog bit me. ~
It (*not be*) my dog; he was with me all day. It (*be*) my brother's dog.
8 I feel terribly ill today. ~
You (*not eat*) those mushrooms yesterday. Mushrooms don't agree with you.
9 I wonder why he didn't answer? ~
Possibly he *didn't understand* the question.
10 I *gave* him a tip, **which was not necessary.**
11 The prisoner (*escape*) this way, for here are his footprints.
12 You *lied* to him, **which was wrong.**
13 I didn't recognize the voice at the other end of the line. ~
It (*be*) my elder sister; she is often at home at that time. It (*not be*) my youngest sister as she is abroad.
14 Someone (*cook*) a meal here lately; the stove is still hot.
15 I've brought my own sandwiches. ~
You (*not bring*) them. I have enough for two.
16 The burglar went straight to the safe although it was hidden behind a picture. ~
Someone (*tell*) him where it was.
17 The president (*unveil*) the statue, but he is ill so his wife is doing it instead.
18 The plane is late; I wonder what has happened? ~
Possibly it *was* delayed by fog.
19 I have never met him. ~
You (*meet*) him; he lives next door to you.
20 I (*do*) it. (**It was my duty to do it, but I didn't.**)
21 He (*not catch*) the 9.20 train because he didn't leave home till 9.25.
22 I *opened* it, **which was unnecessary.**
23 The police were here while we were out. ~
Someone (*betray*) us.
24 I *drove* at 80 miles an hour, **which was wrong.**
25 When I was your age I (*climb*) that mountain, (**but I didn't**).
26 If a policeman had seen me climbing through your window he (*ask*) me what I was doing.
27 He said that censorship of news was ridiculous and it (*abolish*) years ago. (passive verb)
28 You *boiled* so many eggs; **but** there are only four of us.
29 She (*play*) the chief part in the film, but she quarrelled with the director, so he engaged someone else.

30 This poem (*be*) written by Keats, **but I am not certain.**
31 He (*take*) off his hat in the theatre, **(but he didn't).**
32 People used to walk twenty miles to do their shopping. ~
    They (*have*) a lot of energy in those days.
33 One day he went for a walk up a mountain and never came back. ~
    He (*fall*) over a precipice.
34 I just pressed lightly on the pane and my hand went through. ~
    The glass (*be*) very thin.
35 You *translated* it into French, **which wasn't necessary.**
36 You *looked* at the new moon through glass. It is most unlucky.

74 Perfect infinitive used with auxiliaries and some other verbs

■ PEG 255

Instructions: as for Exercise 73, but where two verbs in italics are
placed side by side, put the second verb into the perfect infinitive
and the first into an appropriate tense.
    This palace (*say*) (*build*) in three years.
    This palace is said to have been built in three years.

1 She (*marry*) my brother but she was killed in a plane crash a month
   before the wedding date.
2 You *repeated* it, **which was unnecessary.**
3 There (*seem*) (*be*) a fight here. Everything is smashed to bits.
4 We (*set*) out today, but the weather is so bad that we decided to
   postpone our start till tomorrow.
5 I thought they were mushrooms. ~
   You (*not eat*) them unless you were sure. They (*be*) poisonous.
6 He learnt the language in six months. ~
   He (*work*) very hard.
7 I *brought* my umbrella, **which was unnecessary.**
8 I (*like*) (*bathe*) but there wasn't time.
9 I've forgotten the address. I (*write*) it down **(but I didn't).**
10 If I'd known your house was so cold I (*not come*).
11 You (*tell*) me you were going camping! If I'd known I (*go*) with
    you. ~
    But it rained all the time. You (*not like*) that, would you?
12 Who gave you my address? ~
    I don't remember. It (*be*) Tom. ~
    It (*not be*) Tom; he doesn't know it.
13 You *bought* flowers **but** we have plenty in the garden.
14 After two years of his teaching she knew absolutely nothing. ~
    He (*not be*) a good teacher.
15 My sister has just come back from abroad. She (*seem*) (*enjoy*) her trip
    very much.

16 Life (*be*) very uncomfortable in the Stone Age.
17 You (*stand*) still when you were being photographed, (**but you didn't**).
18 I (*go*) to a foreign university but the war prevented it.
19 I (*like*) (*photograph*) it but I had no more film.
20 There (*be*) a bad accident here. Look at all the broken glass.
21 **It is possible that** prehistoric cave drawings *were* connected with religion.
22 I have been driving for 20 years. ~
   You (*not drive*) for 20 years. You are only 30 now.
23 It (*take*) years to dig the Suez Canal.
24 He walked past me without speaking. ~
   He (*not recognize*) you. He is very short-sighted.
25 I (*like*) (*go*) to the match but the tickets were all sold.
26 He says he saw you at the theatre yesterday. ~
   He (*not see*) me. I wasn't there.
27 This picture may be a fake; on the other hand it (*be*) painted by one of the Dutch masters.
28 **It is possible that** the fire in the ship *was started* by a bomb.
29 She walked 300 miles, carrying her child. ~
   She (*have*) great courage.
30 **It is possible that** he (*read*) it in the papers. ~
   He (*not read*) it. He can't read. Someone (*tell*) him.
31 I told them to meet me under the clock but they didn't turn up.
   Perhaps they *were waiting* under the wrong clock. There are two in the station.
32 He told me his name was Johnson. ~
   You (*mishear*) him. His name is Jones.
33 I said that I couldn't find my pen and he said that **perhaps** somebod
   had borrowed it.
34 I (*like*) (*ask*) a question but I was sitting so far back that I didn't think I'd be heard.
35 There (*be*) a fort here at one time. You can see where the foundations were.
36 The dinosaur (*be said*) (*be*) rather a stupid animal.

7 Gerund, infinitive and participles

75 The gerund

☐ PEG 257

Put the verbs in brackets into the gerund.

1 He gave up (gamble).
2 Try to avoid (make) him angry.
3 Stop (argue) and start (work).
4 The children prefer (watch) TV to (read).
5 I am against (make) any complaints.
6 It's no use (cry) over spilt milk. (*proverb*)
7 I suggest (hold) another meeting next week.
8 He finished (speak) and sat down.
9 He was fined for (drive) without lights.
10 It is difficult to get used to (eat) with chopsticks.
11 If you can't turn the key try (put) some oil in the lock.
12 He lost no time in (get) down to work.
13 You can't make an omelette without (break) eggs. (*proverb*)
14 We are looking forward to (read) your new book.
15 They escaped by (slide) down ropes made of blankets.
16 They don't allow (smoke) in here.
17 He is thinking of (leave) his job and (go) to America.
18 After (read) this article you will give up (smoke).
19 If you put your money into that business you risk (lose) every penny.
20 Imagine (live) with someone who never stops (talk).
21 Is there anything here worth (buy)?
22 He was accused of (leak) classified information to the press.
23 You'd better consult your lawyer before (decide) to buy the property.
24 I don't enjoy (go) to the dentist.
25 Would you mind (put) your pet snake somewhere else?
26 The hostages were rescued without a shot (be) fired.
27 By (work) day and night he succeeded in (finish) the job in time.
28 He has a scheme for (make) grass grow in winter.
29 I don't feel like (work); what about (go) to a disco instead?
30 Would you mind (write) your name and address on the back of the cheque?
31 If a thing is worth (do) at all it is worth (do) well. (*proverb*)

32 I hate (borrow) money.
33 He was furious at (be) mistaken for an escaped convict.
34 After (talk) for ten minutes I succeeded in (convince) him that there was no danger.
35 I remember (read) a review of that book and (think) I'd like to get it.
36 As a result of (listen) at keyholes he learnt many facts which he had no hesitation in (use) to his own advantage.

76 Gerund and infinitive

■ PEG 266–71

Put the verbs in brackets into the correct form (gerund or infinitive).

1 I am looking forward to (see) you.
2 He dreads (have) to retire.
3 I arranged (meet) them here.
4 He urged us (work) faster.
5 I wish (see) the manager.
6 It's no use (wait).
7 He warned her (not touch) the wire.
8 Don't forget (lock) the door before (go) to bed.
9 My mother told me (not speak) to anyone about it.
10 I can't understand her (behave) like that.
11 He tried (explain) but she refused (listen).
12 At dinner she annoyed me by (smoke) between the courses.
13 You are expected (know) the safety regulations of the college.
14 He decided (disguise) himself by (dress) as a woman.
15 I am prepared (wait) here all night if necessary.
16 Would you mind (show) me how (work) the lift?
17 After (walk) for three hours we stopped to let the others (catch up) with us.
18 I am beginning (understand) what you mean.
19 He was fined for (exceed) the speed limit.
20 The boys like (play) games but hate (do) lessons.
21 I regret (inform) you that your application has been refused.
22 I couldn't help (overhear) what you said.
23 Mrs Jones: I don't allow (smoke) in my drawing-room.
   Mrs Smith: I don't allow my family (smoke) at all.
24 He surprised us all by (go) away without (say) 'Good-bye'.
25 Please go on (write); I don't mind (wait).
26 He wore dark glasses (avoid) (be) recognized.
27 Before (give) evidence you must swear (speak) the truth.
28 I tried (persuade) him (agree) with your proposal.
29 Your windows need (clean); would you like me (do) them for you?
30 Would you mind (shut) the window? I hate (sit) in a draught.
31 I can't help (sneeze); I caught a cold yesterday from (sit) in a draught.

32 Do stop (talk); I am trying (finish) a letter.
33 His doctor advised him (give up) (jog).
34 My watch keeps (stop). ~
   That's because you keep (forget) (wind) it.
35 Without (realize) it, he hindered us instead of (help) us.
36 People used (make) fire by (rub) two sticks together.

77 Gerund and infinitive

◪ PEG 266-71

Put the verbs in brackets into the correct form (gerund or infinitive).

1 He hates (answer) the phone, and very often just lets it (ring).
2 If you go on (let) your dog (chase) cars he'll end by (be) run over.
3 I prefer (drive) to (be driven).
4 I advise you (start) (look) for a flat at once.
5 Would you mind (lend) me £5? I forgot (cash) a cheque.
6 (Lie) on this beach is much more pleasant than (sit) in the office.
7 She likes her children (go) to the dentist every six months.
8 By (neglect) (take) ordinary precautions he endangered the life of his crew.
9 An instructor is coming (show) us how (use) the aqualung.
10 I have no intention of (go) to that film; I couldn't bear (see) my favourite actress in such a dreadful part.
11 I suggest (telephone) the hospitals before (ask) the police (look) for him.
12 After (hear) the conditions I decided (not enter) for the competition.
13 Some people seem (have) a passion for (write) to the newspapers.
14 He expects me (answer) by return but I have no intention of (reply) at all.
15 I tried (explain) to him but he refused (listen) and went on (grumble).
16 By (offer) enormous wages he is persuading men (leave) their present jobs and (work) for him.
17 He postponed (make) a decision till it was too late (do) anything.
18 Imagine (have) (get up) at five a.m. every day!
19 Try (forget) it; it isn't worth (worry) about.
20 There is no point in (remain) in a dangerous place if you can't do anything (help) the people who have (stay) there.
21 The horse won't be well enough (run) in tomorrow's race. He doesn't seem (have recovered) from his long journey.
22 At first I enjoyed (listen) to him but after a while I got tired of (hear) the same story again and again.
23 It is usually easier (learn) a subject by (read) books than by (listen) to lectures.
24 It wouldn't be safe (start) down now; we'll have (wait) till the mist clears.

Gerund, infinitive and participles

25 After (discuss) the matter for an hour the committee adjourned
    without (have reached) any decision.
26 It's not much use (have) a bicycle if you don't know how (ride) it.
27 He didn't dare (leave) the house because he was afraid of (meet)
    someone who might (recognize) him.
28 I distinctly remember (pay) him. I gave him £2.
29 Did you remember (give) him the key of the safe? ~
    No, I didn't. I'll go and do it now.
30 Please forgive me for (interrupt) you but would you mind (repeat)
    that last sentence?
31 I know my hair wants (cut) but I never have time (go) to the
    hairdresser's.
32 He made a lot of money by (buy) tickets in advance and (sell) them
    for twice the price on the day of the match.
33 She rushed out of the room without (give) me a chance (explain).
34 He keeps (ask) me the time and I keep (tell) him (buy) himself a
    watch.
35 He has a theory that it is possible (tell) the time in daylight by (look)
    into a cat's eyes.
36 I'd hate (be) beside a volcano when it started (erupt).

78 Gerund and infinitive

■ PEG 266–71

After **like** it is sometimes possible to use either gerund or infinitive,
but there tends to be a slight difference in implication.
like + gerund usually means 'enjoy'; it also usually implies that the
action is/was performed:
    I like skating = I enjoy skating (and do skate).
like + infinitive has more the meaning of 'approve of', 'like the idea
or habit'. In the affirmative it gives no indication as to whether the
action is performed or not, and in the negative implies that it is not
performed.
    I didn't like saying it
usually means 'I said it, unwillingly', but
    I didn't like to say it
usually means 'I didn't say it' (because it didn't seem right or
sensible). The distinction, however, is not rigid. The above notes
are, therefore, only guides which may safely be followed.

Put the verbs in brackets into gerund or infinitive.

1 I used (ride) a lot but I haven't had a chance (do) any since (come)
   here. ~
   I ride sometimes. Would you like (come) with me next time?
2 Most people prefer (spend) money to (earn) it.
3 I resented (be) unjustly accused and asked him (apologize).

4 It isn't good for children (eat) too many sweets.
5 I didn't feel like (work) so I suggested (spend) the day in the garden.
6 Why do you keep (look) back? Are you afraid of (be) followed?
7 Do you remember (post) the letter? ~
   Yes, I do; I posted it in the letter-box near my gate.
8 Did you remember (lock) the door? ~
   No, I didn't. I'd better (go) back and (do) it now.
9 You still have a lot (learn) if you'll forgive my (say) so.
10 It's no use (try) (interrupt) him. You'll have (wait) till he stops (talk).
11 I'm for (do) nothing till the police arrive. They don't like you (move)
   anything when a crime has been committed.
12 He didn't like (leave) the children alone in the house but he had no
   alternative as he had (go) out to work.
13 Why didn't you drink it? ~
   I didn't like (drink) it as I didn't know what it was.
14 I'm very sorry for (be) late. It was good of you (wait) for me.
15 I keep (try) (make) mayonnaise but I never succeed. ~
   Try (add) the yolk of a hard-boiled egg.
16 Do you feel like (go) to a film or would you rather (stay) at home?
17 She told me (look) through her correspondence and (take) out any
   letters that you had written her. I didn't like (look) through someone
   else's letters but I had (do) as she said.
18 He took to (get up) early and (walk) noisily about the house.
19 I liked (listen) to folk music much better than (listen) to pop.
20 The car began (make) an extraordinary noise so I stopped (see) what
   it was.
21 You'll never regret (do) a kind action.
22 He decided (put) broken glass on top of his wall (prevent) boys
   (climb) over it.
23 He annoyed me very much by (take) the piece of cake that I was
   keeping (eat) after my supper.
24 He kept (ring) up and (ask) for an explanation and she didn't know
   what (do) about him.
25 We got tired of (wait) for the weather (clear) and finally decided (set)
   out in the rain.
26 He made me (repeat) his instructions (make) sure that I understood
   what I was (do) after he had gone.
27 I suggest (leave) the car here and (send) a breakdown van (tow) it to
   the garage.
28 She apologized for (borrow) my sewing-machine without (ask)
   permission and promised never (do) it again.
29 I didn't mean (offend) anyone but somehow I succeeded in (annoy)
   them all.
30 She claimed (be able) (tell) the future by (gaze) into her crystal ball.
31 He never thinks of (get) out of your way; he expects you (walk)
   round him.
32 You don't need (ask) his permission every time you want (leave) the
   room.

33 The police accused him of (set) fire to the building but he denied (have been) in the area on the night of the fire.
34 I left my door open. Why didn't you walk in? ~
   I didn't like (go) in when you weren't there.
35 It's much better (go) to a hairdresser than (try) (save) time by (cut) your own hair.
36 I'd rather (earn) my living by (scrub) floors than (make) money by (blackmail) people.

79 Infinitive, gerund, present participle

■ PEG 266–75, 295 C, 295 D

This exercise includes examples of both **ing** forms, the gerund and the present participle. Either present participle or infinitive without **to** can be used after verbs of the senses.

Put the verbs in brackets into a correct form. When more than one form is possible it will be noted in the key.

1 When the painter felt the ladder (begin) (slip) he grabbed the gutter (save) himself from (fall).
2 The snow kept (fall) and the workmen grew tired of (try) (keep) the roads clear.
3 He offered (lend) me the money. I didn't like (take) it but I had no alternative.
4 What was in the letter? ~
   I don't know. I didn't like (open) it as it wasn't addressed to me.
5 Do you remember (read) about it? ~
   No, at that time I was too young (read) newspapers.
6 Did you remember (book) seats for the theatre tomorrow? ~
   Yes, I have the tickets here. Would you like (keep) them? I am inclined (lose) theatre tickets.
7 Try (avoid) (be) late. He hates (be) kept (wait).
8 I didn't know how (get) to your house so I stopped (ask) the way.
9 I wish my refrigerator would stop (make) that horrible noise. You can't hear anyone (speak).
10 This book tells you how (win) at games without actually (cheat).
11 The gunman began (fire). He felt a bullet (graze) his cheek.
12 He heard the clock (strike) six and knew that it was time for him (get) up.
13 I can hear the bell (ring) but nobody seems (be coming) (open) the door.
14 Did you advise him (go) to the police? ~
   No, I didn't like (give) any advice on such a difficult matter.
15 He wanted (put) my chameleon on a tartan rug and (watch) it (change) colour.

16 It is easy (see) animals on the road in daylight but sometimes at night it is very difficult (avoid) (hit) them.

17 The fire seems (be) out. ~
It can't be quite out. I can hear the wood (crackle).

18 I caught him (climb) over my wall. I asked him (explain) but he refused (say) anything, so in the end I had (let) him (go).

19 When at last I succeeded in (convince) him that I wanted (get) home quickly he put his foot on the accelerator and I felt the car (leap) forward.

20 I'm not used to (drive) on the left. ~
When you see everyone else (do) it you'll find it quite easy (do) yourself.

21 It is pleasant (sit) by the fire at night and (hear) the wind (howl) outside.

22 There was no way of (get) out of the building except by (climb) down a rope and Ann was too terrified (do) this.

23 We heard the engines (roar) as the plane began (move) and we saw the people on the ground (wave) good-bye.

24 It's no good (write) to him; he never answers letters. The only thing (do) is (go) and (see) him.

25 Why did you go all round the field instead of (walk) across it? ~
I didn't like (cross) it because of the bull. I never see a bull without (think) that it wants (chase) me.

26 The people in the flat below seem (be having) a party. You can hear the champagne corks (thud) against their ceiling.

27 I don't like (get) bills but when I do get them I like (pay) them promptly.

28 Ask him (come) in. Don't keep him (stand) at the door.

29 The boys next door used (like) (make) and (fly) model aeroplanes, but they seem to have stopped (do) that now.

30 I knew I wasn't the first (arrive), for I saw smoke (rise) from the chimney.

31 We watched the men (saw) the tree and as we were walking away heard it (fall) with a tremendous crash.

32 I hate (see) a child (cry).

33 We watched the children (jump) from a window and (fall) into a blanket held by the people below.

34 It is very unpleasant (wake) up and (hear) the rain (beat) on the windows.

35 He saw the lorry (begin) (roll) forwards but he was too far away (do) anything (stop) it.

36 There are people who can't help (laugh) when they see someone (slip) on a banana skin.

Gerund, infinitive and participles

80 Using participles to join sentences
☑ PEG 276-9

Join each of the following pairs of sentences, using either a present
participle e.g. *knowing*, a past participle e.g. *known*, or a perfect
participle e.g. *having known*. Numbers 17, 28, 33, and 36 contain
three sentences each. Combine these in the same way.
> He got off his horse. He began searching for something on the
> ground.
> *Getting off his horse, he began searching . . .*
> I had seen photographs of the place. I had no desire to go there
> *Having seen photographs of the place, I had no desire . . .*
> The speaker refused to continue. He was infuriated by the
> interruptions.
> *Infuriated by the interruptions, the speaker refused . . .*

These participle constructions are more common in written English.

1 I knew that he was poor. I offered to pay his fare.
2 We barricaded the windows. We assembled in the hall.
3 She became tired of my complaints about the programme. She
turned it off.
4 He found no one at home. He left the house in a bad temper.
5 She hoped to find the will. She searched everywhere.
6 The criminal removed all traces of his crime. He left the building.
7 He realized that he had missed the last train. He began to walk.
8 He was exhausted by his work. He threw himself on his bed.
9 He had spent all his money. He decided to go home and ask his
father for a job.
10 He escaped from prison. He looked for a place where he could get
food.
11 She didn't want to hear the story again. She had heard it all before.
12 They found the money. They began quarrelling about how to
divide it.
13 She entered the room suddenly. She found them smoking.
14 I turned on the light. I was astonished at what I saw.
15 We visited the museum. We decided to have lunch in the park.
16 He offered to show us the way home. He thought we were lost.
17 He found his revolver. He loaded it. He sat down facing the door.
18 She asked me to help her. She realized that she couldn't move it
alone.
19 He fed the dog. He sat down to his own dinner.
20 He addressed the congregation. He said he was sorry to see how few
of them had been able to come.
21 He thought he must have made a mistake somewhere. He went
through his calculations again.
22 I have looked through the fashion magazines. I realize that my
clothes are hopelessly out of date.

23 The tree had fallen across the road. It had been uprooted by the gale.
24 People were sleeping in the next room. They were wakened by the sound of breaking glass.
25 I knew that the murderer was still at large. I was extremely reluctant to open the door.
26 He stole the silver. He looked for a place to hide it.
27 We were soaked to the skin. We eventually reached the station.
28 I sat in the front row. I used opera glasses. I saw everything beautifully.
29 One evening you will be sitting by the fire. You will remember this day.
30 I didn't like to sit down. I knew that there were ants in the grass.
31 She believed that she could trust him absolutely. She gave him a blank cheque.
32 Slates were ripped off by the gale. They fell on people passing below.
33 The lion found his cage door open. He saw no sign of his keeper. He left the cage and walked slowly towards the zoo entrance.
34 The government once tried to tax people according to the size of their houses. They put a tax on windows.
35 I had heard that the caves were dangerous. I didn't like to go any further without a light.
36 She wore extremely fashionable clothes. She was surrounded by photographers and pressmen. She swept up to the microphone.

81 Misrelated participles

■ PEG 280

A participle is considered to belong to the noun or pronoun that immediately precedes it (which usually, but not necessarily, is the subject of the main verb).
> The boy, *climbing* the tree to get birds' eggs, had a bad fall.

If there is no noun/pronoun in this position the participle is considered to belong to the subject of the following main verb:
> *Climbing* the tree to get birds' eggs, the boy had a bad fall.

Sometimes this principle is disregarded and confusion results:
> Climbing down the tree, one of the eggs broke.

This word order makes it appear that the egg was climbing, which is nonsense. A participle linked in this way to the wrong noun/pronoun is said to be 'misrelated'. The sentence should be rewritten:
> *Climbing down the tree he broke one of the eggs* or
> *As he was climbing down the tree one of the eggs broke.*

Other examples of this type of error are given below. Correct the sentences. Sometimes only a change of order is required.

Gerund, infinitive and participles

1 When leaving a car in this car park the brakes must be left off.
2 Wading across the river, the current swept me off my feet.
3 When filling a tank with petrol naked lights should be extinguished.
4 Running into the room, a rug caught her foot and she fell.
5 Reading the letter a second time, the meaning becomes clearer.
6 When carrying a gun it should never be pointed at anyone.
7 When planting these flowers care must be taken not to damage the roots.
8 Riding in his first race, his horse fell at the last jump.
9 When paying by cheque, a bank card should be shown.
10 Knowing me to be the fool of the family, the news that I had won a scholarship astonished him.
11 Believing that his last hour had come, his hands began to tremble.
12 Passing under a ladder, a pot of paint fell on my head.
13 Reading in bed, my hands often get very cold.
14 Leaving the cinema, it seemed to him that the film had been exceptionally bad.
15 Barking furiously, I led the dog out of the room.
16 Having paid my taxes, the amount left in the bank is hardly worth mentioning.
17 Writing my name in the hotel register, a familiar voice attracted my attention.
18 Tied to a post, the sea was tossing the boat up and down.
19 Misunderstanding the question, the wrong answer was sent in.
20 Shining in the sky, we saw the first star.
21 When driving carelessly it is easy to have an accident.
22 Pinned to the door by a knife, the man saw a notice.
23 Written in large letters they read the words 'No Entry'.
24 While cleaning his gun it went off unexpectedly.
25 Wondering where to go, an advertisement caught my eye.
26 Rushing out of the house, a lorry knocked me over.
27 Sitting by the fire, it all comes back to me.
28 Falling from such a height, we thought he would never survive.
29 When changing a fuse the electricity should first be switched off.
30 Towed behind the car, I saw a trailer with a boat on it.
31 While sitting at the foot of a cliff a stone fell on him.
32 Driving to work, the traffic jams infuriated him.
33 Dropped by parachute, the country seemed entirely unfamiliar.
34 Sitting in the dentist's chair, an idea suddenly occurred to me.
35 Weakened by his last illness, I felt sure that another winter in this country would kill him.
36 Getting out of bed, a scorpion bit him.

8 Passive

82 Active to passive

◨ PEG 302-6

Put the following into the passive voice. The agent should not be mentioned except in numbers 11 and 28.

1 You should open the wine about three hours before you use it.
2 Previous climbers had cut steps in the ice.
3 Somebody had cleaned my shoes and brushed my suit.
4 We use this room only on special occasions.
5 You must not hammer nails into the walls without permission.
6 In some districts farmers use pigs to find truffles.
7 Someone switched on a light and opened the door.
8 Somebody had slashed the picture with a knife.
9 They are pulling down the old theatre.
10 Why didn't they mend the roof before it fell in?
11 The mob broke all the shop windows in recent riots.
12 The librarian said that they were starting a new system because people were not returning books.
13 The police asked each of us about his movements on the night of the crime.
14 Someone will serve refreshments.
15 People must not leave bicycles in the hall.
16 Members may keep books for three weeks. After that they must return them.
17 The burglars had cut an enormous hole in the steel door.
18 I've bought a harp. They are delivering it this afternoon. (*Do not change the first sentence.*)
19 Someone has already told him to report for duty at six.
20 They rang the church bells as a flood warning.
21 No one can do anything unless someone gives us more information.
22 People are spending far more money on food now than they spent ten years ago.
23 The organizers will exhibit the paintings till the end of the month.
24 They will say nothing more about the matter if someone returns the stolen gun.
25 It is high time someone told him to stop behaving like a child.
26 A thief stole my dog and brought him back only when I offered £20 reward for him.
27 The judge gave him two weeks in which to pay the fine.
28 They make these artificial flowers of silk.

123

83 Active to passive

◪ PEG 302-6

Put the following into the passive, mentioning the agent where necessary.

Where there is an indirect and a direct object, make the indirect object the subject of the passive verb.

They gave her a clock.
She was given a clock.

The gerund after certain verbs is replaced in the passive by **should be** + past participle:

They advised employing part-time workers.
They advised that part-time workers should be employed.

1 They feed the seals at the zoo twice a day.
2 Who wrote it?
3 Compare clothes which we have washed with clothes which any other laundry has washed.
4 He expected us to offer him the job.
5 They showed her the easiest way to do it.
6 Lightning struck the old oak.
7 Titian couldn't have painted it as people didn't wear that style of dress till after his death.
8 A jellyfish stung her.
9 The author has written a special edition for children.
10 Judges used to carry sweet herbs as a protection against jail-fever.
11 What did he write it with? ~
He wrote it with a matchstick dipped in blood.
12 An uneasy silence succeeded the shot.
13 Did the idea interest you?
14 The lawyer gave him the details of his uncle's will.
15 Beavers make these dams.
16 They used to start these engines by hand. Now they start them by electricity.
17 Most people opposed this.
18 Students are doing a lot of the work.
19 The Prime Minister was to have opened the dry dock.
20 They recommended opening new factories in the depressed area. (*Use* should.)
21 The closure of the workshops will make a lot of men redundant.
22 Anyone with the smallest intelligence could understand these instructions.
23 We will not admit children under sixteen.
24 Boys of sixteen to eighteen are to man this training ship.
25 A rainstorm flooded the gypsies' camp.
26 The howling of wolves kept him awake all night.
27 They suggested making the tests easier. (*Use* should.)
28 Children couldn't have done all this damage.

84 Passive to active

■ PEG 302-6

Turn the following sentences into the active voice. Where no agent
is mentioned one must be supplied.

School notice: This door must be kept shut.

Students must keep this door shut.

1 Why don't you have your eyes tested? (. . . get an optician to . . .
   See 119.)
2 This speed limit is to be introduced gradually.
3 The runways are being lengthened at all the main airports.
4 It is now 6 a.m. and at most of the hospitals in the country patients
   are being wakened with cups of tea.
5 Byron is said to have lived on vinegar and potatoes.
6 By tradition, any sturgeon that are caught by British ships must be
   offered to the Queen.
7 This notice has been altered.
8 The owners went away last March and since then their houseboat
   has been used continuously by squatters. (*Use a continuous tense and
   omit* continuously.)
9 The damaged ship was being towed into harbour when the towline
   broke.
10 Have a lift put in and then you won't have to climb up all these
   stairs.
11 Last year a profit of two million pounds was made in the first six
   months but this was cancelled by a loss of seventeen million pounds
   which was made in the second six months.
12 Evening dress will be worn.
13 The ship was put into quarantine and passengers and crew were
   forbidden to land.
14 Someone will have to be found to take her place.
15 He was made to surrender his passport.
16 This rumour must have been started by our opponents.
17 My paintings are to be exhibited for the first time by New Arts
   Gallery.
18 This scientific theory has now been proved to be false.
19 The car which was blown over the cliff yesterday is to be salvaged
   today.
20 The house where the dead man was found is being guarded by the
   police to prevent it from being entered and the evidence interfered
   with.
21 Why wasn't the car either locked or put into the garage?
22 It is being said that too little money is being spent by the
   government on roads.
23 Your money could be put to good use instead of being left idle in the
   bank.

Passive

24 For a long time the earth was believed to be flat.
25 This copy hasn't been read. The pages haven't been cut.
26 The stones were thrown by a student, who was afterwards led away by the police.
27 Carrier pigeons are said to have been used by early Egyptian and Greek sailors.
28 The referee was being escorted from the football field by a strong police guard.

9 Indirect speech

85 Indirect speech: statements

■ PEG 307–8, 313

1 Students are asked to assume that these sentences are spoken and reported on different days. This will mean that a sentence such as: He said, 'I am coming *tomorrow*,' will become: He said that he was coming *the next day*, and so on.
This applies to all the exercises on indirect speech in this book.

2 With indirect speech, when the person addressed is mentioned, **tell** is more usual than **say to** as an introductory verb. For example:
He told me that he was going away the next day
is more usual than
He said to me that he was going away the next day.

Put the following into indirect speech.

1 'I have something to show you,' I said to her.
2 'Nothing grows in my garden. It never gets any sun,' she said.
3 'I'm going away tomorrow, mother,' he said.
4 'I've been in London for a month but so far I haven't had time to visit the Tower,' said Rupert.
5 'It isn't so foggy today as it was yesterday,' I remarked.
6 'The new underpass is being officially opened the day after tomorrow,' said the BBC announcer.
7 'We have moved into our new flat. We don't like it nearly so much as our last one,' said my aunt.
8 'We have a lift but very often it doesn't work,' they said.
9 'From one of the windows of my flat I can see the Eiffel Tower,' he said.
10 'I've no idea what the time is but I'll dial 8081 and find out,' said his daughter.
11 He said, 'My wife has just been made a judge.'
12 'I'll come with you as soon as I am ready,' she replied.
13 'I have a German lesson this afternoon and I haven't done my homework yet,' said the small boy.
14 'If you let the iron get too hot you will scorch your clothes,' I warned her.
15 'You haven't given me quite enough. The bill is for £14 and you've paid me only £13,' he pointed out.

16 Ann said, 'Englishmen make good husbands because they are nearly always willing to help in the house.'

17 Mary answered, 'I like men to be useful but I don't like them to be too domesticated. I prefer them to keep out of the kitchen altogether. Men look silly in aprons anyway.'

18 Motoring report: The new Rolls Royce runs so quietly that all you can hear is the ticking of the clock.
Managing director of the Rolls Royce company: In that case we'll have to do something about the clock.

19 'I don't know what to do with all my plums. I suppose I'll have to make jam. The trouble is that none of us eats jam,' she said.

20 'We like working on Sundays because we get double pay,' explained the builders.

21 He said, 'I am quite a good cook and I do all my own washing and mending too.'

22 'You can keep that one if you like, Joan,' he said. 'I've got plenty of others.'

23 'I'm going fishing with mother this afternoon,' said the small boy, 'and we are going into the garden now to dig for worms.'
(*Omit* now).

24 'You've got my umbrella,' I said crossly. 'Yours is in your bedroom.'

25 'I know exactly what they said,' the private detective explained to his client, 'because I bugged their phone.'

26 'I'll sit up till she comes in, but I hope she won't be late,' he said.

27 'If you give me some wire, I'll hang that picture for you,' said my cousin.

28 'I have a Turkish bath occasionally, but it doesn't seem to make any difference to my weight,' she said.

29 'This is quite a good model, madam. I use one of these myself,' said the salesman.

30 'My new house is supposed to be haunted, but so far I haven't seen any ghosts,' she said.

31 The advertisement said, 'If you answer the questions correctly you may win £100.'

32 'If I press my ear against the wall, I can hear what the people in the next flat are saying,' he said.

86 Indirect speech: statements

◪ PEG 309–10

Some tenses/forms do not change when direct speech becomes indirect:
'I wish my children would eat vegetables,' she said.
She (said she) wished her children would eat vegetables.

Put the following into indirect speech, being careful to avoid ambiguity:

1 'I couldn't get into the house because I had lost my key, so I had to break a window,' he said.
2 'The mirror is there so that you can see yourself when you are dancing,' the instructress told him.
3 'I wrote to him the day before yesterday. I wonder why he hasn't rung up,' she said.
4 'If the ground is dry on the day of the race, my horse might win,' said the owner.
5 'You'd better slow down. There's a speed limit here,' she said to me. (*Use* advise.)
6 'If Tom wants seats, he'd better apply early,' she said.
7 'We walked 50 miles last night to see the Minister and protest about our rents being raised. He was very polite and promised to do what he could for us,' said one of the tenants.
8 'They should put traffic lights here, otherwise there'll be more accidents,' she said.
9 'It's time we began training for our next match,' the coach said to them.
10 'If you leave home at six, you should be here by nine,' he said to me.
11 'If it rains this afternoon it will be too wet to play the match tomorrow,' the captain said.
12 'I meant to plug in the electric blanket but I plugged in the electric kettle by mistake. I'm always doing silly things like that,' she told her guest.
13 'I was intending to do it tomorrow,' he said, 'but now I don't think I'll be able to.'
14 'Bill should do very well at the university, Mrs Smith,' said the headmaster. 'He's done very well here.'
15 'I don't think your father likes me,' said the young wife.
'You mustn't think that,' said her husband; 'it is just that he is old and finds it hard to get used to new people.' (*Leave* mustn't *unchanged.*)
16 'The steak is overdone again. I'm not complaining; I'm just pointing it out,' said her husband.
'I wish you'd stop pointing things out,' said his wife.
17 'They couldn't open the safe on the spot so they carried it away with them,' the night watchman reported.
18 'If you saw my father, you'd recognize him at once. He is the most extraordinary-looking man,' she said to me.
19 'I found an old Roman coin in the garden yesterday,' he said, 'and I'm going to take it to the museum this afternoon.'
20 He said, 'I got out of my boat, leaving the engine running, but while I was standing on the quay the gears suddenly engaged themselves and the boat went straight out of the harbour with no one on board.'
21 Then Macbeth enters and says, 'I have done the deed.'

22 'Would you like me to go with you?' I said.
   'I'd rather go alone,' he answered.
23 My brother said, 'You may take my car if you like. I shan't be
   needing it tomorrow or the day after.'
24 'Yesterday Tom and I went to look at a house that he was thinking
   of buying. It was rather a nice house and had a lovely garden but
   Tom decided against it because it was opposite a cemetery,' said
   Celia.
25 He said, 'My wife wants to take a job but I'd rather she
   concentrated on our home.'
26 'I don't know what your father will say when he sees what a mess
   your puppies have made of this five-pound note,' said my mother.
27 'It's high time you passed your test; I'm tired of driving round with
   an L-plate on the front of the car,' my sister said.
28 'I wish you'd seen it,' I said to her.

87 Indirect speech: questions

▰ PEG 317

Put the following into indirect speech. The first ten questions
require no change of order:
   He said, 'What is happening?'
   He asked what was happening.

1 'What happened to Mr Budd?' said one of the men.
2 'Which of his sons inherited his estate?' asked another.
3 'Who is going to live in the big house?' enquired a third.
4 'What will happen to his racehorses?' asked someone else.
5 'Which team has won?' asked Ann.
6 'Which team won the previous match?' said Bill.
7 'Who is playing next week?' he asked.
8 'Who will be umpiring that match?' asked Tom.
9 'Who wants a lift home?' said Ann.
10 'Who has just dropped a £10 note?' I asked.
11 'Where is the ticket office?' asked Mrs Jones.
12 'What shall I do with my heavy luggage?' she said. (*Use* should.)
13 'What platform does the train leave from?' asked Bill.
14 'When does it arrive in York?' he asked.
15 'When was the timetable changed?' I asked.
16 'Why has the 2.30 train been cancelled?' said Ann.
17 'How much does a day return to Bath cost?' Mrs Jones asked.
18 'Why does the price go up so often?' she wondered.
19 'How can I get from the station to the airport?' said Bill.
20 'When are you coming back?' I asked them.
21 'Is a return ticket cheaper than two singles?' said my aunt.
22 'Do puppies travel free?' asked a dog owner.

23 'Can I bring my dog into the compartment with me?' she asked.
24 'Does this train stop at York?' asked Bill.
25 'Can you telephone from inter-city trains?' said the businessman.
26 'Does the 2.40 have a restaurant car?' he enquired.
27 'Can you get coffee on the train?' asked my aunt.
28 'Do they bring it round on a trolley?' she said.
29 'Are there smoking compartments?' said the man with the pipe.
30 'Have you reserved a seat?' I asked him.

Extra exercise: read the last twenty questions, using one of the
following prefaces: **I wonder/I'd like to know/Do you know?/Have
you any idea?/Can you tell me?**
  11 *'Do you know where the ticket office is?'*
  12 *'I wonder what I should do with my heavy luggage.'*

88 Indirect speech: questions

☑ PEG 317

A new student, Paul, has come to the college and the other students
are asking him questions. Imagine that he reports these questions
later to an English friend:
  1 *Bill asked what country I came from.*

1 'What country do you come from?' said Bill.
2 'How long have you been here?' said Ann.
3 'Are you working as well as studying?' asked Peter.
4 'Have you got a work permit?' Bill wanted to know.
5 'What are you going to study?' asked Ann.
6 'Have you enrolled for more than one class?' said Peter.
7 'Do you want to buy any second-hand books?' said Bill.
8 'Have you seen the library?' asked Ann.
9 'Do you play rugby?' said Peter.
10 'Will you have time to play regularly?' he went on.
11 'Did you play for your school team?' said Bill.
12 'Are you interested in acting?' asked Ann.
13 'Would you like to join our Drama Group?' she said.
14 'What do you think of the canteen coffee?' asked Peter.

Mary and Tom, with their son, John, aged 11, have recently come to
this area. Mary wants to find a school for John and asks her
neighbour Mrs Smith about the local school.
(a) Later, Mrs Smith reports these questions to her husband:
    'Is it a mixed school?'
    She asked if it was a mixed school.
(b) Alternatively, supply suitable answers to Mary's questions and
    then imagine that Mary reports the conversation (her questions
    and Mrs Smith's answers) to her husband Tom:

36 'Were your boys happy there?' ~
'Yes, they were.'
I asked if her boys had been happy there and she said that they had.

15 'How long has it been a mixed school?'
16 'Do you like the headmaster?'
17 'Is he a scientist or an arts graduate?'
18 'How many children are there in the school?'
19 'How big are the classes?'
20 'Are the classes streamed?'
21 'What is the academic standard like?'
22 'Can parents visit the school at any time?'
23 'Is there a good art department?'
24 'Do they teach music?'
25 'What instruments can the children learn?'
26 'Is there a school orchestra?'
27 'Do they act plays?'
28 'What sort of plays have they done?'
29 'What games do they play?'
30 'Are the playing fields near the school?'
31 'Are they taught to swim?'
32 'Can the children get dinner at school?'
33 'Is the food good?'
34 'Is there a Parent-Teacher Association?'
35 'How often does it meet?'
36 'Were your own boys happy at the school?'

89 Indirect speech: questions

◪ PEG 317

Put the following into indirect speech.

1 'Why are you looking through the keyhole?' I said.
2 'Who put salt in my coffee?' he asked.
3 'Which of you knows how to make Irish stew?' said the chief cook.
4 'Why did you travel first class?' I asked him.
5 'How can I run in high-heeled shoes?' she enquired.
6 'What is your new house like?' I asked them.
7 He said, 'Where am I supposed to go now?' (*Omit* now.)
8 'Whose car did you borrow last night?' I said to him.
9 'What was she wearing when you saw her last?' the policeman asked me.
10 'Who owns this revolver?' said the detective.
11 'Where were you last night, Mr Jones?' he said.
12 'What else did you see?' I asked the boy.
13 'Have you done this sort of work before?' said his new employer.

14 'Can you read the last line on the chart?' the oculist asked her.
15 'Did they understand what you said to them?' he asked me.
16 'Are you being attended to, sir?' said the shop assistant.
17 'Will you go on strike when the others do?' the shop steward asked him.
18 'Do you see what I see, Mary?' said the young man.
19 'Who left the banana skin on the front doorstep?' said my mother.
20 'Have you gone completely mad?' I asked. 'Do you want to blow us all up?'
21 'Why is your house so full of antiques?' she asked. 'Was your father a collector?'
22 'Are you leaving today or tomorrow morning?' said his secretary.
23 'How far is it?' I said, 'and how long will it take me to get there?'
24 'Could I speak to Mrs Pitt?' said the caller.
'I'm afraid she's out,' said the *au pair* girl. 'Could I take a message?'
25 'Are you sorry for what you did?' the mother asked the little boy.
26 'Are you going to see him off at the station?' I asked her.
27 'Would you mind if I looked inside your bag, Madam?' said the policeman.
28 'If someone fell at your feet foaming at the mouth would you know what to do?' said the instructor in First Aid.
29 'Why do you think it may be dangerous?' he asked her.
30 'Do you know that the shoes you are wearing aren't a pair?' I asked him.

90 Indirect speech: commands, requests, advice expressed by object + infinitive

☑ PEG 320

Indirect commands, requests, etc. are normally expressed by **tell**, **order**, **ask**, **beg**, **advise**, **remind**, **warn**, etc., with the person addressed and the infinitive. Change the following direct commands into indirect commands using this construction. Remember that the person addressed is often not mentioned in a direct command:
    He said, 'Go away',
but must be mentioned in an indirect command:
    He told me (Tom/us/them, etc.) to go away.

1 'Switch off the TV,' he said to her.
2 'Shut the door, Tom,' she said.
3 'Lend me your pen for a moment,' I said to Mary.
4 'Don't watch late-night horror movies,' I warned them.
5 'Don't believe everything you hear,' he warned me.
6 'Please fill up this form,' the secretary said.
7 'Don't hurry,' I said.
8 'Don't touch that switch, Mary,' I said.

133

9 'Open the safe!' the raiders ordered the bank clerk.
10 'Please do as I say,' he begged me.
11 'Help your mother, Peter,' Mr Pitt said.
12 'Don't make too much noise, children,' he said.
13 'Do whatever you like,' she said to us.
14 'Don't miss your train,' she warned them.
15 'Read it before you sign it,' he said to his client.
16 'Do sing it again,' he said.
17 'Don't put your hands near the bars,' the zoo keeper warned us.
18 'Buy a new car,' I advised him.
19 'Don't drive too fast,' she begged him.
20 'Don't lean your bicycles against my windows, boys,' said the shopkeeper.
21 'Come to the cinema with me,' he asked her.
22 'Cook it in butter,' I advised her.
23 'Don't touch the gates, madam,' said the lift operator.
24 'Don't argue with me,' the teacher said to the boy.
25 'Pull as hard as you can,' he said to him.
26 'Send for the Fire Brigade,' the manager said to the porter.
27 'Don't lend her anything,' he advised us.
28 'Make a list of what you want,' she told us.
29 'Look at the paper,' he said to her.
30 'Stand clear of the doors,' a voice warned the people on the platform.
31 'See if you can find any mushrooms, children,' she said.
32 'Don't go alone,' I warned her.
33 'Pay at the cash desk,' the shop assistant said to the customer.
34 The notice said, 'Leave this space clear.'
35 'Remember to write to your mother,' I said to them.
36 'Think well before you answer,' the detective warned her.

91 Indirect speech: commands, requests, advice

☐ PEG 320

See note to 90.

Put the following into indirect speech. In most cases the person addressed must be supplied.

1 He said, 'Get out of my way.'
2 'Climb in through the window,' he ordered.
3 'Please pay at the desk,' said the assistant.
4 'Open your bag, please,' said the store detective.
5 'Don't worry about anything, Mrs Pitt,' said her solicitor. 'Leave it all to me.'
6 'Don't use bent coins in a slot machine,' I warned him.
7 'Follow that car,' the detective said to the taxi-driver.

8 'Wash it in lukewarm water,' recommended the assistant.

9 'Have confidence in me,' urged the doctor.

10 'Take me up to the 33rd floor,' he said to the liftman.

11 'Read the notice about life-saving equipment,' advised the air-hostess.

12 'Always cook with butter,' said her mother, 'never use margarine.'

13 'Don't argue with your father,' I said.

14 'Remember to prune the roses,' said my aunt.

15 'Wait for me at the bridge,' said the young man.

16 'Don't eat too much starch,' I advised her, 'and avoid fried food.'

17 'Don't say anything to make her angry,' said my father.

18 Notice: Please do not ask at the desk for change for telephone calls.

19 'Don't forget to feed the goldfish,' Mary said to her brother.

20 'Cross the line by the footbridge,' said the porter.

21 'Write to me as often as you can,' said his wife.

22 'Put your pistol on the table,' said the crook.

23 'Please book me a seat in a non-smoker,' said the traveller.

24 'Don't forget your sandwiches,' said his mother.

25 'Don't go near the water, children,' she said.

26 'Search the house,' said the police sergeant.

27 'Don't make mountains out of molehills,' he said.

28 'Put down that gun. It's loaded,' she warned.

92 Indirect speech: commands, requests, advice

☑ PEG 320

See note to 90.

Put the following into indirect speech, joining the sentences together with **as, and, but** or **for**.

1 'Make good use of your time. You won't get such an opportunity again,' he said to us.

2 'Don't wait till tomorrow,' said the advertisement, 'post the coupon at once.'

3 'Be very careful crossing roads,' she said, 'and remember to drive on the right.'

4 'I can't open it. You have a try, Peter,' he said.

5 'Go and get me a paper, and come straight back,' he said to me.

6 'Someone's coming. Get into the cupboard,' she said.

7 'Give way to traffic approaching from your right,' the road sign warned us.

8 'Please, please send whatever you can spare,' said the secretary of the disaster fund.

9 'Wear a wig if you don't want to be recognized,' I advised him.

10 'Don't bathe when the red flag is flying,' said the lifeguard.

11 'Don't forget to thank Mrs Jones when you are saying goodbye to her,' said his mother.
12 'Watch the milk and don't let it boil over,' he said.
13 'Don't shelter under a tree in a thunderstorm,' he said. 'The tree might be struck by lightning.'
14 'Put the message into a bottle and throw it into the sea,' he said.
15 'Read it for yourself if you don't believe what I say,' he told me.
16 'Don't forget to use your indicators,' said the driving instructor.
17 'Don't drive too fast or the baby'll be sick,' she said to her husband.
18 'Do make the coffee a bit stronger,' I begged. 'It was terribly weak last night.'
19 'Beware of pickpockets,' said a huge notice.
20 'Smell this. Do you think it has gone bad?' she said.
21 'Don't take your coat off. We are going out again in a moment,' she told him.
22 'Stand by the window and tell me if anyone goes into the house opposite,' he said.
23 'Don't move till the policeman waves you on,' said the driving instructor.
24 'Don't touch it. You will only make it worse,' he told me.
25 'Be careful; the steps are very slippery,' I warned him.
26 'Ask your boss to ring me back,' I said. 'My number is 1234567.' 'Could you repeat that, please?' said the girl.
27 'Don't work too fast,' said the foreman. 'If we finish before six we shan't get any overtime.'
28 'Prepare to meet your doom. The end of the world is at hand,' said the placard.
29 'Remember to put the brake on,' the instructor said.
30 'Would you please take off your shoes?' Keiko said to him.

93 Indirect speech: commands, requests, invitations, offers, advice

■ PEG 284–7, 318–20

Put the following into indirect speech using **ask**, **advise**, **invite**, **offer**, **remind**, **tell**, **warn**.

1 'Would you like to have lunch with me on Sunday?' he said to me.
2 'Would you like a cigarette?' said one of the guests.
3 'Would you mind not smoking between courses?' said their hostess.
4 'Take these letters to the post, will you? And shut the door as you go out,' said the boss.
5 'Will you help me, please?' she said. 'I can't reach the top shelf.'
6 'This is a horrible room. Why don't you ask for something better?' he said.
7 'If I were you I'd try to get a room on the top floor,' he said.

8 'I'll wait for you if you like,' she said.
9 'Remember to switch off when you've finished,' he said.
10 'You might check these figures for me,' he said.
11 'You'd better apologize for being late,' said my mother.
12 'Could you check the oil, please?' I asked the mechanic.
13 'I wish you'd sit still!' said the artist. 'How do you expect me to paint you when you keep jerking your head?'
14 'Why don't you go by train? It's much less tiring than driving,' I said.
15 Hotel notice: Will guests please not play radios loudly after midnight?
16 'Would you like to wait here?' said the receptionist, showing me into the waiting room.
17 'You must see this exhibition!' said all my friends.
18 'I should plant daffodils, if I were you,' I said to them.
19 'If you'd just sign the back of the cheque,' said the bank clerk.
20 'I'd be very grateful if you'd forward my letters while I am away,' he said.
21 Police announcement: Will anyone who saw this accident please get in touch with their nearest police station?
22 'Don't leave your room at night,' he said. 'Our host's dogs might mistake you for a burglar.'
23 'Answer this letter for me, will you?' he said. 'And remember to keep a copy.'
24 'Would you mind moving your car?' he said. 'It's blocking my gate.'
25 (in a letter) 'Perhaps you'd let me know when your new stock comes in.' (*Mrs Jones* . . .)
26 Notice on board: The first team will report to the gymnasium for weight-training. (*The coach* . . .)
27 'Could you sew on this button for me?' Tom asked Ann. 'You'd better sew it on yourself,' said Mary. 'Buttons sewn on by Ann usually come off the next day.'
28 'If you will kindly sit down the fortune-teller will be with you in a moment,' the girl said.

94 Indirect speech: questions, requests, invitations, offers, advice

■ PEG 284–7, 318–20, 323

Remember that **Why don't you?** can be an ordinary question or advice/suggestion. Treat it here as advice.

Put the following into indirect speech.

1 'Could you get there and back in one day?' I asked. (*I asked if he* . . .)
2 'I can't open this tin,' said Ann. 'Shall I do it for you?' said Tom.
3 'Could you translate this for me, please?' I asked the official.

4 'Shall we ever meet again?' he wondered.
5 'Will you be here tomorrow?' she asked. 'Yes,' I answered.
6 'Could I lose five kilos in a week?' said the fat woman. 'No,' said the doctor.
7 'Will you have a drink?' he said.
8 'Why don't you install gas central heating?' said the advertisement. (*urge*)
9 'Will you read this very carefully, please?' he said to me.
10 'Shall I tell him what happened?' she asked me.
11 'Wouldn't you like to look ten years younger?' said the hairdresser.
12 'I'm going to Brighton tomorrow,' said Ann.
'So'm I,' said Tom. 'Would you like a lift?' (*Tom said he was too and . . .*)
13 'Can I have a sweet?' said the small boy.
14 'Can we stay up till the end of the programme?' said the children.
15 'Could I have the weekend off?' he asked his boss.
16 'Could I leave early on Friday?' he said.
17 'Why don't you like pop music?' the teenagers asked him.
18 'Why don't you take up the oboe again?' said my friends. (*advise*)
19 'Where shall I hang my new picture?' he said. 'Would it look well over the mantelpiece?'
20 'What shall I do if the car won't start?' I said.
21 'Have you got enough money? Shall I lend you some?' said my friend.
22 'Will you be able to guide me or shall I bring a map?' I asked.
23 'You won't forget to shut the door, will you?' she said. (*remind*)
24 'Would you like to see over the house?' I asked her.
25 'Would you like to peel the potatoes?' said Ann, handing me a knife.
26 'I've got two tickets. Would you like to come with me?' he said.
27 'Can you use a word processor?' he asked. 'No,' I said.
28 'Would you mind living by yourself for six months?' they asked.
29 'Would you mind paying cash?' said my landlady when I took out my cheque-book.
30 'Why don't you trust him?' I asked Ann.
'I never trust left-handed men,' she answered.

95 Indirect speech: commands and questions with **if**- clauses and time clauses

◪ PEG 229, 320–1

Questions with **if**- clauses and time clauses should be reported with the **if**- clause or time clause last.
'When/If I see him, what shall I say?' she asked.
She asked what she should say when/if she saw him.

Commands can be reported by **tell** + infinitive + **if**- clause/time clause.

But sometimes (as in nos. 5 and 10 below) this would produce a rather clumsy sentence. It is then advisable to use **say/said that** + if-clause/time clause + **be/should** + infinitive:

'If /When you see him, ask him to ring me,' she said.

She said that if/when I saw him I was to ask him to ring her.

was to expresses a definite command; **should** implies advice.

Put the following into indirect speech.

1 He said, 'When you are at the butcher's remember to get a bone for the dog.'
2 She said, 'If you feel faint sit down and put your head between your knees.'
3 'If I find your purse what shall I do with it?' he said.
'Keep it till you see me again,' I replied.
4 She said, 'If he arrives before I get back give him something to drink.'
5 'If anyone rings up,' she said, 'say that I'll be back shortly.'
6 'When you are driving always look in your driving mirror before turning right,' said my instructor.
7 'Leave the key under the mat if you go out,' she said.
8 'If you think the room is cold shut the windows,' said my aunt.
9 'If you feel lonely any time ring me up,' he said.
10 'If she doesn't eat meat, offer her an omelette,' he said.
11 'Get the car off the road on to the verge if you have a puncture. Don't leave it on the road,' said my father.
12 'If I am not back by this time tomorrow take this letter to the police,' he said.
13 'When you see Mrs Pitt don't forget to thank her,' she said to her husband.
14 'When the bell rings take the meat out of the oven,' my sister said.
15 'If you are taken prisoner,' said the officer, 'give your name, rank and number but refuse to answer any other questions.'
16 'When you hear the fire alarm, shut all windows and go downstairs as quickly as possible,' said the schoolmaster.
17 'If the lift should stop between two floors press the emergency button,' he said.
18 'Before you allow anyone to use the Turkish bath remember to ask him if he has a weak heart,' said the senior attendant.
19 'If the police stop me, what shall I say?' she asked.
20 'What shall I do if he refuses to let me in?' she said.
'Write a note and push it under the door,' I said.
21 'What will happen if the strike continues?' he said.
22 'If it goes on snowing, how'll we get food?' wondered the housewives.
23 'When the rain stops, can we go out?' said the children.
24 'When you've completed one section, go on to the next,' the teacher said.

25 'If you don't like the programme, switch to another channel,' I said to her.
26 'If I lose my traveller's cheques, will the bank repay me?' I asked.
27 'If the noise gets worse, you'd better complain to the police,' he said to me.
28 'As soon as you find a hotel, ring me and give me the address,' he said.

96 Indirect speech: suggestions

◿ PEG 289 D, 322

Part 1 Write the following in indirect speech, in ordinary narrative form.
Ann suggested having a party on the next Saturday. Mary agreed and asked who they should invite.

Report 'Why don't we . . . ?' as a suggestion and 'Why don't you . . ?' as suggestion or advice. Report 'Why not?' in no. 9 as *agreed*.

1 Ann: What about having a party on Saturday?
2 Mary: Yes, let's. Who shall we invite?
3 Ann: Let's not make a list. Let's just invite everybody.
4 Mary: We don't want to do too much cooking, so what about making it a wine and cheese party?
5 Ann: Suppose we ask everybody to bring a bottle?
6 Mary: Shall we hire glasses from our local wine shop? We haven't many left.
7 Ann: If it's warm, how about having the party in the garden?
8 Mary: Why not have a barbecue?
9 Ann: Why not? We could ask Paul to do the cooking.
10 Mary: Last time we had a barbecue the neighbours complained about the noise. Shall we ask everyone to speak in whispers?
11 Ann: Suppose we go round to the neighbours and apologize in advance this time?
12 Mary: Why not invite the neighbours? Then the noise won't matter.
13 Ann: What a clever idea! Shall we start ringing everyone up tonight?
14 Mary: What about working out how much it will cost first?

Part 2 Put the following into indirect speech.

15 'What about a round-the-world cruise?' suggested Mrs Smith. 'What about renting a caravan? It's all we can afford,' said her husband.
16 'Suppose you complain, Ann?' I said. 'The boss is more likely to listen to you than to any of us.'
17 'You used to be a good tennis player,' she reminded him. 'Why don't you take it up again?'

18 'Shall we talk there? It's not far,' he said. 'Yes, let's,' I said.
19 'What about joining a weaving class?' Ann said to me. 'There's one starting soon.'
20 'Let's organize a sponsored cycle race,' said the children.
  'What about a sponsored silence?' said the teacher with a grin.
21 'Where shall we meet?' I said. 'What about the hotel?' said Bill.
22 'Suppose you ring him, Ann, and ask him what he thinks of the idea?' I said.
23 'I'm doing most of the work,' I pointed out. 'What about giving me a hand?'
24 'Let's leave the washing-up till tomorrow,' he suggested. 'I hate washing up last thing at night.'
25 'Suppose the children go on an adventure holiday this summer?' suggested the father.
26 'Why don't you ask them what they'd like to do?' I said.
27 'Shall we begin training for the next London Marathon?' said Bill. 'I've no intention of running in marathons,' I said. 'Why don't you ask Paul?'
28 'Why don't you put an advertisement in the local paper?' they suggested to me.

97 Indirect speech: mixed types

■ PEG chapter 31 (note especially 324)

Put the following into indirect speech, avoiding as far as possible the verbs **say**, **ask** and **tell** and choosing instead from the following:
accept, accuse, admit, advise, agree, apologize, assure, beg, call (= summon), **call** (+ noun/pronoun + noun), **complain, congratulate, deny, exclaim, explain, give, hope, insist, introduce, invite, offer, point out, promise, protest, refuse, remark, remind, suggest, thank, threaten, warn, wish.**

1 He said, 'Don't walk on the ice; it isn't safe.'
2 'Miss Brown, this is Miss White. Miss White, Miss Brown,' he said.
3 'Here are the car keys. You'd better wait in the car,' he said to her.
4 'Please, please, don't tell anyone,' she said.
  'I won't, I promise,' I said.
5 'Would you like my torch?' I said, holding it out.
  'No, thanks,' he said. 'I have one of my own.' (*Omit* thanks)
6 Tom: I'll pay.
  Ann: Oh no, you mustn't!
  Tom: I insist on paying!
7 'Come in and look round. There's no obligation to buy,' said the shopkeeper.
8 'If you don't pay the ransom, we'll kill the boy,' said the kidnappers.
9 'I won't answer any questions,' said the arrested man.

10 'He expects a lot of work for very little money,' complained one of the typists.
'Yes, he does,' agreed the other.

11 'I wish it would rain,' she said.

12 'You pressed the wrong button,' said the mechanic. 'Don't do it again. You might have a nasty accident.'

13 'Your weight's gone up a lot!' I exclaimed.
'I'm afraid it has,' she said sadly.

14 'I hope you'll have a good journey,' he said. 'Don't forget to send a card when you arrive.'

15 'Hurrah! I've passed the first exam!' he exclaimed.
'Congratulations!' I said, 'and good luck with the second.'

16 'All right, I'll wait a week,' she said. (*Omit* all right)

17 'Many happy returns of your birthday!' we said.
'Thanks,' said the boy.

18 'Your door is the shabbiest in the street,' said the neighbour.
'It is,' I said.

19 'Cigarette?' ~
'Thanks,' I said.

20 'I'll sell the TV set if you keep quarrelling about the programme,' said their mother.
'No, don't do that! We won't quarrel any more,' said the children.

21 'I'll give you £500 to keep your mouth shut,' he said to me.

22 'I'll wait for you, I promise,' he said to me.

23 'I'm sorry I'm late,' she said. 'The bus broke down.'

24 'You've been leaking information to the Press!' said his colleagues.
'No, I haven't,' he said. 'Liar!' said Tom.

25 'I'll drop you from the team if you don't train harder,' said the captain.

26 'If the boys do anything clever, you call them your sons,' complained his wife. 'But if they do anything stupid, you call them mine.'

27 'Let's have a rest,' said Tom.
'Yes, let's,' said Ann.

28 'Ugh! There's a slug in my lettuce. Waiter!' he cried.

98 Indirect to direct speech

■ PEG 307–22

Put the following into direct speech, using dialogue form:
Tom: *Would you like to come for a drive tomorrow, Ann?*
Ann: *I'd love to* etc.

Trip to Stratford

1 Tom invited Ann to come for a drive the following day.
2 Ann accepted with pleasure and asked where he was thinking of going.

3 He said he'd leave it to her.
4 She suggested Stratford . . .
5 adding that she hadn't been there for ages.
6 Tom agreed and said that they might go on the river if it was a fine day.
7 Ann wondered what was on at the Royal Shakespeare Theatre.
8 Tom said they'd find out when they got there . . .
9 adding that it was usually possible to get seats on the day of the play.
10 He asked Ann if she could be ready by ten.
11 Ann said with regret that she couldn't as she had to type a report first.
12 Tom expressed horror at the idea of working on Saturday . . .
13 and advised her to change her job.
14 She told him not to be ridiculous and explained that . . .
15 she had volunteered to type the report in return for a free afternoon the following week.
16 She pointed out that she hadn't known that he was going to ask her out.
17 Tom said he supposed it was all right but . . .
18 warned her not to make a habit of volunteering for weekend work.
19 Ann promised not to.
20 Tom said gloomily that he supposed she'd be busy all morning.
21 Ann assured him that she'd be finished by 11.00 and . . .
22 offered to meet him at the bus stop at Hyde Park Corner.
23 Tom said that it wasn't a very good meeting place and that he'd call for her.
24 Ann said that that was very kind of him and that she'd be waiting in the hall.

Hill climb

25 Tom suggested climbing to the top, adding that the view from there was marvellous . . .
26 but Ann said that they'd been climbing for three hours and that she was too tired to go any further.
27 She suggested that Tom should go on up while she went down and waited there.
28 Tom agreed and handed her the car keys, advising her to wait in the car.
29 He promised to be as quick as he could.
30 Ann said that if he was too long there'd be no lunch left, for she'd have eaten it all.

10 Purpose

99 Infinitive used to express purpose

☑ PEG 334

Combine each of the following pairs of sentences into one sentence using **so as/in order** where necessary.
He sent me to Spain. He wanted me to learn Spanish.
He sent me to Spain to learn Spanish.
He turned out the light. He didn't want to waste electricity.
He turned out the light so as not to waste electricity.

1 I am buying paint. I want to paint my hall door.
2 He tied a knot in his handkerchief. He hoped that this would remind him to meet the train.
3 He opened the lions' cage. He intended to feed the lions.
4 He left his rifle outside. He didn't want to frighten his wife.
5 He has a box. He plans to put his savings in it. (*Omit* it.)
6 We had no cups but he gave us coconut shells. He said we could drink out of them. (*Omit* them.)
7 He rushed into the burning house. He wanted to save the child.
8 He read only for short periods each day. He didn't want to strain his eyes.
9 They got up very early. They wanted to get to the top of the hill before sunrise.
10 He rang the bell. He wanted to tell us that dinner was ready.
11 We must keep our gloves on. We don't want to get frost-bitten.
12 The farmer put a scarecrow up in the field. He wanted to frighten the birds.
13 I took off my shoes. I didn't want to make any noise.
14 Before the carpenter came she covered the floor with polythene sheeting. She wanted to protect the carpet.
15 The boys are collecting sticks. They intend to put them on the fire. (*Omit* them.)
16 He was playing very softly. He didn't want to disturb anyone.
17 I am sending him to the USA. I want him to study electronics there.
18 I sent him out of the room. I wanted to discuss his progress with his headmaster.
19 He fixed a metal ladder to the wall below his window. He wanted to be able to escape if there was a fire.
20 He changed his address constantly. He wanted to elude the police.
21 The police have barricaded the main streets. They want to prevent the demonstrators from marching through the town.

22 They evacuated everybody from the danger zone. They wanted to reduce the risk.

23 I am learning Greek. I wish to read Homer.

24 He sent his children to his sister's house. He wanted them to watch the television programme.

25 He sent his children to their aunt's house. He wanted to have some peace.

26 The town council has forbidden coal fires. They are trying to keep the air clean.

27 They employed a detective. They wanted to learn what I did in the evenings.

28 I am saving up. I want to buy a helicopter.

29 He coughed. He wanted to warn them that he was coming.

30 You should take your holidays in June. In this way you would avoid the rush.

31 I keep my hens in a field surrounded by wire netting. I want to protect them against the foxes.

32 I am learning skiing at an indoor school. I want to be able to ski when I get to Switzerland.

33 The workmen left red lights near the hole. They wanted to warn motorists.

34 He invented a wife and six children. By this trick he hoped to avoid paying income tax.

35 Some women tint their hair when it goes grey. They want to look younger.

36 He didn't tell her he was going up in the spacecraft. He didn't want to alarm her.

00 Clauses and phrases of purpose

■ PEG 336–7

A purpose clause introduced by **so that** can sometimes be replaced by **prevent/avoid** + gerund or **allow/enable/let/make** etc. + infinitive.

The two sentences:

He rumpled the bedclothes. He wanted to make me think he had slept in the bed.

could be combined:

He rumpled the bedclothes so that I should/would think he had slept etc. or *to make me think he had slept* etc.

An **in case** clause is useful when we mention the possible future action we are taking precautions against:

Don't let him play with scissors. He may cut himself.

could be expressed:

Don't let him play with scissors in case he cuts himself.

Purpose

Sometimes an **in case** clause can be replaced by a negative purpose clause.

1 He killed the men who helped him to bury the treasure. He wanted nobody but himself to know where it was.
2 Put the cork back. Someone may knock the bottle over.
3 The airfield authorities have put arc lights over the damaged runway. They want repair work to continue day and night.
4 The girl packed the vase in polyester foam. She didn't want it to get broken in the post.
5 He wore a false beard. He didn't want anyone to recognize him.
6 She built a high wall round her garden. She didn't want her fruit to be stolen.
7 They talked in whispers. They didn't want me to overhear them.
8 You ought to take some serum with you. You may get bitten by a snake.
9 Aeroplanes carry parachutes. The crew can escape in case of fire.
10 I am insuring my life. I want my children to have something to live on if I am killed.
11 Please shut the gate. I don't want the cows to get out of the field.
12 He telephoned from a public call-box. He didn't want the call to be traced to his own address.
13 I am putting nets over my strawberry plants. I don't want the birds to eat all the strawberries.
14 We keep a spade in the house. There may be a heavy fall of snow in the night.
15 We put bars on the lower windows. We didn't want anyone to climb in.
16 You should carry a jack in your car. You may have a puncture.
17 We built the roof with a steep slope. We wanted the snow to slide off easily.
18 The notices are written in several languages. The government wants everyone to understand them.
19 I put my address on my dog's collar. I want anyone who finds him to know where he comes from.
20 She tied a bell round her cat's neck. She wanted the birds to know when he was approaching.
21 Bring your gun with you. We may be attacked.
22 I have put wire over my chimney-pots. I don't want birds to build nests in them.
23 Write your name in the book. He may forget who lent it to him.
24 He chained up the lioness at night. He didn't want her to frighten anyone.
25 Don't put on any more coal. The chimney may catch fire.
26 The burglar cut the telephone wires. He didn't want me to call the police.
27 Take a torch with you. It may be dark before you get back.

146

28 The manufacturers have made the taps of their new gas cooker very stiff. They don't want young children to be able to turn them on.
29 Don't let the baby play with my glasses. He may break them.
30 The debate on education has been postponed. The government want to discuss the latest crisis.
31 If someone knocks at the door at night don't open it. It may be the escaped convict.
32 The policeman stopped the traffic every few minutes. He wanted the pedestrians to be able to cross the road.
33 He had a telephone installed in his car. He wanted his secretary to be able to contact him whenever necessary.
34 Never let children play with matches. They may set themselves on fire.
35 As he went through the forest Bill marked the trees. He wanted the rest of the party to know which way he had gone.
36 Turn down the oven. We don't want the meat to burn while we are out.

Key

1 Articles

Exercise 1 (note that '–' indicates that no article is required.)
1 a, – 2 –, –, –; a 3 a, a 4 a, –; a; a, – 5 A, –, – 6 –, a, an
7 A, –, a, a, –, a 8 –, –; a, – 9 A, – 10 a, a; a, an 11 a, a; –; a,
–, a 12 –, an, an; – 13 a, a; a; a, a 14 –, an 15 A, a; a; a, a
16 an, a; –, an, –, a, a 17 a, –; a, – 18 –, a 19 a; a, – 20 a, a; a;
– 21 A; a, an; a 22 –, a, an, a 23 –, a, an 24 a, –; a 25 a; a, a
26 a, a; – 27 an, a, –, – 28 –; – 29 a, a, –, – 30 an; a, a, a; a; –
31 a, a; an, a 32 a, a, a, a 33 –, a, a 34 a, a 35 a, a 36 –, a

Exercise 2 (As before '–' indicates that no article is required. '(the)'
indicates that the article is optional.)

1 The, –, the, – 2 the; the, the 3 –, –, –, the 4 –, – 5 the; the,
the; – 6 –, –, –; the, the, –; the 7 the, the; –, – 8 –, –, the 9 –;
–, – 10 the, the; the 11 –, –; the, the; the 12 the, the, the, the,
– 13 –, –, – 14 –, –, –, – 15 –, –, the 16 –, –, –, the 17 –,
the, the, – 18 –, – 19 –, –, –, –, – 20 the, the, the 21 the, –;
–, the 22 The, –; the; –, –, – 23 –; the, the, the 24 –; –; the
25 –, the, –, the 26 –, –, –, the, the; The, –, the; the, the, the,
the, –, the, the 27 –, the, the; – 28 the, the; The, the, the, the
29 –, –, the, the, –, – 30 –, –, –; –, – 31 –, –, the, – 32 The,
–; –, –, the 33 –, (the), the, the, the 34 (the), (the); –, –, –, –, the
35 –, – 36 the, the, the, the, the, the

Exercise 3 (Two words separated by an oblique, e.g. the/his, indicate
that either is a possible answer. The first word is normally the
preferred answer.)

1 a, the; a, a 2 an, the, the 3 a, the, –, – 4 the, a, the, –, –, (the)
5 a, –, the, a 6 a, a/the, an, the 7 a, –, an, the, the, the, the 8 a,
the, the 9 a, a 10 the, the, the, the, an 11 –, –, (the), a 12 a, the,
– 13 the, a, the, the, the 14 –; –, –, – 15 The, the, the; the, the
16 the, the, a, –; (the), the, the, – 17 a 18 a; the; a; a 19 a, the; a,
–; The, the 20 –, the; the; a, an 21 The, a, a, –, – 22 the, a, –, the,
a, the, the, the, the 23 a, a, a, the, –, the; The, –, –; The, the, –; –,
the, –, an 24 the, the, a 25 a, the, the 26 –, the; the; –, the; –, a,
– 27 a, the, the, – 28 a, –, an 29 –, –, –, – 30 a, an, an, a; –,
–, –, –, the 31 a; the, the, the; a, – 32 the, an, the; –, the, –; the,
the, a 33 –, –; the 34 –; a, the, –, a 35 –, the; a 36 a, a, a, the;
the, the, –

148

Exercise 4 1 his 2 your, your 3 –, their 4 the 5 his, his 6 his,
– 7 an, the 8 a 9 a, my 10 the 11 a, –, a, his, – 12 his 13 –,
her 14 his 15 the 16 our 17 the, her 18 his 19 your 20 his, the
21 the 22 your 23 –, his 24 –, our/the 25 his 26 the/his 27 your,
the, the 28 a 29 a 30 a, a 31 your, (a) 32 her, the 33 a, his
34 your 35 your 36 my

Exercise 5 1 One, a, a 2 A, a; one; a; one, a; a; a 3 A, a 4 a, a,
an 5 a, a/the, a/your 6 one; a; an 7 a, a 8 One, a 9 (a), a, a; a;
One 10 a; One 11 a/the; a, a/the; – 12 a, a, one 13 one; one; a
14 a; a, a 15 a, one, a, a, a 16 a, a; one 17 One, a, a 18 –, a; a;
one, a; A, a 19 a; a 20 One; an, an 21 a, a/the, a; a, a, an 22 One,
a, an 23 One, a, a, a 24 one; a; a; a; One, an; a

2 Auxiliary verbs

Exercise 6 Negative answers in each case: the auxiliary verb + **not**.
not is usually contracted and added to the verb, e.g. may not/mayn't
cost. **will** + **not** is contracted to **won't**. **can** + **not** is contracted to
can't.

Interrogative answers, except for 1, 13 and 19, are in the following
form: auxiliary verb + subject + infinitive, e.g. Should they eat less?
1 Is it likely to cost/Do you think it will cost? 13 Are they likely to
come/Do you think they will come? 19 Is he likely to be at home/Do
you think he'll be at home?

Exercise 7 Negative: 1 don't have 2 doesn't need 3 didn't use
4 don't have 5 doesn't do 6 doesn't need 7 didn't have 8 didn't
have 9 didn't need 10 doesn't do 11 doesn't have 12 didn't have
13 doesn't do 14 doesn't have 15 don't have 16 didn't dare
17 didn't do 18 doesn't have 19 doesn't dare 20 didn't have
21 didn't do 22 doesn't need 23 didn't have 24 didn't have
25 didn't use 26 don't do 27 didn't have 28 didn't dare

Interrogative: 1 do they have 2 does he need 3 did he use 4 do
they have 5 does she do 6 does he need 7 did he have 8 did she
have 9 did her hair need 10 does he do 11 does she have 12 did
she have 13 does he do 14 does he have 15 do the children have
16 did she dare 17 did you do 18 does he have 19 does he dare
20 did they have 21 did the drink 22 does my watch need 23 did
he have 24 did you have 25 did she use 26 do you do 27 did he
have 28 did he dare

Exercise 8 1 wasn't 2 didn't 3 couldn't 4 had to 5 wouldn't
6 could 7 wasn't 8 wasn't 9 didn't need to 10 hoped that Tom
would 11 did 12 said that Ann might 13 was 14 did 15 did . . .

could 16 could 17 had to 18 dared 19 didn't 20 had 21 were
22 Had you to/Did you have to 23 didn't need to 24 hoped, he'd
25 might 26 Did you understand . . . he was saying? I didn't
27 were 28 might 29 didn't 30 weren't, were 31 thought, might
32 wanted . . . if she could 33 couldn't 34 was, would 35 could,
couldn't 36 didn't, would.

Exercise 9 (Affirmative answers all begin with **Yes** + the first of the
answers given. Negative answers all begin with **No** + the second of
the answers given.)

1 Yes, it is. No, it isn't. 2 I do/don't 3 I can/can't 4 he
does/doesn't 5 it is/isn't 6 I am/I'm not 7 I must/needn't 8 we
are/aren't 9 he did/didn't 10 it would/wouldn't 11 you
may/mayn't 12 it is/isn't 13 she will/won't 14 I do/don't 15 you
should/shouldn't 16 I can/can't 17 I am/I'm not 18 they
could/couldn't 19 it is/isn't 20 they were/weren't 21 she
will/won't 22 you ought/oughtn't 23 you should/shouldn't 24 he
was/wasn't 25 I have/haven't 26 we must/needn't 27 he did/didn't
28 I would/wouldn't 29 it is/isn't 30 I do/don't 31 you can/can't
32 I will/won't 33 I am/I'm not 34 you are/aren't 35 you
must/needn't 36 it was/wasn't

Exercise 10 Part 1 The answers in this section all begin with **So.**
1 So has John. 2 . . . is she. 3 . . . can his wife. 4 . . . ought you.
5 . . . should you. 6 . . .will Tom. 7 . . . was the second. 8 . . . did
my brother. 9 . . . must your son. 10 . . . does that. 11 . . . is my
friend. 12 . . . did I.

Part 2 The answers in this section all begin with **Neither/Nor.**
13 Neither/Nor has Tom. 14 . . . should Tom. 15 . . . must I.
16 . . . can his sister. 17 . . . does Ann. 18 . . . could Andrew.
19 . . . are you. 20 . . .does that. 21 . . . will mine. 22 . . . had the
taxi-driver. 23 . . . did anyone else. 24 . . . would my mother.

Part 3 The answers in this section all begin with **But.** 25 But Mary
wasn't. 26 . . . she was. 27 . . . your brother needn't. 28 . . . I
can't. 29 . . . James did. 30 . . . Stanley must. 31 . . . a dog
would. 32 . . . his wife won't. 33 . . . my neighbour has. 34 . . .
that beach isn't. 35 . . . you needn't. 36 . . . I do.

Exercise 11 Part 1 1 Yes, we must. 2 Yes, you were. 3 Yes, she
does. 4 Yes, she may. 5 Yes, he could. 6 (Oh), so there is! 7 Yes,
he does. 8 (Oh), so it is! 9 Yes, it was. 10 Yes, it might. 11 Yes,
they did. 12 Yes, it is.

Part 2 All answers begin with **No.** 13 No, they don't. 14 . . . he
didn't. 15 . . . it isn't. 16 . . . he can't. 17 . . . it wasn't. 18 . . . it
wouldn't. 19 . . . it hasn't. 20 . . . they don't. 21 . . . they didn't.
22 . . . it hasn't. 23 . . . you don't. 24 . . . he mightn't.

Part 3   25 No, I'm not.   26 Yes, you did.   27 (Oh) yes, they were!
28 (Oh) yes, you were!   29 No, she wouldn't.   30 No, I didn't.
31 No, you can't.   32 No, it doesn't.   33 (Oh) yes, he did!   34 (Oh) no,
they don't.   35 No, they shouldn't.   36 No, she didn't.

Exercise 12   1 are you   2 is she   3 do you   4 did he   5 is it   6 was
she   7 has he   8 will you   9 did I   10 does he   11 do you   12 does it
13 should they 14 are you   15 could they   16 do you   17 was there
18 need I   19 was it   20 did you   21 will it   22 does she   23 did it
24 should he   25 could she   26 are you   27 would you   28 had he
29 were they   30 would you   31 does he   32 has he   33 could he
34 need I   35 were there   36 was it

Exercise 13   1 can't they   2 isn't he   3 didn't he   4 haven't they
5 wasn't he   6 shouldn't he   7 couldn't it   8 isn't he   9 isn't it
10 can't he   11 won't it   12 doesn't she   13 hasn't she   14 didn't
they   15 doesn't she   16 doesn't he   17 didn't he   18 don't they
19 haven't I   20 hasn't he   21 isn't she   22 didn't they   23 mightn't
he   24 mustn't we   25 hadn't you   26 wouldn't you   27 don't they
28 oughtn't she   29 wasn't it   30 don't they   31 won't you   32 didn't
he   33 won't there   34 hadn't you   35 wouldn't you   36 couldn't you

Exercise 14   1 don't you   2 do you   3 is it   4 does it   5 wasn't it
6 was there   7 didn't they   8 wasn't there   9 did they   10 does she
11 doesn't she   12 wouldn't she   13 didn't he   14 did he   15 wasn't
she   16 oughtn't he   17 did they   18 do they   19 can't they   20 does
he   21 is it   22 did it   23 aren't they   24 hadn't we   25 wouldn't it
26 would it   27 isn't it   28 wouldn't she   29 shouldn't they
30 weren't they   31 didn't she   32 does he   33 didn't there   34 is
there   35 will he   36 does it

Exercise 15   1 –   2 to   3 to   4 to   5 –   6 to   7 to   8 –   9 –   10 to
11 to 12 to   13 (to)   14 –   15 –   16 –, to   17 to   18 to   19 –   20 –
21 to   22 to 23 –   24 to   25 –   26 to   27 –, (to)   28 –   29 –   30 to
31 –   32 to   33 to 34 –   35 to   36 –

Exercise 16   1 can/could   2 be able   3 had   4 had   5 must, needn't
6 didn't dare   7 ought/will have   8 used   9 is to be   10 could
11 shall   12 would, might   13 would   14 had   15 don't have/need
16 was to have   17 should/ought to   18 might/should   19 will have
20 used, would   21 should   22 will   23 must have   24 may   25 were
26 have   27 oughtn't   28 might

Exercise 17   (As mentioned in the note, the **do/did** form could be
used throughout except in no. 27, and of course for the future.)

1 hasn't even (got)   2 has (got), has/has always got   3 don't have,
have (got) 4 has (got)   5 haven't you (got)   6 did you have/had you

Key

7 has the alphabet (got)   8 do the houses have/have the houses (got)
9 have you (got), haven't (got)   10 do you ever have   11 he'll have
12 don't usually have   13 have you (got)   14 don't always have
15 hasn't your door (got)   16 have you (got), have   17 haven't (got)
18 has (got)   19 have you   20 has this desk (got), don't ever
have/never have   21 do you ever have   22 do babies have   23 has/has
a pentagon got   24 has, does she have   25 have, won't/don't have
26 do you have   27 have you (got), have (got)   28 have you (got), I
only have/have only (got), will have   29 have you (got)   30 have you
(got), have, haven't (got)   31 hasn't he (got)   32 have, didn't
have/hadn't   33 didn't you have   34 do red-haired people always
have/have red-haired people always got   35 hasn't (got)   36 have you
(got)

Exercise 18   1 are having   2 did you have/had you   3 is having
4 are having   5 does he have, he usually has   6 do you have   7 do
you have, have   8 do you have, have   9 don't you have   10 were
having   11 did you have/had you 12 are having   13 will you have
14 are having   15 had   16 did you have   17 am having   18 are
having   19 was having   20 do English people always have   21 don't
have/haven't   22 are having   23 don't have   24 did you have/had you
had   25 did you have/had you   26 am having   27 does he have
28 did you have/had you   29 had   30 are having   31 didn't
have/hadn't   32 are having   33 am having   34 is having   35 does he
ever have   36 had, did you have/had you

Exercise 19   1 am having   2 will have   3 had   4 am having   5 have
just had   6 am having   7 did you have   8 does he have   9 do you
have   10 don't you have   11 do you have   12 am having   13 have it
x-rayed   14 have it repaired   15 have them shortened   16 am having
them typed   17 have it tuned   18 have the document photocopied
19 had them dyed   20 have it mended   21 have it set   22 have just
had it re-charged   23 to have it enlarged   24 have just had them
sharpened   25 have my car serviced   26 have it seen to   27 had my
watch cleaned   28 is having her portrait painted   29 they had the
man arrested   30 he had the car towed   31 are having a garage built
32 have my windows cleaned   33 had my eyes tested   34 is having
his fortune told   35 had the oysters opened   36 had my ears pierced

Exercise 20   1 is being/will be ruined   2 is to make/is making
3 were   4 being, being   5 were to be/should be extinguished   6 have
you been   7 is being pulled down   8 was to put   9 isn't it   10 are to
stay   11 should be asked   12 were   13 I am to go   14 is being
carried   15 to be   16 were   17 were to have taken   18 is being
taught   19 was, will be, were   20 to be   21 was to have
been   22 should be sent   23 will there be   24 had been   25 is to
open/is opening   26 were being taken   27 was to have been
28 would you be   29 is to be/is being/will be   30 was to have run

152

31 was still being painted 32 should be printed 33 are being/have been translated 34 were 35 was to do 36 is to be

Exercise 21 (Affirmatives are not given in their contracted form but would normally be contracted in speech.)

1 It is, It is 2 is it, It is 3 It was, there were 4 It is, There will be 5 it was 6 It is, it is 7 There are, there is 8 There is; It will be, it is, it is, there will be 9 There is, it is 10 It was, it was 11 There was; There were 12 There was; There were 13 It is, it is 14 It is; There are 15 It is; It is 16 It will be; there will 17 There is; Is it 18 There are, it is 19 It is 20 it was 21 there are; there is; It is 22 It is, it is 23 There is, there are; It is *or* There was, there were; It was 24 Is there; it is; there is/there will be 25 there was; there was 26 There was; It was, there was 27 There are; There is, it is, isn't it 28 It is; there is; There is, there is/will be 29 There are; It is, there is 30 It is; It is; It is 31 there is; it was, wasn't it 32 it was/would be 33 It was; it was, there was 34 Is there; there is; is it 35 There is 36 It is; There is

Exercise 22 1 can, could, can't/couldn't 2 will be able to 3 won't be able to 4 can't . . . can't *or* couldn't . . . couldn't 5 shall/will be able to 6 will never be able to 7 couldn't, can't 8 will you be able to 9 won't be able to 10 could, couldn't 11 can, can, can't 12 can't, can't/couldn't, can't/couldn't 13 could/was able to 14 was able to 15 could/was able to, couldn't/wasn't able to 16 were able to 17 were you able to/could you 18 couldn't/wasn't able to 19 was able to 20 were able to 21 could/was able to 22 was able to 23 was able to 24 was able to 25 could/can, could 26 could, couldn't 27 could, couldn't, can't 28 could 29 couldn't/wouldn't be able to 30 couldn't/wouldn't be able to 31 could/can, can't 32 could, could 33 could/can, couldn't/can't 34 couldn't/wouldn't be able to 35 couldn't/wasn't able to, couldn't/wasn't able to 36 could

Exercise 23 1 may 2 might 3 may/might 4 may/might 5 might 6 may 7 may 8 might 9 may 10 was allowed to 11 might 12 may 13 may/might 14 may/might, may/might 15 might 16 may 17 may 18 may 19 may/might 20 might 21 might 22 may/might 23 may/might 24 may 25 might 26 may/might 27 might/may 28 may/might 29 may 30 might 31 might 32 may/might 33 may 34 might 35 may/might 36 hasn't been allowed to

Exercise 24 1 has to 2 must 3 has to 4 have to 5 must 6 have to 7 had to 8 has to 9 had to 10 have to 11 must 12 will have to/have to 13 must 14 has to 15 must 16 have to 17 have to 18 must 19 must 20 have to 21 had to 22 must 23 have to 24 must 25 has to 26 must 27 will have to 28 must 29 had to

Key

30 have to   31 will have to   32 had to   33 have to   34 must/will have
to   35 must   36 have to

Exercise 25   (Add **not** to each of the following verbs.)

1 need   2 must   3 must   4 need   5 must   6 must   7 need   8 must
9 need   10 need   11 need   12 must   13 need   14 must   15 must
16 need   17 must 18 must   19 need   20 need   21 must   22 must
23 need   24 must   25 must 26 must   27 need   28 need   29 need
30 need   31 need   32 must   33 need   34 must   35 must   36 need

Exercise 26   (**didn't have to** is replaceable by **didn't need to**.)

1 he doesn't have/hasn't (got) to   2 did you have to   3 I don't have
to   4 they will have to   5 we didn't have to   6 we didn't have to
7 you needn't come   8 I never have to   9 shan't/won't have to
10 you needn't   11 shall we have to   12 you don't have to   13 I didn
have to   14 we don't have to   15 have you got to/must you/need you
16 do people have to   17 shall I have to   18 don't have to   19 we
didn't have to   20 you needn't   21 we didn't have to   22 do we have
to/must we   23 did you have to   24 I didn't have to   25 you won't
have to   26 they didn't have to   27 do you have to/have you got to
28 did you have to/had you to   29 didn't have to   30 shall I have to
31 do you have to/have you got to   32 I didn't have to   33 do French
children have to   34 did you have to   35 I didn't have to   36 did you
have to

Exercise 27   1 must have been   2 can't/couldn't have been
3 needn't have helped   4 must have left   5 can't/couldn't have
escaped   6 needn't have given   7 can't/couldn't have seen   8 must
have started   9 can't have been   10 needn't have bought   11 must
have been   12 must have borrowed   13 must have stolen   14 needn'
have done   15 needn't have said   16 can't/couldn't have understood
17 can't/couldn't have done   18 must have been   19 can't/couldn't
have walked   20 can't have been   21 must have been
22 can't/couldn't have had   23 needn't have watered   24 must have
taken   25 can't/couldn't have been   26 can't/couldn't have watered
27 must have been   28 needn't have sent   29 needn't have made
30 must have been   31 must have been   32 can't/couldn't have seen
33 can't/couldn't have come   34 needn't have lent   35 needn't have
spoken   36 must have fallen

3 Present and past tenses

Exercise 28   1 wishes   2 passes   3 helps   4 changes   5 watches
6 worries   7 cashes   8 carries   9 washes   10 goes   11 lays
12 bounces   13 astonishes   14 does he like   15 costs   16 fishes

17 forgets 18 catches 19 misses 20 mixes 21 freezes 22 flies
23 matches 24 realizes 25 uses 26 does he do, does, lies
27 hurries 28 pushes 29 kisses 30 boxes 31 dresses 32 relies
33 snatches 34 fries 35 rises 36 does

Exercise 29 Negative: 1 don't know 2 doesn't have 3 doesn't love
4 don't wear 5 doesn't trust 6 doesn't try 7 doesn't close
8 doesn't miss 9 don't like 10 doesn't finish 11 doesn't live
12 doesn't bully 13 doesn't heat 14 doesn't have 15 doesn't carry
16 doesn't believe 17 doesn't dance 18 don't remember 19 doesn't
play 20 doesn't worry 21 don't work 22 doesn't leave 23 doesn't
arrange 24 doesn't agree 25 don't bark 26 don't complain
27 doesn't enjoy 28 doesn't engage 29 doesn't look 30 don't sell
31 doesn't charge 32 doesn't cut 33 don't pick 34 doesn't leave
35 doesn't relax 36 doesn't refuse

Interrogative: 1 do you know 2 does he have 3 does he love 4 do
they wear 5 does he trust 6 does he try 7 does the park close
8 does he miss 9 do the children like 10 does he finish 11 does he
live 12 does he bully 13 does it heat 14 does she have 15 does she
carry 16 does he believe 17 does she dance 18 do you remember
19 does she play 20 does he worry 21 do these thieves usually
work 22 does he leave 23 does Ann arrange 24 does she agree
25 do their dogs bark 26 do their neighbours often complain
27 does Tom enjoy 28 does he engage 29 does Tom look 30 do
they sell 31 does he charge 32 does she cut 33 do they pick
34 does the last train leave 35 does he relax 36 does she refuse

Exercise 30 1 isn't working, is swimming 2 is teaching 3 isn't Ann
wearing 4 is flying 5 is Tom doing, is cleaning 6 is going, is
someone bringing 7 is it raining, is raining 8 are you mending
9 aren't telling, am not telling 10 is moving, is painting 11 is
sweeping 12 are you reading, am reading 13 is shining, are singing
14 is knocking, am just coming, am just washing 15 is always ringing
up and asking 16 are you making, is someone coming 17 is lying
18 are you using 19 are you doing, am going 20 are having, is
catching 21 am doing 22 are you typing, you are making 23 is
resting 24 are digging, are they doing, are looking 25 is making, are
repairing 26 are doing, are cutting 27 are you waiting, am waiting,
is just getting 28 are saying, is making 29 is always losing . . . and
asking 30 are you looking . . . is something happening
31 am bathing 32 are rushing, are jumping out and unrolling 33 is
pouring, are stopping, is trying 34 is climbing, is helping, are
sliding 35 is waving, is going 36 is coming, is carrying, is/are
cheering

Exercise 31 1 don't build, use 2 is having 3 drinks, is drinking
4 does she do, plays, watches 5 is raining, haven't 6 leaves

Key

7 speaks, don't understand 8 is making, makes 9 wears 10 don't
like 11 am wearing 12 is reading 13 am redecorating 14 is
boiling 15 are you enjoying, am enjoying, want 16 do you get, go,
am going 17 are you putting, am going, are you coming, do you
mind 18 do you owe, I owe, do you intend 19 do you belong, do yc
read, do you change, I change 20 learns, doesn't seem
21 always buy/am always buying, win 22 do you like, am giving
23 promise, promise 24 do you always write 25 do you love, like,
don't love 26 do you dream, dream, eat, have 27 smells, do you
keep 28 are always complaining/always complain 29 are using
30 is always saying/always says, does 31 do you know, falls 32 are
you writing, write, do you want 33 are having, wonder, are talking
34 do you believe, don't believe, do you read 35 is making, do you
think, doesn't matter, makes 36 is smoking, expect, are building,
does, doesn't seem, don't you put

Exercise 32 1 does Tom think, thinks, agree 2 does this one cost,
costs 3 do you hear, is blowing 4 do you see, am looking, don't see
5 listens, is always thinking 6 deserts, goes 7 do you understand,
don't understand 8 do you have, eat, drink 9 rises, see, are
picketing 10 are you walking, walk, am hurrying, am meeting,
doesn't like 11 wish, keeps, think, wants 12 do you recognize,
think, don't remember 13 wonder, waiting for 14 is waiting, want
15 don't you see, see, am not wearing, does it say, says 16 is alway
borrowing/always borrows, remembers 17 do you need, do you fee
18 does it save, take, doesn't matter 19 am saving, am going
20 think, are getting 21 are looking, is just taking 22 does, is
always working 23 is he doing, think, is polishing 24 is coming, d
you want 25 is Peter getting on, seems 26 is Mrs Pitt looking/doe
Mrs Pitt look, is smoking, and (is) dropping 27 leave, arrive, spend
set, sounds, get 28 makes, finds, goes, does not forget, returns,
looks 29 finds, recognizes, coils, kills 30 does the snake feel, don'
know, ends 31 do you end, begins, put, prefers 32 does the word
'catastrophe' mean, means 33 are you waiting, am waiting, doesn't
open, know, want, starts/is starting 34 are you smoking, don't
smoke, am smoking, want, says, removes 35 owns, don't know, us
knows, owns 36 do you mind, ask, depends, concerns, refuse

Exercise 33 1 went 2 met 3 wore 4 made 5 got 6 understood
7 shut 8 spoke 9 left 10 read 11 ate 12 saw 13 sang 14 cried
was 15 knew 16 thought I knew 17 rose 18 took 19 bought
20 dreamt 21 laid 22 felt 23 knew, wanted 24 paid 25 bit
26 smelt 27 cost 28 hurt 29 lay 30 drank 31 grew 32 rode
33 fell 34 fought, met 35 put 36 slept

Exercise 34 Negative: the answer in each case is **did not/didn't** +
infinitive, e.g. 1 did not/didn't see

156

Interrogative: the answer in each case is **did** + subject + infinitive, e.g. 1 did she see

The infinitives are as follows: 1 see 2 hear 3 sleep 4 look
5 drink 6 set 7 think 8 catch 9 hide 10 find 11 bleed 12 choose
13 lend 14 teach 15 hurt 16 break 17 come 18 lose 19 write
20 fly 21 draw 22 lay 23 fall 24 lose 25 forbid 26 send
27 keep 28 ride 29 spend 30 sell 31 ring 32 rise 33 run
34 shake 35 forgive 36 broadcast

Exercise 35 1 were doing, was playing, was listening 2 was
getting 3 were rushing 4 was travelling 5 was wearing 6 was
redecorating 7 were working 8 was running 9 were playing, were
leaning 10 was working, was shopping 11 was sailing 12 were
going 13 were talking 14 was studying 15 was cooking 16 was
dieting, was trying 17 were you talking, was talking 18 was
climbing 19 was working 20 were bathing, were looking, were
playing 21 was he living 22 was standing, was waiting 23 was
practising 24 were carrying 25 were fighting, was trying, were they
fighting 26 was sitting, was reading 27 were doing, was weeding,
was cutting 28 were mending 29 was/were clapping 30 was
making, was saying 31 was learning 32 was repairing 33 was
always trying 34 were fishing 35 were writing 36 was wandering

Exercise 36 1 was burning 2 was writing 3 was making 4 left
5 was just leaving 6 was watching, turned, went 7 stood 8 was
playing, insisted 9 was walking 10 was having, lunched 11 wore,
carried 12 did you think, liked 13 shared, was always
complaining/always complained 14 realized, was travelling 15 was
playing, threw 16 was just opening, blew 17 was opening, heard,
put, crawled 18 was looking, found 19 saw, were you doing
20 were playing, heard, hid, took 21 was cleaning, went, killed
22 didn't allow, was blowing 23 was crossing/crossed, stepped, fell
24 was still lying, saw 25 saw, stopped 26 did you damage, ran,
were driving, were going 27 was getting/got, started, fell 28 called,
was already getting up 29 was mending/mended, got 30 heard,
went, opened, didn't recognize, wasn't wearing 31 were sitting, was
doing, was knitting, were reading, smiled, said 32 were dancing,
broke, stole 33 knew, were looking, hid, went 34 was always
buying 35 told, was spending/spent, listened 36 began, banged

Exercise 37 1 woke, was always getting/always got, went, bought
2 had to, usually grazed/was usually grazing 3 didn't normally chase,
made, was crossing, went 4 annoyed, began 5 was carrying, was
raining, threw, ran 6 stopped, began, was doing 7 awoke, was
sitting, was looking, called, turned, smiled 8 did you interrupt, was
having 9 was carrying, heard 10 was looking, noticed 11 were
walking/walked, heard, turned, held, stopped 12 arrived, was

Key

waiting, was wearing, (was) looking/looked, saw, waved, shouted, was saying/said, was making 13 escaped, was working, was wearing 14 was travelling, began 15 didn't like, was trying 16 was making, felt, brought, was able 17 saw, was painting, did you like, was only just starting, saw 18 took, was being, were still listening, left/were leaving 19 was, had to, was enjoying 20 were coming, stopped, said, was looking, asked 21 saw, were you using, was using, were you riding 22 was knitting 23 was, said, hoped, was enjoying 24 was watering, began, put, went 25 was just writing, remembered, had 26 found, was digging, belonged 27 saw, was hurrying, asked, was going, said, was speaking, wasn't 28 called, was still working 29 came, was smoking, had, threw, hoped 30 noticed, was rising, were you smoking, came, asked 31 was swimming, stole, had to 32 said, were working, wanted 33 said, was building, thought 34 woke, said, thought, was trying 35 did you lend, was still reading, didn't know, were still reading 36 came, woke, started, woke, came, said, said, didn't hear, was barking, went, telephoned

Exercise 38 1 Have you been, I've been 2 have you had, have 3 has the post come, has 4 have you seen, haven't 5 has someone wound, has 6 haven't finished 7 has just gone 8 has taken 9 has stopped 10 have you heard, haven't 11 have just washed 12 has stolen 13 have you explained, have 14 have gone 15 have you had, have had 16 has Charles passed, has 17 has the milkman left, has left 18 have lived 19 have you known, have known 20 have just made 21 has Mary watered, has 22 haven't you made, haven't 23 haven't you mended, haven't had 24 have you dived, haven't 25 have you ever left, haven't 26 have asked 27 has always refused 28 have you ever ridden 29 have bought 30 has he posted 31 hasn't he finished, has had 32 have often seen, have never spoken 33 have you ever eaten, haven't 34 have just heard 35 have recaptured 36 haven't paid

Exercise 39 1 have, wound 2 haven't, ate 3 has, fed 4 haven't, have only repaired 5 have done, did 6 haven't, haven't found 7 have, made 8 haven't, have been 9 haven't, haven't seen 10 have, went 11 have driven, drove 12 hasn't, has, went 13 have, was 14 has, spoke 15 have only spent, have 16 haven't saved, have saved 17 hasn't, went 18 haven't seen, saw, didn't see 19 have, paid 20 haven't, flew 21 bit, has bitten 22 planted, haven't 23 has, wrote 24 haven't, drank, haven't drunk

Exercise 40 1 have you lived/have you been living, have lived/have been living 2 lived, went 3 did you wear, insisted 4 left, cut, have worn 5 wrote 6 has written, has just finished 7 flew, did you see 8 haven't seen 9 hasn't smoked 10 composed 11 did he arrive, arrived 12 did you lock 13 read, enjoyed 14 haven't finished 15 have never drunk 16 have written 17 has stopped 18 have just

cleaned   19 left, got   20 did, was   21 has just gone   22 went
23 have you had, had   24 met   25 did you see   26 began, lasted,
enjoyed   27 has just begun   28 has the newspaper come   29 arrived,
started   30 has been   31 wrote   32 have missed   33 broke   34 has
been   35 worked, retired, went   36 have you been, spent, did you
have, stopped

Exercise 41   1 haven't seen, told   2 bought, did you pay, paid   3 did
you find, found, didn't you leave   4 have lost, have you seen, haven't,
did you last wear, wore, left   5 has just left, has been, has never
bought   6 left, did he go, didn't see, went   7 served, did that war
begin, began, lasted   8 did you vote, voted, wasn't, was, lost   9 did
you like, liked, quarrelled, dismissed, were, was   10 didn't know,
knew, have you known, have known   11 hasn't had, have been
12 did you hear, did, did you think   13 didn't know, were, have you
been, have been, have you been, went   14 have you tried, tried,
found, started   15 have you seen, has anything happened, have
escaped   16 has Mary fed, fed, did she give, gave   17 have you
known, have known, did he do, came, was   18 have you seen, hasn't
been bought   19 has the plumber been, stayed, did he do, turned,
emptied   20 have you been, have been, did you enjoy, took, did you
win, came   21 has that been, has been, have written, has been
22 have just been, have you seen, haven't, haven't read, read, was,
did Tolstoy write, wrote, did he write   23 brought, did he do,
wanted   24 have you been, have been, did he take, did, did it hurt
25 said, hasn't phoned   26 have just received, haven't paid, didn't I
give, did, spent/have spent   27 have you been, have just started, did
you find, answered   28 have you finished, have done   29 have cut,
did it happen, slipped   30 did you get, got   31 did you meet, did,
had   32 lost, has been, did he lose, was   33 has been, did you see,
happened, ran   34 phoned, got   35 did not wear, have worn   36 has
been, have just taken, has bought

Exercise 42   Affirmative: the answer in each case is **have/has** + **been**
+ present participle, e.g. 1 have been making

Negative: **have/has** + **not** + **been** + present participle, e.g.
16 haven't been eating

Interrogative: **have/has** + subject + **been** + present participle, e.g.
6 have you been doing

Present participles are as follows:
1 making   2 ringing   3 overworking   4 cutting   5 looking   6 doing,
working 7 studying   8 waiting   9 raining   10 arguing   11 bathing
12 driving   13 wearing   14 saying   15 trying   16 eating
17 speaking   18 flying 19 playing   20 shopping   21 living   22 eating
23 looking   24 leaking   25 digging, helping   26 asking   27 using

28 driving 29 going 30 snowing 31 crying, peeling 32 making
33 drinking 34 smoking 35 eating 36 trying

Exercise 43 1 have walked 2 have been walking/have walked
3 have been walking/have walked 4 have been making 5 have you
made, have made 6 has eaten 7 hasn't stopped 8 has been
drinking 9 have pulled 10 have been pulling 11 have you been
doing, have been picking 12 have you picked, have picked 13 have
slept 14 has been sleeping/has slept 15 has been riding 16 have
ridden 17 has been making 18 have been working/have worked
19 have heard 20 have been hearing/have heard 21 have been
greasing 22 have been polishing 23 have been working/have
worked, has never said 24 has been teaching/has taught 25 have
taught, have never met 26 have you been, have been pumping/have
pumped 27 have pumped 28 have been looking/have looked,
haven't found 29 has been coughing/has coughed 30 have you
heard, have known 31 have been trying, have said 32 has been
sounding 33 has been raining/has rained, has been postponed
34 has been hoping, hasn't dared 35 have been whispering, have you
been helping, has he been helping 36 have you been making, have
lost, have been trying, have been throwing

Exercise 44 1 for 2 for 3 since 4 for 5 for 6 since 7 since
8 since 9 for 10 since 11 for 12 for 13 for 14 for 15 since
16 since 17 for 18 since 19 for 20 since 21 since 22 since
23 for 24 since 25 since 26 since 27 for 28 since 29 since
30 for 31 for 32 since 33 for 34 for 35 for 36 since

4 Future forms

Exercise 45 1 are starting 2 is making 3 am taking 4 is calling
5 is playing 6 am meeting 7 are not starting 8 are you getting, am
going, is driving 9 is coming 10 are you giving, am giving 11 are
being 12 is coming 13 are having, are going 14 are you going, am
going 15 is not giving 16 am having 17 am buying 18 are being
19 am having 20 is/are meeting 21 are celebrating 22 am lending
23 are returning 24 are opening 25 are moving 26 am not taking
27 are getting 28 are you doing, am going 29 is flying 30 is
starting 31 is giving, are you going 32 is being, am meeting 33 am
catching, are you leaving, am not taking 34 is sending 35 am going,
is taking 36 am lending

Exercise 46 Affirmative: the answer in each case is **am/is/are +
going to** + infinitive, e.g. 1 are going to miss

Negative answers: **am/is/are + not + going to** + infinitive, e.g. 22 am
not going to do

Interrogative answers: **is/are** + subject + **going to** + infinitive, e.g.
3 are you going to pay

Exercise 47 (**be going to** is possible in all these sentences, but where
the present continuous tense is given in the key, that is the better one
to use.)

1 am playing   2 is having   3 am going to light   4 are having   5 is
being, are you putting, am putting   6 are you going, am going, am not
buying/am not going to buy   7 am not going to do   8 am having   9 is
coming, are you putting, am putting   10 is starting   11 am spending
12 is going to build   13 are you going to tell, am going to tell   14 is
starting   15 is opening   16 is speaking   17 is closing   18 are you
having, am having   19 am collecting   20 are taking   21 am giving
22 is singing   23 is going, is he flying, is going   24 is seeing   25 is he
going to wash   26 is ringing   27 is going to ask   28 are giving, are
inviting   29 is playing, is playing   30 are launching, are you coming
31 are you going to do   32 am picking   33 are you going, am going, is
calling   34 am competing   35 isn't coming   36 am going to read

Exercise 48   Affirmative answers: 1st person **will/shall** + infinitive,
2nd and 3rd person **will** + infinitive, e.g. 1 will/shall know

Negative answers: as above with **not**, e.g. 7 will not/won't catch

Interrogative answers: as above with **will/shall** + subject + infinitive,
e.g. 2 will you be

Exercise 49 (**shall** can be replaced by **will** in these answers.
Contractions may be used.)

1 shall recognize   2 will see/am seeing ('am seeing' implies a definite
arrangement)   3 is playing   4 is coming   5 am going   6 shall know
7 shall owe   8 shall believe   9 am having   10 will have   11 is
being/will be   12 is coming   13 is catching   14 are you meeting, am
meeting   15 are you riding/will you ride   16 will Mrs Pitt say, won't
mind   17 will it matter   18 won't forget   19 is leaving   20 shall
remember   21 will break   22 will never forgive   23 will like   24 are
laying   25 will see   26 will grow   27 will understand   28 will
scratch   29 shall be   30 won't pass   31 is going   32 am moving
33 will soon forget   34 will wait   35 won't write   36 will be

Exercise 50 (**shall** can be replaced by **will**. Contractions may be
used.)

1 will go   2 will telephone   3 will send   4 am going to learn   5 are
you going to do   6 will call, will translate   7 are you going to buy, am
not going to eat, am going to eat   8 are you going to redecorate   9 am
going to change, will help   10 are you going to put   11 am going to
put   12 are you going to do, am going to be   13 am going to shorten

14 won't lend 15 will cut 16 am going to attend 17 will ask 18 am
going to open 19 is going to take 20 will ask 21 am going to get
22 am going to develop 23 will make 24 are going to tow 25 am
going to give up/am giving up 26 will say 27 will lend 28 are going
to raffle 29 are going to clear 30 will mend 31 will give 32 am
going to make 33 am going to shorten 34 am going to buy 35 are
you going to do 36 am going to give

Exercise 51 1 will you open 2 are you going to do 3 are you going
to paint 4 will you read 5 are you going to eat 6 aren't you going
to climb 7 will you listen 8 will you put 9 will you have 10 are
you going to make 11 aren't you going to answer 12 will you come
13 are you really going to read 14 are you going to buy, will you
buy 15 will you lend, are you going to fish 16 are you going to
finish 17 will you give, are you going to make 18 are you going to
leave 19 are you going to bath, will you help 20 will you drive
21 are you going to ride 22 are you going to eat 23 will you have
24 are you really going to call 25 are you going to paint 26 will you
be ready 27 will you sit 28 will you do 29 will you be angry
30 are you going to work 31 will you call 32 are you going to walk
33 will you sign 34 are you going to give 35 are you going to
explore 36 will you cook

Exercise 52 Form of affirmative answer: **shall** or **will** ('ll) as
appropriate + **be** + present participle, e.g. I shall/will be sitting.
Negative answer: 19 won't be looking. Interrogative answers:
23 will the children be doing 26 will the tide be doing

Exercise 53 (**shall** can be replaced by **will** in these answers.
Contractions may be used.)

1 will be walking 2 will walk 3 shall be bathing 4 will wash
5 shall be doing 6 shall be working/am working 7 will have 8 will
be looking 9 shall be thinking/shall think 10 will assemble 11 will
meet, shall I recognize, will be wearing 12 will leave, shall be
going/am going 13 will be debating/are debating 14 will go 15 will
be working 16 will post, shall be going/am going 17 will be ·
dancing/will dance 18 will be letting off . . . and making/will let off
. . . and make 19 will remain 20 shall be sitting, won't be reading
21 will be going/will go 22 will be changing/will change 23 will
come 24 will bring 25 shall all be living 26 will be going/will go
27 shall not be playing 28 will be opening/will open 29 will drive
30 shall be entering 31 will hand 32 will be arriving/will arrive
33 will be leaving 34 will be using . . . and leaving/will use. . . and
leave 35 will bring, will catch 36 will put

Exercise 54 (In these answers **I/we won't** can be replaced by **I am
not going to/we are not going to** without any change in meaning. It is

also grammatically possible to replace **you/he/they won't** by the **going to** form, but this would make the negative much less emphatic. **shan't** is replaceable by **won't**.)

1 won't help 2 won't be meeting 3 won't cut 4 won't be cutting
5 won't be coming/isn't coming 6 won't come 7 won't lend 8 won't be speaking/isn't speaking 9 won't work 10 shan't be working
11 won't have 12 shan't be teaching/am not teaching 13 won't speak 14 shan't be writing 15 won't feed 16 won't go 17 won't paint 18 shan't be taking 19 won't borrow 20 won't wash 21 shan't be using 22 won't send 23 won't play 24 won't be singing/isn't singing 25 won't play 26 won't be taking part/isn't taking part
27 won't eat 28 shan't be eating 29 won't ride 30 won't be riding/isn't riding 31 won't give 32 won't be drinking 33 won't open 34 won't tell 35 won't eat 36 won't be wearing

Exercise 55 1 are you going to feed 2 are you letting/are you going to let/will you be letting 3 will you light 4 are you wearing/are you going to wear/will you be wearing 5 will you wear 6 will you come
7 will you have 8 are you having/are you going to have 9 are you going to study/will you be studying 10 will you be speaking 11 will you turn 12 Any one of the four forms is possible here: 'Will you take' implies that the matter has not yet been decided and that the speaker is offering a choice of dates. The other forms would imply that the matter has already been arranged and that the speaker is merely asking for information. 13 will you be listening/are you going to listen 14 will you help 15 will you be staying 16 will you lend
17 are you meeting/are you going to meet/will you be meeting
18 will you come 19 will you have 20 will you translate 21 will you be using/are you using/are you going to use 22 will you be going/are you going, will you get 23 will you come 24 will you be passing/are you going to pass/are you passing, shall be spending/am going to spend/am spending, will you get 25 are you going to keep 26 are you travelling/are you going to travel 27 are you going to repair
28 will you hold 29 are you going/will you be going 30 will you kindly explain 31 will you recognize 32 are you sending/are you going to send 33 will you tell 34 are you going/will you be going
35 are you going to type/will you be typing 36 will you stop

Exercise 56 (**will** and **will not** may be contracted.)

1 shall/will 2 will 3 shall 4 shall 5 shall 6 shall 7 shall 8 will
9 shall 10 shall 11 shall 12 will 13 shall 14 shall 15 will
16 will 17 will 18 shall/will 19 will, will 20 shall 21 will
22 shall 23 will 24 shall 25 will, shall/will 26 will 27 shall, will
28 will 29 shall/will 30 shall/will 31 shall 32 won't, won't
33 will 34 shall 35 will, will 36 shall/will

Key

Exercise 57 (**will** and **shall** may be contracted.)

1 returns 2 are 3 strikes 4 hears 5 shall/will have 6 comes
7 turn 8 gets 9 won't start 10 goes 11 will see 12 will be
13 shall/will lend 14 will wake 15 will he ring 16 goes 17 is
18 shall/will give, comes 19 see 20 get 21 shall/will go 22 have
23 will fall 24 goes 25 arrives 26 lifts 27 will go on 28 will
become 29 won't move 30 will go on 31 learns 32 leap
33 shall/will have 34 get 35 begins 36 arrives

Exercise 58 Answers will all be: **have** + past participle of the verb
in brackets. **shall** can be used instead of **will** for the 1st person, e.g.
1 will/shall have taken. **will** can be contracted to **'ll**.

Exercise 59 (Contractions may be used.)

1 have taken 2 have finished/finish 3 have had 4 have been
5 goes/has gone 6 gets/has got 7 has done 8 have done 9 will see
10 have had 11 shall/will take 12 go 13 have seen 14 goes/has
gone 15 won't let 16 shall/will let 17 sees 18 won't hear 19 has
passed/passes 20 has sold 21 have swept/sweep 22 will get
23 will give 24 says 25 have returned/return 26 has been 27 have
signed 28 won't know 29 have subsided/subside 30 has left
31 shall/will have 32 have had 33 shall/will stay 34 have made
35 has eaten 36 will come/come

Exercise 60 (**should** is replaceable by **would** in nos. 6, 14, 26, 27,
30.)

1 would 2 would 3 should 4 would 5 would 6 should 7 should
8 would, would 9 should 10 would 11 should 12 would
13 would 14 should 15 should 16 would 17 should 18 would,
would 19 should 20 would 21 should 22 should 23 should
24 should 25 should 26 should 27 should 28 would 29 should
30 should/would, would 31 should 32 should, should 33 would
34 should 35 should 36 should

Exercise 61 1 should, should 2 would 3 should 4 should
5 would, would, would, would 6 should 7 should 8 would, would
9 should, should/would 10 should 11 would 12 would, should
13 should 14 should 15 should, would 16 should 17 should
18 would, should 19 should 20 would 21 should 22 would
23 should 24 should 25 would, would 26 would 27 should
28 would 29 should 30 should, should, would 31 should
32 should 33 should/would, would 34 would, would 35 should
36 would, would

164

5 Conditionals

Exercise 62 1 will give 2 stand 3 eats 4 will telephone 5 will arrest 6 reads 7 will steal 8 doesn't open 9 washes 10 needs 11 don't go 12 makes 13 is 14 hears 15 will make 16 will bury 17 won't be 18 doesn't start 19 won't let *or* don't let (habit) 20 goes 21 sells 22 will you repay 23 rises 24 works 25 turns/will turn 26 burns 27 don't like 28 will have 29 see 30 will you promise 31 don't believe 32 likes 33 will make 34 shan't/won't be able 35 knows 36 ring

Exercise 63 1 would type 2 knew 3 would look 4 played 5 wouldn't make 6 were 7 had 8 would you visit 9 gave 10 would buy 11 cleaned 12 would you be able 13 didn't belong 14 won 15 would you do 16 knew 17 gave 18 stopped 19 wouldn't come 20 saw 21 would/should be 22 would not be bitten 23 had 24 did 25 would grow 26 removed 27 would keep 28 lived 29 banned/were to ban 30 would offer 31 got 32 painted 33 changed 34 would you spend 35 had 36 wasn't

Exercise 64 (**should** in the following answers may be replaced by **would**; contractions may be used in the affirmative and negative.)

1 should have visited 2 would have won 3 had arrived 4 had been 5 should have been 6 had not seen 7 would have fallen 8 would you have accepted 9 had had 10 had known 11 should have offered 12 would not have stung 13 had realized 14 should have stopped 15 should have reached 16 should not have lent 17 had not sneezed 18 had put 19 would not have got 20 would not have tried 21 had spoken 22 would not have been 23 had known 24 had tried 25 would not have got 26 would not have put 27 had been 28 would have come 29 would not have turned 30 had looked 31 would have been captured 32 had tried 33 should have taken 34 would have saved 35 had not called 36 would not have burnt

Exercise 65 (In the affirmative and negative **shall** and **should** can be replaced by **will** and **would** respectively; and contractions may be used. **should** in sentences 1, 7, 11 however does not change.)

1 find/should find 2 shall have 3 will happen 4 had had 5 will you stay 6 would you choose 7 gets/should get 8 comes 9 will sit 10 didn't talk 11 shall/should I do 12 had read 13 had 14 shall go 15 would you do 16 run 17 will not be 18 comes 19 would not have 20 had worn 21 leaves 22 will fall 23 don't change 24 should not have bought 25 hung 26 would be able to/could 27 should have brought 28 would have been 29 would not have printed 30 should not buy 31 want 32 won't be 33 would jump 34 would answer 35 had made 36 had known

Key

Exercise 66 Open-ended sentences. No answers given.

Exercise 67 1 could I speak 2 speaking 3 could you come and do
4 couldn't 5 could come 6 could you come 7 could get, would
8 wouldn't, would, leave 9 thought you said 10 could get, couldn't
make 11 having, doesn't like 12 is always trying, cleaning,
thinks/says 13 does she want/would she like you to do 14 would
like/wants me to work 15 says/thinks it would be 16 worked, would
know 17 are you really thinking 18 like, like 19 would get
20 would Wednesday suit 21 would, to come 22 will, let 23 will,
won't 24 will, do

6 Infinitive

Exercise 68 1 do 2 sing 3 to swim 4 to live 5 to go, rain
6 say, understand 7 to see 8 repeat 9 use 10 ask, use 11 to
get, start 12 remember 13 to do 14 to go, wait 15 leave
16 open 17 (to) argue 18 to smoke 19 (to) move 20 play 21 to
accept 22 to arrive 23 know 24 wait 25 tell 26 send 27 go, to
meet 28 to have 29 leave, want, to take 30 to go, make, go
31 go, to visit 32 to know, to live 33 not to inform, (to) disobey
34 come, stay 35 take, make, drink 36 to disappoint, let, have

Exercise 69 1 to be 2 wish to make 3 want, to know
4 remember, look 5 to learn, to know 6 to be 7 not to feed
8 see, to speak 9 to travel, to arrive 10 know, to use, show 11 to
sign 12 open/opening, move/moving 13 to make, believe 14 to
have missed, go 15 shake/shaking 16 to try, to come 17 go,
promise, not to tell 18 like to come, walk 19 to ask, to tell, to get
20 to put, (to) keep 21 to read, answer 22 show, to open 23 say,
to say 24 to be 25 want, to tell, to call, to discuss 26 to give,
see/be seeing, not to forget 27 open/opening, throw/throwing 28 to
carry, help 29 to pick, to handle 30 crash/crashing,
burst/bursting 31 to do, wait, to let 32 crow/crowing 33 tell, be,
to check 34 come, go, be/have been 35 to learn 36 be, look ˙

Exercise 70 No answers given.

Exercise 71 1 too young to have 2 too cold to bathe 3 so kind as
to answer/kind enough to answer 4 too old to wear 5 long enough
to reach 6 enough money to live on 7 too furious to speak 8 hot
enough to boil 9 foolish enough to tell/so foolish as to tell 10 thin
enough to slip 11 too ill to eat 12 too wide to get through
13 strong enough to dance on 14 too terrified to move 15 big
enough to harm 16 strong enough to keep 17 too deep to wade
18 too lazy to get up 19 early enough to catch 20 so good as to

forward/good enough to forward   21 thick enough to walk on
22 too drunk to answer   23 too cold to have   24 rash enough to set
off/so rash as to set off   25 high enough to see   26 old enough to
understand   27 too snobbish to talk   28 too thick to push through
29 too mean to give   30 too impatient to listen   31 too tired to
walk   32 not dark enough to see   33 hot enough to fry   34 too bitter
to eat   35 so kind as to turn down/kind enough to turn down   36 too
selfish to put

Exercise 72   1 to leave   2 only to find   3 You are to go   4 so kind
as to lend/kind enough to lend   5 to mend/to be mended   6 to hear
7 for him to hear   8 It was stupid of me to be rude   9 to play with
10 for everyone to know   11 to sit   12 only to find   13 It was very
brave of him to rush   14 to wear   15 He is expected to broadcast
16 to cook in   17 only to learn   18 to open it with   19 seems to have
been committed   20 Is he likely to arrive   21 just about to leave
22 You are to be met   23 for them to have   24 He is said to have
been   25 to continue the strike   26 kind enough to translate/so kind
as to translate   27 for us to leave   28 It was stupid of you to sign
29 She is said to have   30 to swim   31 He is believed to be   32 He
appears to have been killed   33 to realize   34 The earth is said to
have been   35 only to discover   36 The murderer is said to be
hiding

Exercise 73   (**should** is replaceable by **ought to.**)

1 must have been   2 can't/couldn't have seen, must have dreamt
3 may/might have broken   4 needn't have carried   5 should have
gone   6 were to have been   7 can't/couldn't have been, must have
been   8 shouldn't have eaten   9 may/might not have understood
10 needn't have given   11 must have escaped   12 shouldn't have
lied   13 may/might have been, can't/couldn't have been   14 must
have cooked   15 needn't have brought   16 must have told   17 was
to have unveiled   18 may/might have been   19 must have met
20 should have done   21 can't/couldn't have caught   22 needn't
have opened   23 must have betrayed   24 shouldn't have driven
25 could have climbed   26 would have asked   27 should have been
abolished   28 shouldn't/needn't have boiled   29 was to have played
30 may/might have been   31 should have taken   32 must have had
33 may/might/could have fallen   34 must have been   35 needn't
have translated   36 shouldn't have looked

Exercise 74   (**I'd** is replaceable by **I should. should** (obligation) is
replaceable by **ought to** in nos. 5, 9, 13, 17. **may/might** in the
affirmative is normally replaceable by **could.**)

1 was to have married   2 needn't have repeated   3 seems to have
been   4 were to have set out   5 shouldn't have eaten, may/might
have been (**may** indicates that the danger is still present; **might** that

it is over). 6 must have worked 7 needn't have brought 8 I'd like to have bathed/I'd have liked to bathe/I'd have liked to have bathed 9 should have written 10 wouldn't have come 11 might/should have told, would have gone, wouldn't have liked 12 may/might have been, can't/couldn't have been 13 needn't/shouldn't have bought 14 can't/couldn't have been 15 seems to have enjoyed 16 must have been 17 should have stood 18 was to have gone 19 I'd like to have photographed/I'd have liked to photograph/I'd have liked to have photographed 20 must have been 21 may/might have been 22 can't/couldn't have been driving 23 must have taken 24 may/might not have 25 I'd like to have gone/I'd have liked to go/I'd have liked to have gone 26 can't/couldn't have seen 27 may have been 28 may/might have been started 29 must have had 30 may/might have read, can't/couldn't have read, must have told 31 may/might have been waiting 32 must have misheard 33 might have borrowed 34 I'd like to have asked/I'd have liked to ask/I'd have liked to have asked 35 must have been 36 is said to have been

7 Gerund, infinitive and participles

Exercise 76 1 seeing 2 having 3 to meet 4 to work 5 to see 6 waiting 7 not to touch 8 to lock, going 9 not to speak 10 behaving 11 to explain, to listen 12 smoking 13 to know 14 to disguise, dressing 15 to wait 16 showing, to work 17 walking, catch up 18 to understand 19 exceeding 20 playing, doing 21 to inform 22 overhearing 23 smoking, to smoke 24 going, saying 25 writing, waiting 26 to avoid being 27 giving, to speak 28 to persuade, to agree 29 cleaning, to be cleaned, to do 30 shutting, sitting 31 sneezing, sitting 32 talking, to finish 33 to give up jogging 34 stopping, forgetting to wind 35 realizing, helping 36 to make, rubbing

Exercise 77 1 answering, ring 2 letting, chase, being 3 driving, being driven 4 to start looking 5 lending, to cash 6 Lying, sitting 7 to go 8 neglecting to take 9 to show, to use 10 going, to see/seeing 11 telephoning, asking, to look 12 hearing, not to enter 13 to have, writing 14 to answer, replying 15 to explain, to listen, grumbling 16 offering, to leave, (to) work 17 making, to do 18 having to get up 19 to forget, worrying 20 remaining, to help, to stay 21 to run, to have recovered 22 listening, hearing 23 to learn, reading, listening 24 to start, to wait 25 discussing, having reached 26 having, to ride 27 (to) leave, meeting, recognize 28 paying 29 to give 30 interrupting, repeating 31 cutting, to go 32 buying, selling 33 giving, to explain 34 asking, telling, to buy 35 to tell, looking 36 to be, to erupt/erupting

Exercise 78 1 to ride, to do, coming, to come 2 spending, earning 3 being, to apologize 4 to eat 5 working, spending 6 looking, being 7 posting 8 to lock, go, do 9 to learn, saying 10 trying to interrupt, to wait, talking 11 doing, to move/moving 12 leaving, to go 13 to drink 14 being, to wait 15 trying to make, adding 16 going, stay 17 to look, (to) take, looking, to do 18 getting up, walking 19 listening, listening 20 to make/making, to see 21 doing 22 to put, to prevent, climbing 23 taking, to eat 24 ringing, asking, to do 25 waiting, to clear, to set 26 repeat, to make, to do 27 leaving, sending, to tow 28 borrowing, asking, to do 29 to offend, annoying 30 to be able to tell, gazing 31 getting, to walk 32 to ask, to leave 33 setting, having been 34 to go 35 to go, (to) try to save, cutting 36 earn, scrubbing, make, blackmailing

Exercise 79 1 beginning to slip/begin to slip/begin slipping, to save, falling 2 falling, trying to keep 3 to lend, taking 4 to open 5 reading, to read 6 to book, to keep, to lose 7 to avoid being, being/to be, waiting 8 to get, to ask 9 making, speak/speaking 10 to win, cheating 11 firing/to fire, graze 12 strike/striking, to get 13 ringing/ring, to be coming to open 14 to go, to give 15 to put, (to) watch, change/changing 16 to see, to avoid hitting 17 to be, crackling 18 climbing, to explain, to say, to let, go 19 convincing, to get, leap 20 driving, doing, to do 21 to sit, (to) hear, howling 22 getting, climbing, to do 23 roar/roaring, to move/moving, waving 24 writing, to do, to go, see 25 walking, to cross, thinking, to chase 26 to be having, thudding 27 getting, to pay 28 to come, standing 29 to like making and flying . . . doing 30 to arrive, rising 31 sawing, fall/falling 32 to see/seeing, crying/cry 33 jump/jumping, fall/falling 34 to wake, (to) hear, beating 35 beginning to roll/begin to roll/begin rolling, to do, to stop 36 laughing, slipping/slip

Exercise 80 1 Knowing that he was poor, I offered 2 Having barricaded the windows, we assembled 3 Becoming tired of my complaints, she turned it off 4 Finding/having found no one at home, he left 5 Hoping to find the will, she searched 6 Having removed all traces of his crime, he left 7 Realizing that he had missed the train, he began 8 Exhausted by his work, he threw 9 Having spent all his money, he decided 10 Having escaped from prison, he looked 11 Having heard the story before, she didn't want 12 Having found the money, they began 13 Entering the room suddenly, she found 14 Turning on the light, I was 15 Having visited the museum, we decided 16 Thinking we were lost, he offered 17 Having found his revolver and loaded it, he sat 18 Realizing that she couldn't move it alone, she asked 19 Having fed the dog, he sat 20 Addressing the congregation, he said 21 Thinking he had made a mistake somewhere, he went

22 Looking/having looked through the fashion magazines, I realize 23 The tree, uprooted by the gale, had fallen 24 People sleeping in the next room were 25 Knowing that the murderer was still at large, I was 26 Having stolen the silver, he looked 27 Soaked to the skin, we reached 28 Sitting/Seated in the front row, and using . . . I saw 29 . . . sitting by the fire, you will take 30 Knowing that . . . , I didn't like 31 Believing that she could trust him, she gave 32 Slates, ripped off by the gale, fell 33 The lion, finding his cage door open and seeing no sign of his keeper, left 34 The government, trying to tax people according to the size of their houses, once put a tax 35 Having heard that the caves were dangerous, I didn't like 36 Wearing extremely fashionable clothes and surrounded by photographers and press men, she swept

Exercise 81 1 When leaving a car . . . you must leave the brakes 2 As/When I was wading etc *or* Wading across . . . I was swept off my feet by 3 When a tank is being filled/When you are filling a tank 4 Running into the room, she caught her foot on a rug and fell 5 When I read the letter 6 When carrying . . . you should never point it 7 When planting . . . you must take care 8 In his first race, the horse he was riding fell 9 When paying by cheque, you must show 10 Knowing me to be . . . , he was astonished to hear that 11 As he believed that 12 As I passed/ *or* As/When I was passing 13 When I am reading/When I read 14 As he left 15 I led the dog, barking furiously, out 16 After I had paid my taxes, the amount 17 As I was writing 18 The boat, tied to a post, was being tossed up and down by the sea 19 As the question had been misunderstood, the wrong answer 20 We saw the first star, shining in the sky 21 It is easy to have an accident when one is/you are driving 22 The man saw a notice pinned to the door 23 They read the words 'No Entry' written in 24 While he was cleaning his gun it went off 25 When/As I was wondering where to go, an advertisement 26 As I rushed out of the house, a lorry 27 As I sat by the fire, it all comes back 28 We thought he would never survive after falling from 29 When a fuse is being changed, the electricity . . . *or* When you are changing a fuse you should switch 30 I saw a trailer with a boat on it being towed behind 31 As he was sitting at the foot . . . a stone fell 32 The road was blocked by a huge tree (which had been) uprooted 33 When he drove to work the traffic jams infuriated him 34 As I sat in the dentist's chair an idea 35 I felt sure that . . . would kill him, weakened as he was by his last illness 36 A scorpion bit him as he got out of bed

8 Passive

Exercise 82 1 wine should be opened . . . before it is used 2 steps had been cut 3 my shoes had been cleaned and my suit brushed

4 room is used   5 nails must not be hammered   6 pigs are used
7 a light was switched on and the door opened   8 picture had been
slashed   9 theatre is being pulled down   10 wasn't the roof
mended   11 All the shop windows were broken   12 system was
being started because books were not being returned   13 each of us
was asked   14 refreshments will be served   15 bicycles must not be
left   16 books may be kept . . . they must be returned   17 hole had
been cut   18 it is being delivered   19 he has already been told
20 bells were rung   21 nothing can be done unless we are given
more   22 far more is being spent on food now than was spent
23 paintings will be exhibited   24 nothing more will be said . . . if
the . . . gun is returned   25 he was told   26 My dog was stolen and
brought back only when a £20 reward was offered.   27 he was given
two weeks   28 flowers are made

Exercise 83   1 seals are fed   2 who was it written by?   3 compare
clothes washed by us with clothes washed by any other   4 he
expected to be offered   5 she was shown   6 oak was struck by
lightning   7 it couldn't have been painted by T. because that kind of
dress wasn't worn   8 she was stung by a jellyfish   9 special edition
for . . . has been written   10 herbs used to be carried by judges
11 what was it written with? It was written with   12 shot was
succeeded by an uneasy silence   13 were you interested by the
idea?   14 he was given details   15 dams are made by beavers
16 engines used to be started by hand, now they are started by
electricity   17 this was opposed by most people   18 a lot of the
work is being done by students   19 dock was to have been opened
by the PM   20 They recommend that new factories should be
opened   21 a lot of men will be made redundant by the closure
22 instructions could be understood by anyone   23 children . . . will
not be admitted   24 ship is to be manned by boys   25 camp was
flooded by a rainstorm   26 He was kept awake all night by the
howling   27 They suggested that the tests should be made   28 All
this damage couldn't have been done by children

Exercise 84   1 why don't you get an oculist to test your eyes?   2 the
authorities are to introduce this . . . limit   3 they are lengthening the
runways   4 nurses are wakening patients   5 people say that B.
lived   6 British fishermen must offer any sturgeon that they catch to
the Queen   7 someone has altered this notice   8 squatters have been
using their houseboat   9 they were towing the . . . ship   10 get a
builder to put in a lift   11 The firm made a profit . . . but a loss of
. . . which they made . . . cancelled this   12 guests will wear evening
dress   13 the authorities put the ship . . . and forbade passengers
and crew   14 we shall have to find someone   15 They made him
surrender his passport   16 our opponents must have started   17 the
New Arts Gallery is to exhibit my paintings   18 experts have proved
that this scientific theory is false   19 they are to salvage the car

which the wind blew   20 police are guarding the house where they
found the dead man to prevent anyone from entering it and
interfering with the evidence   21 why didn't you either lock the car
or put it   22 people are saying that the government is spending too
little money   23 you could put your money to good use instead of
leaving it idle   24 people believed that the earth was flat   25 no one
has read this copy; no one has cut the pages   26 the police led away
the student who threw the stones   27 people say that early Egyptian
and Greek sailors used carrier pigeons   28 a strong police guard was
escorting the referee

9   Indirect speech

Exercise 85   (In many of these examples other pronouns would be
equally correct.)

1 told her I had . . . to show her   2 said nothing grew in her garden
. . . it never got   3 told his mother he was going away the next day
4 said he had been . . . he hadn't had   5 remarked that it wasn't so
foggy that day as it had been the day before   6 said that the
underpass was being opened two days later   7 said they had moved
into their flat but they didn't like it . . . their last one   8 said they
had . . . it didn't work   9 said that . . . windows of his flat he could
see   10 said she'd no idea what the time was but she'd dial   11 his
wife had just been made   12 said she'd come with me . . . she was
13 said he had . . . that afternoon . . . he hadn't done his homework
14 warned her if she let . . . she would scorch her clothes
15 pointed out I hadn't given him . . . bill was . . . I'd paid him
16 Englishmen made . . . they were   17 she liked men . . . she didn't
like them . . . She preferred . . . men looked silly   18 The report
stated that the new Rolls Royce ran . . . all you could hear was . . .
The Managing Director replied that they'd have   19 said she didn't
know . . . her plums. She supposed (said she supposed) she'd have to
. . . trouble was no one in her family ate   20 explained they liked
working . . . they got   21 that he was . . . and he did all his own
22 told Joan she could keep that one if she liked as he had   23 said
he was going fishing with his mother that afternoon and they were
just going   24 told her she had got my umbrella and that hers was in
her bedroom   25 explained to his client that he knew what they had
said because he had bugged   26 said he'd sit up till she came in but
he hoped she wouldn't   27 told me that if I gave him . . . he'd . . .
for me   28 said she had . . . it didn't seem . . . to her weight   29 said
it was . . . and that he used one of them himself   30 said her new
house was supposed to be . . . but that so far she hadn't seen
31 said that if we answered all the questions . . . we might win
32 said that if he pressed his ear . . . he could hear . . . were saying

Exercise 86 (See note above key to Exercise 80. Where there is no introductory verb, use '. . . said (that) . . .'))

1 he hadn't been able to get . . . he had lost his key, so he had had to break 2 the mirror was there . . . he could see himself when he was dancing 3 told him she had written to him two days before and wondered why he hadn't 4 if the ground was dry . . . his horse might win 5 advised me to slow down as there was 6 said that if Tom wanted . . . he'd better apply 7 they had walked . . . the previous night . . . protest about their rent. The Minister had been . . . had promised . . . what he could for them 8 said they should put traffic lights there, otherwise there'd be 9 told them it was time they began training for their . . . 10 said to me that if I left . . . I should be there 11 if it rained that afternoon it would be . . . the following day 12 told her guest she had meant . . . she had plugged . . . She was always doing 13 he had been intending . . . the next day . . . didn't think he'd be 14 told Mrs Smith that Bill should do . . . he had done very well at the school 15 told her husband she didn't think his father liked her 16 told her the steak was . . . and said/added that he was not complaining but was just pointing . . . she said she wished he'd stop 17 reported that the burglars hadn't been able . . . had carried it 18 told me that if I saw her father I'd recognize him . . . He was 19 he had found . . . the day before . . . was going . . . that afternoon 20 he had got out . . . while he was standing . . . the gears (had) engaged . . . and the boat had gone/went 21 says he has done 22 asked if he would like me to go with him. He said he'd rather go . . . *or*, I offered to go with him, but he said 23 told me I might take his car if I liked and said he wouldn't be needing it the next day or the day after that 24 that the previous day Tom and she had gone/been to look . . . he was thinking . . . It was rather . . . and had a lovely garden but Tom had decided . . . was opposite 25 his wife wanted to take . . . he'd rather she concentrated on their home 26 she didn't know what my father would say when he saw . . . my puppies had made of the £5 note 27 it was high time I passed my test; she was tired 28 said I wished she had seen it

Exercise 87 1 asked what had happened 2 asked which . . . (had) inherited 3 asked who was going 4 asked what would happen 5 asked which team had won 6 asked which team (had) won 7 asked who was playing the following week 8 asked who would be umpiring 9 asked who wanted 10 asked who had just dropped 11 asked where the . . . office was 12 asked what she should do with her . . . 13 asked what platform the train left 14 asked when it arrived 15 asked when the timetable had been changed 16 asked why the 2.30 had been . . . 17 asked how much a day return cost 18 asked why the price went up 19 asked how he could get 20 asked when they were coming 21 asked if a return . . . was

22 asked if puppies travelled   23 asked if she could bring her dog
. . . with her   24 asked if the train stopped   25 asked if you could
telephone   26 asked if the 2.40 had   27 asked if you could get
28 asked if they brought   29 asked if there were   30 asked if he had

Exercise 88   1 asked what country I came from   2 asked how long
I'd been here   3 asked if I was working   4 asked if I had   5 asked
what I was going to study   6 asked if I had enrolled   7 asked if I
wanted to buy   8 asked if I had seen   9 asked if I played   10 asked
if I would have   11 asked if I had played for my . . .   12 asked if I
was interested   13 asked if I would like   14 asked what I thought

Each of the following will begin: she asked/wanted to know/enquired
15 how long it had been   16 if I liked   17 if he was   18 how many
. . . there were   19 how big the classes were   20 if the classes were
21 what the academic standard was like   22 if parents could visit
23 if there was   24 if they taught   25 what . . . could the children
learn   26 if there was   27 if they acted   28 what . . . plays they had
done   29 what games they played   30 if the fields were   31 if they
were taught   32 if the children could get   33 if the food was good
34 if there was   35 how often it met   36 if our boys had been/were
happy

Exercise 89   (**if** is interchangeable with **whether** except in
conditional sentences.)

1 asked why he was looking   2 asked who had put . . . in his coffee
3 asked which of them knew   4 asked why he had travelled
5 inquired how she could run in high-heeled shoes   6 asked them
what their new house was like   7 asked where he was supposed to
go   8 asked him whose car he had borrowed the previous night
9 asked me what she was/had been wearing when I saw her last
10 asked who owned the revolver   11 asked Mr J. where hè had
been the previous night   12 asked the boy what else he had seen
13 asked whether he had done that sort   14 asked her if she could
read   15 inquired whether they had understood what I had said to
them   16 asked the customer if he was being attended to   17 asked
him if he would go . . . the others did   18 asked Mary if she saw
what he saw   19 inquired who had left   20 asked him if he had gone
. . . and if he wanted   21 asked why his house was . . . and whether
his father had been   22 asked if he was leaving that day or the
following morning   23 asked how far it was and how long it would
take   24 asked if he could speak to Mrs Pitt. The *au pair* girl
answered that she was afraid she was out and asked if she could
take   25 asked the little boy if he was sorry for what he had done
26 asked her if she was going to   27 asked the woman if she would
mind if he looked inside her bag   28 asked the student if he would
know what to do if someone fell at his feet   29 asked her why she

thought it might be   30 asked him if he knew. . .shoes he was wearing weren't

Exercise 90   (The following are possible answers. Other introductory verbs are often possible.)

1 He told her to switch off the TV   2 She told Tom to shut
3 I asked Mary to lend me her pen   4 I warned them not to watch
5 He warned me not to believe everything I heard   6 asked me to fill up the   7 I told them not to hurry   8 warned Mary not to touch the switch   9 ordered the bank clerk to open   10 begged me to do as he said   11 told Peter to help his mother   12 told the children not to make   13 told us to do whatever we liked   14 warned them not to miss their train   15 advised his client to read it before he signed it
16 begged her to sing it again   17 warned us not to put our hands
18 advised him to buy   19 begged him not to drive   20 told the boys not to lean their bicycles against his windows   21 asked her to come with him   22 advised her to cook it   23 warned the lady not to touch   24 told the boys not to argue with him   25 told him to pull as hard as he could   26 ordered the porter to send   27 advised us not to lend   28 told us to make a list of what we wanted   29 told her to look   30 warned the people on the platform to stand clear   31 asked the children to see if they could   32 warned her not to go   33 asked the customer to pay   34 the notice told us to leave the space clear
35 I reminded them to write to their   36 warned her to think well before she answered

Exercise 91   (See note above key to Exercise 90.)

1 told me to get out of his   2 ordered me to climb   3 asked the customer to pay   4 asked her to open her   5 told Mrs P. not to worry but (to) leave it all to him   6 warned him not to use   7 told the taxi-driver to follow the car   8 recommended me to wash
9 urged me to have confidence in him   10 told the lift-man to take him   11 advised the passengers to read   12 told her always to cook. . . and never to use   13 told him not to argue with his
14 reminded me to prune   15 told her to wait for him   16 advised her not to eat . . . and to avoid   17 advised me not to say   18 the notice told/asked people not to ask   19 told her not to forget
20 advised/told me to cross   21 asked him to write to her as often as he could   22 told him to put his   23 asked the porter to find him
24 told me not to forget my   25 told the children not to go   26 told his men to search   27 told her not to make   28 told/warned him to put the gun down as it was loaded

Exercise 92   (See note above key to Exercise 90.)

1 advised us to make . . . our time as we wouldn't get   2 urged the public not to wait till the following day but to post . . . that day

3 warned them to be . . . and reminded me to drive   4 said he couldn't open it and told/asked Peter to have   5 told me to go and get him . . . and to come   6 said someone was coming and told/urged me to get   7 warned us to give way to . . . the/our right   8 begged us to send whatever we could spare   9 advised him to wear a wig if he didn't want to be recognized   10 warned/told them not to bathe when the red flag was flying   11 told him not to forget/reminded him to thank . . . when he was saying   12 told me to watch . . . and not to let it   13 told/advised/warned me not to shelter . . . as the tree might   14 told me to put the message . . . and throw   15 told me to read it for myself if I didn't believe what he said   16 reminded me to use my   17 told her husband not to drive . . . or the baby would   18 begged her to make . . . stronger and said that it had been . . . the previous night   19 warned us to beware   20 told me to smell it and asked if I thought it had gone bad   21 told him not to take his coat off as they were going   22 told her to stand by the window and tell him if anyone went   23 told his pupil not to move till . . . waved him on   24 told me not to touch it as I would only make   25 warned him to be careful as the steps were   26 told/asked the girl to ask her boss . . . and said that my number was . . . She asked me to repeat it   27 . . . told him to tell them not to work . . . as if they finished . . . they wouldn't get   28 The placard warned us to prepare to meet our doom as the end of the world was at hand   29 The instructor reminded me to put   30 Keiko asked him to take off his

Exercise 93   1 he invited me to have lunch with him   2 offered me/her/him a   3 asked if they'd mind not smoking/asked them not to smoke   4 told her to take the . . . and to shut the door as she went   5 asked me to help her as she couldn't   6 said it was a . . . and advised me to ask   7 advised me to try to/and get   8 offered to wait for me/said she'd wait if I liked   9 reminded me to switch off when I'd finished   10 asked/told me to check the figures for him   11 advised me to apologize   12 asked him to check   13 told me to sit/said he wished I'd sit . . . asked how I expected him to paint me when I kept jerking my head   14 advised him to go by train as it was   15 The notice asked guests not to play   16 asked me to wait   17 strongly advised me to see   18 advised them to plant   19 asked me to sign   20 asked me to forward . . . while he was   21 The police asked anyone who has seen the . . . to get in touch with their nearest   22 warned me not to leave my . . . as our host's dogs might mistake me   23 told me to answer the letter and reminded me to keep   24 asked me to move my car as it was blocking his   25 Mrs Jones asked them to let her know when their . . . came in   26 The coach told the first team to report   27 Tom asked Ann to sew on the button for him. Mary advised him to sew it on himself as buttons . . . usually came off   28 The girl asked me to sit down and said . . ./said that if I sat down the fortune teller would be with me

Exercise 94 1 asked if he could get 2 said she couldn't open . . .
Tom offered to do it for her 3 asked the official to translate it
4 wondered if they would ever meet 5 asked if I would be there the
next day. I said that I would 6 asked if she could lose . . . the
doctor said (that) she couldn't 7 offered me a drink 8 urged us to
install 9 asked me to read it 10 asked (me) if she should tell him
what had happened 11 asked if I wouldn't like to look 12 said she
was going . . . Tom said he was too and offered her a lift/asked if
she'd like a lift 13 asked for a sweet/asked if he could have a
sweet 14 asked if they could stay 15 asked for the weekend/asked
if he could have 16 asked if he could leave 17 asked (him) why he
didn't like 18 advised him to take up 19 asked where he should
hang his . . . and if it would look 20 asked what I should/was to do
if the car wouldn't start 21 asked if I had enough . . . and offered to
lend me some 22 asked if he would be able to guide me or if I
should bring 23 reminded him to shut 24 asked (her) if she would
like to see 25 asked me to peel 26 said that he'd got two tickets
and invited me to come/go with him 27 asked if I could use . . . I
said (that) I couldn't 28 asked if I'd mind living by myself
29 asked me to pay/asked if I'd mind paying 30 asked why she
didn't trust him. She said (that) she never trusted

Exercise 95 (See note above key to Exercise 90.)

1 told me to remember to get . . . when I was *or* reminded me to get,
etc. *or* said that when I was at . . . I was to get 2 told/advised me to
sit down and put my head between my knees if I felt *or* said that if I
felt faint I was to put/should put 3 asked what he was to do/should
do with my purse if he found it. I told/asked him to keep it till he
saw me 4 told me/asked me to give him a drink if he arrived before
she got back *or* said that if he arrived before she got back I was to
give 5 told me if anyone rang up to say *or* said that if anyone rang
up I was to say she'd be 6 told me when I was driving always to
look in my mirror *or* said that when I was driving I should always
look 7 told me to leave the key under the mat if I went out *or* said
that if I went out I was to leave 8 told me to shut the window if I
thought the room was cold *or* said that if I thought the room was
cold I was to shut/should shut 9 told me to ring him up if I felt
lonely any time *or* said that if I felt lonely I was to ring 10 said that
if she didn't eat meat I was to offer her an omelette (*the* **tell**
construction would be very clumsy here) 11 told me to get the car off
the road if I had a puncture and not to leave *or* said that if I had a
puncture I was to get/should get . . . and not leave 12 told me to
take the letter to the police if he wasn't back by that time the next
day *or* said that if he wasn't back by . . . I was to take 13 told her
husband not to forget/reminded him to thank Mrs Pitt when he saw
her 14 told me to take the meat out of the oven when the bell rang
or said that when the bell rang I was to take/should take 15 told

Key

them to give their . . . if they were taken . . . but to refuse to answer
or said that if they were taken . . . they were to give . . . but (to)
refuse 16 told them to shut . . . and go . . . when they heard *or* said
that when they heard . . . they were to shut . . . and go 17 told me
to press . . . if the lift should stop/stopped *or* said that if the lift
should stop/stopped . . . I was to press/should press 18 told me to
ask a client if he had a weak heart before I allowed him *or* said that
before I allowed anyone . . . I was to ask/should ask 19 asked what
she should/was to say if the police stopped her 20 asked what she
should do if he refused to let her in. I told her to write
21 asked/wondered what would happen if the strike continued
22 . . .how they would get food if it went on 23 . . . asked if they
could go . . . the rain stopped 24 said that when they'd . . . they
were to 25 advised her to switch . . . if she didn't like 26 asked
whether/if the bank would repay . . . if I lost 27 told me I had/'d
better complain . . . if the noise got 28 said I was to ring him and
give him . . . as soon as I found

Exercise 96 Part 1 (Alternative constructions are often possible.)

1–14 Ann suggested having a party on the following Saturday. Mary
agreed and asked who they should invite. Ann was against making a
list and suggested they should just invite everybody. Mary said they
didn't want to do much cooking and proposed making it a wine and
cheese party. Ann then suggested that they should ask everyone to
bring a bottle. Mary reminded her that they hadn't many glasses left
and suggested hiring glasses from their local wineshop. Ann
suggested having the party in the garden if it was warm and then
Mary put forward the idea of a barbecue. Ann thought this was a
good idea and said they could ask Paul to do the cooking. Mary
remembered that last time they had had a barbecue the neighbours
had complained about the noise, and she wondered if they should
ask everyone to speak in whispers. Ann suggested going round to
the neighbours instead and apologizing in advance. Mary, however,
proposed inviting the neighbours, adding that then the noise
wouldn't matter. Ann thought that was a clever idea and suggested
ringing everyone up that night, but Mary prudently suggested
working out how much it would cost first.

Part 2 15 Mrs Smith suggested . . . but her husband suggested
renting . . ., adding that it was all they could afford. 16 I suggested
that Ann should complain, saying that the boss was more likely to
listen to her 17 She reminded him that he used to be . . . and
suggested that he should 18 He proposed walking . . . as it was not
far and I agreed 19 Ann suggested (our) joining a weaving class,
adding that there was one 20 The children suggested organizing
. . . the teacher proposed 21 I asked Bill where we should meet and
he suggested the hotel 22 I suggested to Ann that she should ring
him and ask him what he thought 23 I pointed out I was doing . . .

and suggested that he should give me/him giving me 24 He
proposed leaving/that they should leave adding that he hated
25 Their father suggested that the children should go
26 I suggested his/him asking them what they would like to do
27 He suggested that we should begin training . . . I said I had . . .
and suggested that he should ask Paul 28 They suggested me/my
putting an advertisement in the local paper.

Exercise 97 (The following are possible answers only.)

1 warned us not to walk on the ice as it wasn't 2 introduced Miss
White to Miss Brown 3 gave/handed her the keys, advising/and
advised her to wait 4 begged me not to tell . . . I promised not
to/promised (that) I wouldn't 5 offered him my torch but he refused
as/explaining that he had one of his own 6 Tom offered to pay. Ann
protested but he insisted. 7 invited us to come in and look round,
assuring us that there was no 8 threatened to kill the boy if they
didn't pay 9 refused to answer any questions 10 complained that
he expected . . . agreed (with her) 11 wished it would 12 pointed
out that I had pressed . . . He warned me not to do . . . I might
have 13 exclaimed that her weight had gone up . . . she
admitted/agreed that it had 14 hoped I'd have a good
journey/wished me a good journey and reminded me to send a card
when I arrived 15 exclaimed with delight that he had passed . . .
I congratulated him and wished him luck 16 She agreed to wait
17 wished him many happy returns of his . . . and he thanked us
18 pointed out/remarked that my door was . . . I agreed (with her)/I
admitted it 19 He offered me a cigarette and I accepted 20 Their
mother threatened to sell . . . if they kept . . . The children begged
her not to do that, promising not to quarrel/assuring her that they
wouldn't quarrel 21 offered me £500 to keep my 22 He promised
to wait for me 23 I apologized for being late and explained that the
bus had broken 24 accused him of leaking . . . He denied it. Tom
called him a liar. 25 threatened to drop us from the team if we did
not train 26 complained that if the boys did . . . he called them his
sons, but that if they did . . . he called them hers. 27 Tom
suggested having a rest and Ann agreed. 30 He exclaimed with
disgust that there was a slug in his . . . and called

Exercise 98 (Other alternatives are possible here.)

1 Tom: Would you like to come for a drive, tomorrow, Ann?
2 Ann: I'd love to. Where are you thinking of going, Tom?
3 Tom: Well, I'll leave it to you.
4 Ann: What about Stratford?
5 I haven't been there for ages.
6 Tom: Good idea!/All right. We might go on the river if it's a fine
day.
7 Ann: I wonder what's on at the Royal Shakespeare Theatre.

Key

8 Tom: We'll find out when we get there.
9 It's usually possible to get seats on the day of the play.
10 Can you be ready by ten?
11 Ann: I'm afraid not, Tom/I'm very sorry, Tom, but I can't. I have to type a report first.
12 Tom: Working on Saturday! What a horrible idea!
13 I'd change my job if I were you.
14 Ann: Don't be ridiculous, Tom!
15 I volunteered to type the report in return for a free afternoon next week.
16 I didn't know you were going to ask me out, after all.
17 Tom: Oh well, I suppose it's all right.
18 But don't make a habit of volunteering for weekend work, will you?
19 Ann: No, I promise I won't.
20 Tom: (gloomily) I suppose you'll be busy all morning.
21 Ann: No, no! I'll be finished by 11.00.
22 Shall I meet you at the bus stop at Hyde Park Corner?
23 Tom: That isn't a very good meeting place. I'll call for you.
24 Ann: That's very good of you, Tom. I'll be waiting in the hall.
25 Tom: Let's climb to the top. The view from there is marvellous.
26 Ann: But we've been climbing for three hours already. I'm too tired to go any further.
27 Why don't you go on up? I'll go down and wait there.
28 Tom: All right. Here are the car keys. You'd better wait in the car./You could wait in the car, couldn't you?
29 I'll be as quick as I can.
30 Ann: There'll be no lunch left if you're too long. I'll have eaten it all!

10 Purpose

Exercise 99 (**so as** is interchangeable with **in order**.)

1 to paint 2 to remind 3 to feed 4 so as not to frighten 5 to put his savings in 6 to drink out of 7 to save 8 so as not to strain 9 in order to get 10 to tell 11 so as not to get 12 to frighten 13 so as not to make 14 to protect 15 to put on the fire 16 so as not to disturb 17 to study 18 in order to discuss 19 so as to be able 20 to elude 21 to prevent 22 to reduce 23 (in order) to read 24 to watch 25 in order to have 26 in order to keep 27 (in order) to learn 28 to buy 29 to warn 30 to avoid 31 to protect 32 so as to be able 33 to warn 34 to avoid 35 (in order) to look 36 so as not to alarm

Exercise 100 (**I/we would** is replaceable by **I/we should.**
would/wouldn't in negative purpose clauses is usually replaceable by
should/shouldn't. Where an infinitive phrase is possible the infinitive
given in the key is not necessarily the only one that could be used.
To save space not more than two possible answers are given for any
one example. Sometimes the **in case** construction would also be
possible. **in case** can be followed by **should** + infinitive, though an
ordinary present or past tense is more usual.)

1 so that nobody should/would know *or* to prevent anyone knowing
2 in case somebody knocks 3 so that repair work may/can continue
or to allow repair work to continue 4 so that it wouldn't get broken
or to prevent it getting broken 5 so that he wouldn't be recognized
or to avoid being recognized 6 so that her fruit wouldn't be stolen
or to prevent her fruit being stolen 7 so that I wouldn't overhear *or*
to prevent my overhearing 8 in case you get bitten 9 so that the
crew may/can escape *or* to enable the crew to escape 10 so that my
children may/will have 11 so that the cows won't get *or* to prevent
the cows getting 12 so that the call wouldn't be *or* to prevent the
call being 13 so that the birds won't eat *or* to prevent the birds
eating 14 in case there is 15 so that nobody will/can climb *or* to
prevent anyone climbing 16 in case you have 17 so that the snow
would/could slide 18 so that everyone may/will understand *or* to
enable everyone to understand 19 so that anyone who finds him
will/may know 20 so that the birds would know *or* to let the birds
know 21 in case we are 22 so that the birds won't build *or* to
prevent the birds building 23 in case he forgets 24 so that she
wouldn't frighten *or* to prevent her frightening 25 in case the
chimney catches 26 so that I couldn't/wouldn't be able to call *or* to
prevent me calling 27 in case it is 28 so that young children won't
be able to turn *or* to prevent young children turning 29 in case he
breaks 30 so that the government may/can discuss *or* to let the
government discuss 31 in case it is 32 so that pedestrians
might/could cross *or* to let pedestrians cross 33 so that his secretary
could/would be able to 34 in case they set 35 so that the rest of
the party would know *or* to let the rest of the party know 36 so that
the meat won't burn *or* to prevent the meat burning *or* in case the
meat burns